TEMPERING POWER

What is the rule of law for? What does that take? Why does it matter? There is little clarity and less agreement about any of these questions. That is partly because they are hard, but it is also because we generally do not think especially well about them. Yet they are rarely more important than today, and there are better ways to think. In this seminal book, Martin Krygier combines an account of conventional assumptions, a fundamental critique of them, and an alternative way of thinking about the purpose, the value, and the significance of the rule of law in light of the goal it should serve: tempering power. In this time of widespread intemperate abuse of power throughout the world, these concerns are not merely analytical, academic, or even legal. They are social, political, and moral, and everyone's business. And the stakes are high.

MARTIN KRYGIER is Gordon Samuels Professor of Law and Social Theory in the Faculty of Law and Justice at University of New South Wales, Sydney. He is the author of *Philip Selznick: Ideals in the World* (2012), *Civil Passions* (2005), and *Between Fear and Hope* (1997). He is also an editor of *Anti-constitutional Populism* (2022), *Spreading Democracy and the Rule of Law?* (2006), *Rethinking the Rule of Law after Communism* (2005), *The Rule of Law after Communism* (1999), *Marxism and Communism* (1994), and *Bureaucracy: The Career of a Concept* (1980). He was the winner of the 2016 Dennis Leslie Mahoney Prize in Legal Theory.

TEMPERING POWER

Beyond the Rule of Law

MARTIN KRYGIER
University of New South Wales, Sydney

CAMBRIDGE
UNIVERSITY PRESS

CAMBRIDGE
UNIVERSITY PRESS

Shaftesbury Road, Cambridge CB2 8EA, United Kingdom

One Liberty Plaza, 20th Floor, New York, NY 10006, USA

477 Williamstown Road, Port Melbourne, VIC 3207, Australia

314–321, 3rd Floor, Plot 3, Splendor Forum, Jasola District Centre, New Delhi – 110025, India

Cambridge University Press is part of Cambridge University Press & Assessment, a department of the University of Cambridge.

We share the University's mission to contribute to society through the pursuit of education, learning and research at the highest international levels of excellence.

www.cambridge.org
Information on this title: www.cambridge.org/9781009775304
DOI: 10.1017/9781009775311

When citing this work, please include a reference to the DOI 10.1017/9781009775311

First published 2026

A catalogue record for this publication is available from the British Library

Library of Congress Cataloging-in-Publication Data
Names: Krygier, Martin author
Title: Tempering power : beyond the rule of law / Martin Krygier, University of New South Wales, Sydney.
Description: Cambridge, United Kingdom ; New York, NY : Cambridge University Press, 2026. | Includes bibliographical references and index.
Identifiers: LCCN 2025053899 (print) | LCCN 2025053900 (ebook) | ISBN 9781009775304 hardback | ISBN 9781009775298 paperback | ISBN 9781009775311 ebook
Subjects: LCSH: Rule of law | Remedies (Law)
Classification: LCC K3171 .K79 2026 (print) | LCC K3171 (ebook)
LC record available at https://lccn.loc.gov/2025053899
LC ebook record available at https://lccn.loc.gov/2025053900

ISBN 978-1-009-77530-4 Hardback

For Ella and Sophie.
With untempered love.

Since the heart of a king ought to be in the hand of God, let him, that he be not unbridled, put on the bridle of temperance and the reins of moderation, lest being unbridled, he be drawn toward injustice. …

Let him, therefore, temper his power by law, which is the bridle of power, that he may live according to the laws, for the law of mankind has decreed that his own laws bind the lawgiver.

Henry de Bracton, *De legibus et consuetudinibus Angliae* (*On the Laws and Customs of England*; written sometime around AD 1250)

CONTENTS

ACKNOWLEDGEMENTS

As I confess in the Introduction (Part I), many of the concerns of this book have been with me for a very long time. Were I to acknowledge all my intellectual debts over that period, there would be no room left for the book. So I will stick mainly to the period since I began writing it, starting with institutions and moving to people.

I started the book in 2019, while a fellow at the National Endowment for Democracy, Washington, DC. After a two-year Covid home stay, I continued it while a visiting fellow at the Institute for Human Sciences, Vienna, in 2022 and as a senior research fellow in the Central European University Democracy Institute, Rule of Law Program, Budapest, in 2023. All three institutions were full of clever and inspiring people, committed to values that I share. I had a lucky start.

In 2024, when the book was beginning to gel, I tried out my then congealing ideas on three discerning audiences: in a public lecture and faculty workshop as Cheng Yu Tung Visiting Professor at Hong Kong University Law School at a particularly poignant moment for partisans of the rule of law ideal; delivering the 2024 Adam Smith Lecture in Jurisprudence (also with a follow-up workshop) in the School of Law, University of Glasgow; and giving the opening plenary lecture to the 31st World Congress of the International Association for Philosophy of Law and Social Philosophy, in Seoul. The subject of the Congress was 'the rule of law, justice, and the future of democracy'. I am grateful to these institutions and the many and diverse participants on these occasions, which occurred at a crucial bedding-down time for this book. Not just bedding down but waking up. The book sped up in the year that followed.

I have also learnt a great deal from discussions in lectures, seminars, and courses I have given over the past few years in Australia, Austria, Czechia, Hungary, Israel, Italy, the Netherlands, New Zealand, Poland, Serbia, Spain, the United Kingdom, and the United States. For many of the participants in these discussions who have had to endure the perils and evils of untempered power, the issues at stake have not been simply 'academic'. They helped me not merely to abhor such power, which I already did, but to understand it a little more.

My home institution, the Faculty of Law & Justice, University of New South Wales, Sydney, has put me up and put up with me for a very long time, with generosity and tolerance. I am grateful to my home and these other institutions and, of course, the many members of them with whom I have talked, whose work I read, and from whom I have learnt.

Research for the book was aided by receipt of the generous Dennis Leslie Mahoney Prize in Legal Theory in 2016, and a 2019 Australian Research Council (ARC) grant to Adam Czarnota, Wojciech Sadurski, and me for an overlapping project on 'Contemporary populism: friend or foe of constitutional democracy?' (Discovery Grant No. DP190102961). That project benefited hugely from the wise and patient shepherding of our omnicompetent research associate, Carolyn Evans. Writing at the same time about the ideal of the rule of law and some of its most significant contemporary enemies had its uses, for understanding both what is going on and what is at stake.

My personal debts are more numerous, and I am bound to miss some worthy creditors. Even within the period to which I confine these acknowledgements, there have been scores of them, and I am grateful to them all. This book would have been very different without them but, alas, they can be blamed for none of it.

They include Richard Abel, Štefan Auer, Petra Bard, András Bozóki, John Braithwaite, Laszlo Bruszt, Bojan Bugarič, Cora Chan, the late Melissa Crouch, Deval Desai, Rosalind Dixon, John Dunn, Hualing Fu, Raimond Gaita, Paul Gowder, Terry Halliday, Marcin Matczak, Stephen Holmes, Ronald Janse, Jeff King, Dimitry Kochenov, Jacek Kurczewski, Sida Liu, Marcin Matczak, Jens Meierhenrich, Randall Peerenboom, Philip Pettit, Gerald Postema, Kristen Rundle, András Sajó, Richard Sannerholm, Paul van Seters, Kim Lane Scheppele, Gregory Shaffer, Sanne Taekema, Brian Tamanaha, Rebecca Tapscott, Veronica Taylor, Renata Uitz, Scott Veitch, Jeremy Waldron, Neil Walker, Michael Woolcock, Mirosław Wyrzykowski, Xiaobo Zhai, Jan Zielonka, and two late, lamented, colleagues and friends, Julius Yam and Emilios Christodoulis.

And then there are the *mates* whom I have enmeshed in this stuff for so long. Over the years they have responded with varying levels of interest, patience and impatience, occasional agreement, acute critique, and sustained fun and friendship: Nick Cheesman, Adam Czarnota, Arthur

Glass, Robert Manne, Whit Mason, David Neal, Gianluigi Palombella, Theunis Roux, Julian Sempill, Wojciech Sadurski, and Robert van Krieken. I owe them heaps.

Over the years I have lost several dear friends and hugely valued colleagues whose influence on these pages, not to mention my life, is indelible: Geoffrey Brennan, David Lieberman, Gianfranco Poggi, and Philip Selznick. I learnt from them all and miss them deeply.

Finally, and most importantly, family. My father, Richard Krygier, died forty years ago. No one has influenced me more. My son, Jonathan, has had to live with this book and its predecessor obsessions for his whole life; my daughters, Ella and Sophie, were only in on the later iterations. I am beyond grateful for their wry tolerance, occasional interest, and sustained, if sometimes mocking, affection. My wife Julie has more than enough on her plate without any of this, but then my plate is her plate, so she has this too. Her serene effectiveness and wise judgement have washed (and watched) over every version, amendment, grammatical slip, word change, wayward comma, and silly idea. My gratitude to them all is only matched by my love. The sentiment of the book's dedication applies to all of them, but this time it's Ella and Sophie's turn.

PART I

Introduction

1

What and Why

Boris Yeltsin, president of Russia between 1991 and 1999, was the first leader ever democratically elected to rule Russia. In 1993, he was involved in a political stand-off with the (also democratically elected) Russian parliament. After seeking to dissolve it by (unconstitutional) decree and after the parliament rebuffed and sought to overthrow him, he ordered the army to storm the House of the Government of the Russian Federation – the so-called White House – which they did on October 4. According to government estimates, in the ensuing ten days of street fighting 187 people were killed and 437 wounded. Non-official estimates were much higher. Small numbers by twentieth-century Soviet standards but the largest toll from street fighting in Moscow since the Revolution of 1917. In December, Yeltsin pushed through a 'Crown-Presidential' Constitution.[1] In 1999, he resigned, to be replaced by his chosen successor, Vladimir Putin. It was the beginning of the end for Russia's flirtation with even a semblance of democracy and the rule of law.

The following observations appeared in my local newspaper, the *Sydney Morning Herald*, on 9 October 1993. They are by the late Robert Haupt, a distinguished Australian journalist and at the time the *Herald*'s Moscow correspondent. Haupt was moved to reflections of a sort rarely evident among Australian political journalists, or among Australians generally, but which are nevertheless distinctively shaped by Australian experience. He wrote:

> Acres of scholarship have been devoted to the question of how Russia – rich, cultured, the bridge between East and West – got to this constitutionless point. Square-inches are given in the Australian syllabus to how we arrived at Federation. Is it time, one wonders, for a comparative study between the thought of Sir Henry Parkes and of Bakunin, the relative achievements of Lenin and Deakin?[2] When one sees Russians killing Russians in a country 88 per cent Russian while Serbs and Croats apparently live in peace in Australia, an explanation must be sought beyond the effects of SBS [multicultural public radio and television station] and surf.

> Here [in Moscow], all the boring things of life are missing. There are no Premiers' Conferences, no shire councils, no chambers of commerce, no solicitors, accountants, real estate agents, no double-entry bookkeeping. There are soldiers everywhere, but very few police, and none you could rely on for help in a sticky situation. There is no head of State, no Scout movement, no civic progress associations and few charitable groups.
>
> All of this, the texture of civic order, strikes an Australian as so natural and ordinary that to investigate its origins seems superfluous, while to speculate on how evanescent it might become is an exercise in sheer wonder, or perverseness. Yet the worth of something can generally be better seen from its absence than its presence.[3]

What 'something' is Haupt getting at, that we might see better 'from its absence'? To introduce the term central to this book, I nominate 'tempered power'.

Of course, Australia has known political crises too. After all, less than twenty years before he wrote the article, Australia was plunged into a major constitutional crisis, indeed the most serious such crisis in the history of the Commonwealth. Its temper is worth recording.

First the Australian Senate – dominated by Opposition members – refused to allow the government's Supply (Money) Bill to pass. While the literal terms of the Senate's powers allowed this, there was much heated debate about whether in doing so the Senate had ignored long-standing, though unwritten, constitutional conventions.

As the government was running out of money and a deadlock appeared unavoidable, civil servants would not be able to be paid, and other complications would ensue, Sir John Kerr, the governor general and the queen's representative as head of state, dismissed the government. He justified this on the grounds of a specific constitutional reserve power to dissolve the House of Representatives given him by the Constitution. He appointed the Opposition leader as a 'caretaker' prime minister until elections could be held. There was again great debate over whether he had a right to interpret that section literally or whether he should have taken account of (unwritten and non-binding but long-standing) legal conventions which allegedly read that power down.

When Kerr informed the imposing and imperious prime minister, Gough Whitlam, of the decision to sack him, Whitlam was furious. I think it is safe to say he would have taken any step he could *imagine* to avoid or overturn that outcome. So what did he do? He strode to the steps of Parliament House, where the governor general's aide read out the announcement of his dismissal, ending it – as was the custom – by proclaiming 'God save the Queen'. Mr Whitlam responded with dramatic emphasis, 'Well may we say "God save the Queen" because *nothing* will save the Governor General.' He exhorted Australians to 'maintain your rage and enthusiasm for the campaign for the election now to be held and until polling day'.

And then he complied with a decision he hated, contested an election he did not want, and – after losing – did nothing to resist a popular verdict he thought unjustly provoked; legally arguable but unjust. While the country was deeply divided over the dismissal, and controversy continues to this day over whether the governor general had correctly interpreted the section of the Constitution on which he based his power, no one thought to call out the troops. No one shelled the governor general's residence.

Some ten years after it happened, I was asked about this crisis by my friend the late and great Hungarian philosopher György Markus, shortly after he had begun his forced exile from his country to mine to spend the rest of his life there. He wanted to know what this greatest-of-all-crises amounted to. So I told him as clearly as I could about the political stand-off and the law, conventions, and proprieties that either side – furiously – invoked. I thought I had done it quite well. But when I finished my disquisition, perhaps boring but I thought accurate, to my surprise Markus, that supremely intelligent man, looked dumbfounded. 'Martin, I find this ununderstandable', he said. For a moment I couldn't understand what he didn't understand, and he in return couldn't understand why I didn't understand what he couldn't understand. He had been told this was a big deal political crisis, the biggest in our recent history, yet not a shot was fired, no one was gaoled, and the talk was all about law and the proprieties and limits of institutional and constitutional behaviour.

Whence the difference between these two stories? One can hardly attribute it to the bipartisan friendliness which has characterised Australian politics. There have been plenty of hatreds, and plenty of ambitious people there. After all, we have the authority of Hansard – the official record of parliamentary debates – that another prime minister of Australia, Paul Keating, considered his opponents to be 'vermin'. He said so and said worse. But we all know – more important *they* all knew – that, though he might shout at them, he never thought to exterminate them. Nor they him.

Australia does not have scenes like those that Haupt witnessed in Moscow. By historical Russian standards, of course, they are rather tame, but they aren't down under. Compared to what is possible – such as the 'wild caprice in politics and violence as a norm in settling disputes' that

Haupt observed in Moscow – use and abuse of power in Australia are not either of them absent, but they are tempered.[4] We are moderate in both the use and abuse of power; the exercise of power is routinely, reliably, and, so far, generally well tempered.

The theme of Haupt's article was that Russia was 'constitutionless', whereas Australia has one. In a literal, legalistic sense that was not true then and it is not true now. Even when he wrote, the last (communist) constitution was still on the books, and arguably it was still legally valid. It did not count for much, but that is another matter, one to which we will return. And even though a new (hyper-centralised) constitution was quickly put into place and remains (with further amendments which centralise power even more),[5] Haupt's observations have not therefore become dated. Conversely, though there is no written constitution in Britain, Britain has a constitution in Haupt's sense, even if it is under greater stress today than when he wrote.

For Haupt's article is not about the absence of a document but of an agreed and relatively widely observed combination of institutional arrangements, traditions, ground rules, conventions, habits, understandings, expectations, and modes of public interaction that somehow together serve to temper the ways in which power is exercised. It is *that* which is pervasively absent in Russia, and not only there, and pervasively present in Australia, but not only here. One can put it the other way around too: there exist institutional arrangements, traditions, ground rules, conventions, and the rest, that support untempered forms and sites of power in Russia and many other states, which do not have counterparts everywhere.

Needless to say, neither of these brief cameos says all that needs to be said about their subject, still less about the country or the times or circumstances in which they occurred. I cite them only as graphic exaggerations of two contrasting tendencies, one of which I oppose, the other which I will endorse throughout this book. Most societies have chequered histories in the ways power is exercised, and there is a lot of movement over time. The movements often surprise, but they are rarely random.

It is not a complete surprise that my example of intemperate use of power came from Russia, but it is far from unique. Many other examples, from many other times and places, could serve. And in relation to Australia, my story is of course incomplete. Above all, Australia's history includes, at its foundation, the dispossession of the Aboriginal inhabitants of the land. That is a tragic story with arbitrary power often at its core. I return to these themes in Chapter 8 and to the contrasts between the ways settlers treated settlers on the one hand and Aboriginal peoples on the other in Chapter 10. Neither element cancels out the other; both need to be woven into any adequate and coherent account of the ways power has typically been exercised. Still, it is a deep and distinctive though not comprehensive fact about Australian history that in many domains and over long periods power has been exercised with comparative and sustained moderation. I almost wrote 'extreme moderation', and there is a case for that, even if the words sit uneasily together.

It certainly beats the opposite. Untempered power can be malign in so many ways. It is a major question of political morality and institutional luck, nurturing, and design how power might be not eviscerated or even in important ways diminished at all but reliably and durably tempered.

One common answer is through 'the rule of law'. I believed that for a long time, and still do in part, but left raw it is inadequate in ways that matter. It systematically puts the cart before the horse. After all, how do you get the rule of law? One initially plausible answer might be: to have had it a long time. And indeed that accounts for many cases on either side: Russia has rarely known it;[6] Australia inherited long traditions where it was significant.[7]

But where do we place the Trumpian, and perhaps post-Trumpian, United States? Where did that come from? After all, while Trump did not shell the Capitol when it endorsed his electoral defeat in 2020, he refused to acknowledge that defeat, then egged on and later praised an armed civilian attack on the Capitol, which caused several deaths. Re-elected four years later, he immediately pardoned all its charged and convicted participants. And, as we now see (at the time of writing, March 2026), that was only the start. Yet arguably the United States was ahead of most of the world in serious, centuries-long, and apparently deeply engrained traditions of institutionalised constitutionalism and the rule of law. What happened to all that?

It would seem that if the rule of law is to be part of the answer, it needs a bit of help. But what sort of help should that be? Where should it come from? And how much help is it likely to be? Once the help comes, what role is left for law? How much is down to law at all, and how much to cultural, social, and political forces and arrangements outside it? Should we start with law or with something, somewhere, else?

Recall Robert Haupt's list of 'boring things of life' that make up 'the texture of civic order' in his own country but are absent from Russia. It is not especially accurate (after all, there was a head of state – he was shelling the parliament; there were accountants, etc.), and it is an intriguing and motley mix, from real estate agents to shire councils to charitable groups, the details of which would not withstand too much scrutiny. Moreover, he does not explain what might link these disparate items, and why they are significant. It is not clear how much he had thought it through. Yet I believe he was on to something. This book is in part an attempt to sort out what that might be.

These are a few of the questions that have led to this book. I have been thinking about them for a very long time, and in the process have wandered – I would say necessarily, critics might think mistakenly – some distance from where I began. I still can't say I have answered them. However, I hope at least that framing and exploring them might move us a bit closer to understanding what is involved, and what is at stake, in answering them.

1.1 The Rule of Law

From the early 1990s, and throughout the world, there has been more said, written, done, and spent in the name of the rule of law than ever before. This English phrase, once only used by lawyers, has circumnavigated the globe, acquiring a kind of radiant rhetorical sanctity, up there with long-established icons of political value, such as justice, liberty, democracy, equality, and constitutionalism, among others. It has come to be unprecedentedly exalted and optimistically proposed for an indefinite, sometimes almost infinite, range of problems.

But quantity has not always generated quality. One eminent writer describes the rule of law as 'a slogan in search of a concept';[8] another observes that often when we talk of it 'we literally don't know what we're talking about'.[9] It would be easy to find evidence for both claims. And as is the way with many ideals that matter greatly to us, their aura tends to obscure any clear shape, detail, focus, or purpose, rendering murky what the concept might mean, what the phenomenon might be, and why anyone should care. Disagreements can be fierce, and clarity is an early casualty.

If we turn from theory to practice, things do not improve. Few of the numerous outfits devoted to rule of law promotion can boast of much success. Years ago one promoter observed that 'we know how to do a lot of things, but deep down we don't really know what we're doing'.[10] After years of busy doing, the condition of the rule of law in the world has not improved. While it is not always obvious that rule of law surveys survey the same things,[11] or the right things,[12] or at the right time,[13] it remains striking that they all report dramatic global declines. The most sophisticated of them, for example, the World Justice Project, in its 2024 report on 142 countries, finds that the rule of law has declined in most of them and that declines have been broader and deeper 'in two critical index factors: Fundamental Rights and Constraints on Government Powers'. More than six billion people, 77 per cent of the world's population, the report estimates, live in countries where the rule of law is weaker than it was in 2016. There are many ways to interpret these findings, and they are not all negative, but there was enough to worry about here, even before Donald Trump came back to slap his thumb on the scales.

There are many reasons for these disappointments. Promoting the rule of law in the places it has recently been most ardently attempted – often in the wake of dictatorships or war or in congenitally fragile states, economies, and societies – was never going to be easy. And as the contemporary United States shows, even maintaining it where it once appeared robust – exemplary even – is not proving to be a picnic.

Though we have reason to be disappointed, we shouldn't be too surprised. Well-tempered power, the goal of the rule of law, is not a natural state of affairs, nor to everyone's taste. It is far from simple to contrive, particularly when, as so often, unruly power comes to be concentrated in the big grasping hands of small numbers. Often despotism is simpler,[14] unruliness easier still,[15] the latter often leads to the former,[16] and the two frequently co-exist.[17]

For *power* is at stake. Often those whose power matters most, and to whom power matters most, simply cannot *imagine* that theirs should or could be tempered. Others understand the idea but reject it, at least when applied to them.[18] Successes occur and some have endured,[19] but they are historically rare and commonly unstable.[20] Pressures, strain, challenge, and collapse are not anomalous contemporary defects but historically common defaults. That has been a perennial challenge to admirers of well-tempered power, such as me, for whom it is a prize almost beyond measure.

Approaching and then sustaining it is always going to be hard, just because of the ways of the world. And there is another reason, which is the focus of this book. While we have come to say a lot about the rule of law, we don't think very well about it. I suggest some ways in which we might think better. We might then even come to do better, which would be a nice surprise. For the stakes are high.

1.2 Recalling the Arguments

In the first volume of his autobiography, Graham Greene recalls:

> My friend Antonia White ... told me how, when she was attending the funeral of her father, an old priest, who had known her as a child, tried to persuade her to return to the Church. At last – to please him more than for any other reason – she said, 'Well then, father, remind me of the arguments for the existence of God.' After a long hesitation he admitted to her, 'I knew them once, but I have forgotten them.' I [Greene] have suffered the same loss of memory.[21]

The combination of faith and forgetfulness that Greene describes in this passage is not uncommon among believers, and not confined to matters that, as we are told, 'surpass all understanding'.[22] It happens often with this-worldly values and ideals as well. If they take hold, as different ideals do for different reasons in different places at different times, multitudes might come to profess or at least approve of them, even if they do not (or no longer) know exactly what they are talking about or why. Perhaps they never did. Sometimes there are good reasons to believe in those ideals, but we have forgotten them. Sometimes there are no good reasons, but we don't know that either.

When we treat such ideals as iconic, we lend them a metaphorical sanctity otherwise scarce in our secular world. But we might be hard put to explain what they involve or why they matter. And things can get worse: the values might go out of fashion, and we come to forget why they were ever in. The faithless don't care, and the faithful don't know why they do. All this has happened to God, after all. Surely it can happen to such mundane ideals and contrivances as the rule of law. There are reasons to think it is happening as I write and/or you read.

In the passage I have quoted, Greene confesses that, like the priest, he too had forgotten the arguments. In fact, it was not really a confession but more a defiant assertion, for he goes on: 'my belief never came by way of those unconvincing philosophical arguments ... [Now] I cannot be bothered to remember – I accept.' Perhaps in matters of faith, acceptance – indeed defiantly unreasoned acceptance of Greene's sort – is all you need. If, however, we are to persuade others that worldly, human, ideals are valuable, important, worth striving for, cultivating, and defending, then it would help to be able to say why. However, it is not obvious that those who wish to defend, or attack, or supplement, arguments for the rule of law are always well equipped. Though they profess the faith, many appear to have forgotten the arguments. Perhaps they never knew them. And there might be new arguments. This book will seek to recall some of them, to revive, refine, reshape, and criticise others, and add a few. And it will try to shift, reframe, and refocus the ways we think about all of the above.

Nothing that follows can draw comfort from faith or revealed truths. Nor indeed is anyone in a position to dictate a uniquely correct meaning for the rule of law, or any incontestable stipulation of the values it serves. It is too late for that, and in any event it would not be enough. Too late because the term has become too protean, the purposes for which it is invoked too many and varied, the freight carried by this short phrase too distant from anything that could be derived from dictionary definitions of its four component words. Not enough because the concept is part of old and ongoing legal, moral, and political arguments about fundamental matters of political organisation, concerns, and ideals much affirmed and much contested.

But we are not flying blind. None of us invented the vulnerabilities for which, and threats against which, the rule of law has been invoked. Nor are we the first to wonder what might be required to deal with them. Discussions about and around values connected with the idea and ideal of the rule of law have been transmitted and contested within traditions of legal and political thought for millennia. They often compete with each other, and within the traditions themselves there are continuing arguments as well. As a result, debate about the rule of law is part of an ongoing conversation about threats, promises, and perhaps even deliverance. We are continuing that conversation, not drawing on a blank slate.

The rule of law is a concept deeply embedded in the philosophical and political traditions of, perhaps not every,[23] but very many cultures. It speaks to important and enduring issues of politics, law, and social life that can be forgotten or ignored by contemporary rule of law enthusiasts, as well as by their opponents. Trying to get some sense of its role and significance will not rule out controversy, but it might give any conception chosen a grounding in common, lasting, and arguably precious concerns.

1.3 A Confession

I have, as I have said, been writing about the rule of law for a very long time. So much so, that in some circles it is taken as what we these days might call my 'brand'. I have written and talked and taught on the subject so often, for so long, in so many places, that I have come to be a sort of easy and cheap default option to fill the 'X … and the rule of law' hole in encyclopaedias and edited collections on something else, almost anything else. When I mention to friends that I'm writing a book, no one asks what it's about. After all, I am a 'rule of law guy',[24] with a 'passion for the rule of law'.[25]

For a long time that's what I thought too. Even when I started to have doubts, it seemed churlish to demur. But I have now decided to come out. After decades of writing about and in praise of the rule of law, I have discovered that my true passion lies elsewhere. I'm still a kind of rule of law guy, but after years of dogged and flaunted devotion, I have discovered that my real love is for something different: tempered power. The two are related, and indeed passion for the latter explains why we should be interested in the former, but that interest is derivative rather than intrinsic.

It is because, and in so far as, it contributes to tempering power that we should be grateful to the rule of law. If prayer would do the trick, I would say less about the rule of law and pray more, but the jury is still out on that. Since I believe tempered power is the *point* of the rule of law, and there are many contexts in which the former could not occur without the latter, the rule of law should be appreciated for that reason, and for other reasons as well. But that is somewhat to decentre and rearrange its place among our attachments.

1.4 Why Now?

The concerns that have animated a great deal of what I have thought and written about, and that eventually led to this book, did not start with law. They stemmed from a hostile fascination with the exercise of wild power by Nazis and Communists in power, and an originally bewildered hope to understand them. For reasons genealogical, personal, moral, and intellectual,[26] roughly in that order, my original focus was on the Soviet Union and its satellites. My parents, refugees from war-torn Poland, escaped the Nazi occupation with difficulty and by a whisker, and when Nazis were replaced by Communists in their homeland, they did not go home. Their lives, families, friendships, and country were ripped apart by the war. They experienced on their skin what I only read about from afar (Australia, i.e. *very* far), but an inherited allergy has dominated my thinking life.

By the time I was born, Nazism had gone but Communism was alive and well. It became a focus of much of my political and academic thought and writing. Well before I had any thoughts about law, I knew of the astonishing arbitrariness, caprice, harshness, and wilfulness of Stalin's rule, the significance of secret directives, the insignificance of public ones, the extraordinary malleability, unaccountability, and brutality of power exercised by the party-state. If one were to seek an ideal type of untempered, ill-tempered power, and of its perils, Stalin's despotism was a good place to start. If one wanted variations of degree still closer to the ideal than any place I had lived, other communist orders would serve well enough. That experience, notwithstanding that it was not my own, and that for a time I only knew it from a great distance, became a focal point of my thinking about matters of public order and morality. In many ways, though it has receded and other abominations (and occasional delights) have come to take its place, it remains pivotal.

Some time later, after studying philosophy and politics, then law, I thought I had left law behind and completed a doctorate in the history of ideas. The subject was Marxism and bureaucracy. Though it was an exercise in intellectual history, a focus of its concerns, since it was the focus of my intellectuals' concerns, was with the ways of power in the Soviet Union – not a happy story, nor one which at the time led me to think much about the rule of law.

I then wandered back into a law school and fell into teaching philosophy and sociology of law, which I have done ever since. In my first year, I was assigned a course on human rights and another on Soviet law, a somewhat quaint combination but not my choice. However, once I dug in, I was drawn to discussions of the rule of law, since they seemed to tell me something about what was missing from the political and legal order of the Soviet Union and other despotisms that I had come to know of. Already believing, like Haupt, that you can learn about something from observing its absence, I thought I had learnt something about the nature and value of the rule of law.

Political scientists and historians of early communism typically said little about law, for to them it seemed insignificant in comparison to raw power. Specialists on Soviet law, by contrast, in taking Soviet 'law in the books' seriously, often appeared wilfully naïve. Nevertheless, there is something to be learnt about despotisms by asking about the role of law under them. Often one is asking about absences rather than presences, but these can be significant. One thing quickly obvious is that though there was a lot of law in the Soviet Union, there was not much rule of law. But what did that even mean? Why was it true, if it was? And what precisely was lacking? What was needed?

If I had tried to answer those questions while European communism still existed, this book would have been very different. Its emotional tone certainly would have been some mixture of loathing and hopeless resignation. More than likely also, it would probably have been much more legalistic than this one has turned out.

But then, to almost everyone's surprise, in 1989 European communism began to collapse, without even being pushed, and, as I argue in Chapter 2 in large part for that reason the rule of law became a global mantra. I was an excited supporter and minor contributor to that eruption of enthusiasms.[27] I came to mix business with pleasure and spent a lot of time in post-communist countries and then in other countries where the rule of law had not been prominent and experiments in 'building' it were in vogue. When I began increasingly to write about the rule of law, though not confident, I was hopeful that it could be successfully grafted onto societies that had not seen much of it.[28] Any book I wrote then would not have been this book. Its subject would have still been the rule of law as commonly understood, and the tone would have been sunnier.

However, increasingly, over the still-triumphal 'end of history' 1990s, I came to think there were reasons to question prevailing understandings of and approaches to the rule of law. That is because both my thoughts had changed and times had changed. What I thought then has developed in ways I could not have predicted over the years. Some of that development has been, as it were, internal: if you think about something long enough, you are liable to have some new thoughts. But changing times also matter. With regard to the themes of this book, the changes have been dramatic, and they have deeply affected what I have come to think, as well as what I believe important to think about. The tone of any book I might have written twenty, even ten, years ago would also have been different from before and since. It would have still been one of hope but tinged with disappointment and apprehension. Positive but anxious.

I do theory for a living, and for a while I thought that is all I was doing in relation to the rule of law, just trying to get things straight. However, I came to believe some of my differences from mainstream approaches might have practical implications.[29] If our understanding of the rule of law was inadequate, so too would be our efforts to generate and sustain it.

Either way, these were arguments with friends, urging them to think more clearly about what together we valued. I still think it's worth getting things straight for purely intellectual reasons, but in the current state of the world I would add reasons grounded in political morality. Arguments about the rule of law are increasingly arguments with its enemies. The urgency I feel stems from the fact that the idea, and even more important the *ideal* of the rule of law as I understand and value it, have come under considerable strain, challenge, and assault, from sources both internal and external. Not just legal forms, indeed not so much forms, since as many modern authoritarians demonstrate and as I will argue particularly in Chapter 8, familiar forms can be, and are increasingly being, bent to many abusive uses.[30]

Rather, in recent years the underlying values which the rule of law has been thought to serve are increasingly contested, eroded, subverted, and rejected. They have been put in question by, among other things, Islamist assault, Chinese and Russian hostility, populist and authoritarian challenge(r)s, lack of interest, not to mention home-grown disillusionment, critique, forgetfulness, incompetence, and rejection. Most recently and dramatically they have been systematically *Trumped*. For a partisan of tempered power, these are not happy times.

In recent years, and to the surprise of many, the rule of law ideal is increasingly abused by regimes that had only shortly before become its apparent beneficiaries and still claim to be its supporters, not to mention at least one, the United States, that had long been taken as an exemplar. As I argue in Chapters 8 and 10, they have come to abuse it, often in its own name and using many of its traditional forms, but with the actual aim of subverting what I will argue is its central goal: tempered power. In such circumstances, I have come to think it a matter of some urgency to try to explain why that matters, and why that requires some significant rethinking of standard positions. Since power-wielders typically need persuading that their power needs to be tempered and if they are not temperamentally open to persuasion, that will need work, today a lot of work, by those who might agree with me.

Of course, the arguments of power are often not intellectual, nor will be those needed to rebut them. Victims of its untempered exercise might be overborne, whatever they think or say. Nevertheless, it is worth thinking better about (and of) the rule of law ideal, if only to understand why power untempered by it has taken you down. There might be other benefits too.

My academic writings over the years have often focused on particular questions about the rule of law and its relationships with other things: how the concept quickly and recently ascended into the global political pantheon of values, its relationship to civility, state legitimacy, legal pluralism, colonial settlement, violence and development, sociology, Marxism and Communism, transitional societies, democracy, constitutionalism, liberalism, neoliberalism, illiberalism, populism, private power, tempering power. I also have an abuser's guide to the rule of law, for anyone who needs it. I cite some pieces on those topics later on,[31] and draw upon them and others throughout the book.

I would be happy for anyone interested in any of these particular applications to look at them. However, now seems to me a particularly important moment to set out their frame and underpinnings, and work out their implications, more than at any time in the decades I have been thinking about these issues. For the values that underpin this book, and more generally concern with and for the rule of law ideal, are being singularly challenged today. So, rather than publish more specific developments of my approach, applied to different problems and different circumstances, as I have in the main hitherto, I have decided to try to distil, reconsider, develop, adapt, extend, and above all reframe the essentials of the argument, in one place, connected and spurred by what is going on around us in many parts of the world.

I am not concerned here to embalm whatever I have written over the years but rather to draw together, reconsider, and develop the underlying and motivating themes as I now understand them, their assumptions, and some of their implications. More specifically, I try to lay out what is characteristic of a particular way of thinking about these problems. Problems change fast, and a central part of the argument of this book is that no general identikit solutions are to be found. But it's not just one damn thing after another. We might be aided by a way of thinking that, while it tries to retain coherence, demands sensitivity to context and variation.

I began writing this book in 2019, and the earlier parts of this introductory chapter were written quite early in the piece. My expressions of apprehension about trends in the world were written long before Donald Trump's second term, spurred by ominous developments both internationally and domestically in many parts of the world. Much though it might disappoint him, he was not the centre of attention. Nevertheless, while I try to keep up with his every intemperate assault (an exhausting task), I have not thought to change the trajectory this book has followed or to give him limelight.

This, despite the tidal waves of untempered, intemperate, ill-tempered power that flood from that source each day, is partly a matter of circumstance, partly deliberate. The circumstance is that, as the Rolling Stones once captured the character of this moment, 'the joint [is] rockin', going round and around'. It's all happening, lurching one way, then another, as we speak. As the journalist Ezra Klein cautioned, 'trying to see this moment from the moment is almost destined to fail'.[32] There is a place for journalistic reportage and another for less event-driven, time-bound, reflection. I respect them both, we need them both, but this book leans towards the latter.

More importantly the choice not to allow Donald Trump to hijack the argument of this book (though his spectre haunts much of it) is deliberate. The malign temptations and tendencies that motivate the concerns of this book existed in many parts of the world long before Trump's first, let alone his second, term – indeed, even before he was born, though that was a long time ago. And the pathologies his regime reproduces, transmutes, parodies, and renders grotesque are ages old. They will recur long after Trump is, as he at present cannot conceive, unremembered. His vulgar additions to the repertoire of intemperance attain world resonance and importance simply because this time it is America that is rockin', and so the world. And of course that matters to us all.

In his wildest dreams, Jarosław Kaczyński of Poland, more intelligent but not obviously less malign, could not have hoped for such resonance and influence. Viktor Orbán of Hungary has ambitions and a following even among non-speakers of Hungarian (destined to be and remain most of the world), but his country has 10 million people. In terms of global reach and significance, no one at present competes with Trump.

His time will pass, but the tendencies, pathologies, and aspirations of which I write are unlikely ever to disappear. It is those that motivate these reflections. I hope there will be something left in the latter, even when their current objects are only an unhappy memory. I have sought to avoid tones of disgust or dismay that could easily supplant the tones of earlier books I have and might have written. If I have succumbed to either, he is in part responsible. But the book is not about him. And I hope the tone never sinks to despair. That is a useless emotion, and not even Donald Trump deserves it.

1.5 The Argument

'The rule of law', a relatively old phrase and even older concept, took off on its spectacular modern rhetorical and programmatic career a little less than forty years ago. I have watched this career as a partisan and have remained so, but that is about the only thing that has stayed stable in my engagements with the ideas and realities the term evokes.

In the 1980s, and before the rule of law was launched on its new career, the subject of my affections was conventional enough; only my partisanship was, in some quarters, controversial.[33] I was for the rule of law, while some of my contemporaries were against, but I had nothing original to say about what 'it' was, where it was to be found, or how best to think about it. I took my understandings of those matters from the shelves where classical analysts, particularly lawyers and legal philosophers, political theorists and, a bit later, the burgeoning profession of rule of law promoters, had deposited them. I embroidered a little but basically you would have to look hard to notice the stitching.[34] Overall, I remain a partisan, for many of the same reasons with which I began, but my understandings of what in the world should be the subject of my (continuing) sympathies have changed – incrementally, cumulatively, substantively, and a lot.

As background for the substantive explorations to follow, Chapter 2 offers a brief account of how and why the rule of law was launched on its recent orbit. It then examines changes in the contemporary world that are likely to affect the trajectory of the concept, the phenomena it directs our attention to, and the ways in which (and the tones in which) we discuss them.

After these two introductory chapters, the argument of the book develops through four stages: Part II 'Approaches' (Chapters 3 and 4), Part III 'Stakes' (Chapters 5 and 6) and Part IV 'Implications' (Chapters 7 and 8) and Part V 'Complications' (Chapters 9–11). It kicks off in the next part by questioning where we should *start* in thinking about the rule of law and how we should go on. Where one *starts* matters, because otherwise discussion threatens to be, in a quite literal sense, pointless. How one proceeds is important, because some questions cannot be answered or even sensibly asked until others have been considered.

Chapter 3 suggests that, however much mainstream approaches differ from each other, they have two unfortunate features in common. First, they all are responses to a prematurely and inaptly posed question – what *is* the rule of law? Second, conventional answers – notwithstanding their many differences from each other – are drawn from within a common, narrowly and legalistically conceived, frame of options – to be sought in some configuration or other of official legal institutions, rules, and practices. They start by trying to delineate the *anatomy* of the rule of law, by specifying its legal tissues and bones. The chapter criticises this sort of approach wholesale, rather than trying to choose retail between one or other example on offer. For, however intelligent and insightful any particular anatomical answers might be, they begin with the wrong question, and so their answers – some extremely intelligent – are, to real if varying extents, beside the point.

Chapter 4 explores some general and theoretical reasons why, to think clearly and well about the rule of law idea and ideal, we should *begin* by asking what we want it for and what we want from it; not by attempting first to define its specific components and then wondering what we might do with them. So, rather than start with any of the numerous anatomical accounts proffered as answers to the question 'what is the rule of law?' we do better to start with a different question: *why* do we want the rule of law? What do we want it for?

Those impatient to cut to the chase might choose to skip this chapter and move on to the more substantive discussions from Chapter 5, which should be understandable without it. But Chapter 4 grounds what follows. For it explains why only if we come to some view of what we are after can we be in a position to explore possible and available ways of getting there. At this point, the role(s) that law might play, the forms it needs to assume, the institutions that would best serve, and what else besides law and institutions would be needed are all in principle open questions, as is the relative salience of whatever particular measures and institutions we light upon. Not completely open, because this is not the rule of law's first rodeo, but open enough, since the world does not always present even the same sorts of problems in the same sorts of ways, different ways require different responses, and there are new problems.

Part III moves from approach to substance. It seeks to identify the problem the rule of law has been thought necessary and able to solve (the mischief) and, secondly, the kind of achievement that might count as a solution (the remedy).

Chapter 5 argues, not originally but not uncontroversially, that there is a distinctive activity and with it a particular problem, a particular kind of mischief, that is the central concern of the rule of law ideal. The focus is not on the *purpose* of power's exercise, for which we have other concepts – justice, equality, prosperity, security, and so on – but the *ways* power is exercised. The rule of law is centrally concerned with a special and widespread disease, arbitrary power, to which the exercise of power is prone and the rule of law is invoked to remedy. The chapter seeks to explicate the notion of arbitrary power and suggest why, when substantial, it is obnoxious.

So what should we seek to avoid, or at least reliably reduce, the availability of such arbitrary exercise of power? I used to think that what this required was adequately captured by the terms commonly employed in this field – limit,[35] constrain,[36] restrain,[37] shackle,[38] and other similarly negative, curbing, shut-down words. In truth I did not much 'think' in those terms but accepted them without thinking, since it was the usual way to talk. As my thoughts changed, however, I came to seek other ways to express them. I came to be persuaded by writings, of Stephen Holmes among others, that this completely missed the positive, often constitutive, and anyway indispensable role of power in social affairs and in what we should hope for if the rule of law was to attain its proper ends. I sought a concept that might capture the ideal of the rule of law within that – once pointed out – inescapable recognition.

For reasons I elaborate throughout this book, and particularly in Chapter 6, this led me to explore the connotations of a term once often used in discussions of the rule of law but rarely explored and with little contemporary resonance. When, after casting around for an adequate term better to evoke the central point and value of the rule of law, I recalled 'tempering power' I was excited. For a self-satisfied moment I thought I had had a new thought. The importance of that thought was reinforced, but my hubris was dented when I discovered the ancient Greek, Roman, Christian, and early common law forebears and origins of the term and the ideas it carried. Still, as Google Ngram reveals, the term has faded from prominence since the early nineteenth century,[39] while the rule of law has soared in the last thirty years or so,[40] and I will be happy if I contribute anything to the former's revival. I am already gratified that my invocations of it have recently met with acceptance and development among several authors I admire,[41] and I hope their ranks swell.

I have no universal linguistic recipe or analytically precise concept to offer, but I suggest that speakers of English and several other Latin-influenced languages learn more from the intimations and connotations of an old but almost disappeared, multifaceted family of concepts derived from the Latin *temperantia* which the Roman Cicero used to translate the Greek terms *sōphrosýnē*. Plato considered *sōphrosýnē* to be a cardinal virtue and its Latin translation as *temperantia* inherited the mantle. The word was used to express the ambitions of those pursuing values then and long since associated with the rule of law. In part a description, in part metaphor, the idea of 'tempering' gives more food to thought and possibility than the defensive, diminishing terms in common use. As I try to show in some detail in Chapter 6, this term evokes a salutary combination of balance, thoughtfulness, moderation, and strength.

Discussion of the rule of law frequently oscillates unannounced and without distinction between end and means. Writers run together whatever institutional arrangements they take to amount to the rule of law, with whatever good they think flows from those arrangements, its alleged elements with its hoped-for achievements. They speak, for example, of 'the rule of law ideal' and then proceed without pause to cash it out in (frequently nationally and institutionally parochial) listings of kinds of rules and institutional arrangements, as though the ideal was uniquely to be identified with a particular notion of what might need to be in place to help attain it. Alternatively, they invoke 'the rule of law' to merge the results they believe such listings generate with the means supposed to achieve them. It is hard to avoid confusion, since 'the *rule* of *law*' suggests both an achievement and its putative ingredients, but I think we need to distinguish between them. At least in principle, and I believe in practice, what we want from 'the rule of law' is valuable however we might reach it, even when some of what is touted as its necessary ingredients might turn out not to be up to the job. In any event, we should not conclude the matter by definition.

At some risk of artificiality, to try to avoid such confusion in this book I will generally try to mark the distinction between means and ends, so it is clear when I am talking of one rather than the other. An analogy might be a distinction between, say, the components of a particular exercise regime, on the one hand, and whatever health benefits we think it might help us achieve, on the other. Pilates, say, is a bunch of techniques and equipment and exercises supposed to improve one's physical fitness. Perhaps they will, perhaps they won't. Still, one can list them. There might, however, be other ways to get there, like going for a run. Similar things might be said about legal arrangements said to compose the rule of law and what we want them for.

When I use the phrase 'rule of law', without more, I am referring to a much-vaunted exercise programme supposed to temper power. When I want to focus on the *achievement* that partisans say should flow from such arrangements, I speak of the *goal* or *point* or *ideal* of the rule of law, not just 'the rule of law' on its own. When speaking more generally of the character of that goal, whatever means might have helped us approach it, I identify it directly by name, as tempered (or well-tempered) power.

Starting with the end in view, which I recommend, tempering power is the ideal; for those who seek it through law it is the master ideal of their efforts; seen more generally, the rule of law is one of the means that might help us attain it.

Part IV examines some implications of this approach and Part V explores complications that arise from it. These move the book more clearly apart from conventional law-centric approaches and indeed from what I had assumed for many years. I have come to believe they should lead us in less commonly charted directions, which I seek to map in the rest of the book, starting with Chapter 7.

The villain of the story, then, is arbitrary power, and its hero is tempered power. Not everyone starts there, but it should not disconcert too many partisans of the rule of law. However, starting there and *then* asking where such problems are to be found, and what might be relevant to dealing with them, has significant implications for where we should look both for problem-makers and for problem-solvers.

As for makers, Chapter 7 argues that if arbitrary power is as obnoxious as I claim, and tempered power such a valuable ideal to pursue, then any serious attempt to approach the goal of the rule of law cannot assume, as is commonly done, that its targets are just governments and the agencies of states. The need to temper the ways power is exercised must be considered in relation to a much larger and more complex force field than that of state power, since arbitrary exercise of power is likely to arise in many places, and so too will reasons to want it tempered. So, we should have in mind much more than the usual rule of law suspects and concern ourselves more broadly with people and entities able to access power substantial enough that its arbitrary use is liable to harm. That will extend to many places we like to call 'private' but whose effects are often palpably public.

That is not to say the rule of law should intrude on everything, everywhere, but rather that where entities command power sufficient to be harmful, questions of how it might be tempered need to be considered. They are not the only questions that might be in play, but they are important and not to be excluded just because power is wielded by some entity other than governments.

Aside from targets, what might we need to call upon and deal with to successfully temper power? These questions are considered in Chapters 8–10. At this stage, at last, it makes sense to focus on the questions that discussions of the rule of law commonly start with: the resources, among them legal, historical, cultural, institutional, and 'spiritual', that might serve, and obstacles that might block, this aim. We have to wait till now, because what means are likely to be appropriate for, and effective in, tempering power will depend upon the particular forms, facts, and circumstances in which problems of arbitrary power present themselves. So too, what obstacles might need to be dodged or surmounted for law to have any useful effects at all.

We should never talk about the rule of law as though it is or can be some unmoved mover in social affairs. No one admits to being so naïve, but too often that is precisely what happens. Legal philosophers expatiate on the effects of formal features of legal rules, almost as though they were the only games in town surrounded by eager citizen-audiences just waiting to be told what to do and how they should do it, or what to avoid and how to avoid it. Rule of law promoters too export legal-institutional packages to 'build' their product in many parts of the world. The results have not often been glorious, and that should be no surprise, for central to many of these problems is that we haven't thought about them in the right way.

Nevertheless, law does indeed have distinctive resources to offer the tempering of power, and Chapter 8 will consider some of them. Law is often likely to be crucial, though precisely *what* in law is so, and for what it is, are not always to be found in the accounts of the rule of law that we are most familiar with.

And whatever law offers, it never does it alone. It always does whatever it does within societies where a lot else is going on. Law has to make its way in various terrains full of obstacles, rivals, and alternatives. Chapter 9 explores some of the consequences of this ever-present buzz, movement, and competition for the ways law works in societies. Chapter 10 discusses the significance of qualitative differences among cultural, social, and political contexts, some of which are likely to support, and others to undermine, the chances of tempering power.

The usual way has been to put law and the rule of law at the centre of investigations. What *is* it, and only then what are *its* problems, goals, and ideal? For so long that seemed so natural that even when I had developed my teleological critique of standard accounts I still brought it all back to *law*.

In my concluding chapter, however, I ask why we should assume, if tempering power is so important, and so much else beyond law is always involved in its achievement, and such things will vary, that law (still less any specific configuration of law) should be our starting point and central focus. Its role and significance will have to be estimated and established, again and again, for they will vary.

Ultimately, the concluding Chapter 11 argues, it makes sense to reconceive the relationship between tempered power and the rule of law. It is the former that is what E. P. Thompson called the latter – 'a cultural achievement of universal significance'. There are few circumstances, *anywhere*, where we should prefer power to be untempered or ill-tempered rather than well tempered. Whether the rule of law, as commonly if variously understood, is of equally general significance – given different circumstances, histories, cultures, traditions – is more doubtful, certainly more variable.

So, substantively, the book argues for a reorientation of priorities between the rule of law and tempered power, better to serve their common purpose. It is its potential contribution to tempered power that makes the rule of law matter, for and to the extent that it is among the possible and variable means that might help us achieve that goal. Thinking this way might involve displacing the rule of law from the centrality it has come to assume in lawyers' offices and international press releases. However, it might help us focus more clearly on what we value it for, and what it might need to do, and combine with, to deliver that valued end. With that end in mind from the start, we might proceed with more specificity, precision, and nuance to ask what – along with other things though perhaps in distinctive, often indispensable ways[42] – it might be able to contribute, where, when, and how.

I hope, then, to persuade readers to think in different ways (to be precise: these ways) about the rule of law itself and about what other actors, arrangements, actions, and interactions might be necessary for successful performance of its role, and achievement of its purpose, and why. Many of those involve and interact with the rule of law, and the involvements and interactions matter as much and often more than the rule of law per se. When they together contribute to tempering power, we've got lucky, and since the stakes can be very high, very lucky.

Ultimately, then, I suggest that we would think better about the rule of law by displacing it from the centrality it has come to assume by those who discuss it. The goal – tempered power – should have that place. There will still typically be an important place for law and the rule of law in considering how to attain that goal, but what that place is, what role it plays, what forms it might take, how it fits with the rest of a temperate ecosystem necessary to support that end, and what importance it actually has cannot be assumed. I hope we can then proceed to ask what – along with other things, but perhaps in distinctive, maybe indispensable ways – it might be able to contribute to achieving the goals we postulate for it. And what else might be needed.

This book offers no recipes for fixing the world or even changing it; indeed, unlike so many in this field it offers no recipes at all. All it does is suggest a different way, ultimately several different but linked ways, of *thinking* about its subject. That is not simply because I'm a lousy cook, though that has been alleged, nor a person of singular modesty, about which there might be reasonable doubt. It follows from the logic of my argument. Thinking will help us work out what we should ask from the rule of law (and other things as well) and why. But whether and how and with what we succeed will depend crucially upon, and vary with, particularities (and novelties) of problem, time, place, circumstance, culture, society, polity, and resources.

So, detailed prescriptions should only be essayed with particular contexts in mind. It is commonly myopic, and can be dangerous, to try to cook them up on the basis of some pre-stocked, often geographically, culturally, institutionally, and temporally parochial recipes that travel poorly but we happen to have on hand.

The world is full of tasteless, occasionally poisonous, concoctions of that kind. Sometimes they disappoint simply because the task is hard, which it often is, or the ingredients are inappropriate to accomplishing it, or we don't have a clue what to do with them, or we have no idea what they should be. Sometimes it is because we chefs are trapped within misguided ways of thinking. This book is aimed to help us think better.

A multitude of works purport to tell us what the rule of law is, what its elements are, what is needed to achieve it, and what multifarious goods might come of it. There are fewer about how to think fruitfully about it, and why. But we generally do better when we think better. Thinking is, after all, itself a key part of doing and a way of doing, and it then affects, or should affect, what else we do. It frames our narratives; includes and excludes possibilities; sets agendas and priorities; focuses and diverts attention; renders some domains foreground, figure, centre of attention, others background; expands and/or limits our imaginative horizons. If it does any of these things in ways that are inadequate or inaccurate or inattentive to matters that require attention, doings suffer. So, if our thoughts mislead and our doings consequently misstep, we would do well to come up with better ways of thinking. Doers might then be better prepared to take their next steps.

Lest my ambition seem too modest, I take courage from two authors who had nothing to be modest about. The first is the seventeenth-century English philosopher John Locke, who claimed for his own *Essay Concerning Human Understanding* that ''tis Ambition enough to be employed as an Under-Labourer in clearing Ground a little, and removing some of the Rubbish, that lies in the way to Knowledge'.[43] In discussions of the rule of law, rubbish removal is no small or simple task.

I also draw strength from another mighty exemplar, the eighteenth-century French genius of comparative political and legal analysis, Charles Louis de Secondat, baron de La Brède et de Montesquieu. Montesquieu's masterwork, *The Spirit of the Laws*, was above all concerned with a desperate and pervasive problem and to suggest what a solution would have to achieve. The problem was how to avoid despotic power, which he loathed. The solution was to discern ways in which power might be reliably tempered, a word he frequently used, so that its exercise would be tempered so as to be reliably *moderate*, a word he used even more often, rather than wild, capricious, despotic, arbitrary and/or fearful.

He is famous for suggesting that a primary source of political moderation was a threefold separation (and blending) of powers – legislative, executive, and judiciary – which he mistakenly thought was part of the constitution of Britain and explained the relative moderation with which political power was exercised there. The founders of the American Constitution, deeply influenced by that book, for good or ill invented and wrote a specific form of such separation into the Constitution's core. Constitutions around the world have followed them.

But although Montesquieu profoundly shaped the Founders' constitutional thinking, the details were theirs. For he left them no manuals, checklists, or blueprints. On the contrary, he deliberately avoided doing so. Instead, he wrote:

> I should like to seek out in all the moderate governments we know the distribution of the three powers and calculate thereupon the degrees of liberty each one of them can enjoy. But one must not always so exhaust a subject that one leaves nothing for the reader to do. It is not a question of making him read but of making him think.[44]

If it's good enough for Montesquieu, it will do for me.

2

Trajectories

> [W]ith the post-cold war rule-of-law renaissance in the early 1990s ... [t]he rule of law became the big tent for social, economic. and political change generally – the perceived answer to competing pressures for democratization, globalization, privatization, urbanization, and decentralization. Rule of law also became the big tent for donor activity to 'rebalance the state'.
>
> Erik G. Jensen, 'The Rule of Law and Judicial Reform'

> This apparent unanimity in support of the rule of law is a feat unparalleled in history. No other single political ideal has ever achieved global endorsement. In the 1980s, when I began to write about the rule of law, it was a rather niche concern. Though the term was not unfamiliar, especially to lawyers, even they rarely asked it to do much work and few others gave it much thought. Law students were told they should respect it; lawyers (particularly English judges) imagined they had invented it and knew everything about it; left-wing critics denounced it; economists, political scientists, and sociologists largely ignored it; and most people thought nothing about it. Notwithstanding the old and often distinguished lineage of discussions relating to it, the concept never had the international, unquestioned rhetorical prominence it came to enjoy from around the 1990s. Flash forward a decade or two, and it had come to be (or, rather, be talked about) everywhere. Why the shift, and where are we now?
>
> Brian Z. Tamanaha, *On the Rule of Law*

2.1 Then and Now

Ideals involving or connected with what we might understand as the rule of law can be plausibly identified in many traditions of thought, in many civilisations, over long periods of time.[1] The traditions differ in many ways, of course, and so too many of the terms and ideas, but there are common concerns and themes that overlap and recur in many different times and places.

They were not all labelled 'the rule of law', of course. Even in English, similar concerns have been expressed over centuries under a variety rubrics, such as 'the supremacy of law', 'government of [or 'according to'] laws', and the 'rule of laws and not men'.[2] Many other languages have overlapping concepts and traditions of concern.[3] Like so many of our most important contemporary ideas and ideals, indeed as the sources of many of them, they can already be found deeply considered by the ancient Greeks,[4] in Rome, in Jewish, Christian, and Muslim writings, in medieval Europe, in thirteenth- and seventeenth-century England, and in many places at many times before and between then and now.[5]

However, the global use of one particular phrase, 'the rule of law', to express some of these ideas is relatively recent.[6] Albert Venn Dicey, from 1862 to 1909 Vinerian Professor of the Laws of England at Oxford, chose to deploy this phrase to explore, adapt, and appropriate for England some of these very old (and frequently encountered) problems, concerns, hopes, and institutional configurations supposed to achieve them.[7] Although he did not coin the phrase, he launched it on a huge career, first among English-speaking lawyers and then in the world. Its current transnational rhetorical sway is even more recent. Not every lawyer, particularly if they spoke French or German, had reason to be persuaded by 'Dicey's unfortunate outburst of Anglo-Saxon parochialism … [whereby] the Rule of Law was thus both trivialised as the peculiar patrimony of one and only one national order, and formalised, by the insistence that only one set of inherited procedures and court practices could sustain it'.[8] Nevertheless, once launched by Dicey, the fortuitous coincidence of English now being 'the default language'[9] of the contemporary world with the (quick waxing and perhaps already waning) moment of international and transnational activities in its name by the United States and its allies after 1989 has given this phrase remarkable global reach in recent decades.

Indeed, the phrase has now so solidified that even one tiny change can be taken to suggest very different things. 'A' rule of law is not 'the' rule of law; rule 'by' law is not the same as rule 'of' law. On their own, however, the words do not tell you much. You won't get to the heart of the matter just by looking them up, individually or together. The ideas, not the words, are the thing.[10] And many of them are good ideas.

However, though ideas around and about the rule of law have had a long life, it has not always or everywhere been a central subject of public discussion and demand. After all, it has to do with law, and not everyone, every time, has found law friendly, central, or even especially close to their concerns. It has thus only occasionally become a concept that could light the public imagination. Moreover, quite apart from its meaning being unclear, its value has rarely been uncontested. Indeed, taken in the round, almost everywhere and everywhen, the ideal of the rule of law has a hard time.

Many rulers and traditions of political thought have warmly accommodated, indeed celebrated, arbitrary power, which I will argue is the nemesis and target of the rule of law. Far from contemplating, still less celebrating, the goal of the rule of law, the idea that rulers' powers should be routinely and effectively tempered has been rejected, often in principle and even more often in practice, in countless polities throughout history and around the world. Even where ideas and ideals of tempered power have had strong constituencies, such as seventeenth-century England in the throes of civil war and eighteenth-century America in and after its war of independence, they found expression as revolutionary fighting words, not Establishment commonplaces. Some have entered into long and strong traditions, but they have rarely been without challengers.

In recent decades, however, 'the rule of law' emerged from the cloistered conversations of specialists and controversies among friends and between foes to be welcomed by a much wider world. Indeed, very recently it came, for however brief a period that turns out to be, to command virtually universal approval, at least at the level of public rhetoric. From the early 1990s, rule of law took on an iconic aura, up there with justice, freedom, equality, and democracy. Vaulting to the top of declared agendas of many organisations,[11] rule of law promotion boomed; international agencies 'programmed' it;[12] thousands were employed to develop it; and billions have been spent on it. It came to be unprecedentedly exalted and proposed for an indefinite, sometimes almost infinite, range of problems.

In the last decade of the twentieth century and the first of the twenty-first, the rule of law came to be lauded as an indispensable condition for economic development, relief of poverty, democracy, human rights, assurance of security, peace, stability, and many other good things. It became a global *project*. In those few decades, rule of law packages for export became standard, central, and pricey elements of international aid for benighted countries thought to lack it and need it. Indeed, more and more international aid and financial packages became *conditional* upon various approved measures being undertaken to achieve the rule of law.

Long marginalised in theories of economic development, the rule of law came to be at their core. A scarcely noticed cliché with little resonance in the imperious rhetoric of international human rights, it came to be said to be a key to achievement of those rights. 'Rule of law promotion' rose to be near the top of the declared agendas of organisations such as the United Nations (UN), the European Union (EU), the World Bank, the International Monetary Fund (IMF), the Organization for Security and Co-operation in Europe (OSCE), Europol, and many others, all of which have dedicated departments charged with developing the rule of law internationally. Rule of law programmes were implemented at vast expense in countries from Afghanistan to Zambia. Asked what was the central failure of 'failed states', a stock answer came to be: absence of the rule of law. And of dictatorships? Same answer.

As the peace-building expert Charles T. Call observed in 2007:

> Among a plethora of development and security agencies, a new 'rule of law consensus' has emerged. This consensus consists of two elements: (1) the belief that the rule of law is essential to virtually every Western liberal foreign policy goal – human rights, democracy, economic and political stability, international security from terrorist and other transnational threats, and transnational free trade and investment; and (2) the belief that international interventions, be they through money, people, or ideas, must include a rule-of-law component.[13]

Those with long memories might think something had been lost in adoption and translation, but the rule of law industry didn't falter on that account. As Brian Tamanaha observed at the peak of its recent resurgence, 'there appears to be widespread agreement, traversing all fault lines, on one point, and one point alone: that the "rule of law" is good for everyone'.[14]

It is worth stressing how new this all was. In world-historical terms, this transformation began virtually a moment ago. In 1992, for example, the rule of law for the first time became an item on the agenda of the UN General Assembly. In 2012 it was, also for the first time, the exclusive subject of a 'High level meeting' of the Assembly, which declared, in its 'Declaration on the Rule of Law at the National and International Levels', that 'human rights, the rule of law and democracy are interlinked and mutually reinforcing and that they belong to the universal and indivisible core values and principles of the United Nations' (even though the Assembly had explicitly begun to register the place of the rule of law in this pantheon only twenty years before, in its forty-sixth year of existence). Over the same period, one writer notes, there occurred

> [a] transformation of the rule of law from curiosity to familiar friend in the term's increasing appearance in the Council's resolutions. During the Cold War, rule of law featured in Security Council resolutions a mere handful of times. By contrast, in the nine years from the beginning of 1998 until the end of 2006, the phrase 'rule of law' appeared in no fewer than sixty-nine Council resolutions.[15]

At least at the level of rhetorical endorsement, by the beginning of this century 'rule of law' had scooped the pool. So much so that transnational supply often outpaced domestic demand, indeed stimulated much of it, and even took on a life of its own. Of course, the rule of law is notably absent from many of the places and predicaments the UN and transnational organisations more generally encounter, so there was reason for demand to have been high in any event, but then that absence was already evident for decades before the UN began to talk about the rule of law. There must have been other reasons for its invocation than the need for it, given that that need has been perennial but rule of law only became such an omnipresent hurrah phrase yesterday.

It wasn't always so, and it might pass. Indeed, I fear it is passing as I write. Over millennia, all sorts of despots and demagogues, tyrants and revolutionaries, military and other adventurers, thugs and crooks, crackpots and criminals, dedicated idealists and ruthless opportunists, gave the ideals of the rule of law short shrift, even as a slogan let alone a reality. That was still true until very recently. Thus, in 1918, Vladimir Ilyich Ulyanov (Lenin), leader of the new Russian communist regime and himself trained as a lawyer, unabashedly proclaimed that his government would institute a 'dictatorship of the proletariat' and 'dictatorship is based directly upon force and unrestricted by any laws. The revolutionary dictatorship of the proletariat is rule won and maintained by the use of violence by the proletariat against the bourgeoisie, rule that is unrestricted by any laws.'[16] This was not an embarrassed confession, still less an apology, but a proud boast. And alas it was for too long close to the truth.

At the turn of this century, Lenin's most recent successor as ruler of Russia told a different story: 'President Putin continues to place judicial reform and the full implementation of the principles of the rule of law among the country's highest priorities.'[17] And recall that a month after seeking relentlessly to overturn his election loss, and a day after enticing his followers to attack the Capitol, Donald Trump was forced to intone on television, like a metronome in pain, that 'America is and must always be a nation of law and order', as close perhaps as he could come to mouthing 'the rule of law'.[18] If hypocrisy is the tribute vice pays to virtue, these are tributes indeed.

At the time of writing, several countries around the world – in the Global North, South, East, and West – are ruled by illiberal 'populists' who have little time for the traditional *ideals* of the rule of law but for many reasons claim to be implementing it, albeit in their own way, infused with their own national 'characteristics',[19] aligned with their particular (sometimes solipsistically conceived), 'constitutional identity'.[20] They might cheat to do so, but, like hypocrisy, this too is a tribute; 'legal cheating is pretending to be faithful while violating underlying principles. It is not a defiant gesture.'[21]

But times don't stop changing. On contemporary evidence, Mr Putin clearly appears to have changed or revealed his mind, and it was plain as day that Mr Trump found it hard to say even the watered-down words written for him; his heart was not in it, and his head didn't understand it. Less than four months into his second term, asked whether he was obliged to uphold the Fifth Amendment of the US Constitution, he replied that he didn't know. Certainly he appears not to care.[22]

Nonetheless, the expression still has global presence and rhetorical force. The UN, World Bank, EU, the American Bar Association, and other international organisations still laud the rule of law and expend much sweat and treasure, and sometimes blood, in efforts to bring it about. Rule of law remains in the foreground of publicly professed political and legal ideals, at least in the West, with such others mentioned above as justice, democracy, human rights, where not so long ago it stood in their shadows. The programmes generated in recent times of enthusiasm have not evaporated, though their promoters today appear less confident that they know what they are doing,[23] and some of those so loud in supporting them only yesterday have gone quiet or AWOL.

Even though the phrase is still everywhere, the reality is absent in many parts of the world. Certainly, inhabitants of Myanmar or Belarus or Afghanistan or Russia or … or … have seen none of it recently. In Hong Kong it is a fast-disappearing memory. In China itself, though the term has had a recent resurgence, it is embraced within qualifiers – 'socialist rule of law with Chinese characteristics'.[24] That term is not empty of significant content, as we will see in Chapter 8. However, its relationship to tempering ruling power is, to say the least, complicated and in relation to the ultimate power of the Communist Party and its leader, Xi Jinping, quite uncomplicated: that is not its point. In the United States, any plausible rendition of the concept has come under sustained assault from the very top.

While autocratic and populist regimes in many parts of the world, including Turkey, Hungary, India, formerly Poland and Brazil, and more recently the United States, deliberately and systematically flout the ideals and assault the institutions associated with the rule of law, typically they deny vehemently that that is what they are doing and invest a good deal of effort in pretending they are doing otherwise. But they do not seem much embarrassed when they are caught out, and notwithstanding heaps of rule of law-based critique, that doesn't seem likely to change.

Even the rhetorical power of the rule of law and professed attachment to its animating values have waned considerably in the last few years. Some of its putative exemplars have let it down, its opponents have muscled up, and its real prospects and significance in the lives of nations are coming under varied, sustained, and imminent threats from many familiar and some unpredicted quarters.

2.2 The Short Twentieth Century

How did we come to be where we are? Of course, any account of the spectacular rise to international modishness of the ideal of the rule of law, and more recent falling away, must be complicated and will be contested.[25] For there is not one story but many. As Ronald Janse, the editor of the *Hague Journal on the Rule of Law*, has noted, 'while the rule of law revival is everywhere, this does not mean that its origins are everywhere the same'.[26] Nor are the reasons it rose to prominence or the challenges it currently faces.

As for its relative rise to prominence, one story might be told about changes in economic theory, and especially the idea – novel to many economists at the time – that particular institutions, prominent among them certain forms and fields of law, were central to economic development.[27] Another theme is associated with attempts to build new international and regional organisations, such as the EU, on a new basis of purportedly commonly accepted values, central among them the rule of law.[28] A third, with ideas of what might help to replace and repair the damage done by dictatorships, internal conflicts, and 'failed states', in the various 'waves' of democratisation that seemed to come to a climax in the late twentieth century.[29]

These ideas might have stayed in the academy, however, were it not for one unplanned and unpredicted world-historical geopolitical development that moved them from theory to practice: the collapse of European communism between 1989 and 1991.[30] That event, or domino-like concatenation of events, bookended what the historian Eric Hobsbawm famously identified as the 'short twentieth century', 1914–1991,[31] that began with the First World War, a war like none before, which transformed the world and ended with the collapse of European communism. One aspect of that transformation was the impetus given to two unprecedented revolutionary ideologies with world-historical ambitions, which came to seize power. The first was Communism, the second Nazism. They warred bitterly (and ultimately for Nazism terminally) with each other most of the time but shared a common already existing adversary – liberal democratic capitalism (LDC) – all of the time.

There was a lot that was special about that century. One was that it was dominated by distinctly *ideological* contests, in which the 'conceptual geography'[32] of the globe was contested by competitive and holistic '-isms'; first three – Communism, Nazism, and LDC – and from 1945, two. Nazism was a far from conventional state power, but it dropped out of the picture in a conventional way: defeat in war. The 'Cold War' between Communism and LDC resumed soon after but ended very differently.

For the first time in history, if perhaps not the last, the globe was fought over by representatives of three secular ideologies. One of them, LDC, had developed in a more traditional fashion, over a long period and with no single founder or leader. The other two, however, were minted scarcely a moment before by specific individuals, Karl Marx and Adolf Hitler, the latter of whom both founded and led his movement until its and his end. These trilateral and then bilateral contests spanned the globe and were fought with every sort of weapon: military, political, economic, and ideological. Moreover, these rivalries were holistically conceived, as between mutually incompatible social, political, and economic *systems* of belief and of life; neither the traditionally recurring power plays between entities of more or less the same sort, jostling with each other for space and power and wealth, nor in service to supramundane religious ideals.

In 1945, when Nazi Germany was defeated, only one of these novel ideocratic creations, Communism, remained. Its influence, as actor, model, and counter-model, was profound. The second half of the short century was framed by the bipolar contest – over ideas as much as territories – between the LDC 'West', dominated by the United States with its allies, subalterns, vassals, and dependants on the one hand, and the Communist – first Soviet, then Soviet and Chinese (and later, Soviet versus Chinese but both versus LDC) – powers, with their allies, attendants, acolytes, emulators, satraps, satellites, and victims, on the other. Of course, other things were happening, but the whole world was affected by this competition: between countries, of course, but more distinctively between views of the world and of life, including political, economic, and social life, that were intense and diametrically opposed.

All that changed with the abrupt end of that short century in 1989–1991. In a moment, the century's great historical struggle seemed all over. As the insightful American student of communism Kenneth Jowett wrote at the time:

> In 1989, the Soviet bloc became extinct; communist parties in every Eastern European country added the loss of political power to their earlier loss of ideological purpose during the phase of 'real socialism'; and the Soviet Union … not only tolerated but instigated its collapse. The result is a gap in Europe's 'conceptual geography' no less significant than that of 1918.[33]

The gap was quickly filled. To put it crudely, in the arena of world history one contestant and an assortment of satellite and client regimes had collapsed, the other was left standing. One was out the window; the other came confidently through the door. And having entered, it seemed keen to fill the room and rearrange (and replace) much of the furniture with its own styles and brands. It had a refurbishment design for export and for a while it was welcomed. It completely dominated the market, at least rhetorically and programmatically. Those who wanted to join the winning team were encouraged to adopt the essential elements of the kit – electoral institutions, political parties, ideological pluralism, market economies, constitutions, new courts, and … rule of law programmes, with institutions to implement them.

Domestically, LDC now seemed the model for any country that aspired to do well. Internationally, it dominated the world, both as a source of support and, for the few apparent opponents around, as the enemy. The task, many came to believe, was now to move rapidly into the future by emulating what were taken to be the lessons of the LDC past and present. Central among those lessons was the rule of law.

2.3 'The End of History' and the Rule of Law

The illustrious recent rise of the concept of the rule of law did not, then, occur in a vacuum. On the one hand, during the short century, the rule of law had no part in the glorifying myths and narratives of one of the two competitors, no role in what Hobsbawm described as 'the special house-style [communism] imposed on its successors'.[34] At best and as a matter of practice not ideological commitment, law was viewed as a piece of (transitional) social technology of subordinate significance in the life of a society, treated always instrumentally, frequently with suspicion or contempt; alternatively, it was often simply ignored.

On the other side, by contrast, law and the rule of law were indeed vaunted, sometimes even considered national treasures, but there were hefty barriers to export, since 'we' only owned a part of things, and no one thought that was going to change in a hurry. On occasion, and especially in the United States' backyard or territories where it sought influence, tentative experiments in law and development (L&D) were tried out. However, L&D was not even a hint of what was to come.[35] Given the competitive struggling and posturing that dominated the world, the rule of law could never be part of any international lingua franca, no common brand of the UN, for example. There was no room then for a global career, for the rule of law to be invoked with reverence by international agencies and the great and the good of all types around the globe. When that changed and the vogue for it began, it is not clear how much that was due to the irresistible charms of the rule of law itself and how much to the package to which it was assumed to belong.

From the beginning, not everyone was persuaded by Francis Fukuyama's famous/notorious 1989 essay on 'the end of history'.[36] Criticisms were plentiful. Still, at the time even those who doubted whether history had really ended found it difficult to think of alternatives. Many key liberal notions, central among them the rule of law, seemed to have crested, if not at the end, then at least on the wave, of history.

Before 1989, no one was predicting that a global network of rule of law promoters and think tanks would be spending billions of dollars and employing thousands of people to promote rule of law most everywhere and for most everything. While not unheard of, it did not draw money or 'promoters', did not serve as a legitimator of one cause after another, and was no conversation stopper. It had no aura comparable to that of democracy, justice, equality, and other such terms of political laudation. That all changed in the 1990s. It was then that rule of law came to be seen as a key asset of the winning side and its lack a major weakness in many unfortunate parts of the world.

Moreover, as the L&D scholar Veronica Taylor has noted:

> Legal reform as a component of multilateral or bilateral development assistance is not new. However, the fall of the Berlin Wall signalled an emphatic 'turn to law' in multilateral and bilateral flows of finance, development aid and technical assistance, to developing and transition economies. Beginning in Central and Eastern Europe but expanding rapidly to other regions, this 'new' wave of legal reform was funded at dramatically higher levels than in previous decades. As a result, over the last two decades, the creation, diffusion and enforcement of law and legal

> institutions has become both a set of free-standing goals and a tool-kit for achieving other policy aims, such as resolving armed conflict, entrenching electoral democracy, restructuring public administration, igniting economic growth, strengthening market mechanisms or improving public health and education.[37]

Within this transformed conceptual geography, the rule of law figured in a range of novel ways. First, there was a new sense of universal *salience*: it came to be claimed that the rule of law was no mere parochial, western, luxury (for those who already possessed many other luxuries) but a key to success in the only game left in town. Secondly, there was a quickening of *interest* in vast newly opened parts of the world. Suddenly and consequently, there were people in plenty of failed or new or newly liberated states that had long, often agonisingly, lacked the rule of law, on *any* definition, for which these were not academic questions but practical and urgent; and there was at the same time lack of ideological competition and hindrance and a sense that this was a global turning point. Third, *range*. There was no principled and determined and strong obstacle to the spread of the good news, no obvious alternative, no determined and attractive competitor. Fourth, *promotion*. Rule of law reform was taken up by major western governments and international agencies, and it came with considerable funds and some pressure attached. The time to propagate the rule of law, markets, and democracy had apparently arrived throughout the world. And finally, the opportunity was taken up widely, for a while with apparent enthusiasm by eager *constituencies*, some because they believed in the ideals and wanted to emulate the practices on offer, others because there was a buck in it, others happy with either or both.

2.4 The End of the End?

Within the relatively short space of three decades all that had changed. The '?' that punctuated Fukuyama's title, 'the end of history?', was little noticed at the time and did not make its way into his subsequent book, *The End of History and the Last Man*. It should have. For the answer seems to be 'no'. It did not take long to became clear that, as Mark Twain said of reports of his own death, the report of the death of history was 'an exaggeration'. Indeed, world history has become more dramatic and contested than expected by virtually any of the '*specialistes du post*' who grew like mushrooms after 'post-communist', 'transition to democracy and the rule of law' rain.[38] And the brief hurrahcious career of the rule of law ideal is suffering, in many places dramatically. It is increasingly clear that it will have to defend itself or be defended by those who value it. For it is being attacked, both directly and by association with regimes and ideals, some of which only yesterday were thought to be luminous bright spots in its moment in the sun.

Everything is a lot more complicated now than it seemed for a moment then, and everyone knows. The early years after 1989 were dominated by a huge 'how-to' literature of 'transition' which assumed a commonly invoked direction and destination: from one package of dictatorship, state-owned economies and 'law as instrument of power' to another of market, democracy, and the rule of law. Now, that 'literature of transition' has largely shut up or dried up. The moment of 'transition' after the short century lasted even more briefly, very much more briefly, than its abbreviated predecessor. September 11, 2001, the financial crisis a few years later, the lengthy, costly, painful, ultimately catastrophic wars in Afghanistan and Iraq, and more recently Ukraine and Israel–Palestine, and Donald Trump's reconfiguring of the rhetoric and realities of geopolitics, challenged both the confidence that the United States specifically and the LDC West more generally had an unrivalled package for success and knew how, or now even wanted, to spread it. All this has put pressure on faith in the cheerful technocratic logic – 'here's the machinery: follow the manual and install' – that had propelled the transplantation of rule of law models and advice to the world.

Many failures and challenge(r)s, not necessarily having to do with the rule of law at all but with what its promoters did in its name, have also diminished its appeal: perhaps the rule of law is not the obvious good that the West has claimed. Perhaps it is not part of the success-bearing economic/technical package of the sort that rule of law promoters have suggested. Perhaps there are other ways to it, uncountenanced by those of the Global North and compatible with antithetical beliefs and practices, found in Cyrillic or Chinese characters. Perhaps other things are more important. Perhaps they deserve and/or depend upon sacrificing the rule of law. Perhaps it is all too hard. Perhaps we just don't know what we're doing (this latter certainly appears often to have been true).

After the shock of September 11, the global financial crisis of 2007 and 2008 further put in question the vaunted virtues of the LDC success package too, this time from another angle; the economic promise of western-style capitalism, whose partisans insisted the rule of law was a linchpin, now seems to many altogether less inevitable and appealing than it had only a short time before. In any event, where was that vaunted rule of law when all these First World financial shenanigans were going on?

Nor did the ravages (including political and legal ravages) of the Covid pandemic and controversies over the various means – including legal and extralegal responses to it – do anything to support the triumphalist confidence of only a few years before. Confidence in the world order or the ways the world comes, repeatedly but not predictably, to be reordered and disordered is not at an all-time high. And now it has all been Trumped.

Moreover, not everyone was just standing and watching while western models were starting to wobble. The monopoly position that LDC seemed to occupy in the 1990s started rapidly to be contested. Today, the liberal democratic world not only has problems; it again has rivals, indeed adversaries, who also and with increasing determination and considerable success compete internationally in undermining their competitors and offering allurements to potential clients. These allurements rarely include the rule of law.

Russia has made a predatory return to the global arena, and notwithstanding earlier pronouncements, the rule of law is not among the values it is seeking to spread. Of likely greater significance is the success (so far) of China in economically catching up to and surpassing most of the West, rivalling the United States in one sphere after another while directly challenging western models of governance and development and also challenging the geopolitical dominance of western countries, institutions, and values.

All this presents formidable challenges to what now seems to have been the premature euphoria of 1989. While western aid agencies made rule of law demands on those they funded, the Chinese Belt and Road initiatives around the globe do not. For many of those countries being courted by both, it might not be obvious which to prefer. Or it may be all too obvious: the suitor who offers more money, seems increasingly powerful, and makes fewer immediate demands – particularly as to how the power of rulers should be exercised. All the more since, as we speak, the United States has dropped both the demands and the aid.

Further, Great Power rivalries aside (though rarely very far aside), there is a new epidemic of populist and authoritarian challenges to rule of law ideals in many parts of the world, among them Hungary, Turkey, Venezuela, Mexico, India, Israel, the United States, and others (whose names are likely to multiply and change). From the point of view of the rule of law, many of these are intriguing and complicating developments, since unlike Leninist (or contemporary Russian) challenges many of their assaults on the rule of law ideal make use of elements that were supposed to secure it, adopt its language, and bear many of its formal attributes.[39]

Overall, both real and rhetorical commitments to the rule of law appear to be weakening by the day. The EU struggles to do anything concerted or substantial about egregious cases of rule of law subversion and when they do Hungarian and (erstwhile) Polish politicians attack these 'imperialistic' and 'undemocratic' assaults on their national sovereignty, democracy, and 'constitutional identity'. And just when we thought military coups were things of the past, recent years have seen what the *Washington Post* described as 'an "epidemic" of coups'.[40] Maybe not everything, but an awful lot that's old is coming to seem new again.

And then there is Trump. I have promised not to dwell more than absolutely necessary on his rise and rise, but whatever one wants to say about other aspects of his regime, one thing is clear: he has no fondness for tempered power, at least his power. That does not bid fair for the ideal of the rule of law in the United States and, because the United States still is what it is in the world, anywhere. His and his numerous loyal supporters' and fixers' assaults on the basic ideals of the rule of law will have lasting consequences. Even if they are ultimately repelled, the damage they have done to multiple institutions and centrally important values will not quickly be repaired.

There is a more general point to be made, which depends less on people's attachment or lack of it to the rule of law specifically than on what is thought, for whatever reason, of its avatars and homes. The prestige of 'the West', and especially the United States, was high after the end of the short twentieth century. All sorts of features, real or imagined, attributed to the available option were considered valuable and important to emulate, just because of their provenance, associations, and success-appeal. This assumption of virtue-by-association is unlikely to continue after these once hallowed sources of influence and prestige have seen their lustre dim in so many aspects, internal and external, justifiably or not.[41] All the more when their leaders come to reject those virtues themselves.

Given all these challenges, one should expect them to be reflected in the future career prospects of the rule of law, both as a slogan with which everyone seeks to be associated and, far more important, as embodying or serving ideals that all should value. Today, after all, it is not only Xi Jinping who believes that 'the East is rising; the West is declining'.

Whatever settles from all these shocks, challenges, and disappointments will be different from what seemed possible, indeed likely, at the ends of both the short and long twentieth century. If these are signs that we might be moving from the end of history to 'no one's world'[42] (or to someone else's world or to another sort of world), this is certain to be reflected in the popularity and career prospects of the rule of law and the ideals associated with it. Some might still mourn the end of the end of history, but they cannot deny that it has been followed by increasing scepticism about, and implosion of, western models, the epidemic rise of populist and authoritarian parties and governments, the increasingly sophisticated and confident development of new forms of 'sharp' as well as old-fashioned and blunt power, too, by rivals with considerable interest in sabotaging and subverting the rule of law, and crises of faith and commitment in once-'model' states. The virtues of western models, among them the much bruited but also now much bruised rule of law, can no longer be assumed to appear self-evidently a good for all. And that, of course, was always a naïve assumption.

If the attractive magic of the ideal of the rule of law seems to be losing some of its spell, one might ask why we should still continue to be concerned with it. My answer is that it is precisely now that we need to think again, rethink, and reimagine what has made people invoke the rule of law and its ideal. We need to revisit their reasons and their arguments, renew them, revise them, criticise them, and where apt add to them. Many of those reasons and arguments are as relevant today as they ever were. However, the world has 'many mansions' and change is relentless, so new and different contexts, resources, and challenges need to be considered and new and different ways to sustain the ideal that has animated and lies behind attachment to the rule of law explored. For the ideal itself is precious. That it is so rarely achieved does not make it less so. Precisely the reverse.

PART II

Approaches

3

False Starts

'What is the answer?' I was silent.
'In that case', she said, 'what is the question?'

Gertrude Stein's last recorded words. Alice B. Toklas, *What Is Remembered*

3.1 Where to Begin?

At first sight, and I suspect to most people, the answer to this question can be brisk and obvious: one begins by saying what the rule of law *is*. As one writer commonsensically puts it: 'Before we can measure how, say, a country fares on the rule of law, we need to define the concept.'[1] And where to look for the content of the concept? Also obvious: the law. Where else would you go looking for the rule *of law*?

And that is typically how and where, over generations, discussions have started. Writings on the rule of law are replete with answers to the question 'what is the rule of law?' that boil down to an enumeration of features or arrangements of official rules and/or institutions said to be its essential elements. The rule of law itself is to be found in particular (approved) forms, configurations, procedures, and arrangements of official legal rules and institutions. As the legal philosopher John Finnis puts it: '[t]he name commonly given to the state of affairs in which a legal system is legally in good shape is "the Rule of Law"'.[2]

The primary task, then, is to discern what elements of legal systems are needed to put them in good shape. The answer to *that* question is a matter of endless contestation, but that that is the first and fundamental question to ask and the official legal order the place to find the answer are not. Not only do accounts of the rule of law typically start there but almost as often that's where they stay. Features of the official legal order are their point of departure and return. If they move anywhere at all, for example to ask what the rule of law is good for, it is out from there: what goods are supposedly generated by legal orders that have these features, that are in good shape in these respects, compared to others that lack them?

3.2 Who Knows?

As obvious as what question to start with and where to find the answer is commonly thought to be whose answers should carry most weight: those of lawyers, of course. After all, who should know better than its adepts about what many of us know least: the law? That too seems to make sense, and to an extent it does. An account of what makes the law in good shape which did not draw on the insights of those who work with law would be missing something, probably a lot. Certainly it makes sense to lawyers. There are important truths there, to be discussed in Chapter 8, but equally important others are likely, not accidentally, to be missed.

It is an old truism (it even has a name: 'Miles's law')[3] that where people stand depends on where they sit. With the rule of law, what they understand seems to follow a similar rule. Lawyers sit in law offices, legal academics in law schools, judges in courts. Legal philosophers spend their sitting time reading lawyers, legal academics, judges, and other legal philosophers. Rule of law promoters try to build working legal orders where they are judged to have been absent, weak, or diseased. Legal institutions and rules are the centres of their working/thinking lives. That is as it should be; it's their job. And in well-functioning legal orders it's an important job.

Moreover, the old proverb 'cobbler, stick to your last' is sound advice, not just for cobblers but for many specialists in complicated and specialised disciplines. They know what they do, usually better than anyone else and commonly better than they know anything else. It's easy to make a fool of yourself if you don't know your way around.

However, there is a downside, particularly if what the specialist knows is only part of what they and we need to know. Every venerable profession has its *déformations professionelles*, members of every specialism a tendency to imagine that the connections between what they do and know, and what matters in the world, are closer, more direct, and more important than they might seem to outsiders. To a man with a hammer, everything looks like a nail. And while such deformations start with the experts, they can spread readily from them to those who acknowledge their expertise. Since lawyers know more about law than laypeople, if the rule of law is what you want, it can seem obvious that it is lawyers, with their insider knowledge, who best understand it and seem best placed to deliver it. And if you ask them, it is only natural that their answer focuses on the law. Why else would people ask *them*? As the hugely influential Declaration of the Congress of the International

Commission of Jurists (ICJ) held in Delhi in 1959 put it: 'the Rule of Law is a dynamic concept for the expansion and fulfilment of which jurists are primarily responsible'.[4]

Law is an intricate and technical discipline, and lawyers tend to treat the rule of law as a technical legal accomplishment. In the case of the rule of law, even though lawyers, legal philosophers, rule of law promoters, and others differ greatly over specifics, they agree on that much. There are many such accounts, but they all have in common this focus on official legal institutions, practices and officials, the character of the rules and principles they make, apply, and enforce, and the official institutions charged with those tasks. Differences among lawyers' accounts are about which features and arrangements of official legal arrangements are key, not whether they are at the core of the achievements we identify as the rule of law.

Lawyers typically, then, focus on particular legal institutions particularly configured: independent courts and judges, say; separation of powers, fidelity to precedents, clear rules literally applied, or some other nostrums drawn from the institutions and arrangements of particular legal orders. Often, they go more local than that: the rule of law is what works where we come from.

3.3 Some Canonical Examples

It has been like this right from the start of the remarkable modern career of the term. As I mentioned earlier, the phrase (but not the concept) was launched into the world of English-speaking lawyers at the end of the nineteenth century by Albert Dicey. First published in 1885, his *Introduction to the Study of the Law of the Constitution* went through nine re-editions (eight in his lifetime).[5] Although not the first to use the term,[6] it was Dicey who launched the career of the modern concept. Lawyers in Britain and throughout the English-speaking world learnt the short form of his account of the constituents of the rule of law, conveniently pared down to three aspects of the English common law (for Dicey thought, as the British often still like to think, that the rule of law is an especially British accomplishment). His account, or rather the three *conclusions* of his account rather than his motivating reasons, were taught to countless anglophone law students over generations. They were frequently drilled into countless anglophone lawyers for much of the twentieth century. So much so that the political theorist Judith Shklar, who was not fond of Dicey's account, nevertheless acknowledged it as 'the most influential restatement of the

Rule of Law since the eighteenth century'.[7] The details of this 'restatement' have been much criticised, but '[l]oved or loathed, Dicey remains a point of departure for thinking about the rule of law today'.[8]

The common law tradition gives a special place to courts, and so does Dicey. He focuses on their allegedly distinctive role, particularly that of what he called 'the ordinary courts', in the legal orders of England and its common law colonies and tributaries, which he regarded as having inherited the singular – arguably uniquely British – blessing of the rule of law. Dicey specified three elements of the English institutional order as accounting for this rare good fortune: inability of authorities to exercise 'wide, arbitrary, or discretionary' powers of constraint; subjection of all citizens, whatever their 'rank or condition', to the same, ordinary, law administered by the same ordinary courts – no special courts for special purposes or people (as found in France, which was therefore *sans* the rule of law); and constitutional principles that flowed up from court judgments in particular cases rather than down from general written constitutional documents. Dicey thought that these three features distinguished the English common law tradition from all others and accounted for the particular, and much noted, prominence of the rule of law in the former.

Practising and doctrinal lawyers everywhere commonly – consciously or unknowingly – echo Dicey's focus on legal institutions, even when they do not adopt, or even know of, the specifics of his account. They identify the rule of law with what they believe contributes to the 'good shape' of their own legal orders, and, like Dicey, it is typical of common law practitioners to focus on courts. The details of his account have been much criticised and its elements refined, rejected, and replaced over time – in Britain itself and more so elsewhere. Nevertheless, family resemblances remain strong. In particular, whatever the differences of detail, the typically unquestioned lawyers' assumption is that the core of the rule of law and the source of the good it does is to be found in some combination of features and operations of official legal institutions and the character of the laws they produce.

Take, for example, *The Rule of Law* by the late Lord Tom Bingham, a hugely eminent former Senior Law Lord of the United Kingdom. According to this immediately acclaimed book, you have the rule of law to the extent that '[a]ll persons and authorities within the state, whether public or private, [are] bound by and entitled to the benefit of laws publicly made, taking effect (generally) in the future and publicly administered by the courts'.[9] The major part of the book explicates features of a legal order suggested as necessary to achieve this goal, among them, as encapsulated in crisp, short, chapter headings and expounded in crisp short chapters: 'the accessibility of the law', 'law not discretion', 'equality before the law', 'the exercise of power' ('nothing ordinarily authorizes the executive to act otherwise than in strict accordance with … laws'), 'human rights', 'dispute resolution', 'a fair trial', and a concluding consideration of how these legal principles might be extended to 'the international order'. Note that while the details differ considerably from Dicey's, they are all to be found in the workings of the same legal institutional domain, precisely and not accidentally where Dicey looked for them.

Legal philosophers add a more abstract and generalising dimension to the institutional focus of practising lawyers. The most influential philosophical accounts focus less on particular institutions of law than on the formal character of the laws they produce. The most influential such account in Anglo-American theorising of the last century is probably that of the late Lon Fuller, professor of law at Harvard University for more than thirty years. The core and character of Fuller's account was further developed by the legal philosopher Joseph Raz of Oxford (and in many respects preceded by the eighteenth- and nineteenth-century polymath reformer Jeremy Bentham).[10] Similar lists proliferate among analytical legal philosophers. These accounts focus primarily on the formal character of legal rules, on aspects of legal craftsmanship that are thought necessary to make law knowable, comprehensible, and predictable and allow the law to be accessible to (and putatively therefore to guide) citizens.

In a book entitled *The Morality of Law*,[11] and its most famous chapter entitled 'The Morality That Makes Law Possible', Fuller composes a parable of a benign ruler, King Rex, who comes to the throne 'with the zeal of a reformer' determined to 'make his name as a great lawgiver'. However, he fails comprehensively, for each of his efforts totally lacks one of eight crucial elements of that morality. With each attempt to overcome a previous blunder, he makes another. The failures have to do, not with the content or substance of his laws, but with their form. Notwithstanding King Rex's best intentions, his efforts fail because they are not, in turn: (1) general, (2) public, (3) prospective rather than retroactive (i.e. they penalise conduct that occurred before the law was passed), (4) comprehensible, (5) non-contradictory, (6) possible to perform, (7) relatively stable, and (8) administered in ways congruent with the rules as announced. Even with the best will in the world, Fuller argued, Rex thus failed to honour law's 'internal morality', a failure that, at the extreme, would amount to a failure to make law at all.

It is important to stress that unlike the *content* of laws – whether they were just, fair, equitable, and so on, which were matters of law's 'external' morality, and which Rex tried to make as good as he could – each of these deficiencies, according to Fuller, amounted to a breach of law's *internal* morality, a kind of morality of legal craftsmanship. Purported laws that exhibited such deficiencies were to that extent likely to be unfit for purpose, and a purported legal order that fails totally in any of these dimensions does not, Fuller argues, deserve the name. One that scores well across the board will be doing well, even though other things matter, life is complex, and perfection in any of these dimensions is neither desirable nor possible.[12]

Though he used the phrase, particularly when citing others using it, Fuller used 'rule of law' relatively rarely.[13] Instead, as we have seen, he more often referred to King Rex's eight forms of failure as betrayal of the internal morality of law, which in my view (but perhaps not for his reasons) is the right way to capture what he was talking about. Whatever its effects in the world, at least one might want to say that no rules supposed to bind citizens should be inaccessible to them or unable to be followed by them. This is an elementary moral obligation, one might argue, particularly in a democracy. Who has the right to push you around for reasons you can't know? Who deserves to be so treated? Whether conformity to such principles adds up to the rule of law, however, or is responsible for the virtues commonly sought though the rule of law are questions we will shortly consider.

However, that is not how discussion of Fuller's account has played out. Instead, countless lawyers and legal philosophers took him, on the one hand, to be offering a succinct account of the necessary features of the rule of law but denied, or the other, that it amounted to a *morality* of any sort. His major critics thought there was nothing especially moral about it; at best it merely captured essential principles of legal *effectiveness*: crudely, if you want people to follow the law, whatever it is and whyever you want them to, they have to know what it says and be able to conform to it. If so, these principles did not add up to a *morality*, just as principles of effective poisoning,[14] blackmailing,[15] golf or safecracking (the put-downs were so frivolous and offhand, one might add wise-cracking),[16] while they might help you in a chosen task, could not be considered moral virtues. Everything depends on the moral worth of the substantive end they are enlisted to facilitate.

Nevertheless, Fuller's list became a kind of template for later accounts of the rule of law, understood primarily as necessary features of law, without which it could not serve a key purpose: to give *guidance* to the activities of citizens. You can't be guided by laws you don't know of, can't obey, or that do nothing to guide those responsible for administering and enforcing them.

Legions of subsequent writers adopted Fuller's list, or created roughly similar ones, as an accurate account of the ingredients of the rule of law, whether or not they thought their lists identified principles of morality or mere effectiveness. These lists have been endorsed, amended, and revised. There are plenty of subvariants, and alternatives as well to choose from, though the differences are often small.[17]

Indeed, as Waldron wryly observes:

> There is a tradition of trying to capture the essence of the Rule of Law in a laundry list of principles: Dicey had three, John Rawls four, Cass Sunstein came up with seven, Lon Fuller had eight, Joseph Raz eight, John Finnis eight, Lord Bingham eight in his excellent book on *The Rule of Law*. (I don't know why eight is the magic number: but it's a slightly different eight in each case); Robert Summers holds the record, I think, with eighteen Rule of Law principles.[18]

Undaunted, Waldron adds yet another list (ten principles) which while differing in important detail – it focuses on *procedures* courts should offer anyone brought before them, required if they are to be treated with respect rather than merely given guidance, rather than the *forms* of rules – shares exactly the same underlying assumption about where in general the rule of law is to be found.[19] The only (but significant) difference is that Waldron concentrates on the character of procedures in courts, while his predecessors stuck in the main to the form of laws. The details of many of these accounts are very different from Dicey's and from each other, but few even ask whether they are looking in the right places to find them.

A common distinction in rule of law discussions is between accounts that do not make reference to the substantive *content* of the law, particularly its moral content, but limit themselves to legal institutions and the formal character of its rules. Such accounts are commonly called 'thin', by contrast with 'thick' accounts that typically agree that some such thin institutional features are *necessary* for the rule of law but insist there must be more: the law must contain specific moral *content* – to do with justice, human rights, or some other esteemed values we believe law should help us attain. Dicey's account is quite thin; Fuller's is thin too, though he hints that a legal order embodying the internal morality is likely to be more congenial to morally acceptable purposes than one that does not. Bingham's is thick. Forms are not enough; the content of the law must include human rights.

I have no wish to join this old debate. My strong advice is: *don't choose*. This is another of those 'pernicious dualisms' that the great philosopher John Dewey railed against that confuse (sometimes useful) analytical distinctions in thought with (simplistic) dichotomies in life. The world often manages, often needs, to include them both. I believe that is true in general, and it is certainly true of the ideal of the rule of law.[20]

So-called thin accounts are at once not thin enough, since they typically assume as constitutive of the rule of law anywhere familiar and favoured institutional features of local set-ups which, even if they appear to work well at home, might not travel well. They are conversely too thin at the same time, since, as will be further discussed, they are compatible with deliberate and systematic violations of the animating and tempering 'spirit' of the rule of law, without which there is little to be said for its alleged institutional components.[21]

Thick accounts, on the other hand, commonly tend to be quite extravagant in what they require for the rule of law to be satisfied – for example, democracy, human rights, social justice, and so on. Famously, modern discussions of the rule of law were propelled by the 1959 Declaration of the Delhi Congress of the ICJ, which proclaimed that the rule of law 'should be employed not only to safeguard and advance the civil and political rights of the individual in a free society, but also to establish social, economic, educational and cultural conditions under which his legitimate aspirations and dignity may be realized'.[22]

Joseph Raz, one of the most prominent 'thin' theorists, with much of whose account I otherwise disagree, aptly notes that 'the report goes on to mention or refer to just about every political ideal which has found support in any part of the globe during the post-war years'. So much so that it threatens to blur any distinction between the rule of law and whatever else we might want, and so to destroy the usefulness of the concept: '[i]f the rule of law is the rule of the good law then to explain its nature is to propound a complete social philosophy. But if so the term lacks any useful function. We have no need to be converted to the rule of law just in order to discover that to believe in it is to believe that good should triumph.'[23]

That is a good point, but it does not save the dualism from being pernicious. One might agree with Raz, and I will, that we need to guard the distinctiveness of the ideal of the rule of law, so that it does not simply wash into values, for which we already have adequate concepts, without denying it any intrinsic substantive content at all. So, to foreshadow, I will argue (unoriginally) that the rule of law is particularly concerned with *ways* of exercising power rather than the *purposes* of such exercise, and the particular ways it is intended to reduce are arbitrary ones. That is a substantive value, but it is a specific one. Although, as we shall see, many activities, actors, and domains have reasons to be concerned with the potential for arbitrary power, law's concern is distinctive (not unique, but distinctive), because law is a vehicle for the exercise of power. But law's special concern is in no way 'a complete social philosophy'.

More can be said about this spurious distinction,[24] but for the time being I just note that either way, whether one's preference is for rule of law 'thin' or 'thick', its source and location are typically assumed to be found in the same place: within the official legal order of institutions, rules, provisions, and procedures.

Finally, apart from domestic lawyers and legal theorists, there is the rule of law promotion industry, which exploded in the 1990s and is still active around the world. Its activities are numerous, its successes are not notorious, and its nostrums have come to be challenged on the basis of harsh experience 'in the field'. They are also derided and undercut, as we have seen, by newly energised authoritarian rivals, for whom the rule of law has none of the charm it had for its promoters. But they are still big business, and were their activities better directed and more successful, I would recommend investing. It's a good cause.

Rule of law promotion is not the province of theorists but of practitioners, charged by their various international agencies with bringing its once undenied, and still much vaunted, benefits to allegedly benighted beneficiaries. Their 'take' on the rule of law is very different from that of Dicey or Raz. Though they too compile rule of law lists, and are aided by rule of law 'indexes', their lists are compiled for a different purpose. For them, 'getting to the rule of law'[25] is not a matter simply of distilling and sieving into the *concept* particular properties supposed to be immanent in existing, often long-evolved legal orders, when well-composed, but actually 'building' such well-designed orders in places where they are thought to be weak, not to have existed, to have dangerous rivals, or to have been destroyed.

Getting to the rule of law has traditionally been recommended to countries, predominantly in the Global South but also East, as an indispensable and central element of 'getting to Denmark' (as Global North as one can get), in the sense explained by Francis Fukuyama: 'The problem of creating modern political institutions has been described as the problem of "getting to Denmark" ... For people in developing countries, "Denmark" is a mythical place that is known to have good political and economic institutions: it is stable, democratic, peaceful, prosperous, inclusive, and has extremely low levels of political corruption.'[26]

Rule of law promotion is, then, an *active project* of 'building' the rule of law where it is supposed that it either never existed, has been undermined or destroyed, or for one reason or another is in poor health. And when it came to be thought that the rule of law might contribute to some valued goal: market economy, development, investment, trade (and also democracy and human rights):[27]

> Rule of law assistance became a multi-billion dollar enterprise that involved massive overhauls of legal regimes all over the world. A central characteristic of this rule of law project was the idea that the formalization of Western-style laws in the developing world was sufficient for promoting economic development. The idea was that implementing the market-based legal framework – or getting the rules right – would create the necessary conditions for growth.[28]

Notwithstanding the important differences, with important implications, between lawyers' and philosophers' attempts to identify rule of law features allegedly immanent in some particular legal systems, on the one hand, and promoting the rule of law as an activist universal project for nominated external purposes,[29] on the other, promoters have continued to draw up 'to-do lists [that] dominate based on remedies working elsewhere'.[30] Again, there are differences among these exporters' to-do lists and the homegrown lists of lawyers and legal philosophers, but they all remain within the extended family of rule-and-institution-centred rule of law compilations. One might argue that, even had Dicey nailed what had sustained the ideal of the rule of law in England, this would not mean (and he half-realised it)[31] that he had discovered a product for export, since the conditions of English excellence might not be generalisable. But that reason for caution rarely tempered the enthusiasm of workers in the promotion industry at its greatest heights. They too distilled what they fancied to be the ingredients of successful rule of law systems and sought to package them for export and transport them to be 'built' in foreign climes.

Thus, the rule of law in RoL interventions has been typically identified with aspects of 'the justice sector', particularly the judiciary and lawyers. And often it has been even narrower than that, for disproportionate attention has been devoted to specific branches and levels of legal rules and institutions, such as contract, property, criminal, and constitutional law, particularly as found in high and visible courts, rather than the mundane working of state administrative agencies, still less social interactions outside state agencies but affected by and affecting rules of law, though these latter enmesh and affect the lives of most citizens for most of the time. As one prominent rule of law promoter lamented:

> It is a simple empirical observation that when and where legal institutions really do matter, that is not where we find the big rule of law players. Global institutions, donor agencies and networks for promoting the rule of law typically attend to capacity deficits in criminal justice and the role and function of judges and other legal professionals. The reach of rule of law interventions is limited to the most symbolic and high-profile aspects of official power and authority. So, making the case over the years for more attendance to rule of law in relation to public administration, the everyday and mundane interactions between individuals and the state, has been an uphill battle, to say the least.[32]

Again, as two participant-observers of the promotion industry observed early this century:

> In legal circles in developing countries and in international development circles, *rule of law* has become almost synonymous with *legal and judicial reform*. Basic questions about what legal systems across diverse countries actually do, why they do it, and to what effect are either inadequately explored or totally ignored. In developed and developing countries, larger questions about the relationship of the rule of law to human rights, democracy, civil society, economic development, and governance often are reduced to arid doctrinalism in the legal fraternity. And in the practice of the international donor community, the rule of law is reduced to sectors of support, the most prominent of which is the judicial sector.
>
> ... During the last seven years, we have witnessed an explosion of literature related to legal and judicial reform. Yet very little attention has been paid to the widening gap between theory and practice, or to the disconnection between stated project goals and objectives and the actual activities supported.[33]

Some of the shortcomings identified here have been reflected upon and rethought in the light of disappointing experience, experiments in practice, and empirical research in subsequent years,[34] but slowly, not by everyone working in the field, and not enough. And donors still want tangible, quantifiable products for their money, preferably in short time frames, which might not be the best way to reach the rule of law ideal. It has certainly led to a lot of anguish in the field.[35]

3.4 The Poverty of Anatomy

For all their many differences, then, the various accounts I have mentioned, and the many people influenced by them and engaging with them, share a common underlying assumption: that to think well about the rule of law one must start by identifying what I have elsewhere called its anatomy or morphology. Or to change the metaphor, writers on the rule of law begin with its putative ingredients and move out from there. 'Ingredients' is an apt word here, for these accounts so often read like formulaic institutional recipes for a somewhat elusive feast.

I think that, notwithstanding its practitioners' more than occasional insights, this is altogether the wrong way to approach the rule of law, still less promote it. In this chapter, I suggest seven such reasons. I could add some, but here are my seven. First, *problems* change. Second, so too do the *circumstances* in which they occur. Third, so must *responses* to them. Fourth, conventional responses rarely pay serious attention to the complex nature of *social causality*. Fifth, partly because of mismatches between responses, problems, and circumstances, and partly because of social complexity and variety, much effort to cook up the rule of law by following established legalistic recipes is predictably *ineffective*. Sixth, the very legal forms typically chosen and crafted to generate the rule of law can be made *complicit* in its abuse. And seventh, if you want to explain to non-lawyers why any of this matters, they are unlikely to follow your explications of institutional detail, controversies about legality and constitutionality, and so on, or at least they are unlikely to follow you very far without asking: okay, okay, *but what's the point?* That seems to me a very good question to ask. To take these points in turn:

First, *problems*: The rule of law is a response to a common pathology that attends the exercise of power in the world. That pathology – which I will later specify as arbitrary exercise of power – can take many different particular forms, with time, place, culture, and circumstance all affecting them. This was always true, and it is arguably more dramatically so today. So much that affects the ways power impinges on huge populations changes so fast, and in so many unpredictable ways, that any particular institutional response is likely to capture only limited slices of the action, and only for a while. I started to think about these matters before artificial intelligence (AI), Amazon, and Bitcoin, and I'm only two letters into the alphabet. A quick skip takes us to Google, a jump to Meta and Microsoft, and before you know it we're at X. So a search for an identikit package of institutions, forms, and practices to respond to potential forms and sources of arbitrary power will often not take us far.[36] And if it does here today, it is unlikely to somewhere else tomorrow.

Second, *circumstances*: Aristotle, who valued the rule of law, lived in a world different in fundamental ways from ours. And I live in a society in many ways different from others not even an age but only a flight away. What might work one way in the Global North and West might do worse or differently (or perhaps better, who knows?) in the Global South and East.[37] My home in the Global South/East is less like many of its neighbours than countries in the North West. So I don't have to fly far to feel far. Differences between societies, within them, and over time – ecological, social, political, economic, cultural, religious, demographic, technological – are multiple, changeable, and cumulative. Since any particular society comes to develop and to share incrementally and intricately patterned ways of acting, thinking, and feeling that gel into (themselves continually changing) ways in which 'we do things here', responses developed in other times, places, and circumstances are often destined to miss their ostensible targets and hit and hurt others that no one had in mind.

Third, *institutions*: These also change and differ. They do so over time and from place to place. The institutions that occurred to Aristotle in ancient Greece, to distinguish 'the rule of law' from 'that of any individual', were not those specified in the Magna Carta of thirteenth-century England; those had little in common with the ones that Montesquieu focused on in eighteenth-century France; what he lit upon was different from Dicey's homegrown nineteenth-century selection; these from Fuller's in twentieth-century America; his (though not so much) from Joseph Raz's; and so on.

Not only do such institutions and practices differ; they are bound to since, as we have seen, the circumstances in which they operate, the forms in which problems present themselves, the capacities, the institutional practices, conventions, traditions, and options from which they draw, differ hugely over time and place. The modern state, for example, thinks about problems differently and does different things and in different ways from other forms of political organisation.[38] Different things are thinkable and much is doable and done by states themselves, for better and worse, that has never been done or doable before. So even if your concern is with one very old problem, for example arbitrary state power, specific ways of dealing with it are unlikely to be those recommended by Aristotle.

Fourth, *causality – social, crucial, and complicated*: We should not be surprised that rule of law promotion in places where dictators have ruled or the state has failed is often disappointing. It is intrinsically hard. But it doesn't help that we are often looking in the wrong places, in the wrong ways, at the wrong things. For whatever the effects of law in the world, they are relayed, or not, by processes of 'social causality', to which we are all subject but which are far from easy to understand, let alone control.

I take the phrase from the legal anthropologist Sally Falk Moore, who points out that 'legislation is based on folk notions of social causality, on ideas of how to make things happen through the use of the power of government'.[39] What she says of legislation is no less true of lawyers' accounts of the rule of law. And though lawyers typically leave the systematic analysis of social causality to others, among them social scientists, they often do, and arguably must, operate on the basis of folk assumptions about what it involves. Indeed much that they say about what the law is and does, and what it should be and do, depends on such notions, notwithstanding that like most folk notions these are typically implicit and not deeply considered. Moreover, the notions of both legislators and jurists are not those of folk-in-general but of legal folk. Such folk often combine strong experience with specific fields of activity, with confident intuitions about how they connect with everything else. No surprise that when they think of law and social causality, state law is assumed to stand front and centre. But it ain't necessarily so.

I have already mentioned the banal truth that lawyers take the rule of law to be centrally (and at times it seems all) about law. In numerous writings,[40] I have also sought to recall what should also be treated as banal but is not often a matter of reflection in writings about the rule of law: what might be called the social face or dimension of the rule of law.

Take rule of law promotion, for example. As Thomas Carothers observed, '[a]id providers know what endpoint they would like to help countries achieve, the Western-style, rule-oriented systems they know from their own countries. Yet they do not really know how countries that do not have such systems attain them.'[41] That is certainly a problem, and I will return to it. But it reflects a deeper ignorance: we do not really know how countries that *do* have such systems attained them. One reason for this is that whether the rule of law is strong or weak in any particular society is usually overdetermined: commonly, so many things seem to have gone right in societies where the rule of law is secure and strong, and so many things wrong in societies where it is weak, that it is hard to separate causes from effects.

It is widely believed, for example, that the ideal of the rule of law has for a very long time been comparatively strong in England, long a relatively rich country with ancient legal institutions and traditions, a legal profession of lineage and power, law-related practices that have developed over long periods, and a strong culture of legality that has seeped into the workings of most people's everyday lives,[42] all interwoven and with little deliberate design to produce the results they have. To pluck out of this dense thicket of institutions, cultures, traditions, mores, and practices merely the formal rules or architecture of legal institutions is to pick at leaves.

Often the usual lawyers' suspects aren't where many of the problems the rule of law is hoped to alleviate occur, nor are conventional legal ingredients always adequate or even appropriate solutions. Even when they are, they depend on social realities and forces that the official legal agencies only ever partially control. Many of the major threats to rule of law values come from beyond the state. And many responses to such threats will also need to be found outside the state and its laws – think media and civil society; and even where the state and law are important or relevant, their significance depends on complex chains of social causality, including the presence, absence, power, and character of social agencies and currents that the law can never completely control. In some circumstances, such agents and media of social causality support the efforts of state law; in others, they undermine it; in many places, both support and undermining take place. The tunnel vision of rule of legal centralism and formalism is not terribly illuminating here. And what is true of threats is equally true of sources of promise. I return to these issues in a larger frame in Chapters 7–10.

Fifth, *ineffectual promotion*: Those who – sometimes with the best of intentions, other times with other intentions – promote the benefits of the rule of law for themselves or for others frequently overlook these elementary truths. And so, promoters' endeavours have been rightly accused of – apologies for the fancy language – 'isomorphic mimicry … adopting the camouflage of organizational forms that are successful elsewhere to hide their actual dysfunction'.[43] As these authors observe of much development assistance more generally, rule of law promotion has often conflated 'form and function … one of the most ubiquitous but pernicious mistakes of development policy over the last sixty years, and is manifest most clearly in widespread implementation failure'[44] Institutions and rules are shipped or copied, but the outcomes expected do not eventuate. Does one then have the rule of law because the institutions appear to be in place, or lack it because nothing works as it should?

Should we say we have achieved the rule of law when we have built courts, installed computers, trained judges, and minted laws imbued from head to toe with Fuller's internal morality, but no one visits them and, more important, they have little effect on what goes on in the wider society?[45] Or what should we conclude when the efforts of so-called rule of law or human rights–focused law reformers to train judges and build courthouses in Sudan, to enlist and reform the law in the service of the poor, turn out not to do much of that but rather legitimise and strengthen the power of a dictatorship that is 'already accustomed to using any available legal tools and resources for political gain'?[46] Have they installed the rule of law, or have they simply issued their best guesses about what institutions are associated with it, which turn out not to add up to much? Or has what they have done got anything to do with the rule of law at all? These examples can readily be multiplied.

When legal institutional tinkering fails to prevent havoc, when people who count ignore the law and those who don't merely suffer it, the rule of law ideal is poorly served if served at all, whatever the laws look like. Often that comes as a disappointing surprise, but while it should be disappointing it should not have been a surprise. On their own, the legal institutional features so often identified with the rule of law are not up to the task. Indeed, on their own they never are but always need supporting circumstances, social and political structures, and cultural supports, which are not always available and are difficult to engineer.

Sixth, *institutional complicity*: The first five problems are typically encountered by people acting with the best of intentions. However, not everyone has those. In recent years, new concepts have entered the lexicon of observers of constitutional politics, among them 'abusive constitutionalism', 'stealth authoritarianism', 'constitutional coups', 'autocratic legalism', 'insulting constitutionalism', 'legal gaslighting', 'twisting and turning of the rule of law',[47] to which I will return in more detail in Chapter 8. This expanding lexicon seeks to keep pace with and capture some distinctive ways many modern authoritarian regimes use law, traditional 'rule of law', and 'constitutionalist' techniques to undermine rule of law values. Thus, the American scholar David Landau presciently analysed what he termed 'abusive constitutionalism'. Old-style authoritarians often staged coups, but that has become considerably less fashionable, and instead has often been replaced by:

> [A] rash of recent incidents in a diverse group of countries such as Hungary, Egypt, and Venezuela [that have] shown that the tools of constitutional amendment and replacement can be used by would-be autocrats to undermine democracy with relative ease. Since military coups and other blatant ruptures in the constitutional order have fallen out of favor, actors instead rework the constitutional order with subtle changes in order to make themselves difficult to dislodge and to disable or pack courts and other accountability institutions. The resulting regimes continue to have elections and are not fully authoritarian, but they are significantly less democratic than they were previously.[48]

Landau's article appeared in 2013, and the rash has not stopped spreading. Add Turkey, Poland, Mexico, India, El Salvador, Serbia, Slovakia, the United States to the expanding list. Brazil, Philippines, and Poland were also on the list but have left it for the time being. But watch this space.

This is not the first time that people need to be reminded of the distinction, and often distance, between the existence of any particular legal institutions, on the one hand, and closeness to the goal of the rule of law, on the other.

Legal punctiliousness is at times strikingly evident in the activities of modern populists in power,[49] and I return to them in Chapter 8. However, the problem of bending often well-intentioned institutions to ill-intentioned interests extends beyond populist politicians. After all, criminals have a vocational interest in taking the law seriously; ruling criminals, it today appears, all the more so.

Seventh, *pointlessness*: It is easy for professionals in any sphere to be so caught up in internal complexities that they forget, or fail to communicate to outsiders, what is at stake in their technical discussions – not to mention that they themselves often won't *know* what's at stake, since the stakes often do not stop with law. That is true at the level of *analysis*: one should always be in a position to know *why* something you are doing, presumably for some reason, matters. It is also true at a very *practical* level, so one can avoid that disease of goal displacement – of which bureaucrats are commonly, often rightly, accused. They can tell you what the rules require but not why. Eventually, often, they themselves forget why, though they don't forget the rules!

This is not merely an issue of experts finding it hard to express their profound and arcane mysteries in language simple enough for laypeople to understand. It goes deeper. Many people who benefit least from the rule of law have good reason to think we are starting and stopping in the wrong place if we confine our attention to enthusiasts' usual suspects: the internal workings of legal institutions, the formal attributes of rules, the procedural configurations of high criminal courts. For most people in most places, these are not where they are ever likely to be able to discover either how close or how distant their order is to the rule of law ideal. But there are many other places where they might value the former and regret the latter.

Many of the world's populations endure political orders (and disorders) where the central institutions of law are far from central in the society. Other forces matter more. At the other end of the scale, the state matters too much, so much so that nothing – least of all law, however handsomely configured and appointed – gets in its way. Billions live close to one of these ends or the other; often a single human life will have to endure both. Where that is so, if citizens demand the rule of law, as often they do,[50] I surmise that their pleas are likely to have less to do with the formal character of legal rules, or internal workings of institutions and practices (though these are often not irrelevant to the relatively few who reach them and whom they reach), than lawyers in rule of law rich countries are likely to find familiar. Pressed for their thoughts on the rule of law, I surmise again, those citizens' concerns will only occasionally overlap with what concerned Lord Bingham in his well-selling volume of that title,[51] an admirable if entirely conventional insider lawyer's characterisation of what the rule of law looks like to him (in the United Kingdom and other similarly privileged countries), recommended for the world. For (a third surmise) the fundamental concerns in societies where the ideal of the rule of law is honoured only or typically in the breach,[52] and/or where power is exercised in ways systematically antithetical to the values that animate it,[53] are not likely to be about legal forms or even procedures. More likely, they will have to do with whether and in what ways those who wield power that can scare and hurt are free to do what they like, in ways those subject to them have good reasons not to like.

To the extent citizens/subjects think of law in such societies, they might be pleased, but are likely to be surprised, if power-wielders have to *reckon* with law at all, for that is not their experience or expectation. If law is taken to matter at all, it is often more naturally to be thought of as irrelevant to what they are able to do, or as part of an arsenal that rulers either wield for their own purposes or regard as sometimes one, sometimes the other. In such places, that is in much of the world, it is not a local assumption that the powerful need to reckon with the law, even if the unpowerful might have to. What might be needed to satisfy the latter's yearnings that things might be otherwise in their societies at this time is unlikely to be found in Lord Bingham's book, or indeed most of the literature by western lawyers that purports to characterise the fundamental nature and ingredients of the rule of law.

3.5 What Is the Question?

Let us return to Gertrude Stein's dying words, quoted in the epigraph at the start of this chapter: '"What is the answer?" … "In that case … what is the question?"' That's a pretty good way to end a life and, even if it came a bit late, it's a pretty good question, for particular questions will frame and require particular sorts of answers rather than others.

Card-carrying contributors to discussions of the rule of law will doubtless continue to debate the merits of their various lists, specifications, and definitions of what the rule of law is. Often a new account comes into vogue because it seems a better answer to the same question. I don't propose to add to or choose between any of them because I believe that, however intelligent and insightful these answers might be, they begin with the wrong question: not a *bad* question but one which needs to be delayed until others are resolved, and then supplemented by other questions, if it is to be a useful response to besetting problems.

4

Ends and Means

> People don't go into a DIY store because they need one of our drills. They go because they need a hole in the wall.
>
> Attributed to (among others) Nolan D. Archibald, former CEO, Black & Decker [Power Tool] Corporation

> If you don't know where you are going, you might wind up some place else.
>
> Yogi Berra

If you look it up on Google, you will find that the first of these epigraphs appears in many versions and is attributed to many parents.[1] It is easy to see why one might claim it, for it captures a deep insight (as indeed does the second), and this book turns on it. More wordy and less homely than these epigraphs, the argument of this chapter is this. The inadequacies sketched in Chapter 3 are not accidental but symptomatic. They point not merely (but of course also) to the complexities of the world, with which partisans of the rule of law must inevitably contend, but to misleading ways of thinking, which make it hard to do so effectively. And Mr Archibald (if it was he) has identified the mistake.

There are at least three reasons his epigram appeals to me so. First of all, drills are enlisted to accomplish something, and we evaluate them by their likelihood of success. If we don't want a hole, we won't want a drill; if we want a hole of this or that size, crisp not jagged, in this or that material, we will choose this or that drill, of this or that size and power, with this or that bit. We need to clarify our purposes before we can specify what might serve them. So, to think intelligently about drills, still more to design them, start with the hole. Presumably, after all, that is how drills came into being.

Secondly, and perhaps less obviously, some purposes are more immediate, more immanent, than others, though not on that account necessarily more important. It is likely to matter much more to us to hang a favourite picture than to put a hole in the wall. And yet the hole precedes the hanging; it is a condition of it. One way of putting this point is to say that immanent goals are what the subject of our inquiry *does*; external goals are what the achievement of that goal might enable and/or support.

Thirdly, not only might immanent goals of this sort be useful conditions for a whole range of further (often more valued) purposes but those purposes might compete with each other without competing with the condition they share. Thus, I might want to hang a picture, my wife a tapestry, my kids a dartboard, and each of us might value one of those further goals without valuing the others. Still, we all need the hole.

Analogies are never exact, of course; that is why we call them analogies, not identities. Nor is this one. In particular, as I argue in Sections 4.3 and 4.4, finding ways to achieve the immanent goal of the rule of law is much more complicated than making a hole, and while drills have long been known and effective, the work of crafting ways to achieve and sustain the goals of the rule of law, in the many ways and places they are under challenge, is still way ahead of us.

With that (far from minor!) qualification, I think about the rule of law this way. Translated from carpentry to political morality, what we want it *to do* should determine how we think about what it needs to be like to do it. What we want it to do that *for* will explain why we want to do it at all. And there might be a range of good reasons to want it, among which partisans of the immanent goal might disagree. Some might want the picture, others the tapestry. If they need a hole to do it, however, they will have to ask how best to make one.

To bring this closer to home, in anticipation of Chapters 5 and 6, I argue that the immanent goal (the hole) for the rule of law is to temper the ways that power can be exercised in order to reduce possibilities of arbitrariness. There are many reasons that goal is valuable. They include securing freedom, protection from fear, enhancement of trust and coordination, encouragement of thoughtfulness;[2] but each depends upon satisfying this prior condition. So we can value that condition, while maintaining different reasons for doing so. Achievement of tempered power, then, is what the philosopher Philip Pettit calls 'a gateway good ... a good whose realization promises to bring the realization of other goods in train'.[3] That makes it potentially valuable even to those not especially excited by it per se, because they value it for what it might make both unavailable and available.

One preliminary caution: while tempered power is the condition of many goods, it is not the only good we want and might be in tension with others we also want. We live in a complex world where choices, even tragic choices, might need to be made. That does not make tempered power less of a good. It just means we might have to make difficult decisions and accommodations.

Back to the hole. To confuse the similes even further, with the rule of law as with drills, we should start by asking: What's the Point?

4.1 What's the Point?

A conclusion of Chapter 3 is that to start discussions about the rule of law with legal institutional checklists, as is typical, constrains thought and blocks imagination. Familiar features of legal rules or institutions, so often those that just happen to be taken to embody the values the rule of law is thought to serve in our own time and place, come to be thought of as default settings for achievement of its ends, even as necessary settings for them, wherever we believe the rule of law is to be sought. So much so that we often fail to consider whether the means we resort to are best to achieve our ends, and merely rehash existing formulae, presuming that once in place they will get us where we want to go. That makes it hard – ruled out, as it were, by definition – to think either that the values of the rule of law might be served in the absence of familiar hardware or indeed that they might be disserved even where the hardware is present. This way of thinking can tie us simply to what we happen to know, rather than allow us to explore whether there are other and maybe better ways of getting where we want to go. Means displace ends in our thinking, indeed might overshadow and obscure them completely.

On this account the starting point for thinking about the rule of law should not be purported anatomies or morphologies of the rule of law, that seek to list its essential legal forms and structures. Rather, we should ask after what the ancient Greeks called its *telos*, its proper purpose or end, before going on to try to specify what might be necessary to attain or approach that end. Less fancily, start with the hole not the drill.[4]

4.2 What Kind of Point?

Many goals that we seek can be described in simple, and purely descriptive, terms. 'Hole' is one such. We might want one dearly, but the concept is not too complicated and it says nothing about the value of holes; like it or not, a hole is still a hole. We talk about the rule of law differently. Though this does not follow simply from the meaning of the individual words in the phrase 'the rule of law' (very different in connotation from '*a* rule of law') is what the philosopher W. B. Gallie calls an 'appraisive concept'[5] rather than a purely 'naturalistic' or descriptive one; it is a concept pervaded by what another philosopher, Hilary Putnam, calls 'the entanglement of fact and value'.[6] Many of our most important political and moral concepts, such as democracy, justice, and fairness, are of this sort. They do not just describe but have an inextricable normative, evaluative element. These are some of the most important concepts we use, and their character generates contention which is, if Gallie is to be believed, 'essentially contested' and never-ending, among people who agree on one thing, and sometimes one thing only: that they involve achievements of high worth and significance.

If the rule of law is appraised as strong in a society, its partisans assume something good has been achieved; if not, if the society 'lacks' the rule of law, it is generally assumed to lack something of value. If we say, for example, that there were lots of laws under Stalin and a lot of rule but there was not much rule of law, we are not making some cute descriptive distinction. We are saying that something valuable was missing in Stalin's Russia. So, at least among the legally and philosophically unwashed, the rule of law means something more than the mere existence of law, or indeed any particular formal or even procedural attributes of laws. Even critics acknowledge such built-in value-laden assumptions, if only in seeking to debunk them.

This is often obscured by the apparently descriptive character of conventional institutional accounts of the rule of law, among them the several lists and catalogues I discussed in Chapter 3. Particularly when they are taken up by acolytes, accounts of the rule of law *begin* with enumeration of features of laws – clear, prospective, non-contradictory, and so on – but they routinely end with endorsements of some achievements or other, attributable to such features, and their authors don't seem to think the links are coincidental. Though that is not the order in which things are usually presented, one might be forgiven for thinking the evaluation has spurred the lists rather than merely followed from them. After all, laws have many features. What guides the selection of just some of them, particularly those that are then argued to support predictability, freedom, security, dignity, and so forth? Why those features? Why those effects?

In fact such concerns are plain in some of the classics of the genre, such as Dicey's, Fuller's, and Raz's. Raz, for example, explicitly derives his eight principles of the rule of law from what he calls the 'one basic idea' that 'the law must be capable of guiding the behaviour of its subjects'.[7] My objection to this account is not to his method but to his basic idea. It is, as I argue in Chapter 8,[8] altogether too thin to capture the ideal of the rule of law. But at least he starts with the right question. However, once a list hits the ground it takes hold and generations of followers just stick to one or another, without asking why. The appraisive concept, the rule of law, is identified with a particular selection of institutions and rules.

Form should follow function. So, rather than start with some or other of the famed 'laundry lists' of postulated elements to make up the rule of law – often inherited from significant thinkers who worried about real problems but were only remembered for their lists – the rule of law needs to be approached *teleologically*, by asking what's the point? And only then: how do you make that point?

Even the harshest critics of the rule of law assume that it is valued, even if not by them. If they say the rule of law is bunkum, or doesn't have the virtues its partisans claim, they are doing something very different from someone who points out that what was thought a vegetable (e.g. a tomato) is really a fruit or what is apparently a hill (Uluru, in Central Australia) is really a large rock.[9] We might debate descriptions of the rule of law as well, of course, but the *value* that partisans attribute to it and opponents might deny is intrinsic to the debate. A lot of facts are involved, but the rule of law involves values all the way down.

But while the rule of law is an appraisive concept, the appraisal involved is of a particular sort. Justice is also an appraisive concept but of a different kind. We might demand justice and condemn injustice for their own sakes, as it were, without thought of consequence, as in the Latin maxim *fiat justitia, ruat caelum*: let justice be done, though the heavens fall. This disdain for consequences makes less sense with the rule of law. Those who appraise it positively do so typically and primarily for its contribution to allaying threats it is alleged to avert and/or supporting goods it helps us attain. Those who praise the law do so because they think its consequences are valuable; those not enamoured deny it has those consequences, or that such consequences are valuable, or point to costs which devalue the achievement. They occupy the same evaluative terrain, even if they take different positions on it.

Our appraisals of the rule of law, in other words, are more instrumental than intrinsic or, to fancy up again, more consequential than deontological. They are more like the gratitude we might feel for a waste disposal system than for justice done 'though the heavens fall'. Its elements might even be quite charm-free in themselves, but if it directs materials we do not want to infect or pollute our lives into channels that are safe, maybe even productively useful, and if it also makes valued amenities (rights, running water, holes) available, for example, then we appreciate it for its capacity not only to resolve problems we want to avoid but also to make available facilities we want to enjoy. Again, this or that fiscal policy might not stir our hearts or loins, but if its consequences help combat inflation, that is welcomed. Covid-19 vaccines are valued for their effects; drills for the holes they make.

Though many of us value the rule of law very highly, it has more in common with plumbing, fiscal management, vaccines, and carpentry than it does with some of the other political concepts close by it, or other things we might value simply for the intrinsic excellence, beauty, or skill they display. We look to the rule of law for its hoped contribution to solving certain problems rather than as a source of aesthetic delight, excitement, or a love-filled life. I know no one, apart from an occasional old lawyer, who is likely to experience anything like Romain Rolland's 'oceanic feeling' in its presence. It is commonly sought for what it helps us avoid and, when avoided, that it then enables us to accomplish.

For the rule of law is what Jeremy Waldron has called a 'solution-concept'.[10] Many contested concepts – 'achievement concepts' – he argues, are held together by reference to some earlier exemplar, our interpretations of which fund our present understanding of what is central to the concept. So, if we are concerned to adhere to 'the Christian way of life', we might glean what that involves by interpreting and following biblical accounts of the life of Jesus; if Jewish, we start earlier in the Bible and skip Jesus.

Some concepts are of a different sort, however. There is no exemplar, but there is an exemplary *problem* to which, if it is sufficiently serious, we seek solutions. Different conceptions of the concept are different suggestions about how this problem might be solved. Waldron suggests the rule of law is that sort of concept, though of a sort more complicated than plumbing, perhaps more like a vaccine: 'Law is a solution-concept, rather than an achievement-concept; it is the concept of a solution to a problem we're not sure how to solve; and rival conceptions are rival proposals for solving it or rival proposals for doing the best we can in this regard given that the problem is insoluble.'[11]

Solution-concepts are distinctive. Before we purport to identify the elements of any solution sought, indeed before we can consider whether it is a solution at all, the first question we need to ask is: what is the problem? For while you can easily identify a problem without a solution, it makes no sense to specify a solution without knowing the problem it is supposed to (help) solve.

So, identifying the problem is the first step. Identifying what would count as a solution comes next. Its nature (and value) is derivative, not intrinsic. These aspects identified, we are only then in a position to move, more specifically to ask how solutions of this sort to problems of that sort might be approached, and what resources are available to us, in the circumstances we confront. That will require subsidiary questions to be asked and answered about the specific forms in which the problem occurs and what means are best adapted to deal with such forms. At this point, the role(s) that law might play, the forms it needs to assume, the institutions that would best serve, *what else besides law would be needed*, are all in principle open questions, as is the relative salience of whatever particular measures and institutions we light upon.

We respond to such questions by drawing on experience, thought, and experiment. Since this is not the first time such questions have been asked, we are not starting from nowhere, which is a plus. But since we always start from somewhere and some time in particular, we need to be cautious about generalising to somewhere else, some other time. All the more is this true with problems (and putative solutions) of the complexity and significance that confront anyone drawn to the ideal of the rule of law – for that is commonly harder to achieve than a hole in the wall.

The central problem we call on the rule of law to help solve, I argue in Chapter 5, is arbitrary power, more precisely arbitrary exercise of substantial power over others, significant enough to cause fear and/or harm. In Chapter 6, I argue more specifically that what we should seek from any promised solution is that it manages to *temper* the exercise of such power. These two suggestions need to be defended, but they start with one advantage over several, besides the fact that I endorse them: I am not the first to think this way, whether they articulate it in this fashion or not. Countless people have suffered from and worried about the harms that arbitrary power threatens, and wished that power's exercise might be reliably tempered (often using precisely those terms). In this respect, I take unoriginality to be a virtue.

The rest of this book seeks to explain these characterisations of problem and promise, justify them, and then draw out some of their implications. However, the *way* of proceeding I recommend does not depend on anyone agreeing with those specific characterisations, justifications, or implications. I hope to persuade readers of the central importance of tempering the exercise of power so it not be arbitrary, and that is the core of the book's argument. However, even if I fail in that ambition I want to insist that to think clearly and well about the rule of law we should *begin* by working out what we want it for and what we want from it, not by drawing on some available/canonical definition of its specific components and then wondering what they might do.

Countless discussions of the rule of law, as we have seen in Chapter 3, start the other way around, with drills rather than holes, often just with one form of drill: 'the rule of law is or requires....' Moreover, it is common to conflate drill with hole, what the rule of law is with what it is hoped to accomplish. In this way, they neatly invert the architect Henry Sullivan's injunction that 'form follows function'. Unless you are Robinson Crusoe, who might happen upon a (presumably cordless) drill on his island and ask what it's good for, that is not a great way to *start*, even though, as Section 4.3 suggests, it might sometimes, in some circumstances, be a sensible way to *proceed*.

4.3 Traditions and Intimations

I have a lot riding on the wisdom of Black & Decker's CEO. But what if he got things the wrong way round? After all, aren't there many circumstances in which it makes sense to see what you can do with the drills you have, rather than speculate from scratch how best one might puncture a surface that lacks the holes you want. Where ways of doing things are familiar, often inherited, and found reliable in the circumstances one anticipates using them, abstract teleological investigations might not be the best way to start. We know what a drill is for and what it is like. Just pick it up and get on with it.

One might argue similarly that even if you do not really understand why, you can still benefit from inherited institutions and arrangements that happen to be on hand and seem to do the job. Thus, Philip Selznick quotes an observation of his friend and colleague, Kenneth Winston, that 'we often don't know what it means to be committed to the value apart from the forms'. Selznick comments that 'we often have more confidence in a particular form or practice, rooted in experience, than in an abstract statement of why the form exists or what values it upholds'.[12] We never start from nowhere, and there is much to be said for the preference of the conservative philosopher Michael Oakeshott for the 'pursuit of the intimations' of existing traditions,[13] over attempts to vindicate, still less impose, some rationalist plan or alien design, which might have come from anywhere and lead nowhere.

Not only might that be more congenial to people happy with what they've got. There is a deep sociological insight there. With social, political, and legal institutions and traditions, where you start is not merely a stepping-off point. It forms contexts and elements of thought and action that stay around to affect, infect, encumber, and inform what its *inhabitants* do, think, and imagine. People do not merely *have* arrangements, traditions, customs, and conventions. We are made up of them, as it were; so too are our thoughts and ways of thinking and feeling, our perceptions and evaluations of what is normal, proper, likely, including what forms risks might take and what are the odds that we will have to run them.

Typically, much of what we make use of, including much of the most important things, is not a product of anyone's design or even thought; it's simply there. Acceptance of established ways, beliefs, canons of judgment, argument, and proof often takes place without those who accept being conscious of doing anything other than acting naturally. This implicit sort of acceptance is crucial to the 'tacit knowledge' which the scientist–economist–philosopher Michael Polanyi saw as the precondition of cultural competence in any particular area or field of activity, the basis on which 'we *attend from* something for attending *to* something else',[14] without giving our crucial starting points any attention. Because these starting points are so often taken to be obvious, they are not referred to as authoritative; just accepted as natural. Indeed, they are often not referred to at all; their power commonly being inversely related to their visibility.

An implication might seem to be, then, that we often do better to start with and work within what we have and what we know (or at least believe) works well, as domestic lawyers typically do within established legal systems, than by speculating about what might work as a solution to some generally stated problem or serve some similarly generally stated goal. That is how many devotees of the rule of law, among them Dicey, think: it is a signal virtue (these days, also a virtue signal) of our legal institutions; we should tend those elements of our institutions that support it and, in societies where it is lacking, propagate them. We're not starting from nowhere, after all.

That conclusion reflects a deep wisdom shared by some of the best sorts of conservatism (Edmund Burke's, for example) and sociology (Philip Selznick's). As to the former, underlying but separable from conservatives' substantive attachment to what they have (or think they have), sophisticated conservatism has a deep sociological message to impart to thinkers of every political stripe.[15] For where conservatism is more than fondness for what one knows and has, there is a *methodological* core that insists that social arrangements are typically inherited, interwoven, and *complex*. That core has two sources: observation of what societies are like and of limitations on what we can know.

Sociologically, methodological conservatives stress the complexity of long-established arrangements, the undesigned nature of many of the most important of them, their multiple interconnections and reciprocal effects, their pervasive shaping and structuring impact on individuals and groups, the only partly chosen environments they find themselves in, and, as a result of all that, the certainty that our social, political, and legal interventions will have unintended consequences. All this can be overdone, of course, but it can also be underdone. It should never be. It is too important.

Second, conservatives stress the appropriateness of epistemological modesty, modesty about what we know, a modesty warranted by the limited degree to which we understand how social arrangements and institutions work, can predict how they will react to what we do, or can even guess how some parts of society will be affected by what we do to other parts. We're not that smart.

Such methodological conservatism does not necessarily entail, though it is often confused with, an unreflective positive evaluation and attachment to the substance of whatever we think of as our established traditions. You don't have to like what you have, to recognise it is there. Methodologically conservative liberals or democrats or social democrats in a society without liberal or democratic or social democratic traditions, values, or institutions might indeed have no sympathy for what they find around them. They should still recognise that these things are there and need to be *taken account of*, and that is a serious business, whether one likes them or not, whether one is out to subvert them or reform them or not. If they are simply *ignored*, there will commonly be a price to pay. There are no clean slates. Drawing on them, you must take account of what is already there. That is so whatever you think of where you are or what you find.

Recognising such complexities, conservatives often say, allows us to draw on socially and generationally accumulated wisdoms, where an insistence on interrogating and judging every practice, custom, tradition, or proposal by the light of one's (often puny) reason tends at best to cleverness, often shallow individual or ephemerally fashionable smarts, rarely wisdom. Consequently, they regard humility in these matters as not merely more attractive than *hubris* but intellectually better off as well.

The implications of these insights themselves are, I believe, profound and every can-do institution-builder needs to reflect upon them and the cautions that they imply. However, those implications are more complicated and ambiguous than they appear.

First of all, not everything we inherit is good for us. Even Oakeshott observes that '[i]f the present is arid, offering little or nothing to be used or enjoyed, then this inclination [to follow the 'intimations of tradition'] will be weak or absent'.[16] Aridity is the least of it. In many times and places the presently inherited past includes traditions in relation to the exercise of power, of great vintage, strength, resilience, local acceptance, and appeal, that applaud arbitrariness, discriminatory uses of power, and exclusion and exploitation of those with less of it. Even a Russian leader of impeccable democratic leanings (exquisitely rare but not quite oxymoronic) would have to face that problem, as do feminists and members of minority religions, races, and poor classes in those many parts of the world where traditions are thick and deep as quicksand. And about as sticky and tasty. There are many such places.

Moreover, even when one has salutary traditions to draw upon, often there are competitors, as we will see in Chapters 8 and 10, and as the Trumpian abuse of many venerable American traditions with the support of others is showing us in real time today. How to choose?

Where something you value is challenged, you need to be able to respond. Unfortunately, a conservative disposition is not always helpful in discriminating between inherited traditions that are good for us and those that are not, between what we should cherish and what we should deplore, between those that can and should persist, and those which will need to change or go. Many conservatives, still more reactionaries, are more inclined to stick to traditions than evaluate them. However, traditions and intimations do not always brim with resources for response to even well-targeted and intended critique, beyond 'that's the way we do things here'. Again, the pursuit of even valuable intimations is often unable to deal well with novelty, variety, hostility, change, and (where, as now so often, that is essayed) transplantation of locally un-intimated modes of being and doing. Yet the rule of law has often been called in aid in a variety of societies, and in a variety of circumstances, where the social and political order is beset with challenge and change, and/or where powerful traditions and traditions of power are hostile to its fundamental values. Indeed, calls for the rule of law often are most urgent and desperate in places where the goal is distant, hostile competitors are present, one wants things to be otherwise, and the legal institutional hardware and software locally available point in different directions to that proffered by metropolitan promoters, who find their drills have difficulty penetrating local walls.

That might mean that one should leave well alone, and often that is good advice. But too many local authoritarian rulers avail themselves of it, while their citizen/subjects struggle for better. In such conditions, there is nothing wrong with seeking to combine conservative/sociological insights, on the one hand, with teleological commitment, on the other. Each should infect the other.

So, on one side, conservatives and sociologists are right to warn that transplantation of hardware from one context to another, though often attempted, will frequently be a fruitless, or even counterproductive, option – particularly since much of the cultural, normative, customary, and traditional software which nurtured tacit knowledge in the homes of rule of law missionaries is harder to ship than the institutional hardware that is sent abroad or the rules that can simply be downloaded from the web and copied. That is partly a problem of identifying, transporting, and transplanting what really counts in the place of origin; a huge problem since the usual institutional suspects – both hardware and software – are often effects more than causes of deeper cultural, social, and political processes and traditions, and in any event are powerless without such (commonly untransported) processes and traditions.

Equally, when one takes the rule of law abroad, one commonly finds that much of the cultural, normative, customary, and traditional software at home is different from what exists in destination countries. To change the metaphor, transplants might simply not take root or might quickly wither or be deformed by inhospitable climes and local, long-established, and often very sturdy growths. They might die or be killed, grow in perverse forms, and/or come to behave in strange ways.

A corollary of the conservative/sociological point I am discussing is that in every society, local traditions, habits, conventions, and circumstances play crucial roles, no matter what one thinks of them, if only because they are there and locals will continue to pursue *their* 'intimations', even where they are inhospitable to values that many people (including many locals) might want to generate. It doesn't even require hostility; reinterpretation in local idioms is often enough to denature even the best-meant presents sent from abroad. They get lost in transportation, translation, and attempted transplantation.

Moreover, pursuit of intimations on its own can be an inadequate response when, as today, familiar ideals are challenged by international and domestic adversaries who respect neither those ideals nor the means traditionally associated with them but seek the 'end' of the rule of law in a literal sense, not meaning by that its *telos* but the more common sense of the word, its eclipse.[17]

One response to challenge might be simply to defend what one has, but even in the once-applauded 'homes' of the rule of law, existing institutions often need removal, renovation, or replacement. As we learn from Lampedusa's great novel, *The Leopard*, 'if we want things to stay as they are, things will have to change'.[18]

Even the best arrangements can come to suffer from internally generated pathologies, such as corrosion and corruption or internal contradictions. Moreover, particularly at a time of overwhelming technological changes in and sources of power, it is far from obvious that standard-issue rule of law technologies and strategies can be counted upon to offer relevant or adequate solutions. They might have, somewhere, once, but that was there and then. Times and places change. Think about the contemporary internally and externally beleaguered United States, only a few years ago found by sophisticated sociological surveys to exhibit a peculiar 'veneration for the rule of law'.[19] Where did that go?

In all these (various but rather plentiful) sorts of circumstances, pursuit of intimations is not enough. We need to think more deeply about first principles and purposes. All the more in contexts where the rule of law has been proposed for many societies where it was not strong or long embedded and/or where it often faces fierce competition from social and political forces that have no wish for it and whose major interests allow no accommodation for it.

Conservatives (and sociologists) are, then, right to emphasise the stickiness and complexity of social and political arrangements. In any particular place, dealing with the application of ideas, institutions, and ideals requires local knowledge; the more the better. That is a key thesis of this book. But it requires other things as well. And conservatives (but not all sociologists) have less to say about those things. For apart from taking into account what exists, one needs to be in a position to reflect upon it and *appraise* it, both affirmatively and critically. So I again recommend starting with function before form, the point or end of the enterprise before the means, the why before the what.

4.4 Legal 'Technologies' and Social Realities

Analogies are always imperfect. So, while I owe a lot to Mr Archibald's insight, there comes a point where we must part. This is that point. The discussion so far suggests we must do more than rely on our familiar drills to take care of every hole we want and might need. However, it has another important implication, not conveyed by the analogy with which this chapter started, though lending even more support to consideration of function before form.

Mr Archibald's epigraph, and the analogy I have drawn, might be taken to suggest that the rule of law should be regarded as a kind of technology, even if a social technology rather than a mechanical one. Indeed, it is often spoken of that way. However, the analogy is liable to mislead in several ways. For drills and the rule of law are different from each other, in ways that matter.

First of all, today, the aptness of drills for making holes is widely known and uncontroversial, and the machinery needed to produce such a result readily manufactured, replicated around the world, and adaptable to most of the likely material contexts in which we want to make holes. Anyone who wants to can grab a drill and get on with it. Of course, the nature of materials varies and so does the nature of drill bits, and so on. But we have the technology and the process pretty well down pat. Not a great deal of reflection needed. Just go to Black & Decker.

However, even with regular mechanical technology, it's not always so easy. Consider the Leveraged Freedom Chair,[20] developed by a team at the Massachusetts Institute of Technology for disabled persons in resource-poor countries, where terrain, architecture, occupations, materials, prices, and financial resources differ dramatically from those available to wheelchair users in Massachusetts. The new 'mobility device' was developed after extensive testing in a range of countries and circumstances, large stakeholder involvement, and high-level neurophysiological expertise and testing. It is made of readily available, replaceable, and cheap bicycle parts, uses levers for propulsion where conventional parts do not operate successfully, and can handle local terrains and other hurdles which regular wheelchairs cannot. It is cheap to buy and fix, in contexts where the materials and costs for repair in Massachusetts would be out of anyone's reach. So contexts matter, even with regular technologies. They even matter for drills: some are good for some sorts of holes, in some sorts of materials, others for other sorts in other sorts. And there are plenty of sorts.

All the more is this so for legal, political, and social 'technologies', such as the rule of law. That, after all, is part of the point that conservatives and sociologists make about social traditions and cultures: there is a lot about the social, political, and legal contexts of legal institutions that develops organically, at least unintendedly, is not designed or made, and is often recalcitrant to manipulation, hard to transport, and not always easy to plug in. Quite apart from whatever surrounding conditions its effectiveness might depend upon, that we identify with difficulty and have even less understanding of how to extract and implant, all this will affect the effectiveness of whatever legal 'technology' one chooses.

After all, the central point of conservative and sociological critiques of transplantational, can-do optimism still stands. Laws and institutions are never free-standing, fully designed tools but in some, usually huge, measure are encrusted with traditions, assumptions, conventions, customs, cultural givens, resources and frames, models and taboos, interpretations, and familiar modes of conflict and management of conflict that their routine workings depend upon. Citizens of any particular society are used to some ways and not others. Expectations derive from experiences, and experiences differ, even within societies at any one time, all the more between them and over time. For it is not only individuals' personal experiences and expectations that matter. Expectations are conveyed by tradition, culture, and education, sometimes over many generations. And then there are *interests*, sometimes welcoming to the ends of the rule of law, often not.

Indeed, as Frank Upham has observed critically, of those professing the (in 2006) 'new rule-of-law orthodoxy': '[l]aw is seen as technology when it should be seen as sociology or politics'.[21] After all, for the billions of dollars spent on reforms that seek to 'install' or 'build' (an assumption-rich success word in itself) the rule of law in Myanmar,[22] say, or Afghanistan or Russia, we don't have many success stories. Sometimes the product – for example, courts that people are willing and able to approach and that do something useful for them, and so on – has turned out to be hard to construct (particularly by foreigners).[23] Sometimes the foundations are hard to discern and the institutions wobble, fail, and fall. Other times edifices are erected but no one pays much attention to what's going on inside; that's not where the action is.

There is a Bulgarian saying that 'law is like a door in the middle of an open field. Of course, you could go through the door, but only a fool would bother.' Where that saying has resonance, the rule of law is not likely to. There are so many reasons, in many societies, not to be a fool. Just think about it. Who are the doorkeepers – ours or others'? Who opens the door? For how much? To whom? What's on the other side? What is in store for me or people like me over there?

And so, on the one hand, as Deval Desai notes in his aptly titled book on rule of law promotion, *Expert Ignorance*: '[t]oday, the rule of law is axiomatically central to global governance. Yet the rule of law is more radically contested than ever before.'[24] On the other, as his book reveals, 'experts remain committed to giving authoritative meaning to the concept of the rule of law, even as they proclaim that they cannot'.[25] While many of these tensions stem simply from the real difficulty of the tasks attempted, we also typically do less well than we hope because we think less well than we might.

Even if it made sense to think of the rule of law as technology at all, it would have to be understood as a distinctive kind of technology: an *interaction* not a production (or with the chair, transportation) technology, to borrow a distinction from the American political theorist Stephen Holmes.[26] Technology intended to shape and direct social and political interaction is typically harder to transplant and to generate than production technology.

To sum up: contexts and patterns of human interaction vary dramatically between societies. If you want to affect them, it is now coming to be admitted by many who have tried,[27] you cannot assume that institutions that work one way in one place will work similarly in another, or that expectations of how they work and should work are everywhere the same. That is implicit in the arguments of Oakeshott and Selznick discussed earlier: the traditions, practices, institutions, and ambitions that I have been 'socialised' into differ from yours. Much of the informing background is taken for granted as apparently natural, indeed typically goes unnoticed. Imported laws and institutions land in territory without much that made them tick and where much that is already firmly embedded, familiar to importers but unknown to the exporters, is often both unprepared and unwelcoming.

In Aesop's fable *The Boastful Athlete*, a visitor to Athens scoffs at local competitors and claims to have witnesses who can confirm that he jumped a stupendous distance in Rhodes. His interlocutor retorts: *hic Rhodus, hic salta* (Rhodes is here, jump here). Such repeat performances are often not easy or successful. Yet the ultimate test for the success of the rule of law has to be present and local.

What it is capable of doing here and now, not what hallowed institutional items it is composed of or what it is said to have done elsewhere or at other times, is the only thing that ultimately matters. New institutions or advocated practices must mesh with a lot else that is going on, and it is often hard even to know what is going on, let alone how to affect it. Societies where the ideal of the rule of law does or does not prevail are not empty spaces ready for missionaries of the rule of law to fill or occupied by eager acolytes waiting for conversion. They are already inhabited by people and groups who are not always interested to convert and/or at times by elites whose existing ways, interests, and power can continue in their current form only for as long as rule of law aspirations can be held at bay, whether by rejection of the transplants intended to redeem them or by cannibalisation or hollowing out of them. The failure to recognise such social and political configurations of traditions, motivations, incentives, interests, and understandings means that a lot of 'international best practice' models that do the rule of law circuit end up as useless junk in places to which they are eagerly exported (and sometimes also eagerly imported) but ill adapted.

The goal of the rule of law, then, needs to be pursued in ways that are in sync with local ecologies, and it needs to be sustained within them. It cannot just be screwed in, though it can be screwed up, and it depends as much on what's going on around it, on particular relationships and interactions in that ecological niche, as on its own characteristics. This is a larger point than it seems, indeed several points, and we will return to them in the following chapters.

I have talked, in general terms, of goals and conditions, but as we have seen, for the ideal of the rule of law, as for many technologies, consequences are key. Whether the rule of law ideal has been approximated in a society is a matter to be found outside legal institutions themselves, in the ways power affects interactions between citizens and the state, between citizens themselves, and, as we will see in Chapter 7, between non-state entities and citizens. For unless the goal of the rule of law is approached in the world around it, all the internal, institutional elegance of design, and conformity to 'international best practice', is not worth a hill of beans.

To conclude, none of this is or can be simple. 'Drill' is a solution-concept too, though not an essentially contested one. There are no huge controversies about what drills are for, nor what is needed to make them work, nor what an acceptable solution will look like, even though holes come in many shapes and sizes, and depending on the sorts and sizes you are after there are plenty of different drills and bits.

But then, the problems the rule of law is called on to help solve come in many forms too, and solutions will need to vary greatly over time, place, and circumstance. Moreover, with the rule of law the problems to be solved are more complex, contested, indeterminate, and difficult to deal with than drilling a hole. Why, how, or whether they should be successfully dealt with at all are matters of continuing debate. I have proposed in general terms how we might proceed in conducting such a debate. I will now try to get into it.

PART III

Stakes

5

Mischief

By and large, the Organs had no profound reasons for their choice of whom to arrest and whom not to arrest. They merely had over-all assignments, quotas for a specific number of arrests. These quotas might be filled on an orderly basis or wholly arbitrarily. In 1937 a woman came to the reception room of the Novocherkassk NKVD to ask what she should do about the unfed unweaned infant of a neighbor who had been arrested. They said: 'Sit down, we'll find out.' She sat there for two hours – whereupon they took her and tossed her into a cell. They had a total plan which had to be fulfilled in a hurry, and there was no one available to send out into the city – and there was this woman already in their hands!

Alexander Solzhenitsyn, *The Gulag Archipelago, 1918–1956*

The hands of one of the men were placed on K.'s throat, whilst the other plunged the knife into his heart and turned it round twice. As his sight faded, K. saw the two men leaning cheek to cheek close to his face as they observed the final verdict. 'Like a dog!' he said. It seemed as if his shame would live on after him.

Franz Kafka, *The Trial*

There is an old English common law doctrine known as the mischief rule. It advises interpreters of statutes to seek out:

> The true reason of the remedy; and then the office of all the Judges is always to make such construction as shall suppress the mischief, and advance the remedy, and to suppress subtle inventions and evasions for continuance of the mischief … and to add force and life to the cure and remedy, according to the true intent of the makers of the Act, *pro bono publico*.[1]

And what is 'mischief'? According to *Black's Law Dictionary*: 'In legislative parlance, the word is sometimes used to signify the evil or danger which a statute is intended to cure or avoid.' This is an apt way to start thinking about the rule of law. Its partisans hope that it will help ward off a particular sort of mischief, and if that fails offer an appropriate remedy.[2] In this chapter, I seek to characterise the kind of mischief that has prompted appeal to the rule of law. What we should seek from a remedy will be taken up in Chapter 6.

What, then, is the mischief that the rule of law has been called to remedy? Better put, since in recent years there have been so many, is there any central and distinctive kind or characteristic of the sort of mischief that should be the special, *immanent*, concern of the rule of law?

I believe there is. A central preoccupation of political and legal reflection over centuries is with ways in which power is exercised, and a central concern has to do with long familiar pathologies associated with such exercise. Of course, we have many fundamental 'thick' substantive concerns with what purposes power might be enlisted for, both negative and positive: war, peace, oppression, justice, human rights, and more. These are concerns of moral and political debate more generally, whatever we think, and whether we think, of law or the rule of law at all. Apart from such overarching questions of moral substance, however, partisans of the rule of law have had another long-standing apprehension – more particular, more instrumental, more adjectival or adverbial than purposive in character. It has to do with the ways in which power is exercised, as distinct from what it is exercised *for*. Some ways of wielding power are objectionable, no matter what the wielder's purposes are. A traditional term used to characterise ways that worry is that they are *arbitrary*. Affection for the rule of law responds to a specific antipathy – to the exercise of power in arbitrary ways.

Many people, in many ages and places, have made this connection.[3] Of course, as with so many other good things, the Greeks got there early. Thus, Aristotle contrasts 'the arbitrary rule of a sovereign over all the citizens' and 'the rule of the law [which] is preferable to that of any individual' on the grounds that 'he who bids the law rule may be deemed to bid God and Reason alone rule, but he who bids man rule adds an element of the beast; for desire is a wild beast, and passion perverts the minds of rulers, even when they are the best of men'.[4] Two millennia later, John Locke insisted that:

> Absolute Arbitrary Power, or Governing without *settled standing Laws*, can neither of them consist with the ends of Society and Government, which Men would not quit the freedom of the state of Nature for, and tie themselves up under, were it not to preserve their Lives, Liberties and Fortunes; and by *stated Rules* of Right and Property to secure their Peace and Quiet.[5]

One does not even have to look to philosophy. As William Lucy points out:

> It aids our understanding of the nature of the rule of law to compare it with what it is not, namely, arbitrary power ... one uniquely relevant hunch exists in ordinary thought and speech that deserves close attention: the idea that if there is some 'thing' that the rule of law certainly is not, then that is arbitrary power.[6]

So, my proposal is deliberately, and I think aptly, unoriginal. I'm hitching my wagon to a long and old line; not merely, however, because it is old or long but because there are good reasons to continue it. In many societies and cultures,[7] thought about the rule of law draws upon long histories of experience of and opposition to arbitrary power, often expressed with that adjective or some other with similar or overlapping connotations. There are probably also equally long traditions that by contrast support arbitrary use of power, though these days its supporters usually avoid the adjective when describing their unattractive ambitions. These are not rule of law traditions. Typically, and naturally enough, they are *anti*-rule of law traditions, often warmly embraced by power-holders and their supporters. That is why the rule of law has often been a slogan of resistance.

On this interpretation, appeal to the rule of law signals the hope that there may be ways, and that the rule of law might be important among them, to diminish the kinds and levels of arbitrary sway available to those who exercise power.

Of course, the dangers that can flow from the exercise of power are much broader than captured by the concept of 'arbitrariness' and extend to the whole panoply of abuses to which power can be turned, which include abusive ways of exercising power and abusive purposes for which power might be exercised. However, abuse is so capacious a category, so empty of specific content, extending both to ways and purposes, means and ends, that we quickly risk falling foul of Joseph Raz's caution lest we elide goals specifically associated with the rule of law with whatever we find good. 'Arbitrariness' focuses on abusive *ways and means*, and their effects, quite apart from the substantive ends the power is enlisted to pursue.[8]

'Arbitrary power' does not reach every way in which power might do harm, but it has been a, indeed *the*, term typically used to convey the central concern of generations of writings about the rule of law, and it covers a lot of ground. If there is more that needs to be covered, I am happy to see the argument and if persuaded seek to reach that too. The borders of the concept of arbitrariness are not the sticking point. Focus on abusive *ways of exercising power*, as distinct and apart from the purposes for which they are employed, marks a distinctive concern.

Neither arbitrariness nor power on their own but arbitrariness *when added to power* is what engages such concern. I can be as arbitrary as I please when I have no significant power over others. Indeed my eccentricities, like those of a pet or a child or a clown,[9] might be part of my whacky charm – until they hurt. The arbitrary beneficiary of a lottery win rarely complains either. Nor is the exercise of power per se necessarily malignant but the (often necessary and salutary, if also often dangerous) stuff of life and, in many forms and circumstances, necessary support for good life. The problem with arbitrary power, then, is neither the adjective nor the noun by itself but their combination. Masochists perhaps aside, few of us want to, and none should have to, endure circumstances where significant power can be exercised over us in arbitrary ways. Though we will never be without power and differences among opportunities to exert it, it is better not to be prey to obnoxious, because arbitrary, uses of it.

Of course, power comes in many strengths, and not every exercise is likely to do much damage. Serious concern is with significant power and significant arbitrariness. And arbitrariness is not the only thing we don't want yoked to power. Other mischiefs, other remedies. But the combination is sinister. Arbitrary power, when significant, is commonly odious. Opportunities to exercise it should be minimised. Easy to say; hard to do. One resource, commended over millennia, has been the rule of law.

We can't leave it there. After all, merely to explain the rule of law in terms of reduction of arbitrary power threatens to collapse one essentially contested concept into two others: power and arbitrariness. So, to avoid just kicking the can down the road, some more specification is necessary. With the caution that these are proposals rather than axioms, and characterisations of concerns rather than analytically precise definitions of concepts, I start with power.

5.1 Power

Writings on power are vast; so too the uses to which the word is put. The term appears far more often and even more indiscriminately than the rule of law. After all, as the sociologist Steven Lukes observes:

> It is not self-evident what talk of horse power and nuclear power, of the power of grace and the power of punishment, of power struggles and the

> power of a group to 'act in concert', of the balance of power and the separation of powers, of the 'power of the powerless' and the corruptions of absolute power all have in common. Moreover, different ways of conceiving power are natural to differing perspectives and purposes.[10]

In this discussion, trying as best as I can to capture the aspects that have generated specific concerns that might relate to the rule of law, I will be selective.

In its broadest sense, 'power' refers to the capacity of anything to produce effects,[11] to 'make a difference'.[12] In that understanding, pretty well everything that moves, and many things that do not, can have and exercise power. Literally from time immemorial, humans have exercised power over nature, which is interesting enough but not my subject until it affects *social* power, power over people. Social power is the capacity of humans to make a difference to other humans – either directly or via human-contrived institutions, organisations, constructions, actions, or effects on nature – or to make a difference to things that make a difference to other humans.

Social power is generated by and within natural and social structures. Who can exercise what powers, when, how, and with what effects depends upon the nature of those structures, their positions, roles, resources, and opportunities; exclusions and inclusions within them; their capacities, talents, and vulnerabilities; and the interplays between and environing contexts in which all the above can be accessed and deployed in the various interrelationships that make up social life. All these things can be moved around (though more by some people than others), but they cannot be eliminated. For social power is not a *thing* that some possess and others do not, nor can societies exist without it. Rather, as the historical sociologist Norbert Elias has observed, power is not 'an amulet possessed by one person and not by another; it is a structural characteristic of human relationships – of *all* human relationships'.[13] Understood in this way, power is not 'a substance one has, but … a facility of which one can avail oneself'.[14]

Writers on social power often distinguish two varieties, 'power to' do things and 'power over' other people. The latter is not simply top-down but always a question of balances,[15] but the balances are rarely equal. Inequalities of power vary, and some can be deliberately diminished, but power over is typically asymmetrical. Some have more than others.

In discussions of power, most people concentrate on 'power over', and many don't like what they see – inequality, domination, exploitation, brutality, suffering. Thus, as Elias remarks:

> For many people, the term 'power' has a rather unpleasant flavour. The reason is that during the whole development of human societies, power ratios have usually been extremely unequal; people or groups of people with relatively great power chances used to exercise those power chances to the full, often very brutally and unscrupulously for their own purposes.[16]

For many partisans of the rule of law, too, there's the rub, and the reason so many people have sought ways to purge exercises of power of their 'unpleasant flavour'. Such purging is unlikely to occur naturally or without resistance, nor is it a simple thing to contrive. A great deal of the history of political and legal philosophy, and discussion of the rule of law, has been concerned with how it might be brought about.

There are, however, forms of social power which are not obviously brutal or unscrupulous or even obviously dominating but which partisans of the ideal of the rule of law should still be concerned about. Thus, the German sociologist Heinrich Popitz, not much cited in English writings, has a more discriminating understanding of such forms than is common. According to Popitz: 'human beings can *directly do something* to other human beings; furthermore they can modify *expectations, standards, and artifacts* that exercise effects upon others. We have an existence open to harm, we depend on artifacts, our action is future-oriented and it needs orientation. Therefore we must suffer power.'[17] Each of these forms of power can be exercised both arbitrarily and not. Each of them can mess with our bodies or heads when arbitrarily exercised. Each of them, then, is a potential focus for concern for partisans of the rule of law's ideal.

However, the problem is *not* that 'power itself has always appeared the archevil',[18] as Friedrich von Hayek suggests was the nineteenth-century liberal view. He may be right that many, too many, so-called liberals and neoliberals have thought that way (though typically more in relation to the power of governments than of private actors), but the view cannot be taken seriously.

Many forms of power, and many ways of exercising it, are not merely necessary evils but genuine, indispensable, goods. Without the ability to exercise power effectively many institutions that we rely upon to serve, protect, and sustain public goods would be unable to do so. Alexander Hamilton put it well:

> Powers must be granted, or civil Society cannot exist; the possibility of abuse is no argument against the *thing*; this possibility is incident to every species of power however placed or modified.[19]

Societies could not do without routine exercises of power in many forms and for many purposes. We should not want to deny the need or emasculate the capacity for power to keep peace, defend populations against abusers, enforce legal judgments, collect taxes, balance other powers, mobilise resources to fight thugs, marauders, and pandemics, protect the vulnerable, supervise those whose acts affect them, coordinate social interactions, regulate institutions with significant public effects, and so on. People who have ever seen, still worse lived in, what are called 'failed states' have witnessed or suffered a terrible experience, in this case *not* because the state's power is too great but because it is too weak to do what we need states to do. Other states, conversely, might be too strong or strong in the wrong ways, of course, and both these tendencies are problems we should seek to avoid.

We do not want ordinary citizens to be impotent either, whether in relations with each other or with those we often call their rulers. One important source of tempered state power, discussed in Chapter 10, is a strong and civil society, able to mobilise to pursue common interests, demand accountability, investigate abuses from overmighty institutionalised powers, including state powers, and require cooperation rather than coercion or corruption from powerful others, including both state and non-state others.

In a spiral of some complexity, the very need to guard against threats from abuses of power requires power, power able to temper power. Who guards the guardians? is an ancient question and a perennial one. More prosaically, and in many settings that have nothing to do with politics or states or threats or dangers, the exercise of power, including power over others, is unavoidable and frequently salutary in many circumstances. Without it many purposes that require coordination and common purpose could not be achieved.

In any event, we're stuck with power. It's not going anywhere. Though they constantly shift and change shape and character and force, power and differentials of power are here to stay. One might dream of a world in which power and disparities cease to exist, but that is not our world and I am confident it will never be anyone's. The rest is Utopia, literally 'no place/nowhere'. No one will ever live there.

So the hunt is on for ways not to eliminate power but to harness, bridle, discipline, moderate, and *temper* – all common terms in rule of law traditions – the ways those with the resources and capacity to exercise significant power can do so. Again, not power itself but *abuses* to which exercise of power is liable are the foes in rule of law thoughts.

When Aristotle wrote of the rule of law as preferable to 'that of any individual', he was not questioning the legitimacy of power per se, or of rule, but suggesting that some ways of exercising it are likely to more legitimate than others. We need to distinguish between more and less legitimate ways. One ground for distinction is between those forms that readily allow or encourage arbitrary exercise of power and those that reduce it; within any particular form, some ways of exercising power are more arbitrary than others.

So long as human relationships are structured in ways that some – individuals, groups, leaders, institutions, organisations – have systematically more power, in any of Popitz's forms, than others do – and that is, I wager, forever – arbitrary exercise of power will remain a matter of fundamental concern. Traditionally the focus has been especially on political power, usually as though it was obvious that the rule of law only applies to states. Those reasons are understandable but ultimately, I will argue in Chapter 7, questionable. Arbitrary power has many sources and respects few bounds.

5.2 Arbitrary Power

Though the term is familiar enough, in both ordinary and specialist legal talk, it is not a simple idea. Examples are more easily recognised than articulated. We are likely to think loosely in terms of examples or synonyms – capricious, whimsical, and so on – rather than precise definitions. A trawl through the scholarly literature reveals little consensus on what it means.[20] Indeed, a common academic way with it is to clear one's throat by confessing it is 'under-theorised',[21] perhaps in the hope that acknowledgement might soothe, at least keep at bay, conceptual pedants. You can then draw breath and keep using it without more, in an 'I know it when I see it'[22] sort of way. I know the temptation, and in many talks and publications I have succumbed to it.

Here I try to reform. I am not a conceptual analyst and do not promise purity or comprehensiveness. As ways of exercising power vary, new ways to exercise power mischievously might be found that cannot be squeezed into the characterisations I offer here, or indeed any plausible definition of arbitrariness. If so, we need to be alert to them and creative in thinking about how to deal with them. Remedies might need to be fashioned and refashioned anew. Nothing I say is intended to exclude that, least of all because they do not fit some familiar definition of arbitrariness. For the moment, arbitrary exercise of power covers much of the ground; if new ways of exercising power, for example through the technological innovations that spring up all around us, do not fit our preconceived conceptualisations we will need to extend old concepts or develop new ones. However, the core idea is unlikely to disappear: there are ways of exercising power, *apart from* the real or ostensible purposes for which that power is exercised, that themselves are liable to cause mischief, that we would be better off without, and that we should try to avoid. If we cannot, we should give thought to remedy and repair.

Power can be exercised arbitrarily – *at source* – when it need be disciplined by no justifying reasons other than its author's choice to do so: 'I can do what I like.' It can also be *experienced* as arbitrary by its targets when they cannot know the reasons, even if they exist, or when those reasons have no reasonable relationship to what they have done: 'Why me? Why that? Why for that?' Often exercise and experience go together, but not always. One who is harmed on the basis of a secret reason is not better off than one on whom harm is inflicted for no rational reason at all. The ideal of the rule of law is that no one be in a position to exercise significant power arbitrarily and no one has power visited on them for no reasons they can apprehend.

I suggest four ways of exercising power, each of which has been a staple of rule of law antipathy as at once common, arbitrary in itself, or liable to facilitate arbitrariness, and for that reason an objectionable pathology – or source of pathologies – of the exercise of power. I think they are four different, though often overlapping and connected, ways in which people are made vulnerable by power exercised arbitrarily or experienced as arbitrary, or both.

The four ways I discuss are not the same but exhibit malign family resemblances, all the more malign when, as is often the case, they are combined or when one involves others. So, exercise of power in any of these ways should be treated with great suspicion, as it has been by partisans of the rule of law. Better still, the possibility of such exercise of power should be reliably circumscribed, and the paths towards salutary non-arbitrary exercise of power opened and smoothed. These four are unlikely to exhaust the field, but they're a start, power-wielders often seek to exercise power in these ways, and, as I have suggested, they cover a lot of ground. Here I will just summarise them, with only slightly strained Mao-style alliteration, as the four 'uns' of arbitrariness.

Power is likely to be exercised arbitrarily or experienced as arbitrary, commonly both, when it is: uncontrolled, unpredictable, unrespectful, or ungrounded.

5.2.1 *Uncontrolled Power*

Power-wielders are not subject to routine, regular control, limit, audit, or accountability to anything other than their own will or caprice. They can do what they like. This sense is nicely captured in the Indian Supreme Court's interpretation of a constitutional provision guaranteeing equality before the law. This provision, the Court held, implied that natural resources could not be handed out 'according to the sweet will and whims of the political entities and/or officers of the State'.[23] This might well have been the original notion of the term. Exercise of power is arbitrary to the extent that it 'is subject just to the *arbitrium*, the decision or judgement of the agent; the agent was in a position to choose it or not choose it, at their pleasure'.[24] The common law tradition from the medieval period to the eighteenth century recurrently warned against arbitrary power in this sense: no one, not even the king, should have arbitrary, that is, uncontrolled, power. Many kings would have disagreed.

Thus, while the seventeenth-century philosopher Thomas Hobbes argued that people would be prepared to agree to give up their independence to an absolute sovereign power in order to deliver themselves from the terrors of an anarchical 'state of nature',[25] his younger contemporary, John Locke, responded, as we have seen, that: 'Absolute Arbitrary Power, or Governing without *settled standing Laws*, can neither of them consist with the ends of Society and Government, which Men would not quit the freedom of the state of Nature for, and tie themselves up under.' He went on: 'It cannot be supposed that they should intend, had they a power so to do, to give to any one, or more, an *absolute Arbitrary Power* over their Persons and Estates, and put a force into the Magistrates hand to execute his unlimited Will arbitrarily upon them.'[26]

The point is important, especially against Hobbes's powerful arguments for unlimited sovereign power, but it was not new even then. Again, Aristotle was way ahead. The 'most typical form' of tyranny, he argued, '[i]s just that arbitrary power of an individual which is responsible to no one, and governs all alike, whether equals or betters, with a view to its own advantage; not to that of its subjects, and therefore against their will.'[27]

5.2.2 *Unpredictable Power*

This second mode is often but not necessarily associated with the first, as in Samuel Johnson's dictionary, where 'arbitrary' is defined as '1. Despotique: absolute; bound by no law; following the will without restraint ... 2. Depending on no rule; capricious'.[28] The notion, very powerful in law, is that power is exercised arbitrarily when those it affects cannot know, predict, understand, or comply with the ways power comes to be wielded. There is no way of preparing for it, abiding by it, adhering to its provisions. It can strike like lightning, out of the blue. That is the kind of abuse typically taken up in the various lists of formal characteristics of legality or the rule of law – clear, prospective, public, and so on – propagated by contemporary analytic philosophers of law;[29] and it is true that if one has no idea how power will be exercised, because the exercise of power is unrelated to whatever rules supposedly govern it, or there are no rules, or they are secret, retroactive, too changeable to know, vague beyond specification, contradictory, or impossible to perform, then one has been treated arbitrarily. One also has been treated without regard or respect. A point to be stressed here is that whether or not the power-wielder is following some rule or other, if the subjects of the exercise cannot know what that rule is, they have been dealt with arbitrarily.

Athenian democracy was more concerned with avoiding arbitrary power (tyranny) in the first sense than in the second.[30] The common law tradition too, from the medieval period to the eighteenth century and most resonantly in the seventeenth, laid more emphasis on avoiding the first sort of arbitrariness;[31] it was less concerned with the law's clarity than with its superiority, even to the king.[32] However, Locke was already onto it, associating the second with the first sort of arbitrariness, absolute power. Thus, to expand the earlier quotation:

> Absolute Arbitrary Power, or Governing without *settled standing Laws*, can neither of them consist with the ends of Society and Government, which Men would not quit the freedom of the state of Nature for, and tie themselves up under, were it not to preserve their Lives, Liberties and Fortunes; and by *stated Rules* of Right and Property to secure their Peace and Quiet ... And therefore whatever Form the Common-wealth is under, the Ruling Power ought to govern by *declared* and *received Laws*, and not by extemporary Dictates and undetermined Resolutions.[33]

Note that Locke is not insisting merely that government be by something that can be called 'law'. Nor does he say anything in this passage about the *content or purpose* of the law. He insists, rather, on the need for laws of a particular – clear, stable, and knowable – *character*, on '*settled standing Laws* ... *stated Rules* of Right and Property ... *declared* and *received Laws*, and not ... extemporary Dictates and undetermined Resolutions'. And the reason for this emphasis on the medium, even apart from the message, is plain. The vice he is most concerned to condemn is not the exercise of power itself but 'Absolute Arbitrary Power', 'Government ... Arbitrary and at Pleasure'. And, as anyone who has suffered such power can confirm, he is right to condemn it.

The increasing turn from judge-made law to explicit parliamentary law-*making* in eighteenth-century England,[34] and the contemporaneous development in Prussia of the concept of the *Rechtsstaat* (legal state; state of law) in Europe, put more emphasis on this second modality of arbitrariness than the first. Particularly as it developed in the late nineteenth century, the *Rechtsstaat* did not know a higher law that limited the power of the state but distinguished between law that was properly so-called because it met certain formal prerequisites, without which so-called laws were not thought to deserve the name.[35]

Often, arbitrary power is identified with *discretionary* exercise of power, because it is assumed to be either uncontrolled or unpredictable. Dicey made the identification explicitly. However, must wide or discretionary powers be arbitrary? It is obvious that they could if the powers were so wide that power-holders could do anything they wished in any way they chose, or discretion so untrammelled that, again, power was quite unconstrained and its manner of exercise able to be capricious and unpredictable. Dictatorships often frame their laws in such ways, and some imagined slippery slope in this direction appears to have underlain the fear of many opponents, among them Dicey, of the welfare state's expansion of governmental powers and discretions.[36] However, it is not self-evident that discretion is of its nature illimitable or that it cannot be reviewed or made accountable.[37] Moreover, width and discretion might indeed be necessary for flexibility in many circumstances of governance, and for many legitimate ends. If they can be effectively framed and subjected to principles, standards, and review, it is not at all obvious that they cannot be controlled or made relatively predictable.[38] Eliding them all, however, does make it easier to oppose an active state.

Many contemporary accounts of the rule of law place most emphasis on predictability. But predictability is never enough. There are many regimes where everyone knows you will never win against the state. You can bet your house on it, and in some regimes you can bet you will lose your house if you seek to resist or question them. You know what's coming. For power to be unarbitrary, predictability must be linked to agency; there must be something you can do about it. You might not win, but you can try. And you're in with a chance. Otherwise you are treated arbitrarily because you are not treated with respect.

5.2.3 *Unrespectful Power*

A third way to exercise power arbitrarily, whether or not it is controlled and/or predictable, occurs where no space or means are made available for those affected to be heard, to question, to inform, or to affect the exercise of power over them; their voices and interests can simply be ignored by those exercising power. They are treated as if they were, in Jeremy Waldron's apt phrase, 'a rabid animal or a dilapidated house'.[39] Kafka's *Trial* exemplifies this way of treating persons (as well as the others). Indeed that is the central theme of that work. It took a long time for its protagonist K to realise it, but from the first to the last he was not allowed to know what was happening to him or do anything to find out or contest the power wielded over him. His cry – 'Like a dog!' – at the very end of *The Trial* – takes its power not primarily from the fact that he was being knifed to death but that this was the *culmination* of a process of demeaning him for the totality of his enmeshment with the law. Of course, disrespect is not a vice limited to law. It is a way of exercising power arbitrarily. And, for those subjected to it, a particularly demeaning experience.

The moral basis for objection to power exercised in such ways, best but far from first or last articulated by Immanuel Kant, is that we all should always be treated at least as *persons* with interests and reason that must be taken into account. Other rationales have been offered, and the intuition is strong. That doesn't mean you will necessarily win, but you are treated as an active, thinking, feeling, hurting *subject* in exercise of powers that can affect you, particularly harm you. It is a large, indeed fundamental, human concern, not merely a legal one.

The notion that power exercised arbitrarily in this sense is objectionable is encoded in many legal procedures, as Waldron stresses, but it is a much larger concern than that, not necessarily limited to law or legal institutional safeguards. Thus the Israeli philosopher Avishai Margalit, in a marvellous work of public philosophy, defined *The Decent Society* as one whose institutions do not humiliate people.[40] His book explores with extraordinary imagination, moral sensitivity, and philosophical, social, and psychological insight the many ways in which the arrangements and activities of social institutions manage to treat people indecently. Many of them stem from ways in which power is exercised disrespectfully towards those dependent on it, even when intentions are honourable (as in many rule-applying welfare interventions of charities and the administrative state); even more when they are not.

5.2.4 *Ungrounded Power*

Finally, a fourth mode of arbitrary exercise of power occurs when power is exercised in ways that are not reasonably grounded in, related to, or derived from whatever purpose is claimed to justify it. Joseph Raz, seeking to identify arbitrariness generally, at least captures this particular form: 'What is arbitrary action generally? It is action indifferent to the reasons for or against taking it. Arbitrary government is the use of power that is indifferent to the proper reasons for which power should be used.'[41]

Of course, the purpose itself might be unjustifiable but that is the concern of a substantive political or moral principle more generally, not necessarily a matter of the arbitrariness of the means of achieving it. However, even where the purpose can be justified, the power is exercised arbitrarily where its manner of exercise does not have a reasonable relationship to, or is not exercised in a manner justifiably proportional to, its achievement.

Montesquieu was perhaps the most profound theorist and opponent of arbitrary power. I have called on him several times and will continue to, for he understood arbitrary power deeply and loathed it. When he observed of criminal punishment '[t]hat liberty is favoured by the nature of penalties, and by their proportion', he enunciated a specific example of a more general principle:

> It is the triumph of liberty when criminal laws draw each penalty from the particular nature of the crime. All arbitrariness ends; the penalty does not ensue from the legislator's capriciousness but from the nature of the thing, and man does not do violence to man.[42]

Well, not *all* arbitrariness, for there are several other kinds, as we have seen. This, however, is an important type, and it is often connected to the others. Philip Selznick captured both the third and fourth senses of arbitrariness thus: 'Rules are made arbitrarily when appropriate interests are not consulted and when there is no clear relation between the rule enunciated and the official end to be achieved.'[43] These two often go together. Government responses to the Covid-19 pandemic potentially raised issues of arbitrary exercise of power the world over, but for most of us they were not whether governments should exercise any of its powers at all in response to the catastrophe but whether they do so by means related to, appropriate to dealing with, and proportionate to the dangers we face. Doing nothing because it's too hard or you don't care or it would be unpopular is a dereliction of duty. However, exploiting the pandemic to garner and wield extraordinary powers unrelated to its management, or imposing penalties out of all proportion to the dangers it represents to citizens, is to act arbitrarily. Some governments, though far from all, were happy to seize the opportunity.[44]

Different thinkers have been more or less concerned with one or another of the forms discussed. Sometimes they have focused on just one; often they have elided them. They should be distinguished, however, at least analytically, and what one does about each might need to differ. Uncontrolled power might not be unruly or unrespectful or ungrounded, though there is a constant risk, difficult to do anything about. Unruly power might be controlled, respectful (of interests other than the right to be on notice), and otherwise fit for purpose. Unrespectful bureaucrats often stick to the rules, are under control of their superiors, and do not act in excess of what is authorised, but they can look through you as though you weren't there, or treat you like dirt or – worse, because dirt doesn't care – like a dog, as K finally discerned. Irrelevant or disproportionate uses of power might have impeccable formal grounding, might be authorised in clear rules, follow established legally policed entitlements and procedures and still have nothing to do with your case, or bear no proportionate relationship to any justifiable way of dealing with it. So, best to avoid all four forms rather than pick and choose among them.

As we will see in Chapter 8, there may well be reasons why the powerful choose not to act arbitrarily in one or some of these ways but retain the power to strike arbitrarily in others. For example, there are all sorts of benefits that might accrue to a ruler who insists in general on stable and understandable rules, as the greatest of social theorists, Max Weber, understood, since acts by its servants can be rendered more predictable to and controllable by *them*.[45] However, if the rules shut out those affected from consideration, subjects – more accurately objects[46] – of power are vulnerable to its arbitrary exercise, as are ones where rules with no justifiable or proportional relationship to any proper purpose are rigorously observed. That is why there should be no free pass for powerful persons or entities just because they score well (low) on one but not another dimension of arbitrariness (as, say, Singapore might on predictability but not on control and, at least in regard to political opponents, not on respect or appropriateness/proportionality of the means chosen to prosecute/persecute them).[47] It is better when the exercise of power does well on all four dimensions. Unfortunately, many of the prevalent 'rule of law indexes', where Singapore scores very highly because its rules are good for business though bad for dissidents, ignore this point.

Because these forms are different from each other and can exist separately, however, it is often more useful to specify the particular kind(s) of pathology, and in what degree they are manifest, than to attempt some single across-the-board, all-or-nothing assessment of whether power is exercised arbitrarily or not. However, while these four forms are distinguishable, power is often exercised in several of these ways at once, and often they are interrelated, with each form of arbitrariness reinforcing the others. As Locke saw, an uncontrolled power-wielder might well have incentives to keep subjects disoriented and anxious, on the hop, and out of the loop. Again, without institutionalised means of holding powerful people or institutions to account, they might well succumb to temptations to exercise their powers in any or all of the other arbitrary forms nominated. And there may well be other forms; the list is not closed and it is unlikely to be short. It is not a likeable list.

5.3 What's So Wrong with Arbitrary Power?

Of course, not everyone finds arbitrary power repulsive. Indeed many powerful people have found it irresistibly attractive, so long as it is they or theirs who exercise it. Such 'arbitrarians', if I may, include those classically called 'tyrants' and 'despots' but many run-of-the-mill monarchs and ordinary leaders as well. Extraordinary ones too, and perhaps especially. In recent times, communists, fascists, racists, terrorists, populists, and Trumpists, just to mention a few of the many types that populate political history, have combined a taste for arbitrariness with technological and propagandistic tools that can make it stick, at least for a while.

Arbitrarians come in a great variety of shapes, sizes, and sorts, but typically they share an insistence that power should be concentrated under their control, to be exercised as they please, unhampered and untempered by institutional tempering or mediation. Arbitrarians are not anti-institutional since they make use of institutions, but they *are* hostile to institutions out of their control and to any idea that these institutions might be independent and mediate, stand between, or temper the ways the powerful choose to exercise power.

In most civilisations, and most of human history, traditional lineage was what you needed and all you needed to get the top job. Many (though not all) who had it faced few (though rarely no) impediments to abusing it. Today, in most of the world, lineage has become a wasting asset. The search is for instrumental justifications. And more than a few have been suggested.

Some partisans of arbitrariness believe power is more efficient and effective when single strong leaders can exert it directly and without interference, in whatever domain and whatever way they consider appropriate. Eighteenth-century 'Enlightened despots', on the cusp of European transformations from what has been called 'an authority of origins' to 'an authority of ends',[48] probably saw this as a way of justifying their reforming mission and maybe their starting-to-be-challenged centrality in the scheme of governance. Again, as Max Weber stressed, it is characteristic of charismatic rulers, wherever they persuade people to believe they have the 'gift of grace', to say and believe they should get away with saying: '"it has been written, but *I* say unto you ..."'.[49] Today, origins don't get you so far, and charisma – real or more commonly manufactured – appears to be staging a comeback. Still, we live in an age of instrumental justifications. Even charismatics these days, particularly those who rely on winning elections, try to convince us they are doing good for us, and not just themselves, or God. So unenlightened despots, authoritarians, and wannabees, of whom there have been quite a number, claim their arbitrary ambitions, positions, and ways of exercising power are justified by what they do for us.

Others, including some (but far from all) conservatives, favour leadership that is free of constraint, for its putative ability to maintain public order, traditions, and ways of being against modern assaults from, among others, individualist, grasping, liberals waving their demands, practices, rights, and insistence that power be reliably tempered by, among other things, the rule of law. In many societies, it has been alleged that it is not only rulers but their subjects too who appreciate, demand, and need a 'strong ruler' able to sort problems, and people, out. The power of 'The People' as embodied in their leaders should neither be tempered nor tampered with. Sometimes 'The People' agree, though it is hard to know for sure, and often a lot of people disagree but lose out.

Not everyone hostile to the values of the rule of law, however, is prosaic, pragmatic, and instrumental in their authoritarian enthusiasms. Some are excited by absolute leaders and by limitless power. They like it not to be merely exercised but wielded, like a sword. Joseph de Maistre, the brilliant French reactionary of the time of the French Revolution, was one such. In his celebration of the Executioner as the font of social order, for example, he explained:

> No moral praise seems appropriate to him, for everyone else is assumed to have relations with human beings: he has none.

> And yet all greatness, all power, all subordination rest on the executioner; he is both the horror and the bond of human association. Remove this mysterious agent from the world, and in a moment order yields to chaos: thrones fall, society disappears.[50]

The (also brilliant) German conservative and later Nazi jurist Carl Schmitt, now disconcertingly back in fashion both in theory and in practice, also had a taste for unbridled sovereign power. Schmitt insisted that the liberal rule of law,[51] with its 'strong guarantees of moderation and an adequately secure protection of freedom and property against arbitrariness and misuse of the legal form',[52] could deliver only an apolitical, anti-political, and mediocre *legality*, ungrounded in any deeper substantive value, fit perhaps for shopkeepers playing for low stakes but unable to match the demands of *politics*, least of all when the stakes are high. There and then, when the chips are down, a state depends upon the wilful *decision* of an unbound and, in principle, legally unbindable sovereign political decision-maker, able and prepared to identify and define the fundamental political distinction – between friend and enemy – and act at the revelatory moment of exception in which 'the power of real life breaks through the crust of a mechanism that has become torpid by repetition'.[53]

One senses a thrill in the air but for partisans of the ideal of the rule of law also a chill. For such partisans reject all of this, many of them – including this one – with disgust. Perhaps the fundamental reasons are general and moral in nature: whatever the consequences that might be thought to flow, and unless there are extreme exceptional or extenuating circumstances, no *persons* should have power arbitrarily inflicted upon them. That has two elements: no person has the moral authority to treat persons in this way and no persons deserve to be so treated. Whatever else happens (and of course even worse can happen), such exercises of power are from the first *insolent* to the victim, who in turn is insulted. When arbitrary power is exercised over persons in such ways, all the more when it is taken as routine that it may be so exercised at any time, and even when it could be but happens not to be, they are denied the respect and moral equality owed to fellow humans. And, as Postema points out, not just the presumption of the offender nor the vulnerability of the victim is objectionable but the very *relationship* between them is perverse:

> Subordination is matter of being vulnerable to the arbitrary will of another in conditions of dependency. The evil of this condition lies not just in the fact that the victim can only do what the dominator permits; neither does it

> reside in the dominator's potential for cruelty, for he may not be cruel. The evil resides more deeply in the nature of the relationship itself. The victim is publicly held to be inferior to the dominator.[54]

This is a general moral claim, and I will argue in Chapter 7 that it stretches more broadly – well beyond acts by states – than is often acknowledged. But it has a special force when the exerciser of power is the state. Because, at least in a democracy, the state has special, extensive, sometimes comprehensive, powers and responsibilities. It is not just another guy; it is supposed to be *our* guy. The state *is* special in these respects, and arguably that generates obligations and responsibilities of special kinds, that not everyone shares, or at least not for the same reasons and not to the same extent. The moral character of the relationship between a state and its citizens flows not merely from its social consequences but also from its extensive reach, the often distinctive means it has at its disposal, and its claim to representative legitimacy. As Lon Fuller argued, a democratic polity should be an order of reciprocity: we obey on condition that we are treated with respect by those who exercise power over us. We should be able to demand from our public representatives, even more than we do from everyone else, that they treat us with respect.

Fuller's internal morality of law focused primarily on the second sense of arbitrariness I have distinguished: unpredictability; but his claims were larger. Recall that each of King Rex's failings as a lawmaker was a breach of what Fuller called the 'internal morality of law', encoded in his eight principles of good legal craftsmanship.[55] What his critics ignored, and what went deeper with Fuller than his somewhat legalistic, and sociologically innocent and inadequate, discussions of the conditions of legal effectiveness, was the *moral* significance of requiring states to act through laws of these kinds. For, effects aside, Fuller had other concerns, more to do with the proper relations between a state and citizens than with speculations about the effects of particular sorts of laws. The moral character of that relationship lies, for Fuller, not merely in its social consequences. It expresses something we should be able to demand from our public representatives. On this account, it is not conjectures about contingent relationships between 'inner' morality and external achievements but rather concerns about the moral character of those relationships *as such*. On this account, the deeper importance of the inner morality of law is that:

> Every departure from the principles of the law's inner morality is an affront to man's dignity as a responsible agent. To judge his actions by unpublished or retrospective laws, or to order him to do an act that is impossible, is to convey to him your indifference to his powers of self-determination.

> Conversely, when the view is accepted that man is incapable of responsible action, legal morality loses its reason for being. To judge his actions by unpublished or retrospective laws is no longer an affront, for there is nothing left to affront indeed, even the verb 'to judge' becomes itself incongruous in this context; we no longer judge a man, we act on him.[56]

The issue here is not merely one of instrumental effectiveness, as his critics assumed, but of intrinsic moral requirements, peculiarly required of states, to act in ways consistent with respect for the persons on whose behalf alone states have rights and duties to act. Fuller spoke of 'trusteeship';[57] others have written of a distinctive 'fiduciary' responsibility of states.[58] And, as one of the best recent writers on the rule of law has remarked, '[o]nce we determine that some law expresses the inferiority of some members of the community, that law is to be condemned on rule of law grounds whether or not anyone (or, indeed, everyone) in that community endorses this message'.[59]

Even though I will argue in Chapter 7 that the ideal of the rule of law must reach much further than acts of states, their role is special. So even apart from consequences in the world, there are good reasons to insist that states incorporate internal means of tempering the character of their laws:[60] rules of the sort Fuller discussed, whose character is intended to allow predictability,[61] procedures that seek to give voice to, and respect the dignity of,[62] people being judged by the law, and exercises of power by means that are appropriate and proportional to their ostensible purpose. One might need to tweak and revise the specifications considerably in various ways to adapt to complexities of and changes in law and society and the variety of laws in play – not all of them directed to citizens at all but to administrators of the laws[63] – but this intrinsic dimension of respectfulness is of distinctive moral significance.

Not everyone, however, is persuaded by considerations of moral principle alone, independent of consequences. Fortunately, there are other and powerful reasons for hostility to arbitrary power that blend moral concerns with empirical/consequential judgments, drawn from what we know about the ways of power in the world. Staying with respect and dignity for a moment, a common actual harm that flows from arbitrariness is the degrading indignity of finding oneself the mere *object* of power-wielders, where one has constantly to guess how one might be treated by them without any effective way of asserting, defending, and claiming attention to one's own interest, stake, or point of view in the face of its exercise.[64] All that flattery, bowing and scraping, those forelocks to tug, caps to tip, favours to curry, to use just some of the more evocative phrases for the imposition on persons of demeaning and undignified ways of being.[65]

Another fundamental value threatened by arbitrary power is liberty, a particular concern of liberal political thinkers, but not only of them and long before liberalism was even an '-ism' at all. The animus and ideal expressed in the concept of the rule of law are not the invention of liberals (who, so described, have only existed for some 200 years) but ideas found in many traditions of political and legal thinking over millennia. They are, however, central to most if not all varieties of liberal reflections on the nature, requirements, temptations, pathologies, and consequences of the exercise of power in societies. The reasons are not difficult to discern. Judith Shklar might have exaggerated in writing that '[l]iberalism has only one overriding aim: to secure the political conditions that are necessary for the exercise of personal freedom',[66] but few liberals would deny that this is a central liberal aim. It goes to the liberal core, as it does to that of the ideal of the rule of law.

Freedom is often directly and palpably imperilled by arbitrary power. Liberal thinkers have thought a great deal about why that is so and what might be done about it. Their apprehensions are amplified by thinkers in the civic republican tradition, whose conception of liberty as *non-domination* is directly counterposed to arbitrary power. This conception has been emphasised by the philosopher Philip Pettit as the central republican contribution to political theory and by the jurist Gianluigi Palombella as the central achievement of the rule of law.[67] It is important to emphasise.

In the republican interpretation, on the one hand, liberty is not infringed by every sort of interference – anti-vaxxers take note – but only by 'arbitrary (reason-independent) interference'.[68] On the other hand, republicans point out, power does not only threaten liberty when it is actually exercised arbitrarily but when and so long as *it is available* for arbitrary exercise. Whenever someone has power to treat you arbitrarily, even if they choose not to, you are subject to domination by them. And that, as people enslaved by even the most benign masters have learnt, is likely to be a deeply demeaning and potentially frightening and constraining condition for a person to be in.

Mary Wollstonecraft, the pioneer feminist of the late eighteenth and early nineteenth centuries, certainly thought so, of wives whose husbands legally could exert their arbitrary, legally unrestrained powers over them.[69] Of course, their legal rights to do so were likely to have had bearing on how many did. But Henrik Ibsen's *A Doll's House* is a portrait of the psychological torture of a wife cosseted and disempowered by a loving but (objectively, though not subjectively) irresistible husband. As Pettit puts it, 'To enjoy non-domination is ... to be possessed, not just of non-interference by arbitrary powers, but of a secure or resilient variety of such non-interference'.[70]

Another reason to value non-domination, often connected to, and perhaps the most basic and elemental consequence of, arbitrary power, is the simple *fearfulness* of life plagued by the potentially devastating impositions of power unrestrained by consideration of anything but the will and whim of the power-holder, or liable to strike like lightning, or exercisable without reference to you, or without connection or proportion to anything you do or any reason that might justify it. Threats to liberty are obnoxious whether or not they cause fear, but if they do, they are doubly so.

This is the fate that Judith Shklar stresses most in what she called and extolled as the 'liberalism of fear'.[71] For a life in circumstances of plausible and sustained fear, often well known to and shared by millions, is a terrible fate. Reduction of reasons for it is a great deliverance. Again, as the civic republican tradition insists, it is not enough if as a simple matter of happy fact one is not actually subjected to acts of arbitrary and fearful power if at any time one could be. On the contrary, as the eighteenth-century scientist, philosopher, and proto-liberal theorist Joseph Priestley observed: 'Having always some unknown evil to fear, though it should never come, he has no perfect enjoyment of it himself, or of any of the blessings of life.'[72] To reduce fear, as well as to augment liberty and respect, the boundaries, channels, and modes of exercise of power must be secure and understood to be so.

These are crucial jobs for the rule of law. Indeed, the link between the rule of law and liberty in this republican understanding depends on law denying the possibility of arbitrary exercise of power. Securities against domination are not likely to occur by accident. Nor will law be enough. They require supports of many kinds, including cultural, political, social, and institutional, as Chapters 8–11 will show.

A common liberal and republican thought has been that, left to their own devices, wielders of power cannot be relied on to avoid exercising it arbitrarily and will constantly face temptations, in many circumstances strong incentives and inadequate obstacles, to throw their weight around as they choose. Some power-wielders might confound such pessimistic expectations, but we should not have to rely on that happy chance. At least we need to hedge our bets. For even were power-wielders' intentions beneficently public-oriented, the possibility of arbitrary exercise of power would still be a perennial concern. There are many other vices that depend on the particular purpose or consequences of the exercise, but arbitrary power is vicious enough even without them and moreover can be so even when intentions are honourable. The tyranny of virtue is perhaps (but perhaps not) preferable to the tyranny of vice, but tyranny is always to be avoided.

All the more because, as Lord Acton was not the first to notice,[73] corruption awaits when power is untamed. If we are left merely to the will or pleasure of power-holders (to use traditional terms of apprehension), arbitrariness will be a constant possibility, and if so a constant and justifiable worry. On this view, arbitrary exercise of power is not a good thing. What might be done about it? There are long traditions of thought about such matters, among them that of the English common law, that explicitly counterposed law to arbitrary power and praised it as a bulwark against that dangerous phenomenon.[74]

A somewhat different reason for hostility to arbitrary power, pragmatic in character, has to do as much with its malign effects on societies as a whole rather than just individuals within them. For, faced with systematic arbitrariness or its possibility in the exercise of power, citizens lack reliable sources of *coordination* of expectations among each other and between themselves and the state. All members of modern, large, and rapidly changing societies find themselves in a predicament that has been best characterised by the eighteenth-century Scottish father of modern economics, Adam Smith: 'In civilised society he [man] stands at all times in need of the co-operation and assistance of great multitudes, while his whole life is scarce sufficient to gain the friendship of a few persons.'[75] We return to this point in Chapters 8 and 10.

Friends, families, and workmates learn whom they trust and whom they don't over long and direct periods of exposure to each other. But great multitudes do not have the same opportunities. Their cooperation depends on the possibility of trust among people who do not and cannot know each other intimately but still must make judgments, however abstract, about the extent to which they can rely on each other, on the institutions that frame their activities and those of other people and institutions. Trust of this sort among multitudes must be *interpersonal*, allowing one to move without fear in a world of strangers, and for that there must exist sources of trust that are *impersonal*, not dependent on direct personal knowledge of the other. That in turn requires *institutional* trust, belief that key institutions – not on their own but as well – are able to restrain arbitrary acts of power by citizens and other institutions and not given to such acts themselves.

Of course, successful social coordination and reasons for impersonal, interpersonal, and institutional trust depend upon much besides clear and reliable legal institutions that cue us into many key rules of the game and contribute to adjudicating and enforcing them. As we shall see in Chapters 9 and 10, to do any of that effectively and reliably law in turn must draw on support from, and be in sync with, many cooperating and mutually supportive social, cultural, and political sources and forces. But in large, complex, and mobile societies at any rate, it is hard to see confident and fruitful social coordination happening without effective sources of tempered power, among them legal sources. One might want more than avoidance of the perils just discussed, and one might want other things. But in the world we know and in any possible world I can imagine, generating and where possible institutionalising frames and channels for the exercise of power in ways that are not arbitrary is a good, foundational, place to begin.

It is common, as I have done so far, to focus on the predicaments arbitrary power creates for its *targets*. However, one final reason to be wary of such power refers back to the power-wielders themselves. The freedom to act arbitrarily often gives licence to act stupidly, ignorantly, or worse,[76] and partisans of the rule of law oppose it for those reasons as well.

One very common, but false, misapprehension about the ideal of the rule of law is that institutionalised constraints on power necessarily undermine effective government. This frustration has long been expressed (and acted upon), for example, by the *de facto* but not *de jure* ruler of Poland between 2015 and 2023, Jarosław Kaczyński,[77] in his determination to overcome what he called the 'impossibilism' of the Polish state – a 'programmed state incapacity to take many steps necessary for the defence of its own interests and the good of citizens'[78] – that frustrated him so much. The state simply can't push through its will. This not only blocks the state, he insisted, but denies the democratic will of the people, as expressed in the decisions of its representatives. This is because Poland had ended up, Kaczyński said (before taking power to correct the situation), in a predicament in which 'without a legal ground no decision can be taken. In this way rational freedom of decision making by various state functionaries is limited.'[79] With a cure much worse than the disease, Kaczyński took many steps to avoid such limitations.

Fittingly, and without any apparent sense of the irony in the statement, when, in the initial years of his post-2015 rule, both the Polish

Constitutional Tribunal and Supreme Court sought to resist the unconstitutional measures taken against them, Kaczyński, himself a doctor of laws, is reported to have said: '[W]e will not permit anarchy in Poland, even if it is promoted by the courts.'[80] His party speedily crushed such 'anarchy' in the subsequently totally suborned Constitutional Tribunal, which became a mouthpiece of the government, and sought to squelch it in the Supreme Court, ordinary courts, and elsewhere. Operating to an increasingly proliferating game plan, governments in Poland, Hungary, Turkey, Venezuela, India, and most recently the United States have indeed sought to eliminate 'anarchy' from independent sources by protractedly targeting, emasculating, and repurposing major public institutions, including courts, civil services, independent central banks, ombudsmen, the media, non-governmental organisations, and non-governmental *organisation* per se. I return to these practices in Chapter 8.

The objection to this common line of defence of arbitrariness is as much pragmatic as moral. As Kaczyński's own government came vividly to illustrate, arbitrary power can be a powerful source and vehicle of stupidity, corruption, even craziness, in the exercise of power. Or just visit Nay Pyi Taw, the 'world's weirdest capital city', the bizarre largely empty, Disneyland capital of Myanmar constructed in secrecy by Myanmar's military junta in 2005.[81] Well, one could visit in the short period of democracy that followed, but since the 2021 coup against the democratic government, again by the military, now no longer. Not surprisingly, not only has much of the population been reduced to fear and misery, which does not matter much to their rulers, but resistance has boomed and the economy has tanked, which does.

Or walk the huge main boulevard of Bucharest to the grotesque but enormous presidential palace built for and once occupied by the tight-knit rulers of 'socialism in one family', built by 'the genius of Bucharest', the 'source of our light', 'the treasure of wisdom and charisma', Nicolae Ceaușescu for his wife Elena and their profligate children. Streets, roads, and houses were razed and some 40,000 residents were ejected from their homes with twenty-four hours' notice and minimal compensation for this absurdity.[82] Alas, it is not at all hard to find evidence of what arbitrary power, which never has to answer a question or conform to an institutional requirement or listen to the views of those with most skin in the game, can conjure up. And I have not even mentioned Mao Tse Tung, Vladimir Putin, or even one Kim, the earlier ones of whom indeed were models for the genius of Bucharest. Donald Trump is not shaping up well.

Authoritarians invoke the anti-impossibilist justification at any time, but it is particularly called upon in 'times of exception', such as anti-terror campaigns or war, when, or so it is argued, executive power needs to loosen normal restraints in order to be effective. There certainly are special circumstances, where normal operating procedures come under strain. But even then, or especially then, it is important to keep in mind that very often arbitrary power is not only incompatible with citizens' rights; it also threatens intelligence. It does so in both the old-fashioned meaning of the word and the new security services narrowing sense, in extremity and without it. Unrestrained power, to put it bluntly, is typically dumb or, even if smart, ill-informed and open to inflicting catastrophe.[83] On this reading, tempered power is not a curb on effective government but a condition of it.

Arbitrary power is never – or if not never then so rarely as to be in need of explanation and strenuous justification – a good thing. More precisely, there is a huge presumption against it. Anyone seeking to justify it carries a huge burden, extremely hard to discharge. Perhaps there are extreme circumstances where untempered power is necessary, but even then – and one should examine the claims closely and sceptically – these are extremes. They should not, *pace* Schmitt, serve as models for the norm.

Moreover, even where one might feel the need to contemplate the use of arbitrary power, one should recognise that harm has been done. As Simone Weil wrote, about sacrificing one value where it's incompatible with another, 'even in such a case a crime is committed if the obligation so sacrificed is not merely sacrificed in fact but its existence is denied in the bargain'.[84]

This last point raises complex issues of governance, especially in times of emergency. Exceptions can truly be … well, exceptional. One cannot always carry on with business as usual. But the temptation to shed constraints is a constant one, needs strenuous justification, should typically be questioned, and its costs always put front of mind.

Arranging power so that it is not available for arbitrary exercise, is not one task, nor is it simple. It is not one since the particular sources of arbitrary power, the circumstances in which it is amassed and wielded the technologies – including institutional technologies – apt for any particular incarnation, will vary. It is not simple because reducing the possibilities of arbitrariness in the exercise of power takes a lot of power and not everyone has it or can arrange and deploy it to good effect. It requires resources, institutions, social and political supporting structures, norms and habits, effective technologies, incentives for good acts, and protections against bad ones – and typically time and good fortune. Historically these have come together rarely. So, world- and history-wide, a sturdy regime of power not given to arbitrary eruptions and interruptions has always been exceptional. Where realised in reasonable measure, something significant has been achieved, arguably against the grain of human affairs.

5.4 Aren't There More Important Things to Worry About?

Few people would deny that the rule of law has arbitrary power in its sights, but why pick on that in particular? After all, as Brian Tamanaha has insisted, the rule of law serves many functions, including reduction of arbitrary power, supporting freedom and dignity, security and trust, construction and institution of institutions, enhancement of economic development, and, he allows, likely others as well.[85] And rule of law promoters came to believe that all sorts of goods will come of their efforts: democracy, human rights, economic development, and more. What's special about reducing arbitrary power?

I have no objections to Tamanaha's list of functions, and it can be extended. The rule of law ideal is useful for many reasons. However, I would stress that reduction of arbitrary power is distinctive in Tamanaha's list. It is not just another 'function' of, or consequence, that might be hoped to flow from approaching that ideal. Rather, it is both immanent and intermediate in a way that the other functions he refers to are not. It is immanent because it refers to the *ways* power is exercised, not the *consequences* of those ways. And it is intermediate because arbitrary power stands in the way of, and non-arbitrary exercises of power serve, many other values and functions as well. Whereas we might hope that a legal order will support freedom, dignity, security, trust, and so on, it is unlikely to do so if the wielders of (legal or illegal) power are free to exercise power arbitrarily.

As for the rule of law promotion industry, the alleged virtues of the rule of law were once less ambitious and less promiscuously strewn about than they are today. Reduction of arbitrariness in the exercise of power was uncontroversial. What further goals that achievement might serve has been disputed and varied over time and in different societies. But whether or not one thought that the rule of law was good for the economy or democracy or human rights, no one doubted that you did not have it unless law was able to serve as an effective means of tempering the possible ways in which power could be exercised.

There are many ways to exercise power, and different ways enable different functions to be performed. Power – whether legal or not – can support freedom, dignity, trust, and so on, but it can deny them as well and often does. It does the former more readily when the chances for its arbitrary exercise are reliably diminished and the latter more easily when its wielders are free to exercise it arbitrarily. The hope of partisans of the rule of law is that the exercise of power might be reliably and routinely framed, constituted, constrained, and disciplined in ways that both help guard against abusive uses and require and enable it to be channelled in fruitful directions and exercised in benign ways.

Though the rule of law ideal is often set against power, that is a mistake, as we have seen. Law is a vehicle for the exercise of power; that is what it does. Channelling power through the rule of law, or so its partisans have hoped, is a way of exercising power that can help avoid the pathologies of arbitrariness. So the ways that power can be exercised are a specific, immanent, concern of the rule of law, even before we get to what purposes the wielders of such power have in mind. Whatever their purposes, the *ways* power is exercised are a core concern. The *immediate* ambition of ideals involving the rule of law and associated ideas is to enable power to be exercised effectively and in ways that avoid the vices of arbitrary exercise that I have discussed. To the extent the ambition is achieved, many other possibilities flow, and functions are enabled, that would otherwise be at risk or more difficult to attain. These include various moral, political, economic, and other goals, ideals, and functions, often more obviously enticing than 'mere' reduction of arbitrariness, among them those Tamanaha suggests. Such reduction is not necessarily more important than other goals, then, but it has a specific immediate, foundational, importance, not reducible to other things, is commonly a condition for the best of them, and too often not separately considered.

Ways of exercising power, including non-arbitrary and non-dominating ways, are, in other words, closely tied up with the ideal of the rule of law, immanent in the idea. They are a *feature* (and certainly not a bug) of the ideal, not just a function it might serve or any consequence that might follow its observance. Other goods, say, economic development or democracy, or human rights, or justice, may, as has in recent times commonly been claimed, flow from the rule of law (and are the only reasons many people today are interested in it),[86] but they are simply not immanent in this way. If the rule of law enables them, these are external and contingent benefits that might flow from a well-constituted socio-political-legal order, that is, one in which the likelihood that power will be exercised arbitrarily has been reduced. But communities are often not well constituted – and never so when arbitrary power is rife. For, unfortunately, as we have seen frequently in recent years and will consider again in Chapters 8 and 10, a 'legally ordered community' full of law and awash with arbitrary power is no oxymoron.[87] And where it occurs, the functions that Tamanaha attributes to such a community are unlikely to be well performed.

On the view recommended here, then, one starts by thinking how arbitrariness in the exercise of power might be reduced, not uniquely to favour that goal over all others in the world of values but because arrangements – deliberate and not, legal and other, intended for this purpose or not – that reduce the ability of power-holders to wield power arbitrarily are foundational both in themselves and for the achievement of many other things we might value, not least those we might value more. What I will call tempered power is less an alternative to any of them than a condition for them; at least for many of them. It is less an intrinsic value that should compete for moral superiority with, say, liberty, equality, security, or whatever, than a foundational achievement necessary for the attainment of many other values unlikely to be attained when power is left to its holders' own devices. It operates at a different, prior plane.

Reduction of arbitrariness in the exercise of power is never a matter of on/off, like a light switch. It is always a variable achievement, always a matter of degree: more or less, more here than there, not all or nothing. On this conception, the ideal is well served where and insofar as the exercise of significant political, social, and economic power in a society is effectively tempered, constrained, and channelled, so that non-arbitrary exercises of such powers are relatively widespread and routine, while arbitrary ones are not.

The rule of law, then, serves a value at once modest and precious. That is not an oxymoron but a recognition that, as I have written elsewhere, 'some values are at the same time modest in scope, but precious all the same. If you ignore their modesty, you debase their worth.'[88] It is modest because it will never be all we want, rarely what we most want, and it might conflict with other things we might want. If so, accommodations might be necessary. Nevertheless, it is precious because it is a condition for avoiding many things we should never want, indeed some of the worst things that we can do and can be done to us. It also opens us to many things that we do and should be able to do and have done.

The promise of the ideal of the rule of law is not that power will be exercised for the best ends; that needs a lot more and a lot else. Nevertheless, approach to that ideal is far from irrelevant to ends. Some of the worst things power can be used to do are harder to accomplish where the possibilities for its arbitrary exercise are lessened, and some of the best are unavailable where power is liable to arbitrary abuse. To the extent that the rule of law contributes to reduction of arbitrary exercise of power, then, it also reduces the chances of the former and increases those of the latter. Still, the *primary* focus of the ideal is on the manner in which power is exercised.

Another way of putting it, as I suggested earlier, is to think of reduction of arbitrary power as what Philip Pettit calls a 'a gateway good ... a good whose realization promises to bring the realization of other goods in train'.[89] That makes it potentially valuable even to those not especially excited by it per se, because they value what it might make both unavailable and available. Many other values are more easily attained when power is less arbitrary. Whether or not, as has often been claimed, the rule of law leads to economic growth, or democracy, or the full span of human rights is a (debatable) question about contingent, incidental effects of orders where power, because less arbitrary, is more controllable and accountable, reckonable, respectful, and grounded. These are important questions, but so is the gateway question: is the exercise of power arbitrary? If significant power is exercised arbitrarily, nine cases out of ten (maybe eight, but anyway most) the danger is, simply for that reason, that it will be exercised harmfully – even if the motives for which it is exercised are pure as the driven snow.

Effective reduction of arbitrary power is a complex, practical, and in large part instrumental ideal. It is complex because a lot is needed even to approximate it and that lot varies and changes with the nature of specific problems, circumstances, and available responses. It is practical because it is neither a natural fact nor a Utopian fantasy we might only dream of but a goal intended to be made good (always only partially) in the real world. It is in large part instrumental since, apart from its intrinsic moral connection with treating persons respectfully, it is rarely anyone's ultimate passion but rather is understood as a means to help solve a problem that threatens the attainment of other goals. And it is an ideal, a condition to be approached rather than a simple description of something readily at hand. The concept is normative, the condition supposed to be valuable, worth striving for. A shorthand term for that condition, that I will describe in Chapter 6, is tempered power.

6

Remedy

> Now there are two generic kinds of princely part or principate, the one tempered and the other flawed.
>
> Marsilius of Padua, *The Defender of the Peace*

> In despotic states the nature of the government requires extreme obedience, and the prince's will, once known, should produce its effect as infallibly as does one ball thrown against another. No tempering, modification, accommodation, terms, alternatives, negotiations, remonstrances, nothing as good or better can be proposed. Man is a creature that obeys a creature that wants.
>
> Montesquieu, *The Spirit of the Laws*

6.1 Limited Perspectives

Appeal to the rule of law signals the hope that there may be ways, and that law might play a distinctive and important role among them, to diminish the kinds and levels of arbitrary sway available to those who exercise power. What should we hope from such measures? What should we wish they would do?

The commonest forms of answer cast the role of the rule of law as defensive, negative, often exclusively so. The terms typically used reflect this negative orientation. The rule of law is to limit, constrain, restrain power.[1] Though these negative connotations were not always so prominent,[2] much more rarely is it today suggested that the aim should equally be to create, generate, enable, or encourage good, positive uses of power to flourish, still less to *strengthen* that power. On the more familiar interpretation, the point is to block arbitrary unruliness, lest it inflict predictable harms.

The reasoning is familiar. The world is a tough place where, as has been familiar experience in many times and parts of the world, 'the dominant exact what they can and the weak concede what they must'.[3] The signal contribution of constraints on power is to help the weak by putting limits on what the dominant can do.

There is much to be said for this emphasis on the need for constraints on the exercise of power. The passages chosen to begin Chapter 5 – and one has an embarrassment of choice – tell us part of the reason why. They represent extreme but far from unique forms of arbitrary power. Each has its own peculiarities, in this respect conforming to Tolstoy's observation that happy families are all alike but every unhappy family is unhappy in its own way. But these unhappy stories have one thing in common: the exercise of arbitrary power. Those passages say nothing about what the purposes of these arbitrary acts were, just about their character. Whether it be the careless, callous, and murderous indifference of the NKVD of Novocherkassk or the chilling end, and ending reflection, of K in *The Trial* – a culmination of endless incomprehensible, humiliating, mock-legal arbitrary torments, apparently all carefully choreographed to disarm and demean him. Quite apart from what they lead to in these specific cases – murder, defiling of humanity (and again murder) – the arbitrary *ways* that power is exercised are evils in themselves that enable and are ingredients of further evils. So it is not hard to understand why anyone conscious of these possibilities thinks first of how they might be avoided.

Even without such horrors in mind, the rule of law has typically been thought of in terms of restraint. Thus the historian John Philip Reid emphasises of the English legal tradition: '[f]rom time immemorial the legal heritage of Europe beyond the pale of Roman law had been law as restraint, not law as command'.[4] The means supposed to guard us from arbitrary uses of power changed over the centuries, particularly moving from allegedly immemorial custom that could not wilfully be abrogated to deliberate legislation that had nevertheless to be clear, precise, prospective, comprehensible, and so on.[5] With those changes went different conceptions of what forms law needed to take in order to contribute to the rule of law. However, the identification of the rule of law's purpose with restraint endured.

It still does. A negative understanding of the contribution to be hoped for from the rule of law remains popular among liberals, especially among those 'libertarians' and 'neoliberals' who are particularly concerned to 'free' the market from state incursion. Thus Friedrich von Hayek, who as we saw regards power as the 'archevil',[6] asserts that '[t]he effective limitation of power is the most important problem of social order'.[7] And it is not just 'neos' who think this way. Thus, my intellectual heroine Judith Shklar, who held no brief either for Hayek or for neoliberalism, argued that there are really only two coherent conceptions of the rule of law,

Aristotle's and Montesquieu's. On Aristotle's view, the rule of law is the rule of reason, as manifest in just decisions by men 'of settled ethical character' and intelligence. It is a way of life, but only for an exemplary, elite, few. Montesquieu, by contrast, has a more limited, protective, conception of the rule of law, but it allegedly benefits everyone subject to it. Shklar's money is on Montesquieu.

On this understanding, the rule of law:

> really has only one aim, to protect the ruled against the aggression of those who rule. While it embraces all people, it fulfills only one fundamental aim, freedom from fear, which, to be sure, was for Montesquieu supremely important. … [t]his whole scheme is ultimately based on a very basic dichotomy. The ultimate spiritual and political struggle is always between war and law … The institutions of judicial citizen protection may create rights, but they exist in order to avoid what Montesquieu took to be the greatest of human evils, constant fear created by the threats of violence and the actual cruelties of the holders of military power in society.[8]

Shklar's own choice is clear:

> If one then begins with the fear of violence, the insecurity of arbitrary government, and the discriminations of injustice, one may work one's way up to finding a significant place for the Rule of Law, and for the boundaries it has historically set upon these the most enduring of our political troubles.[9]

As befits a partisan of 'damage limitation', who 'begins with what is to be avoided', Shklar insists that the prevention of evil, rather than a quest for the good, is the signal virtue of the rule of law; its goal, supremely important but negative, is 'damage control'.[10] And when power is doing real damage, it is easy to believe (and often right to believe) that nothing is more important than stopping it.

For such thinkers, and there are plenty of them, this negative, constraining, controlling aspect of the rule of law is fundamental. And though I do not think this aspect exhausts or should exclusively define the promise of the rule of law, I agree that it is crucial. The exercise of substantial power carries terrible risks. It is wise to be aware and wary of them and do what can be done to minimise them, both because they can be directly threatening in themselves and because where the worst of such threats are realised, nothing much else good will occur. Negative conceptions of the rule of law are clearly deeply informed by such thought, which is a form of 'moral realism' in the sense identified by Philip Selznick. Selznick also sounds another more idealistic note, to which I will return at the end of this chapter, but he insists that, for a moral realist it is not enough:

'to think of specific evils as problems to be solved or as obstacles to be overcome. Rather, the perspective of moral realism treats some transgressions as dynamic and inescapable. They can be depended on to arise, in one form or another, despite our best efforts to put them down.'[11]

Moreover, not just 'moral realism' but specifically *political* realism is necessary in the case of constitutionalism and the rule of law, for thinking about such things is not 'just applied moral philosophy'.[12] It must respond to 'the circumstances of politics'[13] as they often, and often painfully, have been found to be. After all, politics and the wielding of power more generally are frequently not just a matter of the ideal ends we should seek but of conflict, violence, oppression, domination, exploitation, their consequences, and what might be needed and feasible to avoid them.[14] The 'liberalism of fear' articulated by Shklar and others is a sober, sombre, response to such realities.

This defensive understanding of the rule of law is not adopted solely by thinkers like Shklar, for whom its negative, blocking, work is indispensable and precious. Many of its ardent opponents object to it precisely because they see its power in negative, curbing, shackling, terms. Hence Kaczyński's furious impatience with 'impossibilism'[15] and Schmitt's with the rule of law's 'strong guarantees of moderation and an adequately secure protection of freedom and property against arbitrariness and misuse of the legal form'.[16] Hence too, populists' hostility to intermediating bodies, including legal bodies, that threaten to constrain the rightly untrammelled power of 'the people', specifically *their* people, more specifically still *them* as embodiment of the people.[17]

Finally, a negative conception of the rule of law has also appealed to thinkers who recognise that it has positive consequences but can only raise a more tepid enthusiasm (two cheers) than either its passionate partisans or, often equally passionate, opponents display. Thus, Joseph Raz, who, as we saw in Chapter 3, identified the rule of law with eight formal features of official legal orders, commended it thus understood but with studied and sustained coolness. For him its value is:

> a negative virtue in two senses: conformity to it does not cause good except through avoiding evil and the evil which is avoided is evil which could only have been caused by the law itself.[18] … the rule of law is essentially a negative value. It is merely designed to minimize the harm to freedom and dignity which the law may cause in its pursuit of its goals however laudable these may be.[19]

Raz's double negative is quadruply misplaced. First, far from the evil which is avoided through the rule of law 'being evil which could only have been caused by the law itself', such evils often do not necessarily arise from law at all. That is often a source of what is evil about them. They arise from arbitrary abuse of *power*, and that can occur in many ways, arise from many sources, and be delivered by many vehicles.[20] The Taliban has wielded arbitrary power every day for many years, both when in government and when at war with it. Even now when back in the saddle, its exercise of power often is tempered by no law. The Taliban and their foes in ISIS both share Chairman Mao's practical judgment that 'political power grows out of the barrel of a gun'.[21] Guns aside, there are many ways in which power can be arbitrarily exercised and abused, even by the state, without any connection to law. All such ways offend against the ideal of the rule of law from the start.

Secondly, this passage makes no mention of all those non-state entities that might arbitrarily exercise huge power with huge effects, albeit usually not through law (see Chapter 7). Limiting arbitrary abuse by such powerholders is no small matter and it must be, I will argue, a concern of any partisan of the rule of law ideal.

Thirdly, given that a primary objective of reduction of the possibilities of arbitrary power, as Raz recognises, is to offer citizens a 'basis for legitimate expectations',[22] indispensable for many good and positive forms of social interaction, cooperation, and coordination, the emphasis added in '*purely* negative' is misleading. Even if interventions of the rule of law were solely restrictive in character and form, their purpose and effect might be of huge positive significance.

However, and finally, approaching the goal of the rule of law has more than indirectly positive *effects*. Directly and significantly, it does not merely limit power but, as the language of its ally, constitutionalism,[23] suggests, it *constitutes* forms of it. Through law, specific forms of power are created, conferred, allocated, and distributed. It is, after all, a long time since Raz's mentor and colleague at Oxford, the legal philosopher H. L. A. Hart, reminded us that the essential task of many laws, what he called, 'secondary rules', is not to command people what to do or not do ('primary rules') but to confer power.[24] Think of the jurisdiction of a court, the legal status of corporations, the creative purpose of laws of property and contract, the powers granted to various entities and officeholders by laws and constitutions. Without power-conferring laws they don't exist. Such laws, and no developed legal system is without them, encourage, facilitate, and 'constitute' entities and powers, often created by them and non-existent without them. Or, like money, just worthless bits of paper without the backing of law.

But though I criticise, I can't be smug. While I have always been sceptical of Raz's tepid 'two cheers' endorsement of the value of the rule of law, my unease was more about the low voltage of his enthusiasm than its direction. For a long time, I also thought of the rule of law in defensive terms, as primarily negative in function, like a wall or a guardrail, not a foundation; a precious but defensive attempt to prevent certain dangers and evils, not as a constructed and constructive basis for building something good. I just valued that function more highly than Raz seemed to. My view of the rationale and justification of the rule of law stopped about where Shklar's did, echoed the urgency she expresses, and largely for her reasons.

There is an autobiographical element in this, directly for Shklar and many others and vicariously for me. Born in Riga, Latvia in 1928, Shklar escaped with her family from the two overweening, unconstrained despotisms, one of the Right (Nazism) and the other of the Left (Communism), that overwhelmed her country and left their profound imprint on her life and thought. Another eminent liberal thinker who also had a profound influence on me, Isaiah Berlin, came from the same city and suffered the same fate, some twenty years earlier. He also loathed arbitrary power. Much of his political philosophy was concerned with illuminating how vicious it can be.

Fortunately for me, born after the Second World War in sunny Sydney, Australia, almost as far as is possible in distance and hardship from it all, I endured none of that. However, as I mentioned in Chapter 1, the same monstrous regimes that scarred, shaped, transformed, and shifted Shklar's life did so to millions of others, among them my parents. Their lives, families, friendships, and country, Poland, were ripped apart by the war and its aftermath. My father never saw his home again; I took my mother there once, in the early 1990s, after Communism had collapsed. And though my own understanding of the catastrophes that shaped their lives is all at one remove and the result of no personal suffering at all, they have haunted most of what I have written and written about for more than fifty years, including this book.

Reflection on these monstrosities led me to wonder why they occurred, why in some places and not others, in some forms and not others, and what might be needed to prevent them. One long-held conclusion was the thought that power needed above all to be reliably and securely limited, curbed, shackled, tamed, and all those other clamping terms, lest it go wild, or, in more moderate language, be open to arbitrary abuse. I came to the rule of law in the hope that it might be able to assist in such defensive endeavours.

I still have that hope, somewhat battered and complicated, as this book attests, but still alive. However, I have been persuaded that a purely negative, defensive, interpretation of the liberalism of fear can profoundly reduce and distort one's understanding of power, of politics, and of the value of the rule of law ideal. Violence and oppression are not the sum of what the tempering of power can and often does deliver, and limitation of power is not the sum of what the rule of law does and needs to do to contribute to the common weal.[25]

6.2 Powerful Virtues

I was first shaken into this new (to me) understanding by my friend, the political theorist Stephen Holmes, by whom I have often been surprised. He has frequently argued that modern liberals, unlike some of their classical forebears, have simply not understood how liberal values depend on state strength and are endangered by state weakness. Holmes has pursued these themes in many contexts, from exploration of the writings of illiberal thinkers of the sixteenth and seventeenth centuries who foresaw the 'liberal paradox' that constraints can enable, to classical writers of the liberal pantheon who abhorred despotism but valued strong states,[26] to rejection of the arguments of many governments post-9/11 that to deal with emergencies such as terrorism they needed to be able to 'throw off the shackles' of the rule of law.[27]

In many and varied writings and contexts, Holmes made plain how much societies depend upon well-marshalled public power, able to draw upon strength and resources, of their own and of the societies they should assist to be strong, to accomplish valuable ends that cannot be otherwise achieved. Once the point is made, and examples of the pathologies of *intrinsically* ineffectual public institutions recalled, I don't know any way round it. So, swayed by Holmes's insight, I have come to believe that any adequate understanding of the goal of the rule of law must accommodate the need to constrain states from abusing power in ways they mustn't while engendering its uses in ways they must. Fortunately, it is possible to do the one in ways that are compatible with, indeed support, the other. It is a fundamental mistake, too often made both by those who believe that salutary strength requires untempered power and by those who believe the goal of the rule of law is to 'shackle' states, to imagine one must choose between them.

Though they use some unfortunate language in doing so, similar insights are explored in *The Narrow Corridor* by the political economists

Daron Acemoglu and James A. Robinson, who argue that that putative corridor, within which citizens enjoy liberties protected both by and against the state and other citizens, has rarely been entered and even more rarely does it endure. One arrives there only with a historically uncommon combination of a state strong enough to do what it should – 'enforce laws, control violence, resolve conflicts, and provide public services' – with 'an assertive, well-organized society' strong enough to stop it doing what it mustn't. Where a state is too weak (an 'Absent Leviathan') societies remain enmeshed in a 'cage of norms' generated and enforced by an oppressively close and demanding society.[28] Where the state overwhelms the society, it will act as a 'Despotic Leviathan'. As the philosopher-anthropologist Ernest Gellner put it earlier and more pithily, commonly human history has offered only one choice: 'Roughly, the general sociological law of agrarian society states that man must be subject to either kings or cousins, though quite often, of course, he is subject to both.'[29]

Acemoglu and Robinson find the conditions of liberty only where there is a different (and uncommon) configuration of power. This they misleadingly call a 'Shackled Leviathan', in which the shackles are imposed by a strong society but the Leviathan state remains sufficiently strong to do what it should.[30] Though their point is well taken, their terminology is unfortunate: nothing much positive is done in shackles (least of all effective exercise of power, which Robinson and Acemoglu rightly insist is indispensable for this form). However, despite their misplaced choice of word, they clearly have something else in mind: the 'Shackled Leviathan' is not *weaker* than a despotic one but empowered to do things that despots cannot, while and in part because it is prevented from doing things that harm.

Late in the book, they reflect on a fourth type of Leviathan, that they find in Argentina, Colombia, and many states of sub-Saharan Africa. They call it the 'Paper Leviathan'. This type is:

> founded on and supported by the weakness and disorganization of society. It combines some of the defining characteristics of the Despotic Leviathan, in being unaccountable to and unchecked by society, with the weaknesses of the Absent Leviathan. It cannot resolve conflicts, enforce laws, or provide public services. It is repressive but not powerful. It is weak itself and it weakens society.[31]
>
> Paper Leviathans have the appearance of a state and are able to exercise some power in some limited domains and in some major cities. But that power is hollow; it is incoherent and disorganized in most domains, and it is almost completely absent when you go to outlying areas of the country they are supposed to be ruling over.[32]

Given a choice, I would never opt for an absent Leviathan (too many nosy cousins, too much constraining ritual) or a despotic one (too intrusive, frightening, and dominating) or a paper one (too unreliable). My money is on a state that exercises tempered power. It would share characteristics with the 'shackled Leviathan' but not the name. For while overweening, despotic power is horrible, so too is a state unable to exercise public powers of the sorts that are needed, when and where they are needed, in ways that sustain the salutary activities of a strong society, also in good shape. The proper contrast with a despotic state, then, is not a *minimal* state, and certainly not a weak one, but one whose power is at once strong and tempered.

We need to be able to deploy power for many good purposes, but not just any form or way of exercising power will do. If the ineffectual character of Boris Yeltsin's Russian state illustrated the first point,[33] the despotic nature of Putin's illustrates the second. Power must be of the right sort, exercised in the right ways, in the right places, to be able to do what cannot be done without it. If powerful people and institutions can exert power in abusive ways, and also if they are unable to exercise it in helpful ways because in both cases they exercise it arbitrarily, those dependent upon them are in deep trouble. The issue, then, is not to get rid of power or even push it down some single scale where more is worse and less is better or the other way around. Rather, it is to reduce possibilities of malignant, while facilitating benign, uses of it.

So, I have come to believe that there is no contradiction between recognising that both 'power to' *and* 'power over' will often be indispensable for the attainment of collective goods and achieving the goal of the rule of law. Indeed, what anyone concerned with that goal must recognise is how much it depends on salutary empowerments, both public and private, that are in turn dependent, in significant if not sole part, on contributions of the rule of law.

Here too we can learn from Holmes, who has long stressed the *empowering* potential of constitutionalism and the rule of law; what, in contrast to the more common negative conception, he calls 'positive constitutionalism'.[34] Partly that flows from the positive effects of rule of law limits themselves. Appropriately configured laws, on this view, provide 'enabling constraints'.[35] The 'paradoxical insight' here is that 'limited power is more powerful than unlimited power. Restraints strengthen. By closing off some options, a ruler can open up others. A king cannot rule effectively without devices to *retard* his action … under certain circumstances, legal and institutional rigidities produce political and social flexibility.'[36]

Holmes suggests we should think of constitutional provisions and the shaping, channelling presence of the rule of law as constitutive, like the shared grammar which enables communication, rather than restrictive – though he doesn't make this analogy – like censorship of what one tries to communicate. Rules of grammar discipline what we can say comprehensibly but they don't thereby weaken our ability to communicate. On the contrary, they are conditions of it: 'It would obviously be inaccurate, therefore, to conceptualize such rules merely as don'ts, prohibitions, barriers, injunctions, no-trespass signs, or purely negative limitations on permissible behaviour. True, the rules of grammar introduce certain rigidities into ordinary language. But rigidities, for a variety of reasons, can be prodigiously enabling.'[37] It is hard to think of the rules of grammar as 'purely negative' constraints, after all, just because they limit the possibilities of meaningless utterance.

Again, a moment's reflection on ordinary life experience will show that there is no real paradox here. Anyone who has learnt to swim will have quickly discovered that effective performance requires mastery of, and in a sense coming to be mastered by, techniques and disciplines to marshal and channel raw, undirected, energy that otherwise would be dissipated. No one imagines that the power of swimmers is lessened by the disciplined constraints within which they ply their craft. So too the ability of institutions to concentrate their powers where and how they should is potentially enhanced by traditions, practices, requirements, procedures, and institutions of law which, among other things, redirect their movements so they don't splash or smash around where and how they shouldn't. Often the same mechanisms achieve both goals.

Sporting metaphors are not bad ones to think with here. Most sports involve the exercise of power – both *to* do things and *over* things and people. In all sports, that power can be exercised to better and worse effect. To exercise it well, one has to learn not to do things one might otherwise do and to do things one might never have thought of doing.

Partly the contribution is a matter of 'enabling constraints'; for as Locke observed in another context: 'that ill deserves the Name of Confinement, which hedges us in only from Bogs and Precipices'.[38] However, it goes beyond constraint. Thus, Waldron has criticised the tendency among constitutionalists to

> think simplistically [of constitutional devices] … just as *brakes* upon the law-making process, ways of slowing things down, points of possible resistance against oppressive legislation. Equally there is a tendency to think of the formal separation of powers between (say) legislature, executive, and judiciary simply as a way of diluting power and making it harder for it to be exercised.[39]

He insists on the positive role and potential of constitutional provisions. Constitutions, after all, are supposed to *constitute* the elements of a polity and *empower* particular institutions. They *distribute* power to some institutions and actors and not others; they establish fora for discussion and decision 'so that public deliberation becomes a structured enterprise'.[40] All this crucial work is given short shrift by a perspective in which '[e]verything is seen through the lens of restraint and limitation'.[41]

These are not new discoveries. Montesquieu was well aware of them. He of course knew well and used the traditional distinctions long made between forms of government on the basis of what the numbers or classes of people were in charge, such as monarchy, oligarchy, democracy, and plutocracy (a new form, 'bureaucracy',[42] was named ten years before he died). However, the originality of his master work, *The Spirit of the Laws*, was to put his weight behind distinctions among the *ways* governments exercised power, whoever ran them and whatever form they took. The whole of the work was bent not to weaken governments but to explore ways of tempering power in order to *moderate* it and recommend institutional ways to ensure it. Indeed Montesquieu emphasised – with profound if also counterintuitive insight – that although restrained government was not fearsome, as despotism was, it was in a crucial sense stronger than any despot could be:

> A moderate government can, as much as it wants and without peril, relax its springs. It maintains itself by its laws, and even by its force. But when in despotic government the prince ceases for a moment to raise his arm, when he cannot instantly destroy those in the highest places, all is lost, for when the spring of the government, which is fear, no longer exists, the people no longer have a protector.[43]

Nevertheless, Montesquieu recognised that moderation in the use of power was not easily won or kept. As we see in the passage that follows, which also serves as the epigraph to Chapter 8, he laments that but finds it unsurprising, because a moderate government is a much more complicated achievement than an immoderate, unmoderated, one:

> Despite men's love of liberty, despite their hatred of violence, most peoples are subjected to this type of government [despotism]. This is easy to understand. In order to form a moderate government, it is necessary to combine the several powers; to regulate, temper, and set them in motion; to give, as it were, ballast to one, in order to enable it to counterpoise the other. This is a masterpiece of legislation; rarely produced by hazard, and seldom attained by prudence. By contrast, a despotic government leaps to view, so to speak; it is uniform throughout; as only passions are needed to establish it, everyone is good enough for that.[44]

The language with which he makes the contrast is suggestive, for it is not a language of impediments but of difficult and complex balancing, tempering, and regulating; not shackling, and certainly not weakening. Indeed, although Montesquieu is famous for advocating the separation of powers in terms so persuasive that the founders of the American Constitution sought to adopt it, the notion of separation betrays a central element of his thought. For, as Craiutu observes: 'Montesquieu in fact favoured a blending rather than a strict separation of powers and referred in his book to *pouvoirs distribués* and not *pouvoirs séparés*'.[45] Such distribution of powers is not meant to lessen the capacity for their effective exercise. On the contrary, by combining the need for a significant measure of 'comity' between institutions, to allow the branches of government to work together for common purposes, with a degree of 'friction' that allows institutions both to correct each other's errors and to complement their capacities and incapacities,[46] it is arguably a prerequisite for it. Perhaps the American Founding Fathers, so influenced by Montesquieu, either misunderstood him or perhaps the evolution of their Constitution, oscillating between beltway gridlock and contemporary assertion of untempered, intemperate, executive power, shifted relations of power in directions which he did not envisage or recommend. It's not the first time a good idea has been waylaid.

Even when Montesquieu had it, moreover, the idea that unlimited power was not necessarily strong power was not new, nor his alone. Holmes has stressed that Jean Bodin, the sixteenth-century forerunner of Thomas Hobbes as an advocate of absolute power, 'understood before any liberals had appeared on the scene, that "unlimited" power is often crudely ineffective for achieving desirable goals, not to mention being personally dangerous to its wielders'.[47] Montesquieu and others learnt from him.

Montesquieu died in 1755, thirty-four years before the French Revolution. Yet he understood that the French king's position was in effect weaker than that of the English monarch, notwithstanding that, as one author has observed, '[a]t every step the absolutist ambitions of the English Crown were thwarted: consent of Parliament was needed for taxes; consent of the law courts was needed for legal enforcement of alternative revenue sources; and, most important, consent of the gentry was needed for daily implementation of monopolies'.[48] Nevertheless, appearances were deceptive. As the same author explains:

> [L]egislation enacted by Parliament was usually implemented, whereas the will of the much stronger executive in France was less frequently carried out. A significant implementation gap existed under absolutism ... there

> were no legal limits on the French king's power or, by extension that of his ministers, yet time and time again his ministers succumbed to cabals within the court … Despite the legal limits on the Crown's power imposed by Parliament, the English king managed to maintain his position and policies. It seemed to many contemporaries that George III's ministers were more powerful and more likely to be obeyed than the unaccountable and theoretically stronger ministers of the French king.[49]

Not only was English government more effective, more able to raise taxes, and more deeply embedded in society than the French but its economy was more powerful and the people of England were freer than those of France. This is probably no accidental combination. And though France had an apparently far more powerful system of centralised rule than England, the French *ancien régime* was swept aside in 1789, while the English system has survived with only evolutionary change since the seventeenth century. The French head of state had enormous discretionary power, which proved worthless when his own head was removed. The English kings, after controversies over their arbitrary power were similarly brought to a head more than a century earlier, were forced to accede to institutionalised limitations on their personal power and thereafter regularly died in bed, in command of the strongest state in the world for at least two centuries.

Montesquieu's insight into the relative strengths of moderate and despotic governments was even more prophetic than this comparison between England and France suggests. Dramatic evidence of it was the house-of-cards collapse of the Soviet Union and its dominions. This was one of the most despotic empires the world has known, and almost no one apart from Montesquieu predicted its destruction. But it was not the first occasion when apparently overwhelmingly powerful despotisms have wilted before forces which hardly seemed up to the task – though it was exceptional in that in this case there was no force, no task.

Like the collapse of Communism, the French and Russian Revolutions, the end of the Marcos regime in the Philippines, the fall of the Shah of Iran, all seemed overdetermined *after* the event. But they revealed that extraordinary fragility of despotisms which keeps taking us by surprise. It should not.[50]

The point is a large one. Even non-despotic leaders can sincerely view any restrictions, particularly in emergencies, as unseemly limitations on their powers. However, as Holmes again aptly observes:

> The rule of law enforces an uncomfortable degree of transparency on the executive. It requires that the factual premises for the government's resort to coercion and force must be tested in some sort of adversarial

> process, giving interested and knowledgeable parties a fair opportunity to question the accuracy and reliability of evidence. That is how due process serves the public interest and helps reduce the risk of error. To reject the rule of law is reckless because it frees the government from the need to give reasons for its actions before a tribunal that does not depend on spoon-fed disinformation and is capable of pushing back. A government that is not compelled to give reasons for its actions may soon have no plausible reasons for its actions.[51]

Contemporary China is a complex case, and the results are not in. Certainly the calamities of Mao Tse-Tung's rule support this argument. So too the successes of self-enforced (relative) moderation that his early successors pursued. Though they did not have the word, they certainly had the ambition to temper state power to an extent unprecedented under Mao's regime. And it had dramatic economic consequences. Equally dramatic is the constitutionalisation of both 'socialist rule of law with Chinese characteristics' and the leading role of the party in many (but far from all) spheres by Xi Jinping. The jury is still out on the implications of this complicated dual commitment, though none of them points to reduction of his or the party's sway over the law, or to his domination over both the party and the law. I am not competent to discern whether the more recent attempts to combine a novel emphasis on ruliness with doubled-down centralised authoritarianism and crushing of dissent and unprecedented society-wide surveillance will succeed. If it does, it might call for revisions of this sort of scepticism about the productive possibilities of despotism, but I would suggest caution.

Partisans of the rule of law ideal have contrived ways of asking decision-makers, among other things, to justify actions before independent bodies backed by long legal traditions familiar with the dangers of corruption and criminality, the temptations of persecution and prosecution, and the virtues of process, examination, and cross-examination. Notwithstanding China's economic successes of recent decades, I would not let go of these cautions too soon. Nor would I forget the *moral* reasons to condemn arbitrary exercise of power, rehearsed in Chapter 5 and to some of which I return in Chapter 8. These do not lose any of their force even in the face of apparent economic success.

As Confucius might have said, governments that act alone and in the dark too often lose their way. They do the wrong things, catch and harass the wrong people, miss the right ones. Often they blunder, and if ill-motivated they do worse than blunder, because they can conceal their blunders.

6.3 Tempered Power

So far I have followed Holmes and many others in using language that seems to measure exercises of power on a single scale – weak/strong, more/less, ineffective/effective, and so on – but his insight, and that of Acemoglu and Robinson, is better expressed, I believe, if we think in terms of qualitative distinctions, different scales not differences on the same one. So I would amend or reconfigure their point slightly, or at least the language in which they express it (since I doubt they would object). Power differs not merely in amount but in quality, and for power to be usefully tempered, quality is key.

Seeking language that does not obscure but conveys such qualitative differences, which allows for the unparadoxical paradox of constraints that enable, limits that empower, mixes and balances that do not merely separate and, still worse, emasculate but blend and render more effective, the term 'tempering power' came to mind. I was, as I have mentioned, pleased with myself to have come up with this 'coinage', though somewhat chastened when I discovered the distinguished lineage of the term and the idea. Looking into its development and connotations further, I found the word has multiple trajectories (music, alcohol, chocolate) not easily connected, at least by me. Were I a philologist like Nietzsche,[52] or a scholar of ancient Greece and Rome like Helen North,[53] and not the *homme moyen sensuel* that I am, I could enrich our understanding and use of this concept in many ways unavailable to me. But several prominent associations and connotations of the English term, with parallels in several other contemporary Latin-based languages, are suggestive enough on their own.

Many languages do not have a single term with the same history and fertility of connotations both literal and metaphorical as 'tempering', so the ideas that follow would have to be parsed and cashed out in other terms. But those connotations are worth pursuing, however expressed. With even a little unscholarly ransacking, I keep finding reasons to applaud my ignorant (but, I plead, innocent) plagiarism: 'tempering' captures, suggests, and allows us to imagine a great deal that we want in relation to the exercise of power. It might not offer conceptual precision, at least not in my hands, but it might help us to think.

To speak of tempering power might today seem quaint but it is not likely to raise alarm, particularly since Aquinas and Bracton in the thirteenth century, and Montesquieu in the eighteenth, not to mention Cicero before them, did so. Still, though only a word, and in several usages a metaphor at that, this is not today the most common way of putting things. Indeed, usage of the term has suffered a steady decline since the late 1700s.[54] And though Montesquieu used the term often, he put more stress on 'moderation', which is also a key quality. However, it misses something of the positive possibilities of tempering, though not nearly as much as is missed in locutions such as limit, restrain, constrain, restrict, shackle, or curb. As we have seen, these are the terms typically used by people who think themselves realists about power, the rule of law, and constitutionalism. Though there is something to their boast, indeed something important as we have seen, I think they are wrong to think so well of themselves. The rule of law can and should serve larger, more positive, ideals as well. Tempering indicates and makes space for some of those.

Of the many contexts in which we speak in English of 'tempering' (I leave aside chocolate and music since I don't see the connections; and alcohol since I can't stand the implications), three seem to me important to think with in relation to the exercise of power. The first is as a dimension of personal virtue, the second of institutional behaviour, and the third as a chemical process. Each can help us think about the complex promise of the rule of law ideal. For the Greeks, the term *sōphrosýnē*, which Cicero translated into Latin and introduced into European tradition as *temperantia*,[55] was one of the cardinal personal virtues. It included restraint, particularly self-restraint, and was the opposite of hubris, but it also suggested and went along with moderation, thoughtfulness, wisdom, and self-knowledge. Helen North writes of the Greek tragedians:

> If the Aeschylean conception of *sōphrosýnē* [from Cicero and thereafter *temperantia*] can be glossed by the Apolline 'Nothing in excess' and 'Think mortal thoughts', the Sophoclean virtue is closer to 'Know thyself.' The failure in *sōphrosýnē* that marks such heroes as Ajax, Antigone, Oedipus, Electra, and Deianaira is a failure in self-knowledge, amounting sometimes to delusion, sometimes almost to madness. The hero is blind to something essential in himself or his situation, and tragedy arises from the interplay between his circumstances and his admirable but imperfect nature.[56]

Lack of *sōphrosýnē* is a personal failing, but already it has institutional implications. As North writes elsewhere of Greek literary traditions:

> From Aeschyles and Sophocles, Herodotus and the grave-epigraphs, we learn that to the Athenian of the late to mid-fifth century *sôphrosynê* implied good sense, moderation, self-knowledge and that accurate observance of divine and human boundaries which protects man from dangerous extremes of every kind. In private life it is opposed to *hybris*, and in the life of the State to both anarchy and tyranny.[57]

As we saw in Section 6.2, many aspects of the disciplining, slowing down aspects of the rule of law are intended to encourage such virtues of moderation and thoughtful self-knowledge.[58]

Institutionally, tempering suggests a moderating blending of powers and of elements (e.g. power with law; justice with mercy; strength with moderation), a *balancing* and *distributing* of powers designed to lessen the severity, the harshness, the tempting capriciousness of unblended, overly concentrated motive or power. Thus Henry Bracton, the first compiler of the English common law in the thirteenth century, was not out to weaken the king, who 'has no equal within his realm', when he wrote the paragraph that opens this book, urging that he should 'temper his power by law, which is the bridle of power'. Again, in the same work (but with some controversy whether actually written by the same author) we find it argued that:

> The king has a superior, namely, God. Also the law by which he is made king. Also his *curia*, namely, the earls and barons, because if he is without bridle, that is without law, they ought to put the bridle on him. [That is why the earls are called the partners, so to speak, of the king; he who has a partner has a master.] When even they, like the king, are without bridle, then will the subjects cry out and say 'Lord Jesus, bind fast their jaws in rein and bridle'.[59]

Saint Thomas Aquinas similarly favoured a 'tempered monarchy' as a form of government, the tempering achieved by a 'mixed constitution'; he sought 'to place legal restraints on the king in order to prevent tyranny, and the practical means by which this is achieved is to "temper" one type of government by the "admixture" of another'.[60] The civic republican tradition similarly is also full of paeans to mixing and balancing powers and institutions.

In early medieval pictorial representations, *Temperantia* held a mixing bowl, 'in keeping with the translation of "temperamentum" as measure/proper mixture/moderation'.[61] In Tuscan representations of the period, she pours liquid from one bowl to another, 'an evident allusion to the belief that wine should be tempered by water'.[62] This was in keeping with the classical tradition that allied temperance with moderation, a tradition that continues.

In the fourteenth century, another theme was launched in 'The Virtues of Good Government', one of Ambrogio Lorenzetti's three remarkable politically commissioned and politically infused frescoes on good and bad government, in Siena's town hall. Among the seven cardinal virtues portrayed there, *Temperantia* (who figures on the cover of this book) holds a sand-glass rather than a mixing bowl. She is immediately flanked by

Justitia on one side holding the severed head of some (presumably justly convicted) felon and Magnanimita freely disbursing coins from a large dish, on the other. The juxtaposition is unlikely to be accidental. Justice and magnanimity are good, but temperance mediates between them with *measured* patience, which allows for deliberation and thoughtfulness.

As several scholars have suggested, here for the first time the sand-glass connects temperance with time, time-keeping, measurement, and measured temperament, patient, precise, and not capricious: *timely*. A good society needs all three virtues, plus another four. And the results are dramatic, as the two accompanying walls of the hall attest. On the one side, 'the effects of bad government', portrays a literally hellish tyranny. On the other, 'the effects of good government', peace reigns, and conviviality and prosperity flourish. 'Limited government' doesn't capture much of that.

As we have seen, one theme of disquisitions on tempered power is the emphasis on the salutary benefits of mixing and balancing. This line of thought can be enriched by reflection on a third sense in which we use the term, which is for the chemical process of tempering steel (and other compounds such as glass) to make it/them stronger and fit for purpose. Tempering involves a measured process of balance and mixture, but it does not aim for weakness. On the contrary, the resulting, tempered, compound of alloys is less brittle and more powerful than its primary components alone. Tempered steel, after all, is stronger than iron or untempered steel; as Wikipedia informs us, it is intended 'to achieve greater toughness by decreasing the hardness of the alloy'.[63] And it does so by judicious blending. As John Braithwaite, who has joined me in exploring this metaphor, observes: 'Tempered steel is more flexible, yet stronger for realising its purposes: it is resilient and responsive. Tempered steel is distinguished from iron by a combination of alloying it with carbon and other checks and balances and testing it with extreme heat that makes it resilient.'[64] 'More flexible, yet stronger for realising its purposes ... resilient and responsive'; on views of the law and rule of law that I commend, these are just what one should hope for from the rule of law. Elsewhere he approaches our common subject:

> According to the Krygier metaphor, tempered steel is made tougher, less hard and less brittle as an alloy (a balance of more resilient metals) in a test of extreme heat. The tempering metaphor of governance means tempered power is less brutal and less brittle, 'infrastructural' rather than 'despotic' ... because arbitrary power pursues whims of the powerful unconstrained by rule of law, while tempered power is improved and matured by accountability.[65]

Tempering, in any of these senses, does not come naturally. It is a process, commonly thought to involve adroit mixtures, balances. It is a *measured* virtue.

I conclude by ringing one change more on the implications of this resonant word. In 2020, I was interviewed by the eminent Polish journalist Jacek Żakowski. The interview was conducted in Polish and appeared under the title 'How to Temper Power'.[66] Asked what was most missing from Polish politics, I suggested institutions that are expected to, and able to, routinely temper the exercise of power. I added that Poland's ruler, Kaczyński, 'like many other populists, does not understand that a limited state can actually be stronger than an unlimited one, because it can effectively do what it should and not spoil what is not its business'.

I speak Polish, with gaps and errors, but my vocabulary has gaping holes. What I did not know until this interview is that there is another dimension to the concept: the Polish word for pencil sharpener is *temperówka*. So Żakowski immediately repeated my point back to me by saying, 'The state should be like a goose quill – sharply tempered, so as to act with precision and not mess everything up with mistakes.' Sounded good to me. Though I did not have a clue how exactly the metaphor had led him there, I replied, 'precisely'.[67] I only learnt when the article was published under a cartoon of a man with his head in a pencil sharpener, out of which came shavings the colour of the Polish flag. Now I know what he meant, I still say, 'precisely'. Like tempered quills, laws should be finely honed and precise, so that they do not mess things up but on the contrary facilitate purposeful and communicative political penmanship.

So the metaphor I commend for thinking about what we should want from the rule of law is *tempering* rather than all those more familiar terms – shackling, limiting, taming, restraining, curbing, and so on – commonly invoked. Not that they are simply wrong, but they can blind one to core features, complexities, and possibilities that might flow from responding well to the challenges of arbitrary power and contained in the ideal of the rule of law. Tempering suggests some judicious combination of mix, balance, moderation, self-knowledge, measure, and precision, all contributing to particular and salutary sorts – but not every sort – of strength. It is something like *that* that we want from the rule of law, not chains or shackles and not only – though they are hugely important – brakes. A 'purely negative', limiting, conception, or even the wise and flint-edged realism of Shklar, is too – well – limiting a way to view the potential ambition of the rule of law ideal. It slights the complexity of its fundamental purpose and diminishes its larger promise. Indeed, negative conceptions of the goal of the rule of law do not merely ignore such promise; they often undermine it.

6.4 A Larger Promise

It is that larger promise that my mentor, Philip Selznick, spent a large part of a very long life thinking and writing about. As we have seen,[68] like the negative constitutionalists I have discussed, Selznick insisted upon the importance and appeal of the defensive, protective role of the rule of law. Thus, he agreed with those political realists who stress the importance of legality as a restraint on, and the rule of law as a precious protection against abuse of, power.[69] But protection is not the limit of what the ideal of the rule of law might offer us. On the contrary:

> In contemporary discussions of the rule of law we find much that goes beyond the negative virtue of restraining official misconduct. ... This thicker, more positive vision speaks to more than abuse of power. It responds to values that can be realized, not merely protected within a legal process. These include respect for the dignity, integrity, and moral equality of persons and groups. Thus understood, the rule of law enlarges horizons even as it conveys a message of restraint.[70]

Selznick is particularly insightful about the dynamic pressures that the rule of law can generate, both when it fails to satisfy subjects' expectations and when it succeeds. For unusually among writers on the rule of law, he was a sociologist, and in part his objection to a purely limited conception of legality is that:

> We cannot really separate the negative and positive aspects of the rule of law. Indeed it would be highly unsociological to try to do so, for we would then miss the moral and institutional dynamics which create demands for justice, and which induce rulers to accept accountability. ... we should not reduce the rule of law to its most rudimentary forms.[71]

In this understanding, both arbitrariness and its antidotes, among them the rule of law, take on a larger meaning, attached to values to be vindicated and striven for, rather than simply to a set of institutions and practices imagined to guard against threats. Arbitrariness is not found merely when a strict rule is overstepped but – particularly from the point of view of those subject to power – equally when law is inflexible, insensitive, or justified *only* by history or precedent.

After all, 'going by the book' generates its own forms of arbitrariness, as anyone who has sought to deal with officious rule-stickling bureaucrats might testify.[72] In particular, it often slights respect for persons whose particular problems don't easily fit the rules and complicate the lives of rule sticklers. To counteract such forms, space needs to be made for a larger conception of what is potentially in play – as goal and means – more open-ended and open to the complex realities and possibilities of the world we seek uncertainly to navigate. That does not leave too much room for sharp-edged definitions, 'thin' versus 'thick' dichotomies, or sure-fire recipes or checklists, as we will see in the next chapters, but it does help us realise (perhaps even in both senses of that word) the values at stake and how they might be approached.

This, then, is the approach and the goal I believe should animate concerns with and for the rule of law, as well as with and for many other things that might serve it. The rest of the book pursues some of the implications and complications of this approach.

PART IV

Implications

7

Power

> Arbitrariness can flourish in non-legal contexts just as much as in private law and public law contexts, but it is usually equally objectionable in all. And what is objectionable about it is, in part although perhaps not in whole, that it subverts or undermines many of the values and conditions the rule-of-law ideal is alleged to serve.
>
> William Lucy, 'The Rule of Law and Private Law'

The general moral of the story so far is pretty simple: if you want to solve a problem, work out what it is, then what you would want a solution to do. Then, but only then, go looking for ways of doing it. Not the other way around. Chapter 5 identified arbitrary power as the perennial and pervasive problem that has led generations of thinkers to the ideal of the rule of law. Arbitrary power occurs in numerous forms and can be found in equally numerous and changeable domains, places, times, and circumstances. When the power is substantial, it can cause real harm. So arbitrary power has the lead part, as villainous anti-hero, in the rule of law drama, or rather, dramas. There are many of them. It would be nice if arbitrary power could be killed off neatly in the first act of them all, but it keeps finding ways to get back on stage, by guile and/or force, in different guises and roles. Where it is prominent, there is rarely a happy ending. Chapter 6 argued that to write this dangerous character out of the script, and render power at once effective and benign, power needs to be tempered.

If those two chapters are concerned with what to look for, the next four are about where to look, first for sites of mischief, then for potential sources of remedy. This chapter identifies some potential sources of mischief in contemporary societies, including the usual suspect – state power – but suggests that there will always be others as well, too often sidelined in rule of law discussions. Chapter 8 surveys some of the internal resources law might offer to temper power, as well as some of their inherent limitations. Chapter 9 explores the significance of the obvious but often ignored fact that law never acts on its own. All legal activity is an intervention in ongoing processes. That has consequences often ignored, which that chapter will explore. Chapter 10 explores some of the most important general sources of temperance that surround legal orders and that will have to conspire with law and other resources if tempered power is to be even a conceivable, and then a real, option. The concluding chapter, Chapter 11, draws out a couple of implications, for understanding and for action, of all of the above.

7.1 State Power

If arbitrary power is as obnoxious as I have suggested, where should temperers (a real word; I'd like to see it more) focus their attention and energies? In rule of law circles, the answer has traditionally been considered obvious; so obvious indeed as not to warrant much consideration at all. The domain, the territory where the problems are likely to arise to which the rule of law is a response, is assumed to be found in the institutions and activities of the public political order. The sources of threat that concern the rule of law come from governments or rather, more generally, from the official institutional and political arrangements of states – their organisations, officials, powers, and activities. For brevity, I will simply speak of 'the state', unless the context calls for more precision. The problems for which tempered power should respond have to do with the exercise of power by states. That is deep in the tradition.

Moreover, on mainstream understandings not only the challenges and challengers to the rule of law but also its resources for response should be sought in the very same place. As we saw in Chapter 3, the rule of law is taken to depend principally (i.e. both in principle and primarily) upon particular arrangements and forms of legal institutions and rules. It occurs, to use the shorthands common in these discussions, where the state rules *by* laws and legal arrangements of particular kinds, and its organs (in most though not all versions) operate *under* and *within* laws of those kinds, that officials of the state have made. Taken as a whole, this might be conceived of as a form of self-restraint (which is the classical way the cardinal virtue of temperance has been conceived), though rule of law traditions are suspicious of the state as a unified 'self'. They prefer to separate particular functions, such as legislation, administration, adjudication, and enforcement, so that the parts can 'check' and 'balance' each other and not simply be submerged in one directing will.[1] But while powers and functions are to be distributed, checked, balanced and counterbalanced, and coordinated, all this is to be organised within the state as a whole, and those vested with such distributed powers are state lawmaking organs.

Many who make the first assumption, about the location of problems, and the second, about the sources of solutions, imagine they are corollaries: since exercises of state power present the prime challenges to the rule of law, those challenges need to be met by funnelling state exercises of power through state-produced legal forms and institutions that can tame them. Sources of mischief and of remedy are taken as interlinked, indeed inextricably interwoven: the actors and activities of the state provide the former, and particular legal channels and configurations of state power, and lawyers to administer them, are required for the latter.

In many European languages, this coupling is settled semantically, rolled into the term.[2] Whether it is *Rechtsstaat* (German), *état de droit* (French), *statto di diritto* (Italian), *estado de derecho* (Spanish), *państwo prawa* (Polish), or *pravovoe gosudarstvo* (Russian), the ideal is a 'state of law'.

The English 'rule of law' lacks such a semantic link partly because, unlike in European civil law legal orders, 'state' has never been a fundamental legal concept in the common law tradition and also because, until at least the eighteenth century, the English common law was said to stem from an 'ancient collection of unwritten maxims and customs',[3] which royal officials were supposed to recognise and 'declare', not make.[4] However, the significance of that (highly mythologised) customary source has faded. In the modern world of law, including the common law world, whatever the sources of the law might have been thought to be, it is only its recognition by state agencies that attests to its legality. Moreover, today statutes overwhelm common law in quantity, override inconsistencies in substance, and states make the statutes.

And so, as the historian and theorist of the rule of law Brian Tamanaha observes: '[t]he broadest understanding of the rule of law, a thread that has run for over 2000 years, often frayed thin, but never severed, is that the sovereign, and the state and its officials, are limited by the law'.[5] That has not changed. As two (of few) authors critical of this view lament:

> a collective effect of … [contemporary] influential formulations of the rule of law, standing as they do in a long philosophical tradition that shares it, is the implicit acceptance that at its heart the rule of law is an ideal concerning the manner in which a government exercises authority, and the institutional structures through which it may do so consistently with that ideal.[6]

The assumption is so widespread and uncontroversial, we might follow Julian Sempill in calling it 'the state axiom'.[7] It is not to be dismissed cheaply; there are reasons for it. However, they are not self-evident, and they can, and often do, mislead. This goes both ways. State power might be the most dangerous animal on the planet, but state laws might not always be the best way to cope with it. A free press or an active civil society or a widespread, deeply anchored culture of restraint in public life, for example, might be more significant. Conversely, one might concede that there can be non-state sources of arbitrary threat but still believe state responses are necessary to cope with them. Or one can countenance other ways options, likely a complex mix of ways and means. What works depends.

Certainly, anyone seriously concerned with tempering power will have to focus on states, but they will also have reason to worry about threats from elsewhere as well. And wherever they come from, official law will only be one, often crucial but still only one, form of response. For if arbitrary exercise of power is to be kept from spoiling the human drama, then we will have to engage with a much larger and more complex set of characters in more various and also complex ways.

7.1.1 What's Special about It?

No one suggests that states alone exercise power, or for that matter arbitrary power. However, many people believe that states are so distinctive, if not unique, that they require bespoke treatment, and the rule of law is tailored to provide that. And indeed state power *is* special, in many ways. Why so?

First of all, there is a question of range: at least in the modern world of centralised political orders, the power of modern states is distinctively *comprehensive*. It purports to govern the whole of the territory within (and many states have defined 'within' rather loosely and expansively).

Secondly, there are the means distinctively at its disposal: arms, more generally means of violence, and people trained and authorised to use them. As Max Weber, perhaps the greatest theorist of the state (and much else besides), writes, '[o]f course, force is certainly not the normal or the only means of the state – nobody says that – but force is a means specific to the state. Today the relation between the state and violence is an especially intimate one.'[8] This combination of range and putative monopoly of violent means gives modern states, with their professional police forces and standing armies, what the political sociologist Gianfranco Poggi calls 'a quality we may call ultimacy. Violence – or the threat of it – appears as the facility of last resort in shaping and managing interpersonal relations.'[9] Of course, criminals in every country, and citizens in many, have access to some of those instruments (though rarely all sorts) as well. But unless the state is in bad shape, it usually has more, and more lethal, weapons than civilians and criminals do; where it does not, we speak of 'failed' or 'fragile' states. The powers of police and security agencies, again unless they are out of control, are authorised by law and so delegated powers of the state.

Thirdly, apart from putative factual control, state exercise of power, especially violent power, has a specific claim on *legitimacy*, which other entities rarely can make.[10] It is not just that states *have* all that power but their representatives claim that they exercise it on behalf of all their citizens, and it is right that they – and they alone – should claim and be able to do so. Arguably, too, along with that unique claim to legitimacy go distinctive duties that other institutions, however prominent or powerful, lack. Their decisions are supposed to be our decisions. Not so with Amazon or X. We know who owns them, and it is not us.

This combination of distinctive attributes gives hefty reason for devotees of tempered power to take states extremely seriously. What, then, should one say about power available to non-state entities of one sort or another? Might that too be a source of the kinds of problems for which the rule of law is proposed as a solution?

The standard answer is 'no'. Thus Tamanaha endorses what he takes to be the exclusive attention of the rule of law tradition to *state* power, arguing:

> What makes rulers and government the particular focus of rule of law limitations is their capacity to marshal overwhelming prosecutorial and police power against private parties to confiscate property, imprison, fine, exile, and execute, and other draconian actions that threaten life, limb, and possessions; significantly, government institutions create and wield the coercive power of law itself, which calls for legal protections against abuses of its legal powers. Private parties, in contrast, typically lack the capacity to engage in coercive actions backed by force against other private parties, and do not create or carry out law, so the magnitude of the threat they pose to other private parties is much lower.[11]

Similarly, in an important and unusually wide-ranging work on the rule of law, and in several subsequent writings, Paul Gowder argues that:

> [T]he rule of law regulates *states* when they exercise their power over individuals. It does not regulate the private use of coercion or violence. Particularly, it does not give us a reason to object to anarchy, nor does it oblige nonofficials to obey the law. … [T]he unique significance of state violence generates a unique principle, the rule of law, to guard against its abuse.[12]

Only states, Gowder argues, satisfy what he calls both the 'Hobbesian condition' (monopoly of coercive force) and the Weberian one (claim to legitimacy), a combination distinctive enough to warrant the special attention of the rule of law.

7.1.2 How Special Is It?

However, even if one concedes that, in the last instance, state power ultimately can trump everything else, it is worth stressing that commonly we do not reach that instance, a good deal of effort is taken so we don't, and it's nice when we don't. As Poggi reminds us: 'Most aspects of contemporary political experience have become distinctly "civilianised," and make little direct use of or reference to the ultimate sanction of violence. Those who normally act as the state's agents, in most aspects of its political and administrative activity are conventionally mannered people, who operate in a most un-military fashion.'[13]

A lot of this civilianising results from the institutionalising and legalising of routine, non-violent, ways of exercising state power, but it also results from the simple fact that, notwithstanding Chairman Mao's famous aphorism, many forms of power, even state power, occur nowhere near the barrel of a gun. And yet we still think the ideal of the rule of law is relevant to routine acts of government, for asymmetries of power abound – many sorts of power, often huge but having nothing to do with violence or even coercive enforcement, but with potentially harmful consequences for those subject to them.

After all, it is not as though the only reasons we have to be concerned about arbitrary state power have to do with its ability to exercise violence. As we saw in Chapter 4 and will see in this chapter, many forms of power asymmetry, both public and those we call 'private' even though many forms of non-state power are far from private in their effects, draw on other resources than physical coercion – economic, ideological, social, and technological. And where asymmetries of power are significant enough to cause harm, the consequences of uncontrolled, unpredictable, unrespectful, and ungrounded uses of such power can be devastating for those on whom they are wrought. Even where less than devastating, but merely distressing or disconcerting, standard accounts usually do not say that the rule of law can be ignored simply because no guns were drawn or fired.

Just recall the contexts in which even the most traditional understandings of the rule of law have been invoked in recent years in relation to state exercises of power. They have to do with regular peaceful administration of governmental powers of all sorts. We don't just worry about the activities of the army and the police, and in many areas of rule of law concern no one imagines they will be called in. Exercise of power tempered by the rule of law is often, and thankfully, useful in altogether more prosaic, routine, and peaceful activities than those. If a government agency cancels your legal entitlement to social security or medical service on a whim, or on the basis of some unannounced policy or no policy, without telling you, on the basis of one legal provision contradictory with another, or retroactively, or capriciously, or secretly, or based on information you don't and can't know, and if you knew couldn't understand, then, on the most orthodox understandings of the rule of law, you have been treated in violation of its animating values. No one had to put, or threaten to put, a gun to your head to mess with you (or with your head, for that matter).

And there are states and states. As Jan Zielonka observed in another context, 'Germany and Cyprus may both belong to one integrated region, yet they are anything but similar in terms of size, wealth, cultural profile or security preoccupations. The gap between states such as China and Panama [more poignantly today, perhaps, Donald Trump's United States and Panama] is even greater.'[14] Among those gaps, one that stands out is in access to means of coercion, which can be far greater between many states than between them and many non-state entities. And yet we, and their citizens, would not find it outlandish to hope that the government of Cyprus or Panama (or Malta)[15] heed the rule of law. Certainly, if we start to think about states such as Cyprus and Panama, the gulf in power between them and say Meta or Google as 'private' entities seems to be the other way around.

As we have seen, Paul Gowder insists on the centrality of the state as the object of the rule of law. However, already in *The Rule of Law in the Real World*, he recognises that there might be other putative claimants, if they are close enough, dependent enough, or similar enough to their state exemplars. Thus, generally and basically, though he is sceptical of suggestions that non-state entities should be subject to the rule of law, he recognises that sometimes non-officials might 'have such power that they genuinely compete with the existing government for monopoly control over the use of force in the jurisdiction';[16] and so, he is prepared to extend the rule of law to non-state actors who are sufficiently like the state, or in the pocket of the state, that they warrant treatment of a similar kind.

Indeed, Gowder acknowledges that 'some private entities manage to acquire – either conferred by the state or by their own efforts – power that begins to resemble the features associated with state power. Then, those features can be taken (if they appear to a sufficient degree) to license the extension of the rule of law to those private entities.'[17] So here, the state is the primary target of the rule of law, but to the extent that other entities share characteristics that make it so, they also might deserve to have their power tempered. Such entities might include private employers and 'dominant internet platforms such as Google and Facebook'.[18] Given the number of and resources available to such entities, that waters down the original limitation considerably. Moreover, as we shall see, there are other reasons than analogy with states that might get you to want to temper power. But let us pursue this route for a start.

7.2 State-Like Power

If you have been accustomed to believe that rule of law problems stem from states, and rule of law solutions are to be found in state law, private power is unlikely to seem to be your problem or relevant to your solutions. And that, in the main, is how thinking about the rule of law has developed over millennia, for the most part unworried that this might be a form of myopia.

Moreover, given its centrality in rule of law discourse and thought, the state tends to dominate thinking even of those who want to insist that it is not the only game in any rule of law town. Among them was Philip Selznick, who pioneered close exploration of what he called 'private government',[19] and more recently the philosopher Elizabeth Anderson, who also uses the term, though without acknowledging her forebear.[20] The term is arresting, precisely because 'government' is typically contrasted with what is private, and so 'private government' might seem self-contradictory, like snowballs in hell. Still, it only departs from tradition in part, since government conventionally understood is the paradigm and foil for this counterintuitive combination. It moves beyond conventional understandings but only with reference to them. Private entities, Selznick and Anderson suggest, can pose problems *just like* those that stem from state power, and so the ideal of the rule of law extends to them.

Such analogies allow adherents of mainstream paradigms to contemplate some ostensibly 'private' entities as proper subjects of the rule of law, without shifting their understanding of the fundamental source, shape, and constituents of the rule of law too much. To states, they might be persuaded to add outfits that seem very *like* states. The move can be a politically significant one too, indeed became a defiant one in a neoliberal age highly suspicious of the state but less so of corporate, non-state, entities. Analytically, however, it does not require fundamental reorientation. Typically, those who find analogies between states and other forms of enterprise do so on the basis that governments and large organisations look and act sufficiently like governments in form and in many aspects of function that considering them appears to require minimal real deviation from existing ways of thinking. It might, nevertheless, generate major shifts of focus.

First, there is the unprecedented pervasiveness, alike in modern government and in the economy, of huge bureaucratic forms of organisation. This is a theme again pursued more deeply by Weber than anyone else: leadership in the modern world is implemented by vast, rule-based hierarchically organised bureaucracies, both public and private, and the power exercised through them extends to us all. Billions spend their lives working in and for them; few escape their influence. Weber is famous for calling modern bureaucratised capitalism an 'iron cage'.[21] With characteristically more moderate tone but similar substance, Selznick observes: 'the large enterprise – the "representative social institution"[22] of modern life – has brought with it new modes of belonging and dependency'.[23]

Moreover, not merely are public and private bureaucracies similar in many features of organisation, form, and power relations but also their *functions* are not always easy to distinguish. Thus, almost sixty years ago, long before the extensive 'out-sourcing' of many erstwhile governmental activities, Selznick pointed out that in many respects there is less and less functional difference between governmental powers and organisations and those of huge corporations. So, he argued, the political morality expressed in the former might well be adapted to and by the latter. This had been a novel and slow-emerging thought, however, and so:

> The most important source of the weakness of public-law jurisprudence is the great growth of large-scale organisation, both public and private. A striking feature of this development is the convergence of governmental and nongovernmental forms of organisation and modes of action. A great deal of government activity is similar to that carried on by private groups. Government today includes many activities and agencies that have little to do with the distinctive functions of a sovereign and to which, therefore the traditional logic of public law may not properly apply. At the same time, discussions of the modern corporation and trade union, in many ways the representative institutions of industrial society, have increasingly stressed their 'quasi-public' status. It is asked quite seriously whether such institutions are really so different from large public enterprises. … This raises the question whether we have a theory of public law adequate to deal with the group structure of modern society.[24]

So, one might argue, as Selznick and Anderson do, that the rise of large corporate organisations, with their huge multitudes of employees and dependents, has diminished the distance between the nature of private and public organisations and the nature and extent of their leaders' powers over those who inhabit them, deal with them, and in other ways depend upon them, to an extent that talking about the rule of law in the latter doesn't require much deviation from the original path. Thus Selznick argued that:

> [W]herever institutional authority is exercised – wherever there is bureaucracy – people need protection from arbitrary rule. Just governance is a moral necessity, in private as well as in public institutions ... When we fail to see the place of law in 'private' institutions we withhold from that setting the experience of the political community in matters of governance.[25]

Selznick believes that is a bad idea, as does Anderson, for whom 'Government is everywhere, not just in the form of the state, but even more pervasively in the workplace. Yet public discourse and much of political theory pretends that this is not so.'[26] Both Selznick and Anderson argue that the ideal of the rule of law needs to extend to private government, though neither imagines it is a simple, mechanical, thing to do.[27] They are right on both counts.

However, what if, at the level of *problems*, analogies are not obvious because different sources of potentially arbitrary power exist that are different from that of states but still pack a punch? And at the level of *solutions*, what if particular arrangements of private power are beyond the ken of the conventional carpenters of the rule of law? What if rule of law ideals are often not accessible by extending traditional existing legal tools to them? What if they need to draw upon non-traditional means, unmentioned in the canon? I believe all these possibilities exist and indeed are proliferating in modern times. They require us to start with different questions that in turn are likely to generate different answers and to look beyond both conventional rule of law targets and weapons. In this chapter, I will stay with targets. The next three chapters discuss weapons.

7.3 Economic Power

Analogies or putative connections, with something other than what you are talking about often get you somewhere, but sometimes it's worth getting rid of the middleman. Just go to place(s) where substantial power is likely to be found and wielded in ways that can hurt, whether they are like or linked to your first-thought, best example, type or not. Whether or not non-state power is *like* state power is not always the right or at least not the only right question. Whatever the answer there, what matters is whether the entity involved can wield significant power arbitrarily. Temperers have good reason to believe that wherever that occurs there is likely to be a problem: *their* problem.

One centre of power that has received huge attention in many fields for a very long time, but somehow is bracketed or even excluded by many partisans of the rule of law, is the economy. After all, it did not take Karl Marx (though he helped heaps) to make us aware of the extraordinary differences in economic power that exist in modern societies and give those with privileged access to it huge sway over the lives of others with less, who are commonly dependent on the former for their livelihoods. Indeed, Marx thought this was the most important fact about all societies. Even in his time when the powers of states were already unprecedented in scope, he regarded the 'executive of the modern state … [as] but a committee for managing the common affairs of the bourgeoisie'.[28] State power, on this view, is categorically less important than, and typically the servant of, the power of economically ruling classes,[29] at least until the revolution, which had not happened then and has not solved the problem since.

Though Marx dramatically, and many of his followers dogmatically, exaggerated its significance, it is hard to deny that economic power – power over things, which translates directly into power over persons which in turn augments power over things which … – certainly *is* and has been structurally and hugely important in most societies. Its arbitrary exercise has been full of perils for those on whom it might be inflicted. Elsewhere I have written critically of Marx's insistence on the universal primacy of economic power,[30] but it is not clear that turning him on his head is the key to wisdom.[31]

We can start with the very base, as Marx would have it, of the capitalist economy, private property. As Postema has argued:

> Defenders of private property argue that it is a bulwark against the intrusion of the arbitrary power of government. Ownership of property sufficient to sustain a decent life can provide a significant degree of protection. Yet private ownership of resources and wealth also poses a potential threat of arbitrary power. The problem posed by private property regimes is not incidental to those regimes; it arises from their very nature. Property regimes allocate decision-making power over the use of resources in a polity. This law-created and law-allocated normative

> power underwrites and amplifies social power. The owner gets to decide how resources are used. This gives power to the owner, power over resources, and so power over persons. In social contexts of vastly unequal ownership, this power can be great.[32]

Of course, not every sort of property gives its owners the same sway over others. However, many sorts have huge power potential and, untempered, huge arbitrary power potential. Those in control of large numbers of massive non-state corporations are able to exert, to borrow Julian Sempill's terms, both *employment* power and *investment* power, with implications for billions (of money *and* people). The arbitrary exercise of either of these powers can cause potential harm to huge numbers.[33] Often it has. Of course, as with many other forms, economic power might cause great good as well, but it would be rash to rely on that always happening spontaneously, or without side effects. Or so we temperers believe.

We have already, with Selznick and Anderson, met employment power. Selznick was convinced that such power warranted tempering, and in 1969 he was cautiously (and characteristically)[34] optimistic (though never certain) that that might happen through a number of emerging 'inchoate', 'incipient' modern social developments that he observed already beginning to generate demands for extension of the rule of law to and within modern organisations. There is little evidence, however, that those hopes have or will any time soon be able to overcome the vulnerability of employees to employers as well as the (common) distance between formal enactment and real achievement.[35] Temperers might be tempted to ask whether such vulnerabilities and limitations need to be considered by those who believe arbitrary power is an evil to be avoided and/or remedied.

Sempill also argues that investment power – 'the freedoms to invest wealth or not, to withdraw wealth from investment, and to change how wealth is invested'[36] – has huge potential to harm and yet, as he also argues: 'At present, both positive law and Rule of Law discourse place corporate power outside the scope of the Rule of Law mechanisms aimed at systematic recognition, creation, and accountability designed to ensure that powerholders give due weight to respect-worthy things.'[37] I do not draw revolutionary implications from this but, as might be anticipated, temperate ones. Any root-and-branch transformation of contemporary economic structures is beyond my expectations and, given the tragic history of many such attempts, it is also beyond my wishes. But reflection on the potential for arbitrary power that might stem from the pervasiveness of such structures, and on what might be done to reduce it (without excluding benevolent and productive exercises of power at the same time), would be a salutary advance.

7.4 Unseen, All-Seeing, Power

Economic power, political power, the power of guns, corporations, organisations ... these are old hat. Continuingly important, but familiar. We have a lot of experience of the shapes in which they typically come and what they can enable those with superior access to do. Also of the temptations, some familiar, others hitherto unimagined, that occur to those able to wield them.

Of course, the past was neither straight nor flat. One might cite the invention of the wheel, the stirrup, or the printing press, which in their different ways changed the world, but they are dwarfed, almost everything else is dwarfed, by two more recent civilisational transformations: the first industrial revolution of the eighteenth and nineteenth centuries, a big deal in virtually every domain of human life; and the 'technological revolution' of the twentieth century.

However, you don't have to be alarmist, or as old as I am, to recognise that we again live in an unprecedentedly fast-changing world, where access to novel forms and configurations of power is concerned. That is even true of old kinds of power delivered in new kinds of ways: drones, blockchain, artificial intelligence, all transform existing ways of doing old things, and they won't be wished away. Already, we have become dependent on countless '"automated authorities" ... used to exercise power over us by substantially determining what we may know, what we may have, and what our options will be'.[38] That will not decrease.

Beyond the modifications they make to ways of exercising traditional forms of power, it is likely that the technological transformations of the past few – very few – years will change the kinds of power available, in polymorphous combinations and ways, beyond contemporary imaginings. Here analogies with old forms, among them state forms, are rarely to the point.

As Scott Veitch has wryly observed, what matters is:

> [n]ot just the holding and exercising of power but the specific *means* of its exercise; eg the big 5 tech companies (google, microsoft, apple, meta (facebook), amazon) have rapidly specialised in this: algorithmic power, cooptive power, it's for your own good power, power you don't know is being exercised power, now you want it now you need it

> power, you're not going to be able to escape this power power, governance by numbers power (etc: How's your child doing? Compared to what?); financial inclusion of the 'unbanked and underbanked' (it seems you cannot be overbanked); global reach power, beyond (and above and below) the jurisdictional borders of sovereign states power. And no doubt many others.[39]

In the face of such fast-paced, novel and huge transformations, it is easy (and for many including myself appropriate) to feel at once underinformed and overwrought. The changes modern technologies bring are many, complex, massive in scale and reach, attach themselves to most domains of life, point in many different directions, have huge benefits as well as costs, and promise as well as threaten. So to focus on any one tendency is likely to shortchange others, which might be countervailing, though equally they might be accelerating. Still, it is already cliché (and therefore likely to be at least partly true) to observe that we are coming to confront, or rather most of us are coming to be confronted by, novel ways of exercising novel forms of power, much of it concentrated in a handful of huge global corporations but reaching everywhere, exponentially changing and multiplying at astonishing speed, over vast domains of human interaction.

If knowledge is power, then at so many levels and in so many ways, so much more than ever before is known about all of us, by programmes and machines and those who harness them, that most of us know little about, understand less, but use without pause. Sergey Brin, co-founder of Google, once said that 'the perfect search engine would be like the mind of God'.[40] Great. But as well as being all-powerful and all-knowing, God is, or so the Bible tells us, all good. With Google it's less obvious.

The novelties of such sources and kinds of power, as well as their ubiquity, are well captured by Gerald Postema in several passages worth quoting in full:

> The speed, scope, and designed-in opacity of the process has far outpaced and made obsolete ordinary social and legal processes of control. What is more, just in two decades, command of the global data-sphere and the digitization of our lives have been concentrated in very large part in the hands of a few dominant digital companies ('Big Tech'), including Meta/Facebook, Alphabet/Google, Amazon, Apple, Microsoft, Twitter, and a few others. These digital platforms are the new Leviathans, the centers of a new form of ruling power.
>
> The power wielded by the new Leviathans rests not on the power of the sword or control of material resources, but rather on control of data and the technologies that produce, collect, process, package, and distribute it.

> This power is immaterial, ephemeral, yet its ability to penetrate our lives and manipulate our behavior dwarfs that of more familiar forms of power.
>
> This power is immaterial in another sense: it is not territorial. As it defies borders of the self and the personal, so it ignores, transcends, and defies conventional national borders. Its scope, in ambition and in reality, is global.[41]

This is a perceptive summation of where, in only a few decades, we have come to be, and it is clear we are just starting. The only thing I would question is the metaphor 'new Leviathans' that Postema, and elsewhere Paul Gowder,[42] chooses to characterise the novelties he sketches so disturbingly. Presumably he is not talking of the sea monsters so named in the Bible. Rather, he is recalling the title of Hobbes's work of political philosophical genius, *Leviathan or the Matter, Forme and Power of a Commonwealth Ecclesiasticall and Civil.* But that book insisted on the need for an unrivalled single political Sovereign (Leviathan), before whose monopoly of (traditional) means of violence all other powers – civil, ecclesiastical, and so on – must bend, lest we fall into a 'war of all against all'.

These new ways of harnessing and exercising power are nothing like that. They are all over the place, as much out of as in government, straddling the divides, moving from one side to another and outside both, invented one place, adopted in others, forces to themselves, above and beyond any location, indeed every location. Many of them, being at once powerful, accessible, reproducible, and free or cheap to use (think search engines, drones) can potentially redistribute powers once monopolised by states to a variety of non-state and extra-state actors, whence they return and recycle. There is nothing uniquely state-bound about them, and no one has a monopoly over them (though a very few very large companies have a very huge hold). As Jamie Susskind writes: 'The future is not Big Brother, in the sense of one government monolith watching us all at once. It is, instead, a "big brotherhood" of hidden, unblinking eyes, some belonging to the state but countless others belonging to private parties who watch us while remaining unseen.'[43] Not only do such other brothers compete with each other but they do many things better and other things differently than the state itself; indeed they do things which the nation state is not well equipped to do or, at least for the moment, to supervise. Any suggestion (which is clearly not Postema's suggestion) that they only pose novel challenges when harnessed by sovereign states for traditional purposes, simply fails to take the measure, or capture the pervasive and protean character, of the challenges these innovatory forms of power represent.

These unseen seers are unprecedented in scope, intrusiveness, complexity, secrecy, and unintelligibility, certainly to those subject to them, often even to those ostensibly in command.[44] They open enormous space for arbitrary intrusions, in all four senses discussed in Chapter 5.

7.4.1 Uncontrolled

Many of the operations of these new powers are uncontrolled, uncontrollable even, by most who are affected by them, both because of the intrinsic complexity and technicality of these processes and because of the secrecy with which the big five (and others that emulate them) 'resist meaningful disclosure, and hide important decisions behind technology, and boilerplate contracts'.[45] The gap between 'black box insiders',[46] who know what algorithmic engines do and enable, for example, and outsiders, who can know little but cannot escape them and can control less of their invasive operations, yawns. For years I imagined that a 'search engine' was an engine with which I searched; I had little understanding that it was an engine which searched me.

The technologies' 'controllers' themselves are hard to control, and they are not always able to predict the output of their digital devices themselves. Even insiders can lose the capacity to direct what they have made and unleashed, particularly when machine learning allows computers to find patterns and structures beyond the ken of ordinary, even trained and expert, mortals.[47]

7.4.2 Unpredictable

With predictability there is an asymmetry. We are more predictable than we have ever been to automated systems that suck up everything that can today be known about us, which is more than ever before. However, the reverse is not the case. A word one confronts in much of the literature on big data governance is 'opacity'.[48] Another is 'illegibility'.[49] It is difficult, often impossible, for the billions of us surveilled, framed, directed, connected, and shaped by these new technologies even to know this is happening, still less what will happen next. Much of what goes into algorithms is unknown, indeed unknowable, to those whose data is mined and options framed by vast data aggregating codes and connectors that we imagine are serving us, while we are (also) serving them in ways we don't even know how to think about: 'when millions of parameters are applied to billions of data points across hundreds of datasets, and processed thousands of times to form probabilistic outcomes, it can be hard for human engineers to answer simple questions like: why did the system reach that answer? ... Systems which deal in predictions are often themselves highly unpredictable.'[50]

7.4.3 *Unrespectful*

Persons' privacy, reputation, financial security, job prospects, physical safety, and more are today unavoidably affected by technologically empowered agencies of information-gathering and decision-making (about them). For these to be handled with respect requires that these 'data points' be able to know the basis on which decisions are made, where the information comes from, what is likely to be done with it, to them, and why; that they can respond (both formally be allowed to and substantively have the capacity to); and that their personal circumstances, and personal views on the matter, are heard, listened to, and taken into account. But many digitally informed decisions are made on the basis of information you do not know you are giving (or even know), then compared with information about others put together on bases you don't understand, which they also don't know or understand. Vast datasets, in which persons are commonly just individually invisible points, are collected in ways unknown to them, to add to vast aggregations the results of which then come to haunt individuals found to share characteristics classified in one way or another by the all-seeing engines of data collection. As Susskind puts it, 'to treat people as mere data points in a larger algorithmic exercise is to risk violating the principle that every person counts. When we stand before a judge, an employer, a parole officer or a mortgage lender, we want to be seen for who we really are, rather than as mere bundles of shared traits.'[51]

7.4.4 *Ungrounded*

What comes out of algorithmically driven decision-making processes depends upon what goes in. This in turn can reflect conscious and unconscious biases, (mis-) conceptions, and false assumptions encoded into programmes by often unaccountable designers and programmers or built within the data themselves and then amplified by internal machine operations on them.[52] These are hard (and for ordinary people impossible) to detect, still less to question or neutralise. They can block access to jobs and finance, thwart careers and life choices, and at the extreme ruin lives.

In the hands of governments, they have at times literally proved fatal.[53] There can be no talk of fair-minded relationship and proportion when the assumptions that drive programmed decisions might be at once systematically and often invisibly flawed and their grounds so hard to decipher.

Like power generally, we would not want to (and anyway could not) eliminate these multiple new ways of generating and harnessing information, connection, and algorithmic power completely, or even limit many of their (so many) welcome applications. We gain lots from them – connection, information, problem-solving at breakneck speed, and much else – and anyway it is already too late to stuff these numerous and multiform new genies back into their digital bottles. These capacities can be used to serve many good purposes, existing ones better, and new ones not yet contemplated.

A question dear to the heart of temperers, however, is how all this is to be contained.[54] Of course, platoons, more likely battalions, of regulators are wondering what to do about such developments, to harness the benefits they promise while diminishing the dangers they pose.[55] They consider many sorts of both. The plea of temperers is that they recall at least one particular kind of threat, that has less to do with ends sought than the ways available to seekers: the dangers of arbitrary use of these unprecedentedly invasive powers.

Just as traditional thinking about the ideal of the rule of law was concerned with the *ways and consequences of the ways power is exercised*, quite apart from the purposes for which it might be enlisted, so too we need to be concerned with the distinctive ways power might be gained and used, as well as what it is used for, in this risky new world. This is especially so since these new automated systems can not only increase existing power differentials of the traditional sorts discussed in the rest of this chapter but add quite new asymmetries via privileged and guarded access to and control over systems that, to repeat, everyone uses but almost no one fully understands.[56]

To be sure, not everything associated with the power of automated systems is new, but to the extent that it involves the exercise of power which is liable to arbitrary abuse, we need to consider ways in which these new powers might be tempered. This will need a lot more than recycling, or redirecting Fuller's or any existing legal principles, *both* because we need new principles – some legal, some not – and because we need much more than law. We do not have an existing repertoire for the looming threats that might issue from technological innovation. What we *do* have, however, are existing, indeed existential and perennial, vulnerabilities, worries, values, and hopes that certain kinds of mischief might be remedied: wherever they come from and however much the remedies might differ from what Fuller, Raz, Dworkin, or Waldron ever had in mind.

Jamie Susskind has remarked that '[w]e cannot tackle the political problems of big tech using the parched vocabulary of twentieth-century economics'.[57] The warning extends way beyond economics (and also beyond big tech).

7.5 Conclusions

Nothing in this chapter or this book is intended to diminish the significance of the pervasive and often unparalleled power of (many) states in the modern world order of territorial states, nor of the importance of considering how such power – with its many singular aspects – might be tempered to avoid its arbitrary exercise. Rumours of 'the death of the state', which had excessive currency at the end of the last century, were greatly exaggerated. In the twenty-first century, many hugely powerful states are well and truly alive. At that time, one might have needed to argue this;[58] today it is inescapably obvious. State power has so many distinctive sources, kinds, and pathologies available to it and obligations appropriate to it, that deserve specific treatment. Their specificity must not be washed away in some general attempt to temper the world. Particularly given the amount of untempered state power that is rocking that world as I write (2025), that is plain and should go without saying. But in case it doesn't, I say it, again. However, that is no reason to confine 'the rule of law ideal' to states.

States *are* special, at least in the modern era. But they are not alone in being able to wield arbitrary power in ways that can frighten or hurt. The list of power-amassers and power-wielders with a potential for arbitrary exercise of power at great social cost is unlikely to be short or stay still. If non-state power is arbitrarily exercised by the sorts of outfits discussed in this chapter, or for that matter by oligarchs, Mafiosi, warlords, tribal elders, al-Qaeda, non-governmental organisations, currency speculators, international ratings agencies and other multiform transnational arrangements, or financial institutions, it too has the potential to bring with it the vices of arbitrariness mentioned here. Reflection on whether and how such power might be tempered should extend, at least in principle, to these sorts of power as well. We should not forget every other source of challenge just because one has traditionally loomed so large.

Where there is significant power, it is appropriate to put the question (which is not yet the same as *answering* the question) whether and how it might need tempering. The test should be the kind and amount of power an entity has and the likely consequences of its arbitrary exercise of that power, not its location.

The point is that wherever there is the ability to wield serious power there is potential for abuse. The ability to do so arbitrarily with harmful effects is not a governmental monopoly. If some category of power-wielder is free at their pleasure, without announcement, out of the blue, for any reason, to arbitrarily lash out and hit plenty of people in the face, it's not to the point that another category of power-wielder can hit even more faces, and harder. Faces should be protected from hits; simple but true.

Often traditional legal measures are weak, sometimes spectacularly weak in dealing with non-state exercises of power. However, as we will see in the following chapters, that is true in relation to both state and non-state powers; in both cases law often does not do very well, and in neither case can it do anything much on its own. So we will need, in both cases, to look further and elsewhere, instead or as well. In both cases, we seek to find what works. Tempering power, which is the 'rule of law ideal' and animates rule of law thinking, is something we consider doing wherever power's arbitrary exercise threatens harm. How we achieve it is something we are not yet very smart about. If we value the ideal, we should try to be smarter. And that will often require us to go beyond the usual legal suspects.

And yes, if you start with the *purpose*, the *goal* of tempering the exercise of serious power so it not be arbitrary, rather than stipulate from the start that it must be achieved by one or another preformed list of putatively defining (state-centred) *means* of fixing up state law so it is 'in good shape', the story develops in a different way from what is commonly found in rule of law traditions. On my view, however, that is the point; in contemporary computerspeak, a feature not a bug.

So temperers must be prepared to explore powers available to other entities than states. If untempered arbitrary power is liable to do serious harm, then partisans of the rule of law ideal have reason for concern. There is nothing a priori about locating the target or deciding what to do about it. It is a matter of political (and legal) morality whether you should care, but if so, it is then an empirical (and theoretical) matter where the problems might arise, where and what solutions might be found, what forms they might take, and (also and often equally or more) whether there are countervailing considerations that might weigh against implementing them. If the problem is arbitrary power, however, it would need to be shown and not simply assumed that the *state* is the one and only place to worry about it.

Put another way, on this approach, the question is not whether thinking of the rule of law ideal as relevant to non-state power is a conceptual category mistake (should vegetarians eat steak?) or whether there might be some *analogy* with the *Ur-culprit* that would warrant extension anywhere out of its normal range. The burden of argument is reversed: not whether the rule of law can be *extended* beyond the domain of state power but rather whether there is any reason to *exclude its reach* from what falls within its basic domain of concern – which, to repeat, extends to any sources of significant power that can be exercised arbitrarily in ways that cause harm. For what one is dealing with is not *extension*, which might or might not be justified, but *direct implication*, which might or might not be narrowed for other reasons. But then you need to provide the reasons, not assume them.

Perhaps the philosopher Michael Walzer exaggerates a little in saying that 'plutocrats and meritocrats … are tyrants as much as autocrats are',[59] but why assume that their tyrannous potential is of no account to those who value the ideal of the rule of law? All over the world, there exist many entities with, and activities that generate, huge power and consequences, and often their power is not tempered; indeed they typically resist tempering and have powerful resources to enable them to do so. The struggle to temper power must extend to these sorts of power as well, and often traditional legal measures are weak, sometimes spectacularly so, in dealing with them. We should not forget every other source of challenge just because one has traditionally loomed so large.

It is not as though we are entering uncharted territory. We already regulate all the areas of life mentioned in this chapter and hosts of others, in one way or another, for one purpose or other, to achieve one goal or other. Temperers simply ask that we focus *as well and seriously* on the dangers that these sources of power might be exercised arbitrarily.

And so, people who rightly identify arbitrary power as a problem in need of a solution must cast their nets more widely. Where power is sufficiently substantial that its arbitrary exercise is likely to harm, questions of how it might be tempered need to be considered. They are not the only questions that might be in play, but they are not to be excluded just because power is wielded by some entity other than governments.

Of course, there must be limits to, and variations in, how those questions should be answered. One might decide on the basis of competing values, such as the sanctity of the family (somewhat diminished in recent years), that some domains need special protection, even from measures to temper power, or that others are unamenable to tempering in any way we know, or without other effects that make the game not worth the candle. What the social theorist Jürgen Habermas called the juridification of social spheres is not an unmixed blessing in every sphere. Not every exercise of power should be subject to public surveillance and tempering (or tampering). Distinctions have to be made, and matters of scale, character, and consequence really matter. This is equally true in relation to state power, of course.

Again, the ancient Roman legal maxim *de minimis non curat lex*, commonly translated as 'the law does not deal with trifles', is a general one, equally applicable to state and non-state power. Moreover, even where dangers are not trivial, there are often countervailing considerations. The tempering of power is never the only game in town, though where power is substantial it should be an important player in many games.

Public intrusions often come at a price. Not every hurt is or should be a matter of public intervention, though what should be and what thresholds are appropriate are matters on which opinions and judgments will differ, change, and need to be debated. It is fortunately no longer an admissible defence of domestic violence or rape that it happened at home, in the family. Views on boundaries between what is properly a matter of private and what of public concern differ between cultures,[60] and have moved greatly in my own culture over my own (long) lifetime, and even in lifetimes shorter than mine. They will continue to change. I doubt that they will disappear, however, and I do not wish for it.

Even then, there are likely to be (variable and arguable) limits. Neoliberal economists traditionally and strenuously resist incursion on private property and more generally private economic power for many reasons others might contest. They might well do so if tempering power were to be invoked. There is an argument to be had there, but it is an *argument*, not simply a no-go zone where the ideal of the rule of law has by definition no place. How it goes depends upon evidence relating to the magnitude of the power involved, the number of people who might be affected by it, the significance of the effects, the amount and kinds of arbitrariness to which they might be liable, the effectiveness of whatever remedies might be contemplated, the harms interventions might cause, and so on. None of this can be assumed to point exclusively in the direction of states. Nor to state law either, for reasons to which we now turn.

8

Law

> In order to form a moderate government, one must combine powers, regulate them, temper them, make them act; one must give one power a ballast, so to speak, to put it in a position to resist another; this is a masterpiece of legislation that chance rarely produces and prudence is rarely allowed to produce. By contrast, a despotic government leaps to view, so to speak; it is uniform throughout; as only passions are needed to establish it, everyone is good enough for that.
>
> Montesquieu, *The Spirit of the Laws*

If we turn from sources of mischief to ways of avoiding them, few partisans of tempered power will be satisfied to leave things to the personal qualities of individuals, to their innate propensity for virtue, for example. There is no reason to deny or deride the existence or importance of human virtues, among them liberal virtues,[1] and every reason to encourage them. Effective tempering will often need to draw on them and can be lost without them. Nevertheless, worldly-wise temperers believe we would be unwise to rely upon them, certainly not to rely solely upon them.

There are many reasons. Here are three. One is that we might not find enough of these virtues, so we need safeguards against their absence. Another, that even if power-wielders possess them, it would be folly to rely on them alone, susceptible as they might be to seduction, corruption, or erosion. These, after all, are natural enough processes in our fallen world, both tempting and accessible to those with untempered power. A third is that while virtue might well be its own reward, it might not be a reward to everyone touched by it. We need safeguards against its over-assertion, when linked to power. For we have good reasons to fear not only fiends but saints as well – particularly if they are powerful fiends or saints. We need security against empowered excess of zeal from either source, indeed from *any* source.

In the hope that the rule of law might contribute to channelling power in fruitful directions, its partisans have banked a lot on law's ability to do what unaided virtue will not. So the question needs to be put: what might law offer the tempering enterprise. What can it do to refine, channel, and strengthen well-exercised power, while blocking or correcting its wayward and arbitrary counterparts, whether wielded by governments that author the laws or cronies, oligarchs, businesspeople, or power-wielders of any of the kinds mentioned in Chapter 7, to exploit/manipulate/avoid/evade/game/indeed *trump* the rule of law ideal, as has so often occurred and is occurring in many parts of the world, as we speak?

8.1 Lawlessness

Classical writers on the rule of law often contrasted lawful with lawless rule. One common image is of an order in which power is wielded by some 'tyrant', 'autocrat', or 'dictator', without legal authorisation, excuse, tempering, constraint, or frame. This is the thought that underlies the old distinction between lawful government, 'the empire of laws, and not of men', and tyranny. Thus Montesquieu, following long tradition, distinguished among the rule of one person, between monarchies, '*in which one alone governs, but by fixed and established laws*', and '*despotic government [in which] one alone, without law and without rule, draws everything along by his will and his caprices.*'[2] He favoured the former.

Another image of lawlessness often invoked occurs at the opposite extreme: where no one rules but many fight. Such is Hobbes's imagined state of nature, where: 'Men live without a common power to keep them all in awe, they are in that condition which is called war; and such a war, as is of every man, against every man ... and the life of man solitary, poor, nasty, brutish and short.'[3] The state of nature, Hobbes surmised, would be so dreadful that people would willingly agree to submit to the domination of an absolute sovereign, *Leviathan*, who could deliver them from it by means of enforceable laws.

Locke employed the same thought experiment. Life in the natural state as he envisaged it would likely be less brutish, less solitary, and perhaps longer. Still, inhabitants would be minded to leave it, because:

> *First*, there wants an *establish'd*, settled, known *Law* ... *Secondly*, ... there wants a *known and indifferent Judge*, with Authority to determine all differences according to the established Law ... *Thirdly*, ... there often wants *Power* to back and support the Sentence when right, and to give it due *Execution*.[4]

Remedy those three defects, he suggests, and you have moved some way towards what we now call the rule of law.

Though these images of tyranny and anarchy stand at purposefully dramatic and idealised extremes, there are plenty of examples to suggest they are not simply dystopian fantasies. There is a huge difference between orders where rulers do exist and appear able to exercise power when and how they like, in favour of what and whom they like, and against whomever they dislike, on the one hand, and ones that approach anarchy (from the Greek *anarkhia*, without a ruler), on the other. Both defy the ideal of the rule of law, however, because they lack reliable ways of tempering power.

On the one hand, past and contemporary examples abound of power exercised arbitrarily by absolute rulers, juntas, revolutionaries, and charismatic leaders who either draw on or consider themselves bound by no law. Many have got away with it, at least for a while. Often when they fall, similars rise. Towards the other end, there have been numerous 'failed states', 'Absent Leviathans' in Acemoglu and Robinson's rendition,[5] where disorder rules, and certainly not law. And then there are 'paper Leviathans', where states are strong enough to act arbitrarily but too weak to tame the power of monsters and others, free to prey on hapless populations. Full of despotic power, they have few infrastructural capacities.

There are many stages in between, and societies can shift, usually messily, from one to the other. Recall Communist China before, during, and after the Cultural Revolution of 1966–76: in turn, unrestrained despotism, uncontrolled lawlessness, and 'socialist rule of law with Chinese characteristics' (which are hard to pin down, change, and have quite other concerns than the tempering of ruling power).

Another option is an order so composed that rulers rule but their exercises of power are framed, channelled, constrained, and also facilitated by norms, entities, mechanisms, common social understandings, political arrangements, and felt obligations (among them legal).

What resources might law offer to support that latter, happy, state of affairs? I should stress that 'offer' carries specific weight in this question since, as we will see in the rest of this chapter, the mere existence of law does not mean such offers will be forthcoming, and as we will see in the next two chapters, even when they are made, they might not be well communicated, or received, or understood, or taken up, in whatever senses are intended by their authors. Nevertheless, partisans of the rule of law believe, our lives would be fraught without them.

8.2 Letter

The 'letter of the law' is obviously a place to start. On the one hand, where power is exercised without any apparent legal warrant, rule-of-lawyers know what to say. On the other, where those with power stick strictly to what is encompassed by the letter of the law, it might seem we know what to say about that too. The written publication of rules, judgments, and other documents of the law is an age-old vehicle of communication,[6] ideally available to all liable to be affected by it, of rules and norms that people can grasp and apply to themselves and their activities. So, if all enemies of the rule of law ideal were of the first sort, its friends of the second, and everyone could see the difference, we would all be – as the Australian horse-racing idiom has it – home and hosed.

Once upon a time it seemed easier to pick winners. Enemies of legally tempered power made their hostility plain. We just had to choose between orders where law was in and where it was out. So, when Lenin proudly declared that the 'proletarian dictatorship' was 'unrestricted by any laws',[7] he was candidly and unapologetically revealing that the letter of the law was not going to count for much in his order of priorities. Countless coup leaders, revolutionaries, tyrants, and thugs-in-power have been similarly and often openly unmoved by it as well. Their exercise of power is rarely well tempered, and that's the way they like it. Nowadays, such candour is less prevalent: dictatorial lawlessness got a bad press in the first half of the twentieth century and many rulers of dictatorial ambition and/or achievement have tried to pretend to be different from their predecessors. Yet even the best of legal words, communicated in the most legible and visible of ways, will not necessarily serve, or be intended to serve, to temper power.

8.2.1 Masks

Perhaps the simplest of complications, at least in hindsight, occurs when authoritarian regimes invest heavily in wordy legal façades intended only to mask and camouflage what is actually happening in other ways and for other reasons. Stalin's orchestrated show trials of former leaders of his own party, in which they faced legalistic accusations and interrogations, and where their assigned roles were as support players in their own prosecution/persecution and assistants in their own execution, are examples. The results foreordained, the rest was theatre. The theatre was important though, since leading communists, whose fate was of interest to a broad and international audience, were on trial and the show had to go on.[8] Millions of ordinary citizens were exterminated, one way and another, without any such fuss. Millions more who survived were ground down into lives that were stunted, hopeless, 'poor, nasty, brutish, and short'. Law had nothing to do with it.[9]

The formally rights-rich 1936 Constitution (Fundamental Law) of the Soviet Union presided over much of this carnage. It lasted forty years (to be replaced in 1977 by another which changed nothing much). It had 146 articles, a chapter (X) on 'Fundamental Rights and Duties of Citizens', including article 127: 'Citizens of the U.S.S.R. are guaranteed inviolability of the person. No person may be placed under arrest except by decision of a court or with the sanction of a procurator.' In the year it was promulgated, several prominent but hapless drafters of its rights guarantees (including the eminent revolutionary Nikolai Bukharin and the pre-eminent Soviet lawyer Evgenii Pashukanis) were executed. Millions of Soviet citizens were imprisoned and died under its watch. As one scholar observes, with studied, perhaps intentionally parodic, moderation: 'One might almost say that, whereas the 1918 Constitution might be faulted for its naïve revolutionary enthusiasm, the Stalin version was deliberately designed to deceive.'[10] Almost indeed.

Façade constitutions, parchment institutions, judges whose only loyalty is to the party; there are many ways in which authoritarian and totalitarian regimes enlisted the letter of the law to impersonate the rule of law and to violate its ideal. Laws can require the impossible, for example, so that anyone of official interest is presumptively guilty of breaking them and thus available to be hauled in at will.[11]

Another very common kind of façade is constructed by laws so capaciously drafted and expansively interpreted that virtually anyone can be accused of violating them. Thus, Alexandr Solzhenitsyn writes of the notorious article 58 of the Soviet Criminal Code of 1926, which laid out hosts of 'counter-revolutionary' criminal activities in such expansive terms that little imagination was needed to find one or other on which to base a conviction:

> Paradoxically enough, every act of the all-penetrating, eternally wakeful *Organs*, over a span of many years, was based solely on *one* article of the 140 articles of the nongeneral division of the Criminal Code of 1926. One can find more epithets in praise of this article than Turgenev once assembled to praise the Russian language, or Nekrasov to praise Mother Russia: great, powerful, abundant, highly ramified, multiform, wide-sweeping 58, which summed up the world not so much through the exact terms of its sections as in their extended dialectical interpretation.

> Who among us has not experienced its all-encompassing embrace? In all truth, there is no step, thought, action, or lack of action under the heavens which could not be punished by the heavy hand of Article 58.[12]

There are many other tricks of the façadist trade. But they are interesting as stagecraft and choreography, not for their contribution to the tempering, or even guiding, of power. Secret rules or rulers' whims override public ones, and such rules as are applied were potentially malleable, 'applied to enemies, but only interpreted as regards friends'.[13] After all, the letter never applies itself but is mediated by powerful operators, and there are many of those and many forms of mediation. As Alvin Cheung observed, '[a]busive legalism is about keeping up appearances: how can one maintain the *appearance* of a rule of law state but frustrate the meaningful attainment of the rule of law'.[14]

8.2.2 Rule by Law

However, while it is common to think the laws and constitutions of despots are 'sham', 'façade', and of no real account, many contemporary *abuses* of the rule of law are truly *uses* of the letter of the law.[15] In such cases, the letter makes a real, substantive, contribution to arbitrary uses of power; it is not a sham. After all, as I mentioned in Chapter 3 and will elaborate in a moment, the letter of the law has often been a genuine and useful vehicle for authoritarian, illiberal exercises of power.

Many regimes have aspired to use law for their purposes but without submitting themselves to it in any ways that matter to them or to those who might have hoped to rely on the law. The letter of the law is to be taken seriously by its human objects but not in the same way, or at times at all, by its author/subjects in the upper reaches of power, at least if it might get in their way. In those circumstances, when those in the commanding heights estimate it appropriate, they have a free hand. And the letter can be enlisted to legitimise such freedom.

Thus, law was often plentiful in communist states, but the power of political rulers there was relatively untempered by it. Often that has not been a corruption of the written law but a principle of it. The party was above the law, even as a matter of legal theory, and all the more so in practice. Law was conceived of purely as one among a range of instruments of power, all subservient to the party. Institutions, among them courts in a rather minor and dependent way, trade unions, state officials, and the legal order writ large were all conceived of, in Lenin's terms, as 'cogwheels' or in the term which entered Marxist-Leninist orthodoxy, 'transmission belts running from the vanguard to the mass'.[16] There was in principle no room for notions of independence or institutions of restraint, at least in matters that mattered to the Party. In the former Soviet Union or contemporary China, regular legal constraint on the power of the ruling party never existed even in law. That 'leading role' was somewhat belatedly inserted in the Constitution of the Soviet Union in 1977 and in China in 2018, but in fact it was assumed from the start.

These polities are not lawless, since there is plenty of law about, and as we shall see in some of them, particularly China, its role is not merely decorative but, particularly in recent years, taken very seriously. However, the law's legally enshrined subordination to a supra-legal authority vitiates the key feature of what, under the conception of the rule of law ideal advanced here, it is for: tempering the exercise of power, *especially* ruling power.

Of course, sham and real can be combined, as in the current Russian Constitution. As William Partlett shows in detail, that constitutional edifice has been purposefully constructed to centralise all political power in the elected president, while the elections themselves are sham and so too the democratic principles and individual rights enshrined in the Constitution itself.[17] The combination of real and sham is central to the 'dark arts' that Partlett claims underlie the structure and furnish 'the populist leader [in Russia and elsewhere] with more than just tools to dominate politics; they also allow centralised authority to justify their actions as democratic and rights-promoting'.[18]

To capture this way of using law, it has been common to distinguish between rule *of* and rule *by* law.[19] Where the second phrase applies, it is conventionally taken to mean that though political power is exercised by legal means, at least those who direct that power are not subject to those means. They are not a frame within which dominant power is exercised and a way of tempering or moderating that exercise but rather an instrument, frequently a very flexible, malleable, instrument, of those who wield it.

The distinction is, of course, a simplification. Wherever there is rule of law there is rule *by* law as well. Today's governments are not sporting umpires, simply enforcing unchanging rules of a game made elsewhere and elsewhen. They are active in pursuing their own purposes and make laws to implement and communicate them. That, after all, is what they are supposed to do, and it is good in the main when they do it by public laws rather than lawlessly.[20] So rule by law is unavoidable wherever law is the vehicle through which power is exercised. Recall the adjectival/adverbial quality of the ideal. It is not opposed to the exercise of power but qualifies the ways in which it occurs: power is to be tempered, not shackled.

Moreover, the distinction is idealised. Whatever one hopes for from the rule of law, one will never get it all or unmixed. Similarly, with rule by law. The very fact that it is *law* which is the instrument of choice places some constraints on how one exercises power, both because law has forms and because even the most ruthless instrumentalisers will often need to take some account of whether, if it was obviously of no account, it would serve their purposes.

However, if the distinction oversimplifies reality, it also has a point. To the extent that it is the expectation and the reality (and in the workings of power expectations are also realities) that those with power can ultimately wield the law as they choose, the core of the rule of law ideal is missing. To be consistent with that ideal, the exercise of power will *include* rule by law, but if it is only that (or that and rule without law), law is disconnected from the rule of law ideal.

Within this chastened understanding of the contrast, a regime rules *by* law when it treats law as its pliable and unresisting instrument with which to direct subordinates. If appearances require camouflage, it builds in legal escape hatches that allow leaders to subvert or ignore the law in ways that matter to them, when they wish or feel they need to. And/or it takes control of crucial institutions and functionaries, so that they know and are willing to do what they are told.

Rule by law can be formally authorised: the Communist tradition of insisting that the party is above all laws is one way of doing this. Informal means are also available. Here a regime promotes law and even fidelity (of officials and citizens) to law, but there are limits to how high the law will reach, which the regime can set and change. Subordinates, including most officials, should act in accordance with laws, citizens must obey the laws and might be granted specified rights under them against other citizens and even some officials, but not in circumstances deemed sensitive, and not against just *anyone*. What is deemed sensitive and who is exempt are decisions for the leaders to make.

Again, this is far from lawless. Under such a system, while the upper reaches of power have a free hand, they may often choose for tactical and strategic reasons not to exercise it, and lots of law and lots of life never reach that high. Authoritarians know that and have come to find it useful to live with it rather than have undirected chaos or unruliness below.

Citizens, particularly those who have experienced lawless alternatives, might appreciate the difference too. Still, its lawfulness is often brutally selective, and it could all turn on a dime. And knowing that is a poison that courses through the system and affects everyone who deals with it.

The simplest forms of rule by law are, like military commands, top-down, a law of duties without rights, or at least rights of subjects against rulers. But there are more complex forms. Thus, Singapore scores high on rule of law indexes for its punctiliously observed civil and commercial law in non-politically sensitive domains that are economically valuable. However, the definition of those domains is decided by the government. Beyond their flexible boundaries, as Jothie Rajah has vividly exposed,[21] the political order is policed by illiberal uses and abuses of rule of law rhetoric and machinery. Rajah shows how the regime of Lee Kwan Yew and those after him cemented their power, destroyed opponents, and 'emasculated' restraints on state power via legal procedures, practices, and rhetoric, all in the likeness and name of the rule of law. Indeed, as befits a former British colony whose ruler read law at Cambridge, 'a liberal account of the rule of law informs Singapore's very existence as a nation-state and is incontrovertibly a part of Singapore discourse'.[22]

Elsewhere and more recently under the government of President (now legally for life) Xi Jinping, China has invested enormous energy and expertise in talking up and muscling up the role of law. The Constitution of the People's Republic was amended in 1999 to provide (in article 5) that: 'the People's Republic of China shall practise law-based governance and build a socialist state under the rule of law'. In 2014, the party announced that a central committee plenary session would address the topic of rule of law for the first time. According to its Plan on Building the Rule of Law in China (2020–25), by 2025 'the party leadership will have a more complete system of governing the country according to law … significant progress will have been made in the construction of a rule of law society, the legal system within the party will have been improved, and a socialist legal system with Chinese characteristics will have taken shape'. By 2035, 'a rule of law country, a rule of law government, and a rule of law society will be basically completed, a socialist rule of law system with Chinese characteristics will basically have taken shape'.[23] At the party's Central Conference on the Work of Comprehensive Law-Based National Governance, a new overarching term of legal art was introduced: 'Xi Jinping's Thought on the Rule of Law'. It is now everywhere on everything; compulsory in law schools, nationwide training courses, instruction for the whole legal complex. As

Randall Peerenboom observes, 'for now, and into the indefinite future, there is no escape from Xi Thought on Rule of Law'.[24]

Some writers see in these developments a major 'turn towards law' with legal, if not liberal, trappings. While no one denies that since 2014, Xi has concentrated extraordinary power in himself and the top party leadership many note that 'at the same time, [the party] has championed law-oriented governance as a pathway to stability, growth, and development'.[25]

Whatever one makes of it, this new emphasis on law's importance is a real development rather than a façade, and some argue that it is not merely a top-down arrangement to serve the interests of the Communist Party. Rather, according to Zhang and Ginsburg, the turn responds at the same time to 'bottom-up, demand-side incentives for legality [that] are at least as strong as the supply-side ones, and are likely more durable over the long run'.[26] If that (contested)[27] prediction proves accurate it will represent a significant change in the way power is exercised in China (especially for anyone who recalls the wild and terrible years of the Chinese Cultural Revolution).

Whether it has much to do with tempering power, at least of China's rulers, is another matter. For at the same time, the leading role of the party has been written into the Constitution (article 1) for the first time, and strenuous, systematic efforts are under way to strengthen the already pervasive presence, power, and formal recognition that, as Xi put it in a report to the 2017 19th Party Congress, 'the Party leads everything'.[28] And, according to the rewritten Party Constitution, he leads the party now for as long as he or fate chooses. This combination of dramatically increased emphasis on the leading role of the party might be taken to pull in the opposite direction to the new ideologisation of the rule of law. However, there is another, plausible, interpretation: 'in the Party's view, legality must be taken seriously in all areas of governance because it embodies the Party's norms, practices, and ideology and thus serves as the expression of the Party's normative authority'.[29]

Certainly, while Beijing now says and does a great deal to promote 'socialist rule of law with Chinese characteristics', none of those characteristics has to do with tempering the power of the ruling party, and none that of the ruler(s) of the party. On the contrary, the commander of the commanding heights has centralised his power to a degree unseen since Mao Tse Tung. And it remains the case, not accidentally or coincidentally but deliberately and systematically, that these characteristics include unprecedentedly intrusive surveillance of the whole population, unhindered repression of dissenters or anyone the regime considers or names a dissenter, harassment of criminal defence lawyers who 'work in a minefield filled with trenches and bombs, sometimes with their hands cuffed',[30] the mainland's tightening stranglehold on Hong Kong, and legally unconstrained oppression of Uighurs, including the incarceration of an alleged million or more of them in 're-education camps'. The list is not short, nor is it finite. And so, notwithstanding their determination to emphasise the extent of the 'turn to law' in contemporary China, even Zhang and Ginsburg concede that:

> This kind of legal reform – driven, as it is, by a desire to establish personal political dominance – is unlikely to trend towards political liberalism, nor is it likely to overtly constrain the ruler in a true 'rule of law' sense. In the Chinese case, what it has produced is simply 'legalism': stronger compliance with written legal rules, even as the rules, on their own terms, fail to constrain the Party leadership in any substantial way.[31]

8.2.3 Dual States

Such attempts to combine untempered ruling power with the benefits of order and obedience to law by non-leaders in non-sensitive domains was rarely remarked upon in classic portrayals of despots and tyrants as 'lawless'. However, while it has become more obvious in recent years, it is not news. Like so many pathologies we imagine are unprecedented, rule by law too has been around for a very long time. Certainly Locke was onto it:

> *In Absolute Monarchies* indeed, as well as other Governments of the World, the Subjects have an Appeal to the Law, and Judges to decide any Controversies, and restrain any Violence that may happen betwixt the Subjects themselves, one amongst another. ... this is no more, than what every Man who loves his own Power, Profit, or Greatness, may, and naturally must do, keep those Animals from hurting or destroying one another who labour and drudge only for his Pleasure and Advantage, and so are taken care of ... if it be asked, what Security, *what Fence* is there in such a State, *against the Violence and Oppression of this Absolute Ruler?* The very question can scarce be born.

In direct response to Hobbes's insistence that nothing less than the absolute Leviathan could keep people from the horrors of life with just each other in a state of nature, this passage continues:

> As if when Men quitting the State of Nature entered into Society, they agreed that all of them but one, should be under the restraint of Laws; but that he should still retain all the Liberty of the State of Nature, increased

> with Power, and made licentious by Impunity. This is to think that Men are so foolish that they take care to avoid what Mischiefs may be done them by *Pole-Cats*, or *Foxes*, but are content, nay think it Safety, to be devoured by *Lions*.[32]

Much more recently, and also surprising to many, was the exploration of law in Nazi Germany by Ernst Fraenkel,[33] the German-Jewish analyst and practitioner of law under the Nazis. Fraenkel showed with his courageous contemporary investigations from within the belly of the beast that the Nazi state at least between 1933 and 1938 was not lawless, as his more famous friend Franz Neumann argued,[34] and many assumed. Rather it was what he called a 'Dual State': on the one hand, a 'Normative' State' in which, for many parts of life and of law, legal business among citizens who were not Jews, homosexuals, Roma, or political dissidents seemed to go on largely as usual, with a 'Prerogative State' which did what it chose, as arbitrarily as it liked. The combination was not accidental or a reluctant concession but useful to the regime. And so, several contemporary scholars of Chinese law interpret the socialist rule of law with Chinese characteristics in these terms.[35] Formal legality is certainly not the whole of the story, but it is a crucial part of it. However, as in contemporary China, the prerogative and the normative never functioned on the same plane. Rather, as Fraenkel insisted:

> The Normative State ... is by no means identical with a state in in which the 'Rule of Law' prevails, i.e., with the *Rechtsstaat* of the liberal period. The Normative State is a necessary complement to the Prerogative State and can be understood only in that light ... The Prerogative State's jurisdiction over all other jurisdictions guarantees that the efficiency of the state shall have priority over the liberty of the individual. In National-Socialist Germany the 'gospel of efficiency' has been substituted for the worship of liberty.[36]

Many contemporary analysts of the Chinese legal order bend more to Fraenkel's analysis than Zhang and Ginsburg's.[37] A non-specialist might guess the truth is some combination of both, neither of which has tempered power, at least of the top power-holders, prominent among its aims.

8.2.4 Authoritarian Populism

Totalitarian regimes, as we used to call them, are rare. Even authoritarian dictatorships are only one variant of challenge to the rule of law idea. Thus, in recent years, new political movements of a decidedly 'anti-establishment' character have taken many countries by storm and many observers by surprise. Among the characteristics these movements share is that they, and more particularly their leaders, claim uniquely to represent the true, real people of the country, a claim that frequently seeks confirmation in electoral victory. For unlike standard-issue coup-ists and putsch-ists, communists and fascists (also anti-establishmentarian until they become established), these movements are not shy of elections. They feed off them.

They are different in other ways too. In particular, and so far, they have a strong involvement with law. Along with more democratic legitimation and less oppressive action than the harshest of repressive regimes, they also display close attention to forms, rhetoric, and institutions of the rule of law and constitutionalism. All this combined with scant commitment, indeed anti-commitment, to the tempering purposes for which these ideals were traditionally invoked. As Wojciech Sadurski has observed, for example, Jarosław Kaczyński, the leader of the populist party that governed Poland from 2015 to 2023 (named, with typical populist Newspeak, the Law and Justice Party (PiS)), was 'no Leninist: just like Orbán [of Hungary], he knows and skilfully uses the legitimating value of formal legality – except when the political costs of legality are found by him and his advisers to be too high'.[38]

Under Kaczyński's rule, apparently earnest and typically pedantic arguments were raised by regime lawyers, in both domestic and international fora, about interpretation, inclusion, or exclusion of this or that provision, sacking and packing, dismantling or inventing, this or that court, all replete with poker-faced legal argumentation, typically of a highly formalistic sort. If critics alleged that an institutional innovation was intended to threaten judicial independence, say, the hunt was on for any ostensible, context-free cherry-picked in-any-way-similar arrangement in Germany, Liechtenstein, Luxembourg … anywhere that might serve. That these comparisons and purported borrowings were radically superficial, selective, torn from their original contexts, and hostile to liberal-democratic purposes is rarely obvious to laypersons and never, naturally enough, emphasised by their perpetrators.[39]

Thus, from the start the Polish government under PiS packed the courts by means of institutions that they reconstruct for the purpose to give them control, filled the leadership of the procuracy with their faithful and when in power literally hateful servants,[40] completely took over the constitutional court, the procuracy, the public television network, and assaulted many other centres of social and political contest, criticism, and independence.

To mistake constitutional fraud and chicanery for genuine contestation over shared goals is a serious mistake. It is an easy mistake to make, however, for many polities that only a few years ago were feted for ushering in a 'third wave'[41] of democracy and the rule of law have become increasingly skilled in processes now dignified with the expanding collection of neologisms that I referred to in Chapter 3: 'abusive constitutionalism', 'stealth authoritarianism', 'constitutional coups', 'autocratic legalism', 'abuse of the constitution', 'twisting and turning of the rule of law'.[42] Many commentators focus solely on the threats such activities pose to democracy, but that is not all that is threatened. As the constitutional scholar Kim Lane Scheppele has pithily observed, 'buried in the story of [democratic] decline, … there is a story of constitutional malice'.[43] The malice involved might be invisible to those for whom the rule of law is a checklist of legal forms, but it is readily apparent to anyone concerned with tempering power.

These forms of legal use and abuse often slip under the radar of much conventional rule of law promotion scrutiny, since rather than rejecting law they bend legal devices originally designed for and widely associated with liberal, or at least 'rule of law', purposes to authoritarian ends.

Legal formalists do not quite know how to deal with its subversive spirit. For where the point of the rule of law is undermined in such ways, what we are seeing is not vulgar authoritarianism, still less totalitarianism, but rather an often-refined form of legal abuse. This is something very different from defiance or ignorance or rejection of the law. On the contrary, contemporary illiberal populists in power are more given to what András Sajó describes as *usurpation*. He tellingly calls in aid Benjamin Constant's observation, made already at the start of the nineteenth century: 'Despotism banishes all forms of liberty; usurpation needs these forms in order to justify the overturning of what it replaces; but in appropriating them it profanes them.'[44]

Of course, there is a lot of straightforward vulgar abuse and gaslighting as well: accusations, insults, and threats hurled, constantly and from on high, at the 'castes' of judges and lawyers and any who would support them. Opponents, and even apolitical 'servants of the law', are intimidated, disciplined, and sued (by lawyers appointed precisely for such purposes). The genre is becoming a norm in Donald Trump's United States, but it did not start or end there. And while vulgarity is becoming normalised, it is also combined with sometimes highly refined 'dark arts'[45] of kinds well identified in other contexts by law, whereby one pretends fealty to formal rules to achieve purposes alien to their underlying (often unwritten but assumed) aims. What we are seeing is an often-refined form of abuse of the rule of law but in its own name. Law is *used* precisely so that the ideal of the rule of law can be abused.[46] It is thus possible to be a rule of law success story in formal terms while systematically violating the underlying values of the rule of law – not simply possible but helpful to those who would resist the tempering of their power.

In the populist rendition of this art, law is used precisely so that the purpose and the fundamental principles of the ideal of the rule of law can be abused. Moreover, because that purpose and those principles have no weight with these leaders, they can at one moment be constitutional pedants when it serves their ends and at another be 'constitutionally shameless'[47] when pedantry does not work for them.

The details and techniques of the various forms of manoeuvres employed to serve while concealing this malice have been rehearsed in many places. The repertoire is extensive and is found in an increasing number of states. For many modern populists-seeking-or-in-power and contemporary practitioners of 'competitive authoritarianism'[48] find they can enlist ostensibly orthodox, originally liberal, legal and constitutional provisions for deliberately illiberal ends. All they need to do is cheat.

Indeed cheating, as examined in András Sajó's two excellent recent books,[49] has a claim to become a technical term of legal art, so apt is it to describe the contemporary legalistic abuse of the rule of law. For the rule of law can never be reduced to formal instrumental legal rules alone. It has an immanent ideal: the tempering of power. Those who use the rules to defy the ideal are not playing the game, but *cheating*. And that is what we have in much of the world today: cheating in the rule of law game by using the forms of law. Use is elided with abuse, and the principles of the rule of law are deliberately and systematically trashed in its own name.[50]

Thus, with regard to the Polish judiciary under the 'Law and Justice' party government between 2015 and 2023, Lech Garlicki, former judge of the Polish Constitutional Tribunal and European Court of Human Rights, has exposed the combination of government practices intended first to 'neutralise' the courts so that they could not check government initiatives and then to 'absorb' them so that they actually rendered assistance to them.[51] In regard to the Constitutional Tribunal which outlasted the government whose servant it was and continued to be, Wojciech Sadurski similarly plots the move from 'paralysing the Tribunal by Court-Packing', 'Legislative Bombardment', and refusal to publish judgments, to turning the Constitutional Tribunal 'into the Government's Enabler'.[52] The Polish government became the chief petitioner to the

Tribunal, since others could not anticipate independent judgments, and sent political hot potatoes to the Tribunal it had come to make its own, so that with all the pomp, regalia, and apparently serious consideration of constitutional provisions and argument it could serve up a diverting decoration of a politically predetermined result.

Those neologisms springing up in the literature like mushrooms after rain draw attention to some distinctive ways many modern regimes use (in order to abuse) formal legalities in the process of deliberate undermining of the rule of law ideal. Not always, but not rarely, formal punctiliousness is strikingly evident in the many forms of legal cheating that modern populists have developed. When challenged for cheating, they do not respond 'so what?' but rather: 'it's legal'. And since they have worked systematically to take over institutions, neutralise those they cannot, and then pack them with loyalists, all by means of law, they can do so with a poker face.[53]

Deliberately and insidiously, anti-rule of law, legalistic populists make it difficult to tell, from the start, that anything particularly sinister is happening. Institutions are 'deflated rather than demolished by populist authoritarians'.[54] The rule of law is typically brought down by 'a thousand cuts',[55] many of them small and often unseen, while the cumulative result is blood-letting of the idea of tempered power, often on a torrential scale. All done with the active assistance of law.

Contemporary populist governments have sought in these and other ways to undermine key legal and other sites and processes that might temper their power. Such governments are not necessary 'anti-institutional', as is often claimed, since they are keen to use institutions to serve their own purposes. What they are anti is *independent* institutions, in law, administration, media, and society. Typically (though not always), they do not destroy such institutions but hollow them out in order then to fill them with their own people, principles, and policies. Donald Trump's second administration is a classic in the field, but he was preceded by some years. That, presumably, is why Viktor Orbán has been welcome in the White House.

Populists of such malicious intent are, then, at once 'constitutional' in that they pay much attention to constitutional documents and institutions, but subversively so, for their engagements take forms and have effects that are relentlessly hostile to the values, practices and institutional constraints that were taken to be the *raisons d'être* of those institutions, principles, and practices. This sort of constitutional but anti-constitutionalist ambition requires not the neglect of those institutions, practices, and principles but their transformation. And this transformation occurs without apology: after all, who are 'elite' members of legal and other self-interested and malevolent 'castes' to interpose their unrepresentative strictures on the bearers, indeed the embodiments, of the people's will?

These governments have disdain for the notion that their power should be tempered, though they claim to be serving the rule of law in their own way, in line with authentic national 'constitutional identity',[56] 'Chinese characteristics', and so on. Their attempts to eliminate competing sources and resources of power and the destruction of opposition are often complex in form but their purpose is not difficult to understand. They have to do with undermining and subverting the *point* of the enterprise.

Sadurski has shown many Polish examples of exactly this occurring '*without a formal change* of institutions and procedures, so they are invisible to a purely legal account'.[57] For example, government laws were introduced as private members' bills, so avoiding requirements for consultation, expert assessments, or audits; or opposition MPs were allowed to speak in debate but given one or two minutes for their speeches. Courts were gutted, neutralised, packed, and then mobilised for the regime, all in the name of court reform and the rule of law. Procedures and institutions do not disappear but they 'become hollow'.[58] 'Become' is too soft a word. It is not simply a matter of institutional degeneration but an active assault: they are hollowed out.

Again, this is not some empty façade. One can actually adhere to the letter of the law without satisfying the demands of the ideal of the rule of law. There is, for example, much similarity between the ways in which the former government in Poland and the Fidesz government in Hungary abused the spirit of constitutionalism and the rule of law. But there is a difference as well. The Polish PiS government never had a constitutional majority in parliament; the Hungarian ruling party, Fidesz, did. So where the Hungarians could do virtually what they wanted within the existing constitution, and could change the constitution and its provisions whenever they chose to within textual constitutional bounds, the Poles had to resort to legal trickery more obviously and more often. Occasionally, though a lot of noise was made about the constitution and the law, they simply ignored it and judgments by courts both Polish and European when they would stand in their way. As constitutional law scholars Scheppele, Kochenov, and Grabowska-Moroz observe:

> [W]hile the two countries share certain similarities, the legal tools used in the two countries are not the same. In Poland, ordinary legislation violates the Constitution but since the Constitutional Tribunal has

> been captured, there is no mechanism to bring this legislation into line with constitutional (and for that matter EU) values; in Hungary, a new Fundamental Law and numerous constitutional amendments permitted the Rule of Law to be 'lawfully' dismantled without violating the domestic constitutional order. In both cases, however, formerly independent institutions were captured, power was consolidated in very few hands and the rights were violated.[59]

Does this mean that the Hungarians honour the ideal of the rule of law more than the Poles did, as they constitutionally dismembered legal and constitutional constraints and generated new ways of facilitating their common goals? Not if the concept has any substance. These are merely two different opportunistic routes to a common destination.

Many other exercises of power by law evade tempering without obvious breaches of the law. Discriminatory legalism through multiple strategic lawsuits against public participation (SLAPP) defamation, corruption, or other trumped-up (apologies for the word but it existed before 2016) allegations and litigation against opponents and other tricks of the authoritarian trade blossom. Much of what really matters occurs behind heavily closed doors, or is authorised by open-ended, quickly changed, or deliberately opaque provisions, procedures are at the same time observed as they are mocked in their literalistic abuse, and so on. Whether one therefore wants to call the formal vehicle 'law' or not might well be an important issue of jurisprudential controversy, but it is unlikely to make much difference to the benighted subjects of such 'legal' and 'constitutional' regimes. The question is whether the law operates as a means of tempering, moderating, channelling, and limiting power. Often it does nothing of the sort. Indeed the imprimatur of legality serves as a support for the dis-tempering of power.

At the time of writing, the mechanisms of Donald Trump's assaults on rule of law ideals are still revealing themselves, and doubtless they will grow and change. They include regular law, outdated law, intended-for-other-purposes law, pressures on law and lawyers, packing, sacking and intimidating, weaponisation of law against critics of any kind, and hosts of other ingenious legal and extra-legal operations. Whether they graduate to explicit lawlessness, time will tell. In the meantime, citizens (and others) face an anxious wait, and the help they can get from the letter of the law in tempering the resolutely intemperate power of the state appears equivocal at best. I hope it will prove useful, but it will never do it alone. So far it seems a weak reed, poorly embedded in thin soil.

8.3 Character

Perhaps, then, the key is to move quickly beyond the mere existence of the letter of the law and focus on the *character* of legal rules and institutions, as contemporary legal philosophers commonly do. Recall our discussion in Chapter 3, of accounts that attributed the rule of law not to the mere existence of a legal order but to the character of its rules and procedures. Many thinkers have believed such arrangements to be key. Take one of the best and most influential anatomical accounts – Lon Fuller's 'internal morality of law' and the profusion of only slightly variant adaptations of his list that have been taken to constitute the rule of law.

As we saw in Chapter 3, Fuller distinguished eight features of the formal character of laws, rather than the substantive content of law, and these, or small variants of them, have been taken by hosts of later writers to be the rule of law. According to Fuller, the internal morality of law requires that it be expressed in general rules rather than simply ad hoc pronouncements; publicly available to affected parties; prospective not retrospective; comprehensible; not contradictory; not requiring the impossible; not so changeable that they cannot provide guides to action; and be administered in ways that conform to their terms.

No legal system achieves perfection in any of these dimensions nor, Fuller stresses, is perfection a salutary ideal for a practical art. All depends on degree, overachievement is not necessarily superior achievement, and sometimes compromises need to be made, at times to protect and preserve the internal morality itself. However, a 'legal' system that does systematically poorly in any of these ways suffers degradation and degeneration in the character of its institutions and its output. The integrity of legal forms, captured in these eight 'principles of legal craftsmanship',[60] according to Fuller, is denied by such degraded 'laws', and with that denial, in extreme forms, so too the moral ground for obeying them. This, Fuller insists, is true quite apart from the substantive goals governments seek to achieve, though he also believed that governments which respected these principles were less likely to violate 'external' morality as well.

Two apparently simple factual assumptions underlie this and similar sorts of catalogue. One is that the rule of law, which involves law serving as a reliable and trustworthy source of guidance to its subjects, depends upon people being able to know the law that applies to them when they are choosing how to act. The second is that these principles are necessary for people to be able to do so. The link between the two is often dependent on lawyers' intuitions rather than empirical demonstration, as I argue in Section 3.3.[61] However, even if you accept both assumptions, what follows from them?

As we saw in Chapter 3, legal positivist critics of Fuller commonly accept the list, or some variant of it, and the assumptions that underlie it but deny that there is anything intrinsically moral about his 'internal morality'. It amounts, they say, merely to principles of efficacy, necessary for the law to serve any purpose but equally open to moral and immoral uses. Fuller responded,[62] and Jeremy Waldron has recently reiterated,[63] that if law is required to conform to the formal and procedural constraints of legal character that they enumerate, its contribution to law's tempering of power might indeed be considerable. Having to exercise power according to general rules that are public, prospective, comprehensible, clear, consistent, stable, possible to obey, and so on would seem calculated to block a lot of ways tyrants prefer to move. Just watch how executives, even in successful constitutional democracies, chafe against exposure or constraint.

Tyrants often have good reason to conceal what they do from, among others, those to whom they do it. *Their* purposes may not rely on subjects' ability to know the provisions of the law, understand precisely what it prohibits and permits, plan their lives according to it, still less know what to do to avoid its sanctions or object to abuses of it. It might be enough that they are terrified, knowing that whatever is done to them cannot be resisted, or that rulers have maximum flexibility and/or subjects maximum uncertainty. Evil regimes, Fuller believed, will avoid the use of laws that embody law's internal morality, at least when they do their worst.[64] Conversely, denial of Fuller's principles, often systematic, can help them attain their purposes, and they have not been unaware of it.[65] Nor was Fuller.

This underpins a more general point. Fuller insists on a distinction between 'managerial direction', a 'one-way projection of authority, originating with government and imposing itself upon the citizen',[66] and law properly so-called, which depends upon *interaction* between lawgiver and citizen. The manager wants jobs done at least cost to best effect; efficacy refers to the degree of success in achieving managerial goals. Elements of institutional character are subservient to such goals and are therefore contingent – appropriate to, and only to, the extent to which they help in the achievement of centrally directed goals. If it would help achievement of such goals to keep things quiet, allow unfettered discretion to decision-makers, or change rules rapidly, there is no intrinsic managerial reason to object. Interaction has a different logic. For law to provide a reliable basis for reciprocal (not to mention mutually respectful) interaction between lawgiver and legal subject, the trade-off for their obedience must be that the latter are able to predict and rely upon the routine ways in which power is exercised. Unlike managerial direction, interaction requires substantial adherence to the internal morality of law as a matter of principle, Fuller believes, not merely contingent and revisable practice.

And finally, this distinction between ways in which governments treat citizens in turn rests upon a less instrumental, moral, claim. It has to do with what Fuller calls 'the view of man implicit in legal morality'.[67] Here again, as we saw in Chapter 5, the objection to deviation from the internal morality has in the first instance to do *not* with the external substantive purposes that might be pursued. Rather it concerns whether, in the very ways power is exercised (for whatever purposes), one treats persons with respect. To return to the passage I quoted in Chapter 5: 'Every departure from the principles of the law's inner morality is an affront to man's dignity as a responsible agent. To judge his actions by unpublished or retrospective laws, or to order him to do an act that is impossible, is to convey to him your *indifference* to his powers of self-determination.'[68] 'Indifference' is a good word to use here, since it can span both intentional oppression or repression and well-meaning authoritarian direction. Even where the former is absent, there is a lot of the latter in modern societies, even those governed with the best of intentions and with a large measure of the rule of law.

There is a lot to be said in favour of Fuller's 'internal morality'. But at times too much has been said. To invoke again the distinction between necessary and sufficient, while Fuller's principles might be *necessary*,[69] they are nowhere near *sufficient* for rulers to treat citizens respectfully. To be sure, if governments cause harm to subjects without warning, in unpredictable ways or circumstances, on the basis of incomprehensible rules or ones with which it is impossible to comply, they treat them without respect. But governments can make their requirements plain to their subjects while still treating them disrespectfully. After all, the old admonition – 'just do as you're told' – rarely brims with high regard. So, if the rule of law is reduced to formal features of legal rules that help them guide action,[70] it is hard to argue that it need be the antithesis of tyranny that has traditionally been supposed. Some positivist rule of law ascetics, such as Joseph Raz and many of his followers, are happy with this deflationary implication, but for many – and for me[71] – the ideal of the rule of law requires more.[72]

Recognition of subjects as purposeful *agents* is compatible with denying them *respect* as *persons*, as laws of slavery make clear.[73] It is also a way that many colonial or otherwise autocratic and oppressive regimes have liked to operate.[74] As we saw in Section 8.2, formal clearly communicated laws can be a useful vehicle for autocrats, as many have learnt.

There are many sorts of authoritarian regimes and, as we have seen, while some have little use for legality, others find that channelling some of their power through formally predictable and ascertainable laws serves many of their purposes and interests. As the German exile from Nazism Otto Kirchheimer wrote of law under the Communist German Democratic Republic: 'Judged by its result rather than the modes of action it embodies, legality is like the twin but respectable brother of terror, to whom a more specific task is assigned: ensuring the regularity and predictability of behavior.'[75]

Indeed, as Julian Sempill has argued powerfully, with telling illustrations from Nazi 'miscegenation' laws and American Jim Crow laws, immaculate formal and procedural requirements of law can exacerbate the deepest indignity when allied with laws of evil content. The former 'were intended to dehumanise, degrade and humiliate their victims'. One way they did so was to require those victims to apply to themselves rules which no one should ever have even to consider. He quotes an appellate judgment against a Jew accused of 'polluting' a woman of German blood. The accused had had to claim 'lack of intent' in the lower court where he succeeded, but that was still not enough. The court held 'a Jew who seeks extramarital relations with a German woman in Germany has the legal obligation conscientiously to seek information about the race to which she belongs'. Thus, Sempill argues, 'the lawmakers' demand that their victims engage in self-application promoted a special, grotesque form of degradation and humiliation'.[76]

This goes against the grain of many writings on the rule of law which, as often happens among lawyers, bridge the spaces between features of law and what happens in the world with little more than professional intuitions. Thus the legal philosopher John Finnis argues that '[a] tyranny devoted to pernicious ends has no self-sufficient reason to submit itself to the discipline of operating consistently through the demanding processes of law, granted that the rational point of such self-discipline is the very value of reciprocity, fairness, and respect for persons which the tyrant, ex hypothesi, holds in contempt'.[77] I once had a similar view:

> [I]t is common for there to be a 'general and drastic deterioration in legality'[78] when despots do their worst and there is no surprise in that. There is nothing in the logic of despotism that draws it to respect the rule of law, and many costs in doing so for which there is no despotic rationale.[79]

This simply ignores the many uses of certain kinds of laws and lawfulness, to authoritarians and wannabe authoritarians, a few of which I've sketched in this chapter.

Gerald Postema too blurs a moral ideal with a prudential assessment of the facts. Unlike Finnis, he does not deny the potential uses of legality to authoritarians, but he argues that it only helps them if it is masked to look as though it were governed by the principle he calls 'reflexivity': 'that the law applies to and tempers ruling power, and second, it does so by subjecting the exercise of power to institutions and arrangements of accountability'.[80] Unless the people are so fooled:

> When rulers can exercise political power more efficiently without submitting to the fussy technicalities of law, they see no reason to use law. But this willingness to ignore law when it serves their purposes cannot be widely known in the political community without jeopardizing the benefits of ruling with law that they seek. The formalities of law prove useful to those in power precisely because it is widely believed by those subject to their governance that law constrains the exercise of that power. That is to say, those who are inclined to rule with law realize that law is an effective tool of governing just insofar as it is possible to mask their use of it.[81]

Postema offers no evidence for this claim, and perhaps it is true. But I suspect it would come as a surprise to citizens of Xi Jinping's China and to Xi Jinping himself, as he insists upon the untouchable, constitutionally enshrined, primacy of the Communist Party in 'the rule of law with Chinese characteristics', not to mention his own rule over the party.

Clear comprehensible prospective laws can be useful to illiberal authoritarians: they can tell far distant subordinates what they must and must not do, they beat knocking on every door or supervising every interaction, can lend support to legitimating stories, shift blame to designated and often hapless officials who can only do what they are told, sort out politically unthreatening but socially important activities, lubricate routine and unthreatening social interactions, and more. Since the despots still ultimately call the shots, why not save troops and bullets for when they are necessary? That is true whether or not the law also functions as a constraint on ruling power, not to mention that it can be done selectively, applied in domains where it is useful to rulers, and ignored where it conflicts with their self-chosen purposes.

More generally, the problem of bending even well-crafted rules to ill-intentioned purposes extends beyond authoritarian and proto-authoritarian regimes. As we have seen, contemporary populist regimes are much given to techniques that, as Kim Lane Scheppele observes, show 'careful attention to constitutional form while hollowing out liberal constitutional content'. This broken-backed legalism distinguishes what she calls 'democratorships as a special category among competitive authoritarian regimes'.[82] It is thus possible to be a rule of law success story in formal terms while systematically violating the underlying point and values of the rule of law. Another way of putting it is that the letter and even the character of the internal morality of law is honoured while the spirit is defiled.

Moreover, this can happen to laws of good character, even when that character is not being abused by its makers. Many legalistic exercises of law are routinely and without difficulty 'gamed' by powerful non-state entities. Indeed, John Braithwaite argues that where powerful interests are involved and in circumstances of complexity and rapid change, the Fullerian/Razian canon lends itself particularly easily to being so gamed.[83] Precisely because of its precise and legible character, those who wish to game the law know what is coming, and if they have the resources, skills, and time to avoid it, the character of the rules can work in their favour – particularly where legal formalist insistence on the supremacy of the letter of the law is strong.

Indeed, often the more precise the law the better able are those with resources to work around it. That, cynics might say, is what high-priced lawyers are for. As John and Valerie Braithwaite pointed out, a long time ago in another context: 'Detailed laws can provide a set of signposts to navigate around for those with the resources to employ a good legal navigator ... Marching under the banner of consistency, business can co-opt lawyers, social scientists, legislators and consumer advocates to the delivery of strategically inconsistent regulation of limited potency.'[84] A further implication of the Braithwaite argument is that 'when rules are gamed to conflict with the principles that motivate them, the rule of rules undermines the rule of law. Increasingly professionalised gaming of rules supports arbitrary power.'[85]

In circumstances of complexity, instability, and high stakes, legal rules closest to fashionable formal laundry lists of the rule of law are particularly open to being gamed. For formal rules lend themselves to what the legal sociologist Carol Heimer has called 'creative compliance, in which people or organizations follow the letter but not the spirit of the law' and 'feigned compliance [where people] do not even bother with the letter of the law except to use it as a guide for creating an appearance of compliance'.[86] Heimer's observations raise a very old concern, that 'the written words of a constitution may be followed to the letter in ways that undermine the spirit of the law'.[87] That is true far beyond the letters of constitutions.

8.4 Spirit

Contrasts between letter and spirit have a distinguished genealogy. They reach back to the Bible, are common in Shakespeare, and legal tomes are full of them. And notwithstanding a hint of the supranatural, there is nothing ineffable about them. Purpose and intent cover some of the same ground as 'spirit' though their connotations are narrower and explicitly instrumental; 'immanent ideal' is more complicated and less familiar but moves in the same direction. The mischief rule, cited at the start of Chapter 5, is an example of a practical search for the spirit of a law. Arguably, though the spirit of the law is harder to tie down explicitly, it is ultimately more important, anyway more basic, than the letter, in a well-functioning legal order. For it frames the ways we interpret, understand, and implement the law.

In relation to particular laws, the contrast between letter and spirit asks interpreters to reach beyond or behind or beneath the literal words of a law to seek what it was intended to do, what it was for, but also how – in what spirit – we are to interpret and apply it. If words interpreted themselves, if those interpretations were universally known, commonly understood, and agreed, and if those to whom the words are addressed all deferred to such shared understandings, there would be little more to say. However, that is notoriously not, and can never be, the case, given long-known truisms about the open texture of language, the vagaries of application of laws to unanticipated problems,[88] and so on. Though this evident truth is denied frequently by 'strict constructionists' and legal formalists the world over, there is no news here. For, even when interpretation is undertaken with the utmost devotion to the text and the best will in the world, legal texts do not and cannot determine what is made of them or done with them.

Sometimes interpretation is pretty simple, as with many rules of the road. In such cases, it typically goes without saying and without fuss or contention what the spirit is. However, often simplicity is unavailable and controversy cannot be avoided. What then, besides the words on the page, gives these terms specific meaning? More particularly, what lends plausibility, coherence, and authority to some interpretations rather than others? Invocation of the spirit of a law is an invitation to interpret its words in light of its purposes and the values that stand behind it.

Where do you look to find the spirit? There are internal controversies in legal systems about the role of the intentions of the lawmakers, earlier interpretations by courts, doctrines of interpretation, and so on. These in turn have to be interpreted, and the standard answer – and in stable well-tempered orders much of the truth – is that this occurs on the basis of shared legal norms, conventions, values, and understandings – often unspoken or unwritten but nevertheless key – among major players and members of authoritative interpretive communities.[89] As we shall see in Section 8.5, these frequently draw upon, and only make sense within, long institutionalised interpretive traditions.[90] Those might generate understandings within an interpretive community of what particular words mean, how to interpret ambiguities, fill gaps, infer 'the intentions of the founders', apply immobile words to mobile realities, and so on. There will be understandings of what the *kind* of text one is interpreting requires, how as a text of this sort it needs to be read, and what authority it should have. In stable orders, though dissent is common, such understandings frame, inform, and discipline what might otherwise be random. Sound interpretation, it is often repeated, will be informed by both letter and spirit, with the former being interpreted in keeping with the latter, the letter according to the spirit.

Beyond specific laws, the spirit of *the rule of law* needs to be understood more expansively than does the specific purpose of a particular law. On the interpretation advocated here, but not merely here, it is animated by the goal of temperance in the exercise of power. In many legal orders, the law itself, its makers and executors, are animated by other spirits, even when the letter of the laws they produce are unexceptionable in formal terms. So, not everything that is available according to strict interpretation of the letter will accord with the spirit of the rule of law. Impeccably formed laws that make way, or pave the way, for arbitrary exercise of power violate that spirit.

The various neologisms recently invented to capture the distinctive abusiveness of modern populists are different ways of saying that however formalistically kosher the stacking of a court or the attempt to glue one's people onto official positions even after elections and transfer important powers to them just in case of loss might look, they are affronts to the spirit of the rule of law, the immanent core of which, to repeat, is not service but hostility to arbitrary power. That matters politically and morally, and it matters legally too.

Often, even intelligent observers might think they are watching a contest between competing interpretations of constitutionalism and the rule of law ideal, rather than conflicts between their partisans on the one hand and enemies on the other. This misunderstanding is furthered by traditions of formalistic legal reasoning, strong among members of the legal complex in several of the countries under discussion, and readily and often enthusiastically exploited by those enemies.[91]

This is the case both when such enemies seek to cement their control over institutions and people in positions of power and when they seek to render their achievements reform-proof by successors. Thus, in Poland, though much of the sustained take-over of institutions between 2015 and 2023 was designed for immediate use, it had a second function as well: to thwart opponents in case of electoral defeat. With institutions they had formed, full of functionaries they had selected, they had fashioned fortresses of legally armed resistance. Then, with heroic shamelessness, from the moment they lost the election of 2023 they became the most punctilious of formalists, wielding the letter of the law that they had crafted for such an eventuality against any attempts to reform the institutions they had systematically hollowed out and subordinated, leaving them full of loyalists to the former regime. As a result, their successors are faced with what Sadurski describes as 'a situation of deep entrenchment – largely by statutory means, but not open to easy statutory changes – of the remnants of the *ancien régime*'.[92] These remnants he aptly calls 'mine-fields', 'traps', 'ambushes', trying to capture the standard Polish metaphor – *zabetonowany*, cemented, concreted.

Not a comma can be changed, lest the rule of law fall! And if the letter of the law is what it boils down to, it is often hard to argue with them. The only thing lost in a debate conducted in these terms is the point of it all. The letter becomes holy while the substance is profaned. And if one believes that law is exhausted by its letter, or even letter and character, those attempts will succeed. The rest, their authors might say, are just matters of taste and those, we all know, cannot be disputed.

However, formalistic impotence or external and moral condemnation are not the only answers. As Samuel Issacharoff points out, '[c]onstitutionalism has never been exclusively reduced to the written text either in terms of its commands or its interpretation'.[93] Laws designed to free power-holders to act arbitrarily might still be 'laws' in some reduced legal positivist estimation but they are flawed by their flagrant abuse of the rule of law ideal. People committed to the rule of law should insist on the difference. And it is not always so complicated. After all, as András Sajó points out, 'an apple and a rotten apple are both apples, but you don't eat the rotten one'.[94]

As Sajó shows in detail, many legal traditions contain plenty of 'spiritual' resources, standards and principles hallowed within regular legal doctrine, that enable formalistic abuses to be identified and rejected, without falling into 'the legality trap' on the one hand or leaving the law behind on the other. In normal circumstances, one might not think to reach for them, and doing so can take some argumentative effort against the simplisms of formalists. However, populists-in-power and just-out-of-power do not make for normal circumstances, at least with regard to the rule of law ideal, for they have no patience with the tempering of their power.

In many legal traditions, however, there are established legal warrants and resources for invoking the spirit of the law against formalistic strategies of abuse. Sajó advocates what he calls 'militant rule of law', which appeals to accepted principles in the spirit of the rule of law to respond to formalistic abuses that deny that spirit in what amount to extraordinary circumstances. Such militancy is not, he emphasises, without risks but 'calls for caution. It operates on the basis of widely accepted RoL [Rule of Law] techniques and exceptions and its use must be justified by the principles of the RoL.'[95] However, such techniques, exceptions, and principles exist in many long-established legal orders, and the stakes are high.

Anatomical accounts of the rule of law have difficulty responding to formalistic abuse of its spirit. Few of the fashionable lists make much space for spirit, which is one reason even sophisticated rule of law enforcers like the Venice Commission of the Council of Europe have often found it difficult to see or say what precisely is wrong in the legal manoeuvres of populist abusers in Poland and Hungary,[96] and what might be right in the attempts of their Polish successors to navigate the 'minefields' they have been left.

Viewed teleologically, however, what is at stake for the rule of law in the contemporary proliferation of proper forms with subversive substance is easier to see. As Sajó observes: 'Calling a spade a spade is not a violation of constitutional neutrality … The logic of calling a spade a spade dictates that both a review of the political consequences of reform – particularly those affecting democracy – and of those consequences' compatibility with the RoL would have been appropriate in the circumstances.'[97] I am very much in sympathy with Sajó's argument, and those of other scholars who tend in similar directions.[98] Kim Lane Scheppele invokes 'the rule of law writ large', as found in international and transnational law to which offending states have bound themselves. Wojciech Sadurski draws on supra-statutory law, such as constitutions, European law for members of the EU, and international legal standards. Though this book is not the place to rehearse them all, it is the place, and the contemporary proliferation of anti-constitutional populism an occasion, to be reminded that any serious engagement with the rule of law ideal must take us well beyond the letter and even the formal character of laws, to their spirit. What Sajó calls the 'mimetic' character of populist rule of law will not be revealed or resisted by a purely formal reliance on the letter of the law, since that has often been the pliable vehicle of the abuse. This should be exposed, as a matter of simple legal and public morality. How effective it is likely to be, without parallel militancy in many other realms,[99] is less clear to me, given the considerations raised in the next three chapters. But it has moral, political, and legal justification of its own. Independent of its effects.

8.4.1 Absences and Presences

Apart from its internal role in legal argument, there is a more encompassing reason to pay attention to the spirit that animates legal orders, with which I will conclude this section. It has to do with another common misconception, discussed in Chapter 4 but worth another look. That misconception is identified in a passage I quote there from Frank Upham: too often '[l]aw is seen as technology when it should be seen as sociology or politics'.[100]

An example might help. For a long time, when rule of law promotion went global, promoters treated the problem they were purporting to solve as primarily a technical-legal one; epistemological, a problem of knowledge. It was to be addressed by legal professionals with legal means, designed by experts and taught to those less expert. So, if things didn't conform to the rule of law, recipients of rule of law largesse were taken not to know what the rule of law is or what it requires; we do know, so the job is to educate them and provide technical-legal and institutional training and models to follow. After all, we were not starting from nowhere; we have our own practice as well as 'international best practice' to draw upon. And that is how westerners typically operate, even though their intentions are good and colonialism is supposed to be in the past.

Over time and after disappointment, some reformers came to believe their addressees' ignorance was not the whole explanation of the distance between teachers and learners in the rule of law enterprise. So some of them started – some twenty-five years after they had got into the business – to talk about moving from 'best practice' to 'best fit', again conceived in primarily epistemological ways. This time in a partial *mea culpa*, reformers admitted that the problem was that we, proto-reformers, need to know more than the earlier generation did of recipients' culture, social relationships, ways of dealing with disputes, and so on. And doubtless, that was often also true. But while each generation found a different locus of epistemological limitation, what both shared was the belief that it was gaps in legal knowledge and understanding that primarily accounted for the difficulties in promoting the rule of law.

This epistemological assumption meshed with another feature of common approaches to 'building' the rule of law reflected in some of the language often used. Where the rule of law was to be 'built' one often found oneself plagued with 'absences' and 'lacks': they lack the rule of law and understanding of the legal arrangements the rule of law depends upon, and/or we don't understand what they have, lack, and need. How big are the gaps, how large the absences? Well, that can be marked on a metaphorical scale – rule of law is higher, rule by law lower, lawlessness lowest – or literally, on one of the 'indexes' compiled by the various rule of law indicator-generators that now proliferate, which purport to rate whether a country does well, middling, poorly, and so on, in achievement of the rule of law, or putative elements of the rule of law, drawn from many numerically weighted 'indicators'.

However, what is involved when the rule of law ideal doesn't do well is often not a *lack*, an absence of understanding of the rule of law, or not merely or primarily that, but rather the *presence* of something else: a contradictory agenda, a different spirit, often anchored in a quite different and often hostile *Weltanschauung*.

Often those in pursuit of such agendas are not at all epistemologically challenged. They know what they want and they don't want the rule of law in any plausible approximation of the ideal, even though they might use the term and accept all its promoted and associated institutions, because they need the halo it bestows, the money it draws, the facilities it offers, and the sanctions it might help one avoid. So they might mimic the techniques, pick out existing 'worst constitutional practices'[101] to follow, to shield them from legalistic international and national criticism. But they have other ideals, antipathetic to the tempering of their power. And that is often true where rule of law promotion is energetically pursued. Indeed, they might even be pleased to encourage enthusiastic rule of law and human rights promoters to improve the effectiveness of their laws, all the more to impose their will on their subjects.[102]

An important book, *Opposing the Rule of Law: How Myanmar's Courts Make Law and Order*, carries a message of direct relevance here that applies well beyond its particular geographical focus. Its author, Nick

Cheesman, found in Myanmar, and argues one often finds elsewhere where rule of law promoters merely see gaps for them to fill, that:

> If [rule of law] scholars and practitioners use rule of law criteria to measure the practices of institutions captured by other ideas, then we are liable to misunderstand and misrepresent them. ... We mistake the problem for a gap between principle and practice, between aspiration and reality, to be rectified by better training, laws, and funding, when the problem is of a different nature. Partisans of law and order are not the occupants of low rungs on a ladder to the rule of law; they are climbing a different ladder.[103]

His central point is that the 'absence' of the rule of law in many of the countries in which it has been promoted is not an empty space, ground zero, indeed not an absence at all. Often, and in Myanmar in spades, those with power are imbued with a spirit quite contrary to that of the rule of law ideal – with its own motivations, rationales, instruments, and consequences. It is not well characterised as an absence because it is an actual and active presence that needs to be understood on its own terms. It is often not that people, particularly political leaders and their legal servants, are more or less interested or informed or adept in achieving the rule of law, and so higher or lower on some scale of rule of law attainment. Rather, they frequently have purposes and ambitions-sometimes personal, sometimes corporate, commonly long-term and strategic, frequently highly institutionalised-for which law is employed, often centrally, that are systematically, institutionally, and practically antithetical to the rule of law. This not as a matter of accident or ineptitude but deliberately. In Myanmar, law is to be used not to temper rulers' power but to help them impose 'order' or 'tranquility', understood roughly as Montesquieu understood it: 'the principle of despotic government is fear, its end is tranquillity; but this is not a peace, it is the silence of the towns that the enemy is ready to occupy'.[104] Other polities, other aims, but very often tempering is low, or not, on the list of any of them.

8.5 Tradition

If letter and character are unlikely to temper power on their own, without the spirit that should inform them, where does that come from? It doesn't come from nowhere but it does not waft in on the breeze, nor indeed is it a breeze to make up and make stick. Nor will it necessarily emanate automatically from the installation of those parts of the law – particular kinds of rules and institutions, however well crafted – where people, including rule of law people, are likeliest to look. Instead, its sources are likely to be borne by vehicles less obvious but frequently of much deeper importance: the legal traditions which underpin the legal order. One is well off if a spirit of temperance is embodied and transmitted within and through them. However, that is not always so.

The philosopher Michael Oakeshott has observed that 'a tradition of behaviour is a tricky thing to get to know'.[105] Quite so. Typically, significant traditions span generations, partly accreted and inherited, partly crafted, typically indistinguishable, their elements sometimes visible, sometimes invisible though no less influential for that. Legal traditions, moreover, are never just one thing but rather intricate and complex orders of evolving and interrelated elements, some explicit, many implicitly assumed, some containing injunctions about matters of substance, others instructing participants how to regard, read, and respond to such injunctions, what questions to ask, what answers to give.

Not only are traditions highly complex, but theirs is frequently a layered complexity where insiders learn authorised ways of understanding how to deal with elements of other layers – ways of reading, interpretation, application, and so on. They are also tricky because so much that matters in complex traditions is just part of that background framing, tacit knowledge, that novices in traditions come to learn by osmosis, as it were, on the way to becoming adepts. Norms, understandings, rules of the game become taken for granted and all the more powerful for their unnoticed obviousness. This complicates many transformative ambitions, let alone – as we saw in Chapter 4 – transplantational ones.

To return to Oakeshott: 'All actual conduct, all specific activity springs up within an already existing idiom of activity … The questions and the problems … spring from the knowledge we have of how to solve them, spring from the activity itself.'[106] The idiom of activity *within which* – not simply with which – lawyers learn to think and speak is that of their particular legal order and it is transmitted in the traditions of that order, sometimes over extraordinarily long periods of time. Learning to 'think like a lawyer' – which is what law schools profess to teach when they despair of teaching anything specific, and which is perhaps the only lasting thing they do manage to teach – is only a particular way of saying 'learning the idiom of activity of law', though even then the phrase is not absolutely accurate. One does not learn to think like *any* lawyer but rather like a lawyer from a specific legal tradition, one at home in a particular legal idiom, expressing particular legal norms, injunctions, values, prescriptions, and proscriptions. Different traditions, different spirits, different idioms.

Traditions are everywhere, and notwithstanding the conceits of modernity, which even the great Max Weber shared, we don't get rid of them easily. Particularly not when, as in law and religion, they are cultivated and policed within dedicated, authority-bearing institutions that preserve, supervise, adjudicate, implement, cull, add, and keep score.

Legal traditions differ greatly, and not just in their particular rules and institutions. They come to be manifest, not simply as particular precepts of law, or particular canons of interpretation or even in particular ideals, but in broader and more overarching interwoven tapestries of thoughts, values, and ways of seeing that have often been called and are called here, with only a slight excess of mystery, 'the spirit of the law'. Different cultures, different spirits.

Beyond particulars of machinery and rules, different legal traditions embody characteristic and distinctive styles and visions of law: what it is, what it does, how it should do it, and why. Particular legal orders embody and presuppose distinctive ideologies in a broad sense, distinctive 'ways of viewing both law and the world'.[107] These incorporate particular constellations of values, views of how the world works and should work, through which lawyers see the world: particular 'legal sensibilities'[108] which are pervasive and inform legal goals, means, doctrines, and machinery. These sensibilities are not seamless or monolithic, and they are subject to strain, corrosion, conflict, and change, but again it is typical that such challenges have deep roots in what has gone before. And finally, it is not merely values and sensibilities within the law that matter. Societies differ in the importance, role, and value that dominant traditions and their bearers place on law. Such differences also endure.[109]

As the comparative lawyer J. H. Merryman has noted: 'A legal tradition ... is a set of deeply rooted, historically conditioned attitudes about the nature of law, about the role of law in the society and the polity, about the proper organization and operation of a legal system, and about the way law is or should be made, applied, studied, perfected, and taught.'[110] One such 'set of deeply rooted, historically conditioned attitudes' has to do with the role (and rule) of law in relation to the exercise of power. That is a distinctively significant question for legal professionals, standing as they do 'between rule and power',[111] a choice that is not presented as starkly to many other professions. How it is posed and answered is only partly traceable to the activities of contemporary actors, or to particular rules and institutions, though these count too. They give form, focus, and texture to what might otherwise be unworkably diffuse. However, they are buttressed and made to endure, made part of public culture, by less obvious but no less important, indeed indispensable, larger political and social traditions, ideologies, familiar practices, and notions. These underpin, institutionalise, and transmit the values and practices (many unwritten) that accompany them. This is generally true and it is true of the ideal of the rule of law.

Elsewhere, Adam Czarnota and I have distinguished analytically between two ideal types of traditions: 'legal' and 'state'.[112] In the former or more realistically, since the ideal types are never realised in full, where elements of the former are strong, law and legal traditions have been distinctive and important elements of society and culture, with their own authoritative institutions and writings, which inducted cadres and officials are required to sustain, vet, and contribute to. Adepts talk to each other, (and come to talk like each other). It makes sense to talk of the distinctive identity and integrity of specifically legal institutions, doctrines, and ways of thought and practice. Law developed as a practice which had an independent significance that counted and was thought should count in social life and was understood as a source of reciprocal rights and duties among those it affected.

Where such salutary traditional frames of practice and imagination exist, and tempering institutions and rules of restraint are strong, a large part of that strength typically flows not directly or solely from the institutions and rules themselves. Rather, it stems from the values embedded within the traditions in which they developed and from the broader political and legal cultures and social practices which they themselves generated and which grow around and encrust them. These come to form and shape the routine expectations of participants and observers.

Where practices and ideals of tempering power through law are strong, they not only are evident in doctrines, principles, and provisions of the law itself but contribute more generally to the ways that power is exercised and thought apt to be exercised. They *count* and are thought appropriately to matter in the everyday workings of a society. Usually much less than lawyers imagine, and with all sorts of byways and hurdles and competitors we met in Chapter 7, but still significantly. They contribute to framing, channelling, and limiting the ways power is exercised and expected to be exercised, often as much by limiting the imagination of those who implement it as by limiting what can be done with it. Exercising power in tempered ways is 'the way we do things here', and people would be shocked if we did otherwise. That can be a significant constraint on those tempted to do precisely that. It is the difference between Yeltsin and Whitlam, with which this book began.

Distinctive and strong traditions, incorporating ideas of legally patrolled tempering of power or indeed regular tempering of dominant power by any means, are not natural facts. Where such traditions are strong, within and without the law, good inheritance is likely to have conspired with good management, good sense, and good luck. As we will see in Chapter 10, there is no guarantee that luck won't change. Still, it is salutary where it exists and should be tended. For in many societies and cultures over long periods of time, those whose power matters most, and to whom power matters most, simply cannot *imagine* that theirs should or could be tempered. If any powers are to be tempered (and usually harsher words are more appropriate), it is only that of others. And if dominant power is to be tempered at all, there is no human agency whose job it is. Only God is qualified, and His will is for the powerholder to interpret.

8.6 Law's Offerings

A legal order that comes out on the right side in the ways sketched in this chapter – clear letters, borne and tended within institutions and officials of good character, imbued with a spirit of temperance, solidified by congenial legal traditions – does indeed have the potential (though, as we will see, it is an uncertain, qualified, rarely uncontested potential) to contribute fundamentally to the quality, ease, productivity, and security of social life. It is a complex combination, rarely achieved and never more than somewhat, but it is way ahead of its opposites.

Among other virtues, it can help solve the basic challenge that, to cite Adam Smith again, modern societies face: that each of us 'stands at all times in need of the co-operation and assistance of great multitudes, while his whole life is scarce sufficient to gain the friendship of a few persons'.[113] Such cooperation and assistance depend upon frames, conditions, forms, and consequences that a legal order can help provide, and without which we would be at a loss, with every new encounter facing the possibility of having to start from scratch. That's no way to run a society and not a pleasant way to live in one.

The sociologist Émile Durkheim underscored the significance of this contribution when he wrote of the fundamental social significance of the 'non-contractual elements of contract'. Libertarians and neoliberals might imagine that societies are constructed by free individuals coming to agreements that generate social bonds and the state should just get out of the way. The reality is very different and must be. As

Durkheim explains, criticising such theories of social organisation, particularly those of the nineteenth-century English polymath Herbert Spencer, that would base societies on foundations of individual contractual choices:

> Most of our relationships with others are of a contractual nature. If therefore we had each time to launch ourselves afresh into these conflicts and negotiations necessary to establish clearly all the conditions of the agreement, for the present and the future, our actions would be paralysed …
>
> But contractual law exists to determine the legal consequences of those of our acts that we have not settled beforehand. It expresses the normal conditions for attaining equilibrium, as they have evolved gradually from the average case. Epitomising numerous, varied experiences, it foresees what we could not do individually; what we could not regulate is regulated, and this regulation is mandatory upon us, although it is not our handiwork, but that of society and tradition. … We co-operate because we have wished to do so, but our voluntary co-operation creates for us duties that we have not desired.[114]

Durkheim's observations can be generalised well beyond the law of contracts. Thus, in his rich and insightful discussion of what he calls 'Law's Toolbox',[115] Gerald Postema emphasises that law does not merely direct and constrain power but 'constitutes and grounds' it. You can draw on it and apply it to your own decisions and actions, taking into account much that it leads you to be able to expect from others.

And when you don't like the ways things are going, law provides institutions and procedures and professionals used to drawing upon experienced reflections on common problems and solutions, stored over generations, sometimes millennia. The promise is that law 'creates *ways* of doing or accomplishing things that are, in a sense, artificial but not pointless', even and frequently through written formalities which 'are often seen as "mere" and hence in a way arbitrary, beside the point, indifferent to the real merits of actions. However, this is shortsighted, for law's formalities order behavior in public; they contain and constrain power.'[116]

Where the rule of law ideal is approximated, the spirit made flesh, a signal feature of such arrangements is not merely that they provide pre-tested answers to common questions; they also offer a common language and a depository of norms, values, conventions, and arguments on the basis of which one can deliberate and argue, often over subjects of angry dispute. Participants can have a voice and a hearing within them, aided by people expert in them, even against forces of great power arrayed against them. And the weapons of choice are words and argument, at least in the first instance, not the violent powers readily accessible to the powerful but not to us all.

When all of this is in good shape, and hostile forces are kept at bay, we can hope that, as Justice Brandeis of the US Supreme Court put it, 'deliberative forces prevail over the arbitrary',[117] for as Postema who quotes this passage from Brandeis observes, it is characteristic of a legal order in good shape that '[t]he law, through its courts, proceeds deliberately and deliberatively'.[118]

A point emphasised by Jeremy Waldron and that splendid person and philosopher Neil MacCormick, who influenced Waldron as he did me, is that at its best 'law is an argumentative discipline',[119] and that is not through accident or misadventure. Nor is the argument left unstructured by the law. Even if the space legal institutions create for interpretation, reinterpretation, and argument might well diminish the legal predictability (too often miscalled 'certainty', which is rarely available), that is a price worth paying. For arbitrariness comes in many guises: one is law that is unpredictable, another that it is disrespectful. We want a considerable degree of predictability, though perfection is never attainable, and we should not sacrifice respect for persons to gain it.

People with legal interests at stake need to be able to speak for those interests, whether they accuse or are accused. This requires a good deal of provision from legal orders by way of procedures that require impartial third-party hearings, defences, ability to speak, examine witnesses, present evidence, see evidence relied upon by the other side, and so on. It also depends on shared traditions of argument and value, for the powerful have a tendency not to wish to hear from those they want to bring into line.

As might be expected, Montesquieu had important things to say about what law could offer to the tempering of power. Even more important than his specific proposals, many (but not all) of which have lost bite over time, is his fundamental insight into the point of it all and what is needed to make that point:

> Political liberty … is present only when power is not abused, but it has eternally been observed that any man who has power is led to abuse it; he continues until he finds limits. Who would think it! Even virtue has need of limits.
>
> So that one cannot abuse power, power must check power by the arrangement of things.[120]

How is that to come about? Montesquieu believed that particular forms of government depended on particular quasi-moral qualities in citizens: republics on 'virtue', monarchies on 'honour', and despotisms on fear. However, he did not rely on these qualities, still less on the personal qualities of governors, to restrain governments. He insisted that tempered power depends, in considerable part, upon complex institutional arrangements designed with just such 'checks' in view. One was the separation of powers that he thought was part of the British constitution and which, on that revered misunderstanding, the Americans sought to institute. And then the world emulated the Americans, with legally binding written constitutions that Montesquieu (and the world) didn't know: bills of rights, courts with powers of legally decisive interpretation of the constitution, and so on. A great deal of attention has been given to the detail of constitutional provisions, doctrine, and conventions that might serve the ideal known as constitutionalism, which I take to be a sub-branch of the rule of law ideal.[121]

As we have seen, there are vast legal literatures devoted to these matters and, no doubt, thoughtfully designed legal institutions and craftsmanship, based on experience and reflection, are better than bad ones. There are technically preferable ways to deal with many problems which have occurred in societies familiar with them and may well occur in societies to which they are new. Apart from those already mentioned, adequately trained lawyers, with an ethos of independence and lawfulness, independent and adequately paid judges, a police force trained in some ways and not others, open to some incentives and not others, and so on, are no doubt better than their opposites. All this matters. If, even taken together, it is not sufficient to deliver the rule of law ideal, much of it is necessary.

There has been a lot of serious thought about such issues, and it would be silly not to reflect on it and seek to learn from it. When the spirit is willing, such institutional arrangements can be salutary channels and vehicles for well-tempered performance. And if they stick around long enough, they might well enter enduring traditions that infect the spirit in turn. These are all salutary elements of a legal order in good shape, and nothing in this book is intended to deride the attractiveness of such good shape.

However, even if those involved in a legal order have all their legal ducks in a row – letter, character, spirit, tradition – pointing in the same and a good direction, there is a long way to go, and a lot to do, before power can reliably, confidently, and enduringly be tempered. For quite apart from the quality of the law, we need to think more deeply than is common about something that everyone knows but legal theorists so often manage to ignore: even in the best of times and circumstances, law will often not be at the centre of the action, nor in a position to direct much of that action. It is *never* the only game in town. In the next two chapters, I will turn to some of the other games, and players, with which it unavoidably has to play. Sometimes they are on the same side, but that cannot be guaranteed.

PART V

Complications

9

'And' or 'In'?

> Laws do not walk themselves.
>
> Chinese saying. Cited in Liu, 'Between Rules and Power'

The rule of law is a crisp phrase: four words, all short, leaving no doubt which one is in charge. Achieving its ideal is more complicated. Even if the letter is clear, character upright, spirit willing, traditions congenial, the ways it works and the effects it has depend on its interactions with structures, agents, and forces of many kinds. In any one society and time, some of these might be 'in sync' with each other and with the intentions of the masters of the law, others less so or not at all. And it can all change.

The ways of power in the world are also complicated. It has many faces and appears in a huge variety of places but never in a vacuum. It is generated within complex, labile, and overlapping ecosystems, which provide many kinds of resources and challenges and are populated by different, changeable, and occasionally novel species, occupying a variety of different niches and acting and interacting in multitudes of ways.

The workings of law and power will necessarily be affected by all this surrounding colour and movement. Whether and how people will interpret state law and respond to it, how highly it will rate for them in comparison with other influences – these things depend only partly on what it says, how it says it, what the law is intended by its makers to do, and what those involved in its operations do with it. How, in what form, and with what communicated and received residue of initial purpose, salience, and force law is able to penetrate all these intervening media; how attuned to it putative recipients are; how dense, competitive, resistant, or hostile to its messages they might turn out to be; what intervening forces are and do – all these factors are constantly in play and on the move.

So temperers need all the help they can get, and the continuing puzzle is just what forms such help should take. The institutional artillery familiar to lawyers and legal philosophers is unlikely to solve that puzzle, or rather those multitudes of puzzles, unaided. For while the ideal of the rule of law remains precious, its attainment is an extraordinarily complex achievement, so complex indeed, so dependent on so many factors in so many domains, that it is peculiarly miscast by lawyers' often solipsistic understandings and renditions.

9.1 Law in Society

Once upon a time, when it was it was still somewhat *outré* to suggest thinking about law might be enriched by thinking about something else, 'law and' became a cautiously fashionable locution: law and literature, law and economics, law and religion, and – of course – law and society. The umbrella organisation of socio-legal studies, headquartered in the United States but with worldwide membership, is the Law & Society Association (LSA). The Society's journal is the *Law & Society Review*; Britain has its own *Journal of Law and Society*; there are centres for the study of law and society at universities around the world.

This apparently natural and innocent copulation implies more perhaps than its users intend, in at least two ways. First, it suggests that law and society are separate, independent from each other. 'Law' on one side, 'society' on the other. They are not even intertwined as in a marriage, just juxtaposed like, say, meat and potatoes, oil and water. Second, law comes first. Three words, two mistakes.

Lon Fuller disapproved of the phrase. His objection was to the separation. He insisted that law was *part* of society, not merely a partner of it. So, 'law *in*' not 'and'. As Philip Selznick, himself founder of one of the first law and society centres,[1] was somewhat chastened to admit, Fuller 'disliked the phrase "law and society." He objected to the "and" as a distancing imagery; it seemed to counterpose what should be understood as wholly intermingled. We may not wish to indulge that bit of purism, but the point is well taken.'[2]

It is a rather general point, of course. Fuller adorned it with little detail and not everything he wrote followed through completely on its implications. His principles of the 'internal morality of law', discussed in Chapters 3 and 8, could have been designed – by a lawyer – for the moon, or anywhere else where nothing would be likely to intervene between the character of official law and its effects. Nevertheless, it is an insight.

An anecdote might help; anyway, it helped me. Some years ago, I spent a stimulating year at an interdisciplinary centre for social science research.[3] One of my colleagues was James House, a sociologist and social psychologist who studied the US health system. Our substantive research interests had nothing in common, but we spent time together because, neither of us being adept at the volleyball which our peers played with energy and enthusiasm, we retreated most days to gentle games of ping pong.

When not pounding the table, one thing I was trying to understand was the experiments in rule of law promotion which had begun in post-communist societies and had come to span the world. I wanted to work out whether and how the rule of law might be introduced, and then sustained, in countries that were getting a lot of exhortation, advice, and money to develop it but had not much experience of it (and, it appears in retrospect, were to achieve uneven success with it).

House was trying to explain why, though the United States spent much more on health care and insurance than any other country in the world, absolutely and per head, its health results were worse than those of many countries that were comparable in other relevant respects. Indeed, at the time, US outcomes were declining. He argued that this problem would not be fixed by spending more on the usual suspects – hospitals, health care, medical technology, drugs. America led the world there already, but the results of all this money, technology, research, and expertise were disappointing. Remedies would have to be sought elsewhere: in education policies, social welfare, improving distressed socio-economic circumstances, and so on.

The results of that research were later published in a co-authored book, *Making Americans Healthier: Social and Economic Policy as Health Policy*, which explored 'a growing paradox between [the US's] declining levels of population health relative to other wealthy nations – and even some developing ones – and its burgeoning spending on health insurance and medical care'.[4] If your aim was to improve health care, you needed to understand that it would not come from any one, even the apparently obvious one, central, dispensary; it needed a lot of help from many different social, political, and economic domains, not customarily identified as, or obviously connected with, health at all.

I was struck by parallels between House's argument and the core assumptions of some strands of socio-legal research which I was beginning to try to integrate into thinking about the rule of law. A theme of that work, varyingly carried out by legal anthropologists, investigators of 'legal pluralism', and writers on 'societal constitutionalism', was well captured by the title and text of Marc Galanter's remarkable – in my view classic – essay 'Justice in Many Rooms: Courts, Private Ordering, and Indigenous Law'.

Galanter argued there that:

> Just as health is not found primarily in hospitals or knowledge in schools, so justice is not primarily to be found in official justice-dispensing institutions. People experience justice (and injustice) not only (or usually) in forums sponsored by the state but at the primary institutional locations of their activity – home, neighborhood, workplace, business deal and so on.[5]

Of course, we might readily concede that *justice* could be found in many locations but still draw back from seeing implications for the rule of *law*. After all, it is common to observe that law and justice often go their own ways; the former does not necessarily produce the latter and the latter appears (or fails to appear) in many domains other than official legal ones. Legal positivists and 'thin' theorists of the rule of law insist on distinguishing the two. And recall the lament of the former East German dissident Bärbel Bohley after the collapse of communism in the 1990s: 'we wanted justice; we got the rule of law'. She seems to have felt shortchanged.

However, Galanter's point goes deeper than that, directly to the second assumption in 'law and society'. Why should law come to mind *before* society? If we are thinking of the law of states, chronologically the order was otherwise. Sociologically, it is arguably so as well. Societies come first. Or perhaps it makes no sense to assign priority. At least the mix(es) deserve close attention. As Galanter goes on to argue:

> The mainstream of legal scholarship has tended to look out from within the official legal order, abetting the pretensions of the official law to stand in a relationship of hierarchic control to other normative orderings in society. Social research on law has been characterized by a repeated rediscovery of the other hemisphere of the legal world. This has entailed recurrent rediscovery that law in modern society is plural rather than monolithic, that it is private as well as public in character and that the national (public, official) legal system is often a secondary rather than a primary locus of regulation.[6]

Neither the state nor its laws ever makes all the running nor runs alone. They cannot avoid interference, or do without assistance, from many other activities in many social domains. How much interference? How much assistance? It depends.

These were themes already pursued in some of the earliest socio-legal writings, particularly from Central and East European multinational empires before the First World War, where the distance between imperial codes emanating from Vienna or St Petersburg might have said one thing while locals of varying regions, languages, ethnicities, and religions lived, valued, thought, and listened to other sounds. Later observers of settler colonial legal regimes witnessed similar, typically more pronounced, patterns. It has dawned on some more recent observers that even western metropoles are not on another planet in these respects.

Among the pioneers was the Polish-Russian legal sociologist Leon Petrażycki (1867–1931), who originally wrote from within the Russian empire. He distinguished and gave priority as law to what he called people's 'intuitive law': the felt sense of right and obligation, which had many sources and existed whether or not mandated by official law.[7] The professor of Roman law Eugen Ehrlich (1867–1922), teaching in Czernowitz (now Chernivtsi), part of the Austro-Hungarian empire until 1914, then Romania, then the Soviet Union, again Romania, and now Ukraine (though it never moved an inch), had reason to be sceptical of the centre's pretensions to dictate effective norms of living to its disparate subjects, particularly given that the centre kept changing but was always somewhere else, far away. He sent his students out to find what the 'nine [ethnic and religious] tribes' of the city thought and did about ostensibly 'legal' problems, what was their 'living law', as distinct from what Vienna might have mandated. He insisted that 'the center of gravity of legal development lies not in legislation, nor in juristic science, or in judicial decision, but in society itself'.[8] While the theories of Petrażycki and Ehrlich were very different, both stressed that there was a huge gap between the official centres' (and their lawyers') fantasies that their laws were the fundamental normative sources of what happened on the ground and what actually governed most people's lives most of the time in most places.

Such insights travelled far. The Polish social anthropologist Bronisław Malinowski, educated in Kraków, Poland, also within the Austro-Hungarian empire till 1918, transplanted these Central European ways of thinking about law to 'discover' in Papua New Guinea that law could exist without 'central authority, codes, courts and constables'.[9]

Students of colonial and postcolonial countries provide countless similar examples of distant and foreign-dominated capitals affecting to dominate societies that handle the *vast* majority of their affairs with no reference to those states' law. Indeed, it is still common to observe, as the World Bank legal department has, that 'in many developing countries, customary systems operating outside of the state regime are often the dominant form of regulation and dispute resolution, covering up to 90% of the population in parts of Africa'.[10] Percentages might differ in and out of Africa but the phenomenon remains and they are high everywhere. So perhaps it is appropriate that some of the best writing on the sources and varieties of normative orderings both in colonial *and* non-colonial settings comes from the legal anthropologist Sally Falk Moore, who did fieldwork in Africa but wrote with extraordinary insight about the 'semi-autonomous social fields' that generated and mediated authority everywhere.

Students of colonial and postcolonial societies contributed greatly to the study of 'legal pluralism', the idea that any social order contains multiple normative domains and sources of 'law'. There are disputes over whether that word is always appropriate, but often it clearly is, and the name does not matter much. Moore's writings are key here, though she preferred not to use the term and took over the French 'reglementation', as an overarching concept for 'all those attempts to organize and control behavior through the use of explicit rules'.[11] She reserved 'law' specifically for state law in complex societies, on the ground that this accords with common usage, preserves significant distinctions, and is less confusing. But if she chose not to call non-state reglementation law, she repeatedly and illuminatingly revealed how significant such often very varied, very law-like, but not state-produced, kinds of rules and normative practices are for the normative regulation of societies – *all* societies – and in particular how variable and complex were the interrelations between various sorts of non-state reglementation and between them and state law.

I am not particularly interested in the conceptual question of whether the various non-state sources of norms should be called 'law' or not, though some – for example, religious law, customary law – should be fairly uncontroversial. In any event, it is enough to recognise that they perform many functions that elsewhere we entrust to, and too often associate exclusively with, official law. If one's concern is the tempering of power, Moore's and other legal pluralist writings draw attention to just how many sources beyond emanations from the state really can and do matter, how they will differ with context and circumstance, and how many circumstances there are in which state law matters less, or differently, than its authors and administrators imagine.

Though it often does, this should not come as a surprise. It reflects Durkheim's observation, discussed in Chapter 8, that society is not just a mass of people who happen to live together. It depends upon the existence of common bonds, norms, traditions, prescriptions, proscriptions, and understandings that people who live connected lives come to have, and that mark the difference between a society and a random collection of individuals.

To live in a society is not merely to have a lot of neighbours, but nor is it to be part of some vast undifferentiated blob into which one sinks without agency or trace. On the one hand, individuals are profoundly affected by their social relations which mould and connect them, teach them what they should and should not do, and check whether they are doing it. To the extent that we are 'socialised', moreover, these norms are not just external injunctions but parts of who we are, or what we have to reject (often with some pain) to be who we are. They are never of no account.

On the other hand, society is not a *thing*, and certainly not just *one big* thing. Its individual members typically inhabit what Moore has described as 'semi- autonomous social fields',[12] usually several simultaneously – home, friends, work, belief, party, and so on. Participants in such overlapping fields, or perhaps in today's language networks, are affected – some more some less, in one way and another – by interactions with other people, structures and norms, official and non, from other fields, but not without reinterpretation, reconfiguration, and competition from within. Norms and patterns of interaction, dispute, resolution, and so on emanate from within our fields of core attachments and operation (and so are, to that extent, 'autonomous') but also from other overlapping fields as well (and so, 'semi'). Not only do the norms and so on of any one field have direct significance of their own upon their own, but they mediate other norms and relationships, and so contribute to the shape, penetration, and measure of significance those latter are liable to have. They have no single, central source, and they have reciprocal effects on the character of other fields.

Semi-autonomous fields include the organisations in which we work and with which we deal – families, localities, people we trust, ethnic and religious communities where these matter, and so on. Particular influence comes from what Avishai Margalit calls 'encompassing groups', where these exist. An encompassing group is 'a group whose culture stands out, encompasses many aspects of life, and covers important and varied areas of its members' lives, especially those significant for the well-being of the people belonging to the culture'.[13] Encompassing or not, all of these generate normative imperatives and social connections, some strong some weak, sometimes loose sometimes tight, sometimes open sometimes closed, sometimes egalitarian sometimes clientelistic, sometimes honest sometimes corrupt, sometimes law-abiding, sometimes not. Apart, perhaps, from Robinson Crusoe, no one escapes them.

Semi-autonomous fields generate distinctive ways of viewing and handling affairs including those inside the field and those with people in other fields. Also, distinctive ways of hearing, interpreting, valuing, attending to, official law. Even in the most law-observant societies, these informal norms have sources other (and closer) than state laws, and they will affect much that happens in the fields, sometimes without more; sometimes in interaction with external norms, including official ones; sometimes by redirecting the interpretation and effects of those laws and norms in unpredictable ways; sometimes in ways that block or frustrate their legislative or curial formulators. Sometimes such blocking and frustration is intentional, or would be if their targets knew what official lawmakers were asking (or commanding) with their laws. Often they don't.

Much that official laws might in theory relate to never comes within the purview of state institutions. It will be handled on the ground, sometimes 'in the shadow of the law',[14] other times under various other shadows, often without reference to state laws at all. Such dealings may at times be innocent of the injunctions of state law, or reflect idiosyncratic interpretations of that law, or simply reject it. Distant official law is often beside any local point. We have other concerns, other questions, other answers, and other regulators of our behaviours. Local responses will have effects that mediate, refract, often redirect and refashion the significance and consequences of state law, whatever lawmakers intended it to accomplish. And there might not be any relevant state law. Even if there is, local networks find, or don't find, ways to deal with it.

These, it should be stressed, are general truths that occur simply because the normative orderings of societies are complex, and in large, plural, modern societies dramatically so. They are not just what happens in countries with weak states or defective legal systems or little or no rule of law; they happen everywhere. Orders of local 'governance' are often not within central cognisance or competence.[15] In many countries thought to be deficient in state competence and the rule of law, however, where the rule of law industry is hard at work, the balance between 'semi' and 'autonomous' frequently favours the latter, organically and dramatically, and the disjunction between official and not is often extreme. Sub-state networks are often more autonomous and powerful in such countries and lead to greater and more dramatic deviations from official aspirations. The state and state law are often correspondingly weaker.

Nevertheless, it is a common mistake to compare a society thought to be awash with 'informal practices' (as obstacles to legal interventions in benighted countries are often characterised)[16] with some idealised model of an impersonal and sovereign western legal order, with the state at the centre and nothing between its laws and 'its' individual 'subjects'. As we all know except when we play at legal philosophy, sociologically there is no such order. People have many other things to do than wait to interpret state law in the ways its creators had in mind, or to evade or subvert it. It may just not be on their minds or particularly salient in the orders that organise their lives.

The character, impact, and salience of informal practices in relation to official law are almost infinitely variable. And apart from them, there are the *actors* in these variously choreographed scenes: '[s]ocial transactions usually take place in the service of objectives to which legal rules are merely ancillary shapers, enablers, or impediments. Conformity to the rule is seldom in itself the central objective.'[17] How might recognition of these truisms affect how we should think about the place of the rule of law in tempering power?

9.1.1 Legislation

As we have seen, much legal and philosophical discussion of the rule of law focuses on the character of official legislation: it should be clear, public, prospective, non-contradictory, and so on. And why not? Who would want it otherwise?[18]

However, though no one denies that there's a world out there, much discussion proceeds as though it made no difference that the distance between laws and life is often great and heavily populated with other things, including law-like things, that do and have to do many of the jobs we attribute to state law.[19] Against this background, Moore makes the very obvious point, the implications of which are so often overlooked, that '[l]egislation is intrusive. It is a tinkering with an ongoing social field that has areas of relatively autonomous activity and self-regulation.'[20]

In another idiom, legal interventions in existing social fields are what social systems theorists such as Gunther Teubner call 'irritants',[21] sometimes in some places more able and likely to irritate, at other times and in other places less; sometimes with predictable effects, often not; for reasons as much dependent on qualities of the irritated as of the irritator, the chemistry between them, and what exists and what happens in the spaces between. This is most obviously true of deliberately introduced laws from other jurisdictions (transplants) but it is, as he argues, an intrinsic quality of the relationships between law and the increasingly functionally differentiated and fragmented segments into which modern societies are split.

To be sure, in some societies, much state law has been around long enough and accepted well enough that it forms a central part of the generally accepted, often unconsciously assumed, normative background of everyday life. It no longer irritates everyone painfully, though it is unlikely to soothe everyone equally. Even in such societies, however, new laws can open new wounds,[22] or reopen old ones, and in modern societies the continuous introduction of new law frequently irritates and unsettles existing practices. In societies which have, or have come to have, great plurality within, it will encounter and generate many social antibodies. All the more so in societies where the state-source of the law is distrusted and/or regarded as alien. And anyway, what does the state know about 'the way we do things here'?

An upshot is that again unless state laws are brutally enough administered to pulverise everything in their path – a rare event, even in totalitarian countries, likely to generate workarounds, and hard to sustain – their effectiveness will be heavily dependent on their degree of synchronisation with the 'indigenous' orderings generated from within social fields. Indeed in totalitarian and authoritarian polities, the very *lack* of synchronisation between exercise of state power and social realities and possibilities often stimulates the development of informal practices in the society, which at the same time subvert the official order and try to make up for its inadequacies.[23] Both in these situations of chronic lack of sync and ones where the mesh is smoother, one can talk as much of 'the law in the shadow of indigenous ordering'[24] as of the more familiar bargaining in the shadow of the law.

While the points made here are generally true, their weight and salience also vary greatly in significance and implication. Whenever law stakes a claim to rule, the upshot of the many potential sources of normative, structural, cultural, and institutional overlaps, collaborations, and competitions in every society will differ markedly between (and often within) societies. Whether and how people interpret the state's law and respond to it, how highly it will rate for them in comparison with other influences – these things depend only partly on what it says, how it says it, what the law is intended by its makers to do, and how rigorously attempts to enforce it are made. So much writing on 'the state' and 'law' ignores, however, how various are the phenomena and relationships clumped under these apparently simple and single concepts and what happens in between.

Moreover, lest one think this is only significant in pre-modern or developing societies where social connections are strong and state law alien and weak, there is a sense in which the complexity of the roles of semi-autonomous fields is even greater in developed societies with overarching states than elsewhere. Recall one of Max Weber's central insights about the distinctiveness of social modernity: it separates and fragments spheres of life – political, economic, spiritual, family, work, administration, ownership, and so on. These spheres develop different modes of valuing, understanding, and regulating. And so, even if we return to the political centre, to borrow from Moore yet again:

> It seems incontrovertible that the more complex a society, and the greater the appearance of rational control, the more delegation there will be in government and administration and the more areas of discretion and semi-autonomous activity there will be in the subparts of the society, formal and 'informal' ...
>
> This view of complex society, or of any society, leads one to a paradox. Formal reglementation can control certain behavior, but not the aggregate of behavior in a society. The more 'rational' a society seems in its parts, and its rules, and its rules about rules, the thicker the layer of formalism and ideological self-representation to be penetrated to find out what is really going on. ... over time, reglementary control can be only temporary, incomplete, and its consequences not fully predictable. The study of reglementation is therefore the study of the way partial orders and partial controls operate in social contexts.[25]

It might be frustrating for lawyers to learn that so much that matters is not amenable to the application of some hallowed legal checklist or another, that none of it is easy, and a lot of the hard work involves stuff they don't know. But how many lawyers and legal philosophers think it is even their business?

International rule of law promoters have started to think so after repeated disappointments in the field. Since the industry is relatively new, that has only happened recently (though with some, at least intellectually, disruptive force),[26] even though sociological reflections on social causality are actually quite old and have not been far to seek. Much of the disappointment found in rule of law cultivation in fallow fields abroad could well have been predicted ahead of time, as indeed it was – but by thinkers to whom promoters didn't listen. And neither sociology of law nor the experiences of rule of law promoters has had much resonance among legal philosophers who concern themselves with the rule of law. And yet, to quote Moore one last time:

> Ordinary experience indicates that law and legal institutions can only effect a degree of intentional control of society, greater at some times and less at others, or more with regard to some matters than others. That limited degree of control and predictability is daily inflated in the folk models of lawyers and politicians all over the world.[27]

9.1.2 Courts

What about courts and their procedures, on which Dicey and Waldron, and most common and constitutional lawyers, set such store? Doubtless they and the particular ways they operate are important for those who find themselves there, as well as for those many more who anticipate such a possibility at some time in their lives, whether or not it eventuates. However, much that has already been said about society and legislation applies, virtually without remainder, to the significance of what happens in courts as well. Here too, what in socio-legal studies might be counted as truisms are relevant and often ignored by writers on the rule of law. I will again draw on the literature I have sketched earlier, which has been around long enough to figure centrally in discussions of the rule of law but too rarely does.

Given the significance of social fields and orderings in every society, an enormous amount of social activity to which state law might relate will not come anywhere near the institutions in which lawyers are employed and on which legal philosophers focus. It will be dealt with, if at all, elsewhere and without the intervention of officials. This is common knowledge, but its proper acknowledgement requires a rearrangement of the conceptual maps many of us rely on to understand the positions and roles of official agencies in society.

An early generation of law and society research explored what was then called the 'dispute pyramid', plotting the combination of rare approach, relentless winnowing, occasional ascent, and continual transformation that faced the vast majority of disputes to which the law might apply. The base of the pyramid is the broad terrain where people experience some hurt or injury, real or perceived. Much of this will be put down to accident or fate. But perhaps this time we notice a particular hurt and give a name to it. Naming transforms a simple 'unperceived injurious experience' (unPIE) (apologies for the acronym; it's not my invention) into a perceived one (PIE). Then might come, but frequently will not, a next stage, of 'blaming' someone or thing and further, again frequently not: 'claiming' vindication.[28] All this can occur long before anyone thinks to seek a professional intermediary to whom they might entrust transforming a private grievance into material fit for recognition (and often transmutation) by definitions, criteria of relevance and seriousness, and procedures, for presentation before formal institutions. Longer still before anything reaches such an institution. In the meantime, and often for all time, local specifically relevant normatively influential orders and actors might deal with things. Some time later, for a few of those who have lasted this far, might begin the often costly and perilous ascent up the ladder of the law. Few go very high. On the way, many rungs have to be climbed, and the number of climbers is not only attenuated but skewed, depending on a vast range of resources, skills, determination, and stakes.

So, the vast majority of questionable behaviours and even the smaller number of legally relevant disputes never reach official agencies. This is not to say rules and institutions have no influence until they are directly and explicitly engaged, but it does mean that their influence has plural interpreters, mediators, supporters, opponents, and rivals, other than those on which law-talk typically concentrates. More than that, there are other stages, variously institutionalised and effective, where things might stop.

Even were official rules and procedures to do what is often conventionally assumed, how much they do it, and with what consequences, is rarely just up to them. The effects of legal rules, then, cannot be in any direct way read off from their formal character or even their informal intent or governing spirit. All the more, in the light of more recent suggestions that the metaphor of a 'pyramid', which posits a linear ascent, miscasts what is more like a 'tree' with many branches other than official ones, that channel and deal with many matters we think of as legal, bearing a range of flowers and fruit unlikely to have been contemplated, still less cultivated, by Dicey and his successors.[29] All often without any official recourse ever being available or contemplated.

What follows from this? Certainly not that dispute settlement by courts is unimportant. The fact that 'health is not found primarily in hospitals' is not an argument for the unimportance of what happens in hospitals. Even if I have only one heart attack in my long life, it matters that I can reach specialised institutions able to deal with it. And so with courts. Treated for the moment just in terms of what they do for those who reach them, this will include serving many who found nowhere else to go, or no other independent institution capable of doing justice to their claims. There is an incalculable difference between societies where this possibility is available to citizens and ones where it is not, or is available only to certain categories, or deals so badly with them that they have no use for courts, or costs so much that they can't afford to use them. All of this has to do with the ways power is exercised, and so all of it has to do with the ideal of the rule of law. Not to mention that unsupervised state power is a singularly bad option.

Moreover, whether or not one ever has occasion actually to use such institutions, they can still matter. The absence of a real, even if distant, possibility of enforceable intervention by a third party independent of the parties to disputes (and with institutionalised quasi-independence from the states that pay them) can have tragic social consequences. In such circumstances, people do not merely, as we often do, fend for themselves in the first instance but are liable to do so without curb or limit on one side or both, if they lack even the in-principle anticipation that they might call on official agencies if all else fails.

So nothing I say is intended to detract from the strategic, ultimate, and salutary significance of state institutions – where they exist and operate effectively and well – to hear and do justice to the parties who make their way to them, and of procedures to vindicate the dignity of those who appear before them.

And yet, this acknowledgement of the crucial significance of an effective state legal system (where it exists) must remain consistent with two other truisms that I would stress. On the one hand, a key part of the social importance of state legal institutions stretches well beyond what it does to any specific litigants in legal proceedings. On the other, that significance can only be assessed in the light of other sources of social influence than the law itself. These may support, refract, re-channel, transform, totally block, or simply not be accessible to or visited by it.

Legislation, of course, is always directed outwards,[30] but court proceedings too have fundamentally important effects that radiate well beyond their direct participants. If they were to be judged simply by the numbers of social disputes they suck in for official treatment, they might well be accounted failures everywhere, given the very small proportion of disputes that reach them. But apart from citizens' (generally rare) direct invocations of official channels, there is the extent to which they are able and willing to use and to rely upon legal resources as cues, standards, models, authorisations, immunities, what the socio-legal literature identifies as 'bargaining chips' or 'regulatory endowments', in relations with each other and with the state. In this respect, as Galanter has emphasised, courts act less as magnets than beacons. In the very process of dealing with those disputes, they send signals about law, rights, costs, delays, advantages, disadvantages, aggravation, anguish, and other possibilities into the community. This is what gives meaning to 'bargaining in the shadow of the law'.[31]

So it matters to at least two constituencies (apart from those – lawyers – who make their living from them) how legal institutions settle disputes. The smaller and frequently atypical constituency is the litigants themselves, whose days in court are nevertheless often of extremely highly charged significance to them and therefore significant in themselves. They are also part of the second, much larger, constituency affected by law: all those who, often subconsciously, act and react, in their relations with other citizens and with the state itself, on the basis of their interpretations of signals that emanate from those institutions or their attitudes towards those signals and to their sources.

However, even when official signals are bright and visible, they do not necessarily signal or beckon engagement of the sort the signallers intend. Not everything depends on the message or the messenger. And here we have come full circle. Once we get to message sending, everything said earlier about fields, orderings, and legislation applies equally to messages that emanate from courts. The legislators' and judges' jobs are done when the messages are sent; those of interpreters, evaders, ignorers, and scrupulous obeyers have just begun. And, to switch the metaphor slightly, there are many other messages, from many other sources, that fill the airwaves. People listen to different ones, in different ways, and don't listen to some because they listen to others. And there are plenty of others.

Overarching all the official activity, then, is the fact that official agencies are only some of the reglementary sources in play in *any* society, whether religiously or ethnically plural or not. Who can know *in general*, when, where, and how one centre should be picked as the key from all this mix?

Again, none of this is to say that that we should simply upend legal centralism and put some vaguely characterised 'society' in its place. In modern circumstances, and virtually the whole of the developed and undeveloped world is affected by those circumstances, the state has pivotal importance in modern societies, and its laws are often crucially important in tempering its, and others', powers. But how important, and even if important, in what ways acts of state work out in the world, are questions whose answers are necessarily and heavily dependent on the plural and complex social, economic, and political contexts in which they occur and into which they intervene.

These are general truths, and so those interested in the ideal of the rule of law need to come to terms with them. Where official law fits, and what it does in relation to them, depends on how effective it is in affecting chains of social causation, many links of which precede it, outlast it, and at any particular moment are more powerful than it is. How all this is likely to pan out will differ from place to place and time to time. It cannot be decided a priori but only after social investigation and theorisation. Jurists attracted to the rule of law have not been prominent in either. That has never appeared, however, to lessen their confidence that it is 'law' conventionally understood which must stand at the heart of the achievement of the ideal of the rule of law.

9.2 Tempering Outside Law

In all societies, then, even the most highly law-abiding, the significance of law for those who receive it is commonly very different from the imaginings of those who send it. The bottom line, even when all institutions have been imported and officials trained, retrained, and equipped, is that to be more than purely decorative, the rule of law requires the law to *count*, as a temperer of power, in the thoughts and activities of both wielders and wieldees of social power.

What is involved when the law counts in such ways is a complex sociological question on which the law bears. It is not in itself a legal question, for it depends as much on characteristics of culture, society, and polity as of the law, and on their interactions. All the questions asked in this chapter have a sociological dimension, this one above all. It asks about the social reach and weight of law, and the answers, whatever they are, will have to attend to questions of sociology and politics as much as of law. Unfortunately, in many discussions of the rule of law, more thought has been given to the character of laws than to what might be necessary to make them count. If no one is listening, however, it doesn't matter too much what the law is saying or indeed how it is said. The most important question to ask – *the* question about law, but not a legal question – is: what makes anyone listen? And that question still needs an answer.

Social and political questions are central to the place of law in a society, and they will be answered differently in different societies, whatever the written laws share or say. This is not because the law has no significance but because the nature and extent of that significance cannot be inferred from the law itself. Where the law really does seriously count in ways its authors intend, when the law is socially and politically significant, the legal position will bear closely on the factual position and the hour of the lawyer is at hand. But that is only because what lawyers don't know, the conditions of legal effectiveness, gives significance to what they do, the law. When those conditions are lacking, lawyers' talk is beside the point.

State law should be viewed, then, not as the always-necessary centrepiece of power-tempering craftsmanship to which other measures are inferior or supplementary addenda but as one implement among several, in some respects and particular circumstances of potentially distinctive importance, but dependent for its success on many other things, and often arguably not more important for the achievement of its own goal than they. That, again, does not make state law unimportant, but it might enable us to see its importance in perspective and as variable with time and circumstance.

To say that the ideal of the rule of law is in good health, that is, power is effectively and widely tempered, is to appraise a state of affairs – cultural, social, political, legal – with complex, multilayered elements of various provenances, rather than simply to characterise any particular set of public and legal institutions. You have more of it insofar as power is routinely exercised in ways consistent with the ideal, and certain other ways of exercising power – capriciously, wilfully, arbitrarily, wildly – are rare. Since many of the major threats to the ideal of the rule of law come from outside the state, and many means of achieving that ideal are also to be found in the wider society, the rule of law must be sought there too.

Recognition of the importance of social fields might complicate our understanding of the ideal, but it does not undermine it just because law may not play its customarily assumed role. Indeed, it might well give us more grounds and more resources to support it. For there is no reason to deny the possibility of tempered power in non-state contexts, drawing from non-state resources, just because they fail to emanate from the sovereign Hobbesian source of all. Viewed teleologically, the end, not the means, is the thing.

How that end might be approached depends on the particularities of the setting, the character of the problem, the alternatives open within specific contexts, and what sorts of arrangements are specifically appropriate there. They will often spring up from within the domain of the problem itself, which is commonly a better way of dealing with it than wheeling around institutions designed for other contexts or not designed for any particular context but simply familiar.[32] Such experimentation beyond state and official law is plentiful and often successful, but it takes many different forms where other structures, forces, 'rationalities', and sources of legitimacy dominate – and where state power and its official vehicles are often not the major currency of exchange. Rather, such settings need and often come to develop:

> rules not only against the negative externalities produced by the power imperative of politics but also against those coming from the profit imperative of the economy, the reputation imperative of science, the innovation

> imperative of technology, the news imperative of the information media, the health imperative of the medical system, and the juridification imperative of the law.[33]

Arrangements beside official legal ones will certainly need to be taken into account, and they often do good work, providing standards, agreements, incentives, and constraints effective in the particular contexts for which they are designed, and in which the writ of official law does not run, or stumbles ineffectually. This, for example, is the burden of explorations of both domestic and transnational 'societal constitutionalism' by Gunther Teubner and others in his orbit and influenced by him.[34] One does not, fortunately, have to buy (nor indeed understand) the whole conceptually and linguistically intimidating theoretical juggernaut which underpins the explorations of societal constitutionalism to find plausible its central contention: that, within both domestic and transnational social fields, institutional experimentation and creativity are unavoidable in the many different settings and *sorts* of settings where needs and demands for new forms of 'constitutionalisation' emerge. Often such constitutionalisation will have little to do with law.

Parallel researches into modes of non-state orderings can be found in the work of Shaffer and Halliday on transnational legal organisations,[35] the researches of Clifford Shearing and his colleagues into 'nodal governance',[36] and John Braithwaite's far-flung researches aimed explicitly at finding how power might be tempered in a huge range of very different contexts by a huge range of means.[37] Old-school 'formulaic checklists' of the features of legal rules might have little foothold in these settings, but teleologists are concerned with attaining a goal rather than sticking to a list. How that goal might be approached, attained, and reliably secured is a task that the institutional artillery familiar to lawyers and legal philosophers will not solve on its own.

10

Contexts and Connections

> Even when we consider development in a particular sphere, such as economic development or legal development, the instruments that are needed to enhance development in that circumscribed sphere may not be confined only to institutions and policies in that sphere … If this sounds a little complex, I must point out that the complication relates, ultimately, to the interdependences of the world in which we live. I did not create that world, and any blame for it has to be addressed elsewhere.
>
> Amartya Sen, 'What Is the Role of Legal and Judicial Reform in the Development Process?'

Apart from 'law and society', it is common for those uneasy with 'unmoved mover' images of law to speak of 'law in context'. That is the title of several books and journals, part of the titles of many more, and the rubric of a Cambridge University Press book series, running since 1970, billed as part of 'a movement to broaden the study of law'.[1] The noble intention of such publications appears to be to remind lawyers that there is more than law in the world.

If one's primary focus is law, this phrase answers Lon Fuller's objection to 'law and society'. Law is still the focus, but it is not apart or alone but in. However, if one's primary interest is the ideal of the rule of law, the tempering of power, this phrase still does not get quite to the point. Why should temperers assume that law is necessarily at the centre of the relevant context? Power is, but law might not be.

Where power is concerned, and law too for that matter, contexts matter. In this chapter, I focus on three overarching and inescapable contexts, frames of human interaction, which necessarily means power-full interaction. I distinguish three – cultures, societies, and polities. The distinctions between these three are of course artificial, artefacts of the words we use, not distinctions we find in the domains themselves. What we seek to capture with these words is always and inextricably mixed: no cultures without societies or societies without cultures, no societies without arrangements for dealing with common matters of value, dispute, defence and social control, and so on. The phenomena we pick out with these terms overlap, interact, and are interwoven in multiple ways, with each other, with power, and with law, which is part of the point of the story. These are merely aspects of collective human life that we choose to distinguish within multi-element and multi-form wholes. Moreover, there are other aspects. Still these three have profound effects on, and are profoundly affected by, the play of power in the world. If I were competent to discuss other aspects, such as economies, it would amplify the range of contexts and connections I want to stress, but it would not nullify them.

When I speak of 'cultures' I have in mind the common, collective frames and contents of thoughts and values shared by members of particular societies. 'Societies' are groups of people characterised by patterns of interaction, cooperation, and communication distinct from those among members of other societies and shared among members of the group. 'Polities' are modes and institutions of government of the public affairs of a group.

Whether the tempering of power is on any agenda, how high it rates, to what extent it develops beyond agenda to realisation, what competing agendas are in play, these are hugely influenced by how our cultures frame them, how our societies enable and encourage us to interact, and how the official ordering of public values, choices, and decisions is framed, led, and conducted. Societies, and the rule of law ideal, are well served if they allow, still more encourage, activities and intra-inter-domain complicities of tempering kinds. It can seem that there's not much left for us to do, but that is a mistake. Even well-tempered societies are never necessarily so. Surprises happen, distemper comes to thrive, in places one never expected. Parts of the world are discovering that today. Moreover, certain patterns of cultures, societies, and polities do not favour the tempering of power, and it is hard for temperers to know what to do. Either way, we cannot escape our cultures, societies, and polities, and we need to be aware of that if we are to do anything about them, to them, within them.

This chapter examines some kinds of cultural, social, and political contexts and some of the virtuous and vicious circles in which they are likely to be entwined. An implication is that partisans of tempered power should not start with the assumption that law will be central among the relevant contexts for tempering power, though it will often turn out to be important. Law provides another particular kind of context and content for engagement with power, distinctive but not necessarily more (nor less) important than others with which it must mix. What results is always a product of the mixture, and of what we contrive to do, not of any of its elements alone.

10.1 Cultures

When I was young, and so a long time ago, a remarkable controversy erupted over the last eleven and a half pages of a book by the eminent British historian, ex-communist, unorthodox Marxist, and peace activist, E. P. Thompson. The work, *Whigs and Hunters: The Origin of the Black Act*,[2] was a close reconstruction, from masses of fragmentary evidence, of the origins, social meanings, and significance of a law passed by the UK Parliament in 1723. The Whigs of the book's title governed Britain for much of the eighteenth century, the hunters were mainly forest dwellers and farm labourers who sought game in parks and forests owned by the king, nobles, and gentry. The 'Black' of the Act referred to the camouflage used by these hunters/poachers ('Blacks') on the job, and the Act 'at a blow' created around fifty new capital offences. It provided, Thompson writes, 'a versatile armoury of death apt to the repression of various forms of social disturbance'.[3]

As might be expected from the author of a classic work of Marxist history, *The Making of the English Working Class*,[4] Thompson had no sympathy with this Act nor with the ruling class to whom he attributed it. The bulk of his book is a detailed and excoriating critique of their motives, character, and actions, revealing ways in which this and other laws were made and used by the government and those whose interests, particularly economic interests, they served.

In a conflict between 'users', 'petty predators' often asserting customary rights, and 'exploiters' and 'great predators' who ignored those rights, the Act was crafted and employed, Thompson argued, by the latter. They had all the cards, as Donald Trump might say:

> At the level of affrays between poachers and keepers there was some equality in the contest. But at the point where the petty seriously inconvenienced the great, then the entire apparatus of power and law could be brought to the side of the latter. The Black Act put unprecedented legal power in the hands of men who had not a generalized, delegated interest, such as the maintenance of order, or even the maintenance of the privileges of their own class, but a direct and personal interest in the conviction of men who were a nuisance to them.[5]

Had Thompson stopped there (which he almost did, given that the offending section starts halfway through page 258 of 269),[6] his readers could have emerged edified and instructed but not surprised by the direction the narrative took. Ruling classes exploited the ruled; who knew?

However, to the dismay of erstwhile comrades and the (occasionally pleased) surprise of erstwhile opponents, unused to Marxist books ending in this way, Thompson concluded his exposé of ruling class manipulations with some immediately notorious reflections in a section entitled 'The Rule of Law'. At their heart was his insistence that 'there is a very large difference, which twentieth-century experience ought to have made clear even to the most exalted thinker, between arbitrary extra-legal power and the rule of law'.[7] Notwithstanding all the distasteful legal and extra-legal machinations and manipulations he had chronicled:

> the notion of the regulation and reconciliation of conflicts through the rule of law – and the elaboration of rules and procedures which, on occasion, made some approximate approach towards the ideal – seems to me a cultural achievement of universal significance.[8]

A page later, he explains that:

> I am insisting only upon the obvious point, which some modern Marxists have overlooked, that there is a difference between arbitrary power and the rule of law. We ought to expose the shams and inequities which may be concealed beneath the law. But the rule of law itself, the imposing of effective inhibitions upon power and the defence of the citizen from power's all-intrusive claims, seems to me an unqualified human good. To deny or belittle this good is, in this dangerous century when the resources and pretentions [*sic*] of power continue to enlarge, a desperate error of intellectual abstraction.[9]

Few who had learnt from Thompson over the years were happy with these conclusions, least of all coming from him. The arch-liberal, Friedrich von Hayek, might be expected to say such things, but who in the mid 1970s, and on the Left, cared about him?[10] From Thompson, however, this came as a shock. The puzzled reaction of contemporary and former allies was summarised by a later scholar who reviewed the controversy: 'He [Thompson] had shown throughout the book – convincingly and repeatedly – that the law was being used to the benefit of "the ruling class" … Why, then, did he turn around at the end of the book and call the rule of law "an unqualified human good?"'[11]

The heat of that controversy had to do not with Thompson's characterisation of the rule of law as 'cultural' – which few seem to have noticed – but with his praise of it as any sort of achievement, let alone one of 'universal significance'. Elsewhere I have endorsed both his characterisation and his praise (though not as 'an unqualified human good'; I know none of those).[12] Since my views on the value of reducing arbitrary power are obvious by now, I will here stick to culture. What could Thompson have meant by describing the rule of law as a *cultural* achievement? He gives us some clues, both negative and positive.

Perhaps fortunately, Thompson was not a lawyer, legal philosopher, or rule of law promoter. Note where he starts: not with any particular selection of hallowed legal institutions or rules. He did not identify the rule of law with any particular checklist, recipe book, or template of legal and institutional hardware. Rather, he began with the 'obvious point' that 'there is a difference between arbitrary power and the rule of law'. It was *that* difference which mattered for him. Thompson does not explicitly make the distinction I have argued for, between rule of law means and tempered ends, but what matters most for him, as for me, is the end.

Instead of some Diceyan attribution of the good he identified to any particular arrangements of British institutions, Thompson focuses on that *specific achievement*, that is, both specific and an achievement. *Specific*, because it has to do not with the overall substantive purposes or outcomes of the exercise of power; it is not a 'thick' account but one concerned with the ways power is exercised. *Achievement*, because it is attained only to the extent that something substantive has occurred: 'the imposing of effective inhibitions upon power and the defence of the citizen from power's all-intrusive claims'. It is that, not any particular array of legal bits and pieces that might (but also might not) achieve it, which he characterised as the rule of law. His approach, in other words (though not his words), is teleological, starting with the point of the enterprise, rather than anatomical, stipulating institutional forms and features taken to amount to some legal configuration anointed with the title 'rule of law'. In my terms the concern is with the tempering of power. That, one might predict, seems to me a good approach.

Indeed, although Thompson believed law was crucial for the achievement he lauded, he expressed disdain for many of the particular English offices and officers he was discussing. On his interpretation, the Black Act itself, and the many laws that supported and extended it, was spawned by an ascendant and obnoxious ruling Whig oligarchy 'which created new laws and bent old forms in order to legitimize its own property and status',[13] 'inventing callous and oppressive laws to serve its own interests'.[14] It was 'a bad law, drawn by bad legislators, and enlarged by the interpretations of bad judges'.[15] More generally: 'The law when considered as institution (the courts, with their class theatre and class procedures) or as personnel (the judges, the lawyers, the Justices of the Peace) may very easily be assimilated to those of the ruling class.'[16]

Thompson's account started, then, by specifying a valued accomplishment, and though he stressed that it was a *legal* accomplishment, more was involved. Thus, when he acknowledged that the specific institutions of eighteenth-century English law could easily and rightly be seen as instruments of a ruling class, he went on: 'But all that is entailed in "the law" is not subsumed in these institutions.'[17] So what else was there, and what was 'cultural' about it?

10.1.1 Lawyers' Traditions

First, and to return to Chapter 8's discussion of traditions within law, while Thompson says little about legal institutional hardware, he has a great deal to say about legal cultural software, the stuff in our heads. He begins with lawyers and sets some store by the 'forms of law'. They are important in themselves, he thinks, for 'It is inherent in the especial character of law, as a body of rules and procedures, that it shall apply logical criteria with reference to standards of universality and equity.'[18] Already there is cultural fodder here, since these are intellectual criteria, part of 'thinking like a lawyer',[19] routinely passed down by tradition in their writings, thinkings, and practices. Individual lawyers don't invent them, and they don't apply themselves. They must be learnt, thought about, and applied by members acculturated and thinking within a common language with other members of shared legal traditions.

According to Thompson:

> In the case of an ancient historical formation like the law, a discipline which requires years of exacting study to master, there will always be some men who actively believe in their own procedures and in the logic of justice. The law may be rhetoric, but it need not be empty rhetoric. Blackstone's *Commentaries* represent an intellectual exercise far more rigorous than could have come from an apologist's pen.[20]

As I have argued already, there is considerable evidence that legal traditions, training, and practice do tend to dispose lawyers in many societies to a particular range of values – among them attachment to civil and political (but not socio-economic) rights, protection of legal forms, and a 'moderate state' – and that not just lawyers themselves but those involved more broadly in the administration of the law, members of what Karpik and Halliday call 'the legal complex', are likely to be similarly acculturated to share such notions, as well as thoughts and practices tied up with them.[21] No small thing, where it occurs.

10.1.2 Rulers' Ideologies

All that might be true about *lawyers* and their attendant complexes, but how many (armed) divisions do they have?[22] They are typically not rulers. They serve them. So what larger significance does their culture have and why, particularly if they might thwart powerful interests?

Not enough, on their own, but they are not always on their own. Here we start to move beyond the traditions and culture of lawyers themselves and the legal complexes that surround them to more commanding heights.

Marxists were familiar with the idea that law supports ruling classes not simply as their sharp or blunt sword but – full of handsome and self-justifying words as law typically is – as legitimating *ideology*, often with powerful social effect.[23] English lawyers were typically members of, or closely allied with, ruling classes, went to the same schools, spoke a common language. They and the rulers' ideological convictions converged and served them both.

Thompson accepts, indeed emphasises, these ideological components but gives them a twist. For he insists that, as ideology, law is two-edged. To be effective in legitimating power an ideology must be plausible, both to those subject to it and even to those who benefit from it. As to the latter: '[I]t is not often the case that a ruling ideology can be dismissed as a mere hypocrisy; even rulers find a need to legitimize their power, to moralize their functions, to feel themselves to be useful and just.'[24] Moreover, as Thompson writes elsewhere, the English ruling class had its own reasons to want to temper at least the state's power:

> [The] Whiggish ruling class ... feared the central monarchy and its powers and feared the institutions of state. These gentry did not like the Crown to have too strong a power, nor a large standing army, nor a system of spies ... So they were jealous of the power of the central state and they hedged that state around with fences of law. In doing so we have the origin of a complexity which is not exhausted to this day.[25]

So, even though it is not false to identify law as 'ideology' and 'rhetoric', those very characteristics make it possible for law more than occasionally to constrain the powerful and strengthen the powerless.

10.1.3 Social Practices

All the more was this possible because, quite apart from the cultures of rulers and their servants, ordinary Englishmen shared many beliefs with their rulers. In the period and among the people he was discussing, he insisted, law was not merely a bunch of thunderbolts thrown by Whig oligarchs from on high but was deeply embedded in everyday ways of life and thought, 'often a definition of actual agrarian *practice*, as it had been pursued "time out of mind" ... deeply imbricated within the very basis of productive relations which would have been inoperable without this law'.[26] Beyond a matter of commands which one needed to know how to obey or avoid, then, the law was taken as a source of felt entitlement and, when thwarted, grievance. For the law was not an alien incursion into some social vacuum. At least, and especially, in eighteenth-century England, Thompson insisted, 'this law, as definition or as rules (imperfectly enforceable through institutional legal forms), was endorsed by norms, tenaciously transmitted throughout the community'.[27] Such norms, as Sally Falk Moore might have observed, are likely to have social significance, whether or not lawyers and rulers respect them.

Though the law of eighteenth-century England was full of ruling class rhetoric, as Thompson acknowledges, 'so far from the ruled shrugging it all off as hypocrisy, some part of it at least was internalised by the plebeian crowd, part of what it meant to be a '"free-born Englishman" with his inviolable privacy, his *habeas corpus*, his equality before the law':[28]

> [T]hough those in power used the law for their purposes, this is not the same thing as to say that the rulers had need of law, in order to oppress the ruled, while those who were ruled had need of none. What was often at issue was not property, supported by law, against no-property; it was alternative definitions of property-rights ... For as long as it remained possible, the ruled – if they could find a purse and a lawyer – would actually fight for their rights by means of law; occasionally the copyholders, resting upon the precedents of sixteenth-century law, could actually win a case. When it ceased to be possible to continue the fight at law, men still felt a sense of legal wrong: the propertied had obtained their power by illegitimate means.[29]

Particularly after the revolutionary turbulence of the previous century, much of its rhetoric focused squarely, explicitly, and centrally on the dangers of arbitrary power; English public culture was particularly law-suffused. This was true in comparison both with earlier ages (where, for example, religion was more important) and with many other societies where laws and notions of tempered power in general, and tempering power by means of law, had less cultural resonance.[30] And a central theme of the English focus on law was that it should ensure 'an empire of laws and not of men'.[31]

10.1.4 Notions

The concluding pages of *Whigs and Hunters* are usually taken to be a full-throated paean to the achievement that Thompson takes the achievement he calls the rule of law *itself* to be. And it is that. However, he also makes another, subtler, claim, which, so far as I know, has gone unnoticed; certainly I only noticed it recently even after decades of returning to these eleven and a half pages. When he writes of the rule of law, he several times focuses not on the actual achievement itself but on what he calls the *notion* of it. Thus, he remarks, 'Turn where you will, the rhetoric of eighteenth-century England is saturated with the *notion* of law.'[32] Again, it is 'the *notion* of the regulation and reconciliation of conflicts through the rule of law – and the elaboration of rules and procedures which, on occasion, made some approximate approach towards the ideal – [that] seems to me a cultural achievement of universal significance'.[33] When we see Whigs manipulating the law, 'we feel contempt for men whose practice belied the resounding rhetoric of the age. But we feel contempt not because we are contemptuous of the *notion* of a just and equitable law but because this notion has been betrayed by its own professors.'[34] And finally, while Thompson is usually remembered for saying that 'the rule of law' is an unqualified good, he also says that it is 'the *notion* of the rule of law [that] is itself an unqualified good'.

10.1.5 Discussion

What should we make of these few pages of 'inchoate afterthought',[35] about the significance of legal traditions, ideology, cultural and social practices, and 'the notion of the rule of law', pegged at the end of a book of somewhat different tenor, saying other things?

I am no historian and Thompson was no philosopher. I cannot tell if his portrayal of eighteenth-century England is accurate, and his arguments do not march in cumulative succession, one building upon and strengthening the other. He moves back and forth between a number of themes, in a fashion more literary than logical, rhetorical than rigorous, polemical than professorial. And yet I have found myself drawn back to these few pages time and again. They figured in many courses I have taught over decades, and in many things I have written. Apart from what they might tell us about eighteenth-century England, I think they can help throw light on current, indeed perennial, quandaries. In any event, I propose to enlist them in that effort.

Unless it is five minutes old, every society has cultural and legal traditions that frame and inform the ways those who inhabit them (and whom cultures inhabit) think about, expect from, and respond to ways in which power is exercised. Of course, as we have seen, the legal complex itself extends well beyond lawyers themselves. Stephen Toope has an allied phrase, 'legal communities of practice', and he points out that they 'encompass far more people than would be included in the concept of the legal "profession", and may include students, civil society actors, journalists, professors, civil servants in government, politicians, business people, trade unionists, think tank researchers and writers, diplomats, criminologists, and many others. The boundaries of the community are porous.'[36] Many in such communities are aware of and affected by traditions of and about law, and in many it is expected, at least hoped, to temper power. In some societies, moreover, such hopes and expectations are prominent themes in much broader cultural traditions, not just those of lawyers.

Where legal traditions are strong in dominant cultures, they are not merely found among lawyers but have been distinctive and important elements of society and culture. Law was not seen purely as a unidirectional instrument of rulers against members of society. On the contrary, one of the most important roles attributed to it was as a medium – of protection, communication, understanding, and argument between rulers and society *and* between the different, plural, important and legally recognised constituents of the society itself[37] – cities, guilds, estates, regions, and individuals. Law came to have significance not simply – to borrow a distinction from the social philosopher Jürgen Habermas – as a political or economic 'steering medium' but as an institution of the everyday 'life world' itself.[38] Western legal traditions are strong cases, but they are not unique.[39] In traditions and cultures of these sorts, the idea that law should temper power is at home.

Temperance has never been the only theme in such traditions. It has mixed – at times victoriously, at others not – with competitors, its significance is often exaggerated, it is often horribly compromised, as when colonisers go travelling, but even then it is rarely totally shed or left behind.[40] Allowing for all these sources of slippage, hypocrisy, and self-service, there has been something significant, real, and highly institutionalised there to build exaggerations upon.

Where what Adam Czarnota and I have called 'state' as contrasted with 'legal' traditions are culturally prominent and widespread, things are different.[41] Thus it has, for example, been argued by numerous scholars that for most of their history neither Imperial China nor Russia knew Thompson's 'notion' that law might temper rulers' power, still less that it should, as anything more than heresy.[42] In the Russian imperial tradition, for example, law was not a central cultural symbol and to the extent that it counted it did so as an arm of central power. The notion that power should be tempered by law, or that law should have a *horizontal* role among members of the society, or that it should do anything but transmit central orders, was at least heretical, more commonly alien, and late and weak in developing, if it developed at all. And where its partisans stuck their heads over the parapet, they often lost them. When any conception of tempering ruling power was known, it was rejected, at least by those in key positions of power. None of this is past history.

Where such state traditions are long and strong, law has existed, at times in bulk, but primarily as a subordinate – indeed servile – branch of political, administrative, and at times quasi-theocratic power. That is how it was and that is how it was widely conceived naturally to be. Such law is extremely permeable, at least to pressure from above. Where the political centre is powerful, the role of law is conceived of in almost exclusively instrumental terms, either as a repressive instrument of social control or as an executive instrument of centrally determined goals, values, and decisions. Law is dominated by political requirements, and it lacks institutional, social, political, and ideological sources of autonomy. There might be considerable social and institutional differentiation, but the idea that law is and should be distinct from the exercise and demands of political or religious rulers is either unthinkable or strongly rejected.

In some countries, such as Russia, these state traditions were endogenous. In others, most particularly Poland under the 120 years of partition between Austria, Prussia, and Russia, they were imposed from without. In some, they dominated both state forms and social consciousness. In others, they rode uneasily over indigenous non-state traditions – indeed, in the 'noble republic' of Poland from the sixteenth to the eighteenth century, quasi-anarchic traditions. These latter traditions tended, on the one hand, to mollify state impositions – compare, say, Polish and Russian communism. There are many other versions and combinations.

Where state traditions are strong, societies and polities do not lack their own dominant 'notions' about law and power, but they are very different from those that Thompson lauded. Rather, they often have taken, and long taken, what Nonet and Selznick describe as 'repressive' (as distinct from 'autonomous' or 'responsive') forms:

> [T]he courts and legal officials are the king's ministers. They are perceived (and perceive themselves) as pliable instruments of the government in power. Legal institutions serve the state: they are not a counterfoil within it. The idea of sovereignty pervades legal imagery … Legal rules give power the color of authority, but their use is qualified by criteria of political expediency. *Raison d'etat* requires that unchecked discretion be preserved; rules remain weakly binding on the sovereign; the recognition of rights is precarious.[43]

In many societies and cultures, it is not just that notions of tempered rule are weak. There are strong traditions that reject the notion that ruling power should be tempered. In many polities, tempering power is simply not the name of any official or public game. In such societies, notions of tempered power seem simply implausible. Those with power have no felt obligation to submit to its tempering or even pretend to, and subjects/citizens have no expectation of it occurring. Few have what the legal philosopher H. L. A. Hart called an 'internal' attitude to law that treats it as 'as a general standard to be followed by the group as a whole'.[44] Rulers use it for their purposes and citizens regard it as something to be exploited or avoided, used or abused. 'Informal practices' not only exist, as they do everywhere, but often contradict or ignore or supplement or replace law, assuming it will be gamed by the powerful in any event and every event.[45] Recall the Bulgarian saying, which has counterparts in many parts of the world, that likens the law to a door in an open field.[46] Only a fool (or perhaps a lawyer) would enter. And why? Well, there is a Russian answer: 'The law is like the shaft of a wagon; it goes wherever you turn it.'[47] Trouble is that 'you' are very rarely me.

Such notions do not die quickly, even when the regimes that spawned them do. As one Polish legal philosopher (and later head of the Polish Supreme Administrative Court) wrote of the already softened inheritance of Polish lawyers in the 'transition to democracy and the rule of law' of the immediate post-communist period: 'During this period … [l]awyers played the role of "guardians of law" whose main task was to recognize law as the content of the Sovereign's will and possibly to explain it.'[48] We also know of destructively anti-legal currents as well (for instance, the Chinese Cultural Revolution, Pol Pot's Kampuchea). These particular examples did not last long enough to establish traditions, and all the better for that, but it is conceivable that they might, as others have.

A culture strong on tempering power, particularly ruling power, is not, then, as explicit legal rules might be, some sort of machinery or cultural Esperanto, which can simply be isolated, identified, shipped, and taught, to operate identically wherever it is transported and assembled. Institutions may well be shipped and copied, and very often are, but something will be lost – perhaps even gained but anyway changed – in the process. For like any other complex and enduring cultural tradition, legal traditions involve what Clifford Geertz calls 'local knowledge': 'local not just as to place, time, class, and variety of issue, but as to accent – vernacular characterisations of what happens connected to vernacular imaginings of what can. It is this complex of characterisations and imaginings, stories about events cast in imagery about principles, that I have been calling a legal sensibility.'[49] It is harder to create such a sensibility than a rule. Typically it is not created but grows, though it can be encouraged and discouraged, added to and taken from. If, however, it has been damaged or destroyed, or if it never existed, thought must be given as to how it might be encouraged to develop or redevelop. So must time. And failure is common.

Needless to say, the distinctions drawn here are idealised. Like most ideal types, their elements are never totally present and rarely totally absent. Legal traditions are rarely as independent or self-generating as their proponents imagine or profess. Nor are they ever free of traces of reasons of state, and other reasons. Conversely, states rarely can exercise the sort of central control necessary to achieve rulers' goals completely. And there are always cross-currents, competing demands, and other cultural traditions. Nevertheless, again like most ideal types, there are moments and places where they are more closely approximated than others. The 'moment' of cultural traditions in which law is supposed to have a tempering role has been long in several countries in western Europe, as was that of state traditions in the Russian, then Soviet, empire, and now its successor. As a result, there are systematic and deep differences between the role that law has played in the former and that played by it in the latter.

And of course, even within legal traditions and cultural traditions writ large, there are complications and contradictions, sometimes tragic. Thus, one place the 'notion' that Thompson writes of was exported was my own country, Australia. Its early history – which, as one chronicler argues, moved from penal colony to free society (for white settlers), by any then contemporary standards, in the space of some fifty years – might serve as an example of some of the characteristics (and limitations) of such 'notions'.

On the one hand, it was not just convicts (among them Luddites, Levellers and indeed 'Hunters' themselves) who were transported to the other end of the world but particular notions about the legal rights of 'free-born Englishmen' that they (and their rulers) carried 'as part of their cultural baggage'.[50] Central to that baggage was the notion, and the understanding that their overseers shared it, that laws should be respected and that they could and should form the basis of rights that could be asserted against them. 'A cluster of ideas known as the rule of law provided the major institutions, arguments, vocabulary and symbols with which the convicts forged the transformation.'[51]

Notwithstanding all the hypocrisies in which British colonial rulers indulged, and easy temptations to which they readily succumbed, there was something truly substantial in the notions that they shared with their prisoners. And unlike the Indigenous inhabitants of the land, whose land (and many lives) they took, their convict subjects knew the score, were familiar with the law and its cultural connotations, and reminded their commanders of both, often to their benefit.[52]

Convicts fought battles for status and recognition in terms of what they believed to be their entitlements under the law, believed that the rule of law should apply to them, insisted that the authorities should respect it, and demanded rights that they believed flowed from it. A great deal flowed from these beliefs. Convicts were rather liberally granted legal rights; and they made use of them, often to good effect. When they won, it was because their opponents' hands were also tied. One reason (not the only reason: who else would do the work in a penal colony?) is that they too, after all, had the same baggage in their heads. And even where governors and marines did not, the courts often did, insisting on their independence under British law and the subordination of the apparently (and in many ways really) autocratic governors to that same law.

It did not have to be like this. What if the convicts and their governors had come from eighteenth-century Russia? There would have been fewer tricky arguments making their way through the courts about the legal rights of free-born Russians. Indeed, the penal colony would likely not have had – from the very beginning – courts in which convicts could sue their masters, and oftentimes win, and this for two reasons: courts would not have been provided and, had they been, few people would have thought to use them. There would have been no fuss about trial by jury, still less about who had a right to serve on juries. Nor would the governors have constantly had to battle against prickly judges, conscious of their independence and attached to their traditions, or free settlers against far-too-smart ex-convict ('emancipist') lawyers, who were often able to best them in court. This was not because those who landed here were more virtuous than the notional Russians I have just whisked to the Antipodes, but because their cultural baggage in relation to these matters was very different from that of Russians of that time (and arguably, of many at this time).

Not only did it not have to be like this but for Australia's Indigenous inhabitants it *wasn't* like this, from the very beginning. To say the least, not everyone benefited equally from the law and cultural understandings the British exported to, and imposed upon, their new colony. The civilisational calamity and tragedy of Australia's First Peoples, about which I have written elsewhere,[53] had many sources and was indeed overdetermined, but it was without doubt the harshest example of that human blindness also and equally part of the cultural baggage that English colonists brought with them.

Far from undermining Thompson's argument, however, this poignantly confirms its two-pronged point: the rule of law *is* a cultural achievement, not a matter simply of legal rules and institutions (which as a matter of law were for some time the same for settlers and Aboriginal peoples). In England itself, as everywhere, the haves came out ahead,[54] and the notion of the rule of law was unevenly recognised. In Australia, in relation to Aboriginal peoples, however, the cultural ground for that notion was dramatically, spectacularly, split. They knew nothing of the settlers' law and for a long time had no way of making sense of it or use of it, and settlers typically cultivated it only for their own benefit and had no cultural basis (nor, it must be said, any evident basis in their own self-interest) to extend its culturally derived ameliorations to those they were conquering.

The differences in availability of the rule of law to convicts and Aboriginal peoples derived, in considerable part, from a complete absence of cultural common ground between Indigenous and settler Australians, as well as from a deep split and limit in the cultural and moral imagination of the dominant early Australian lawmakers, enforcers, and, more generally, settlers. In early contact with Aboriginal society the cultural baggage that convicts shared with their rulers and benefited from was simply not extended or made available to Aboriginal peoples, even where the will to make it so was. Commonly it was not, nor for a very long time did the latter have access to any of the resources – cultural, economic, social, political – necessary even to be able to seek advantage from it.

That did not in the first instance depend upon the forms or institutions of the imported law but underlay it and conditioned the ways it worked in the world, and more generally the ways *power*, both legal and extra-legal, worked in that world.

This then made its way – often, one imagines, unconsciously, as part of obvious taken-for-granted settler views of the world – to be reflected in the practices, character, forms, and obligations embodied in the institutions of law and in the entitlements, or lack of them, of its subjects. Better: its subjects and objects. Among the former and between them, the 'notion' of the rule of law was remarkably strong. Between the former and the latter, it often had no bite at all. The notion of the rule of law occasionally (and over time increasingly) had some purchase, but commonly not. It took a long time for that to change, in many respects it has yet to be fully achieved, although the constituency for 'the notion' – both among Aboriginal peoples and the (now multicultural) majority – has expanded, certainly ideologically, and to a considerably extent actually as well.

Similar culturally embedded contradictions have occurred in most colonial settings, including quite obviously the United States, in relation to Native Americans. And it does not need to be a colony. Hostility to arbitrary power, drawn in part from English traditions,[55] was strong in relations among 'insiders' of ruling groups, for example white Protestant Americans. It fuelled the American Revolution and was encoded in the Federalist Papers and the Constitution. Often without any apparent cognitive or moral dissonance, such notions have been ignored or rejected in relation to numerous others, for example indigenes, blacks, Japanese, Muslims, Venezuelans, immigrants.[56]

Moreover, as this history also illustrates, even powerful and established cultural traditions often have equally strong rivals with equal or stronger pedigrees. Even among majority groups themselves, many contemporary, polarised societies are culturally divided precisely on such issues, with particular constituencies committed to notions of tempered power, while others starkly reject them. As historian Stephen Hahn has shown in rich detail, the famed American 'liberal tradition'[57] was preceded by illiberal traditions deeply embedded in local cultures, which did not die but paralleled and competed with it through time, sometimes marginalised, at times ascendant. Often, as with Thomas Jefferson and Abraham Lincoln and many others, contradictory elements of both were housed in the same breasts.[58]

Such contradictions are becoming increasingly evident in recent years, and not only in the United States. For some time to come, in several countries around the world, the cultural sway of the rule of law ideal, even when apparently long and deeply anchored in large parts of the population, will depend on who wins the next election. That might also be true of its actual fate in the world.

In the United States, as much as the need to temper power has been enshrined in legal, political, and cultural history and legend, it is today assaulted from many quarters, including the most powerful in the nation. Its fate as a ruling ideal is uncertain. It is neither ascendant nor irrelevant in public culture but explicitly at stake. Losers are not merely divided from winners over matters of politics or spoils but over fundamental notions about the proper role, limits, and character of the exercise of winners' power in public life. Donald Trump did not come from nowhere.

Again, as I write this in mid 2025, the Polish presidential elections have been won by a candidate, known a few months before by almost no one but anointed and supported by the former governing party PiS whose sustained assault on institutions that might temper power I discussed in Chapter 8. He appears to be an ardent supporter of all such assaults. The margin was 50.89/49.11 per cent. That split reflects profound cultural divides between north and south of the country, east and west, urban and rural, tertiary-educated and not. It will not disappear soon.

10.2 Societies

In a critique of Friedrich von Hayek's *Constitution of Liberty*, Raymond Aron observed that 'before a society can be free, it must exist'.[59] That is a profound point, though it would make no sense to Hayek's self-proclaimed disciple, Margaret Thatcher, who famously asked, 'who is society?' and answered, 'There is no such thing! There are individual men and women and there are families.'

It was, of course, Hobbes's point. His solution was political: for individuals living in a 'state of nature' to become a society, he insisted, they must come to be ruled by a sovereign with absolute power. However, apart from the dangers of such a solution, the sociological truth is it wouldn't be enough to hold.

For, notwithstanding Thatcher's scepticism, there *are* such things as societies, and it is a good thing too. They depend upon much more than the existence of individuals (and their families), and the latter would not last very long without them. So Durkheim taught and he was right. Though he never defined 'society', it is his master concept. A collection of individuals only forms a society, on Durkheim's view, to the extent that those individuals are connected, formed, and bound together by shared 'collective ways of acting or thinking'[60] that they do not invent but learn in common with other members of the same society, from myriad sources: human, institutional, cultural, political, legal. While some of these ways are optional, many are socially enforced by norms, customs, religions, expectations, institutions, laws, and other members of the society who share them. These shared, customary, inculcated, often policed, apparently 'natural' and 'obvious' ways allow individuals to recognise themselves and others as parts of the same society. They think many of the same, or at least familiar, mutually intelligible thoughts, behave in many recognisable ways, in many ways different (or believed to be different) from 'ways of acting or thinking' found and formed in other societies.

Such ways of acting, thinking, expecting, and valuing are never monolithic or univocal, there is argument over them and within them, but it is rare, if ever, that members of a society are unaffected by them. That is as true of those who seek to reject them as those who imbibe them. No one comes from nowhere, and no one rebels against nothing. Even when individuals reject prevalent ways of acting and thinking, as happens all the time, they know what they are rejecting. As Gianfranco Poggi felicitously expressed it, though society for Durkheim is not a tangible substance itself, and in this he might agree with Thatcher, it is 'a process, a reality, real performance, an *in so far as* reality'.[61] It exists '*in so far as* certain things go on'.[62] Different societies, different things go on. That is true at the level of particular norms, values, common understandings, available cognitive and normative repertoires, of course, but it is also true of the general character of social relations, how people interact with others.

One might extend the thought to our subject by asking what sorts of societies are likely to support the rule of law ideal. With no pretence to precision or comprehensiveness, I will distinguish between three ideal type social formations. Reality will always be a varied, mixed, and incomplete approximation and mixture of such (and other) types, but some distinct tendencies can be identified and clarified this way.

The first type, a 'sack of potatoes', has little defensive capacity and is inclined to invite domination. For if 'power must check power by the arrangement of things', a sack of potatoes is not up to the task. For members of society to be able to mobilise collectively to check and temper the power of those who might seek to exercise it over them, they need sources of, and resources to support, independence, connection, interaction, and mobilisation.

Even these features, while indispensable, are not enough. Both the second and third types I distinguish – 'civil society' and 'polarised community' – have them all but only one is likely to give support to tempering agencies or to be supported by them. Civil society enables and encourages temperance among citizens, favours it among those with power, and is supported by tempered and tempering politics, states, and law. Though a polarised community, or a society composed of polarised communities, on the other hand, does not necessarily lack independence, connection, interaction, and mobilisation *within* its hostile parts, it is unlikely to favour tempered relations between them. It is also likely to favour, and be favoured by, leaders of firmly (and usually stridently) intemperate disposition. And its institutions are unlikely to stand in the way. At the time of this writing, polarised communities are on the rise.

10.2.1 A Sack of Potatoes

In one of his most brilliant essays, *The Eighteenth Brumaire of Louis Bonaparte*, Karl Marx sought to explain the success of the great Napoleon's lower-grade nephew, Louis, Napoleon III, who followed the socialist uprisings of 1848 by winning the French presidential elections that same year and then staging a coup d'état in1851 to became emperor.[63] Both with overwhelming popular support.

Marx's practical question was 'how a nation of 36 millions can be surprised and delivered unresisting into captivity by three swindlers'.[64] More theoretically perplexing, how could the state come to dominate the society, including its ostensible ruling class, the bourgeoisie? That was not the standard Marxist script, according to which the economically ruling classes rule.

Notwithstanding occasional attempts to distance himself from his followers and deny it,[65] Marx was a Marxist. So the answer had to be sought in economic class structure. That of mid-century France he believed to be distinctive and pathological. Partly, splits and divisions within the ostensible ruling class, the bourgeoisie, contributed to Napoleon's dominance by threatening their overall economic interests and weakening the political power of the class. As a result:

> [T]he bourgeoisie confesses that its own interests dictate that it should be delivered from the danger of its *own rule* … that in order to preserve its social power intact, its political power must be broken … that in order to save its purse, it must forfeit the crown, and the sword that is to safeguard it must at the same time be hung over its own head as a sword of Damocles.[66]

This analysis formed the model for later Marxists' invocations of 'Bonapartism' to explain bourgeois support for dictators such as Mussolini and Hitler, even at the price of losing all political control and, for some, their property and their lives. There was some surface plausibility in the explanation, though here as elsewhere it was a forced plausibility which assumed priority of economic factors over others, even when the others are running the show and there are more direct, non-economic, grounds to explain that.[67]

Another and central factor that Marx needed to explain was the support Bonaparte received, both in the 1848 elections and after the coup, from the largest class in France, the peasantry. For: 'Only under the second Bonaparte does the state seem to have made itself completely independent ... And yet the state power is not suspended in midair. Bonaparte represents a class, and the most numerous class of French society at that, the *small-holding* [*Parzellen*] *peasants.*'[68] Marx found the answer in the dispersed and unconnected character of this 'class', which was not quite a real class, able to connect its members, articulate its own interests, and act in its own name. Rather:

> The small-holding peasants form an enormous mass, the members of which live in similar conditions but without entering into manifold relations with each other. Their mode of production isolates them from one another instead of bringing them into mutual intercourse. ... In this way, the great mass of the French nation is formed by the simple addition of homologous magnitudes, much as potatoes in a sack form a sack of potatoes. In so far as millions of families live under economic conditions of existence that separate their mode of life, their interests and their culture from those of the other classes, and put them in hostile opposition to the latter, they form a class. Insofar as there is merely a local interconnection among these small-holding peasants, and the identity of their interests begets no community, no national bond and no political organization among them, they do not form a class. They are consequently incapable of enforcing their class interest in their own name ... The cannot represent themselves, they must be represented. Their representative must at the same time appear as their master, as an authority over them, as an unlimited governmental power that protects them against the other classes and sends them rain and sunshine from above. The political influence of the small-holding peasants, therefore, finds its final expression in the executive power subordinating society to itself.[69]

Historical accuracy and doctrinal contortions aside, there is something in the account for our purposes: an atomised, dispersed, unconnected, passive population is fertile ground for untempered dictatorial rule. Moreover, an implication that Marx does not draw is that, even if dictators do not find such populations when they come to power, they often strive to make them so. Even if, once in control of 'the commanding heights' as Lenin called them, they can do without active support, some, particularly those once called 'totalitarian', stifle their subjects' chances actively to oppose. A method of choice is to break up independent sources of connection, to 'atomise' them.[70]

And that is precisely what led the architects of the most important and successful revolt against communism to focus their energies, not on converting or subverting the power-monopolising communist state – which was uninterested in the former and too powerful for the latter – but connecting, and thereby strengthening, society.

Early dissidents in communist countries had focused their efforts on the state, hoping to influence its activities and perhaps even to transform it – either because they believed the state was reformable, or the society was not, or both. In some countries, such as Hungary after the calamity of 1956, many kept doing this until 1989. In the mid 1970s, however, dissidents in several communist states focused on a new target for their endeavours – not the government which was now considered unreformable, nor the economy which was owned by the government, but *society* which was the victim of both. In Poland, this refocussing was manifest in a disillusionment with what had been called *revisionism*, which between 1956 and 1968 had sought to reform communist rule from within.

In 1976 Adam Michnik, one of the leading figures in the democratic opposition to the communist Polish state, articulated a novel strategic target for people interested in social and political change in communist countries: no longer the state but society. In a very influential article, he wrote: '[W]hat sets today's opposition apart … is the belief that a program for evolution ought to be addressed to an independent public, not to totalitarian power. Such a program should give directives to the people on how to behave, not to the powers on how to reform themselves. Nothing instructs the authorities better than pressure from below.'[71]

A central part of the opposition strategy was to encourage the establishment and re-establishment of connections among members of the society, horizontal links which were independent of the state and which that state had sought to destroy. This was sought as a brake on the state and as an end in itself rather than as a means of wresting state power. The very fact that the communist state sought to monopolise everything made any autonomous, horizontal, relations among citizens politically significant.[72] But this broad political significance was not to be translated into political power conventionally conceived. As Michnik wrote in another essay:

> Such actions are unique in that they do not aim to win power but to help society organize itself through the gradual emancipation of groups and individuals from the grip of the all-powerful apparatus. The people have to look after their own interests, the independent flow of information, free learning and culture. Society must transform itself from a 'sack of potatoes' (we owe this apt metaphor to Marx) into the executor of its own interests and aspirations. Only such a society can effectively oppose totalitarianism and become a real partner in power.[73]

And so the famous slogan of Michnik's colleague and mentor, Jacek Kuroń: 'Don't burn down their committees. Found your own.' Though no one knew it then, this was the source of that unprecedented movement of society against the state: *Solidarność* (*Solidarity*), which took Poland – and the world – by surprise in August 1980.

The movement was apparently shattered when, on 13 December 1981, martial law was imposed and almost the whole of the leadership of *Solidarność* was scooped up overnight. But after some years of apparent stalemate, and an extraordinary amount and range of illegal and underground opposition activity, the government and the leadership of *Solidarność* agreed to talk at the famous Round Table negotiations of early 1989. There, among many other things, they agreed to elections in June of that year where, to the bewilderment of both parties, *Solidarność* candidates received overwhelming, astounding, support. The electoral system agreed upon had made it impossible for the communists formally to be in a minority, but after two months of trying, the communist leadership could not form a government, and representatives of the former opposition were asked to do so. Something had to give. And so, in 1989 it did. The rest is history, often written as a triumph of *civil society*.

10.2.2 Civil Society

The concept of civil society has a long and cosmopolitan history,[74] though discussions of it had largely subsided until it was revived at roughly the same time by dissidents in Central and East European communist (and Latin American dictatorial) states, as a contrast with what they had. Their efforts captured the attention and admiration of many, and their slogan began echoing round the world in the 1980s. After more than a century of relative neglect, 'civil society' seemed a concept whose time had come. Shortly before 'rule of law' became the revived international slogan *du jour*, and for similar reasons, civil society held the spot for several years. All the more so when it moved from being a symbol of the apparently powerless to being hailed as the epochal victor over a system which had relentlessly sought to crush and oppose it.[75] It had, after all, paved the way for the end of history. Democracy, markets, and the rule of law would follow. A bit like the rule of law which began its global career soon afterwards, no one would say anything against it, even while it was not always clear what they were talking about.[76] Four qualities that deserve to be talked about follow.

10.2.2.1 Distinct

The specific observation of dissidents in communist states, which fuelled their renewed interest in the old idea of civil society, was that they lacked something found in what they used to describe as the 'normal' societies of the West: social relations which had their own agendas and rhythms, relations which were distinct from not penetrated, pulverised, or distorted by a state which knew no bounds. In civil societies, people went about much of their business in activities and associations which they, not the state, chose and which they and not the state directed. There was no need to ask for permission. They rose and fell at the initiative of their members, not as a result of political command. That seemed an extraordinary possibility among those to whom it was deliberately and systematically denied, however prosaic it might appear to those who have never known it to be questioned. For communist societies were special in this regard.

This was not merely the hyperbole of opposition. It was so. To an extent unmatched in any other form of socio-political order, communist societies were penetrated, overseen, and dominated by the party-state. So, by the 1970s, having despaired of wresting or modifying state power, dissidents in East and Central Europe turned their attention elsewhere: to reviving the independent activities of members of their societies by encouraging people to engage with each other without asking permission, 'as if' they lived in a free and civil society.

Long after the excitement of *Solidarity* had waned, this emphasis on 'the significance of the social' remained central to prevailing conceptions of civil society. Indeed, often when it is spoken of today, the adjective in '*civil* society' has no distinctive role to play. The noun carries the whole load. The term has come simply to point to what is specifically *social*, apart from the state. The point, made in a multitude of ways, is that independent social connections, following their own rhythms undirected or penetrated by the state, matter.

Partly the stress is defensive and reminiscent of Marx: without independent social connection, citizens are playthings of those more powerful.

Partly it is positive: cooperative, self-chosen activities and associations are alleged to be associated with better government and better societies.[77]

Partisans of civil society draw attention to, and advocate, horizontal links among citizens and bottom-up connections from citizens to governments, rather than top-down, vertical links from governments to citizens. They point to salutary consequences of joining, of voluntary associations, of informal institutions, of cooperation, trust, 'social capital', of activities that build up from society rather than trickle down from governments, and of organisations involved in such activities. These are good things to stress. They do not occur in sacks of potatoes.

10.2.2.2 Plural

However, a society distinct from the state, and capable of mobilisation against it, is not enough for it to be civil. For there are at least two kinds: unitary and plural. For obvious and good reasons, societies engaged in war or its like stress unity. The *Solidarity* experience demonstrated with unprecedented drama, passion, and eloquence the incompatibility between despotism and independent social activity. Something had to give. And so, in 1989 despotism did, to what appeared to be an unprecedentedly unified society.

But while this could plausibly (though not completely accurately, even in Poland, and less elsewhere) be portrayed as a triumph of 'society against the state', it was not obviously a triumph of *civil* society.[78] For such a society did not yet exist. *Solidarity* had sought an organic unity of 'us' (*społeczeństwo*, society) against a demonised (and at times demonic) 'them' (*władza*, the power, the government). The very name of the movement suggests as much. Though the leaders of *Solidarność* spoke constantly of the development of civil society, they were more Spartan than modern – more ethical (often religious) than civic – in their conception of it. The movement sparked and came to embody a sense of national and social unity unparalleled in any communist country, indeed virtually anywhere outside of wartime. It mobilised and united vast numbers of Poles who had little else in common than a national church, a traditional, organic national ideology, a common social and political predicament, and a common enemy. The consequences of this movement were profound, but not especially civil. To fight *for* society may well be more attractive than to argue *within* society, but it is quite a different idea.

It is different in two crucial respects. First of all, society was conceived of as a united body, which is unlikely to be a long-standing prospect and threatens central constituents of civil society as traditionally understood:

civil liberty, pluralism, and tolerance. Secondly, it is conceived not just as a body but as a *movement* focused on common goals, goals which depend on having a common opponent. As a result, while it might have been a *prerequisite* for the achievement of civil society in the circumstances of communist Poland, as a *model* of such a society, which it was so often taken to be, it was seriously lacking.

Moreover, when 'they' collapsed, so did the unity of 'us' and it became time to think afresh about both. With victory rapidly came disintegration, the dissolution of solidarity, and another lesson about civil society. As Poland went on to discover but the solidary ethos of *Solidarity* was not the place to learn, a civil society in 'normal' circumstances is not just a society independent of the state but a 'society of societies' (also distinct from the state). It comprises multitudes of independent and semi-independent actors and associations, with their own various ends, going about their individual or freely chosen cooperative affairs, able to choose to associate and participate (or not) in an independent public realm. A central feature of such a society is the existence of a plurality of different, often competing, often self-chosen, *intermediate associations* and social institutions,[79] with different interests, aims, and membership. For a civil society is a plural society, not a monolith. Indeed the very idea of one integrated whole society, thinking the same thoughts, valuing the same things, is a distinctly uncivil idea, heroic and inspiring as it more than once turned out to be.

Alexis de Tocqueville and before him, though without the term, Montesquieu, both emphasised the importance, as brakes on despotism, of a multiplicity of groups that are independent of state power and intermediate between the state and private and intimate groups. A society is civil to the extent that it contains numerous self-chosen forms of association, and it is those groups rather than the society as a whole that are properly identified as the civil elements in society.

In the most popular and influential recent writing on civil society, these themes are often repeated. The point, made in a multitude of ways,[80] though rarely so simply, is that plural entities, with non-governmental, social, connections, matter. Apart from top-down, vertical links from governments to citizens, contemporary partisans of civil society draw attention to, and advocate, horizontal links among citizens themselves and bottom-up connections from citizens to governments. They point to salutary consequences of joining, of voluntary associations, of informal institutions, of cooperation, trust, 'social capital', of activities that build up from society rather than trickle down from governments.

This pluralist conception of civil society is ancestor to all those contemporary activities which focus on non-governmental organisations (NGOs) as indicia of civil society. It contains truths, but still it is not enough. All the more when, as recently and unfortunately, this pluralist strand of thinking has been reduced simply to designate a particular subcategory of organisations within society at large: NGOs, or 'not-for-profits'. Indeed this understanding of civil society is so prevalent that many who speak of it have in mind only how much that goes on can be categorised as the business of the 'non-governmental sector'. Some lay stress on what governments cannot do, some on what citizens can. Either way, attention is directed to social networks and socially generated initiatives, most commonly by contrast to projects initiated by government. For those newly struck by the 'significance of the social', civil society is simply a contrast term to point to what is not governmental but social. Like an appendix or fifth wheel, it is hard to know what the adjective is there for. This might be what led to the lament by the Hungarian former anti-communist dissident Ferenc Miszlivetz: 'what we dreamed of was civil society. What we got were NGOs.' One senses he hoped for more.

The existence of social groupings separate from the state is undeniably preferable to their totalitarian suppression and it is a *condition* for a society to be civil. It is necessary both to allow scope and freedom for individual choice and to curb, by dispersal, the resources and power available to would-be despots and other uncivil powers. But it is not obvious that groups independent of government will necessarily have all the charms claimed for them, nor that support based on independence of government is even the best-targeted approach to supporting civil society. A society abounding with NGOs might well be one with feuding mafia groups or warlords and their clients fighting with each other. Within the plurality of groups, individuals might be trapped with no exit short of treason, no mode of recognition of or by outsiders except as enemies. This can even happen when the groups are not mafiosi or warlords but altogether respectable, with honourable names like Montague and Capulet. The result might be a large 'civil society sector' but not much civility. If the claim is that the proliferation of such groups of itself has salutary effects, it has to be made out. It does not follow from their mere existence.

In this context, civility in a society cannot simply be inferred from the number of groups, or number of people joining groups, in a society. That is all the more clear in the light of Sheri Berman's researches into Weimar Germany, which reveal widespread associational life which, she argues, far from encouraging democracy 'served to fragment rather than unite German society'[81] and were hospitable breeding and recruiting grounds for Nazism. Similarly Dylan Riley argues that fascism more broadly had 'civic foundations' in active social organisations.[82] These are salutary cautions. Berman is quite justified in turning the understanding of civil society held by many of its contemporary proponents against them. But something has been lost when the growth of Nazi-producing groups is taken as evidence of '[t]he vigor of German civil society'.[83] What in particular is lost is any attention to the *texture* or *quality* of social relationships.

For making clear what is lost when horizontal linkages among citizens are suppressed, then, we have to thank anti-communist dissidents. But such linkages can exist and exhibit many dreadful qualities.

10.2.2.3 Civil

Adjectives matter. The modern career of the concept linking 'civil' to 'society' began when Scottish Enlightenment thinkers used it to characterise distinctive aspects of emerging modern societies. It was taken up by Hegel and Marx for similar purposes, each stressing different elements. The German of Hegel – *bürgerliche Gesellschaft* – is in part, and as interpreted by Marx centrally, economic – a society of *Bürgers, bourgeois*. When the Poles revived it, their rendition – *citizens'* society – was primarily and explicitly political.

The English adjective they were appropriating speaks, among other things, to something else than politics and economics: a particular character and temper of social relationships – civility – which is much more than mere etiquette.[84] It has to do with what Hobbes called 'manners': not what he distinguished as '*decency of behaviour … the small morals*', 'how one man should salute another, or how a man should wash his mouth, or pick his teeth before company', but rather 'those qualities of mankind, that concern their living together in peace and unity'.[85] It sought particularly to capture characteristic *textures, scope, and boundaries* of social relationships among strangers, more generally non-intimates, which were becoming more necessary and routine in modern societies. A civil society on this interpretation is one in which routine relations among citizens are both not dominated by the state and also actually, and typically expected to be, routinely civil, rather than hostile, warlike, full of mutual contempt, and/or worse.

A special charm claimed for societies in which civility is widespread is that instead of suspicion, hostility, hatred, or simple fear, routine non-predatory social relations can occur that neither depend upon love or deep connection nor – as is common in uncivil conditions – are fractured by their absence. Cool, civil connections are not the only ones that exist, nor should they be, but in the public realm the possibility of such connections is key. People have familial, ethnic, religious, and linguistic attachments that often matter to them greatly and that differ; but they do not kill for them. Nor is it a realistic expectation that they might.

Compared with love and hatred which are both in their different ways exclusive emotions, civility is moderately inclusive, that is both moderate and inclusive. Civil relations among non-intimates or strangers are not all-or-nothing encounters. They are something but not everything. This is a good way to do business, if not to raise a family or fight a crusade. It is also a *restrained* way. Well tempered, one might call it. Civility in this sense is cooler certainly than love – if all you can say of lovers is that they behave civilly to each other you know the relationship is on the rocks. In its place, however, civility is precious, for it is cooler (and calmer) than hatred as well.

Families and intimate relationships do not disappear with modernity and are not subverted by civility, but they are not all that exists and they are not *distinctive* of what exists. What, among other things, distinguishes a modern civil society in good shape from others is that it includes and comes to depend upon relationships of a novel and special sort: relationships among people whose detailed knowledge of each other is and must remain limited but are not full of suspicion or fear as a result.

Successful modern civil societies are typically large. They involve the routine interaction and interdependence of millions. They thus depend upon the ability of many people to deal easily and securely with many people, whether or not they are well known to each other. For such relationships to be routinely possible, as Durkheim stressed, there need to be distinctive social bonds among individuals. One summary label for the distinctive character of such relationships is civility. Civil society breaks down where civil relations among non-intimates and strangers are impossible.

10.2.2.4 Tolerant

Civility enables relations between non-intimates to proceed, then, notwithstanding the absence of deep connections. The opposite of my friend is not necessarily my enemy but my acquaintance. I can do business with her, and I do not necessarily betray anyone by doing so. In politics, too, civility is 'a mode of political action which postulates that antagonists are also members of the same society, that they participate in the same collective self-consciousness'.[86] A civil society is, then, a shared society, though it may not in any strong sense be a community.

A perennial question in every society is: what to do about difference? Indeed, as John Hall remarks, 'living with difference is as important to the notion of civil society as is the control of despotism'.[87] Civil societies depend upon a large measure of tolerant pluralism. In civil societies differences are tolerated, different organisations and institutions develop to cater for them, and participation in certain institutions is compatible with participation in certain others. In uncivil ones, the idea that citizens should at once belong to a common society and at the same time maintain a variety of different loyalties, affections, interests, associations, and organisations is unavailable or under constant, often dangerous, threat.

10.2.2.5 The Virtue of Civility

Lest this all sound too sweet and uplifting, we should reflect on what is at stake. If everyone naturally was given to trust and respect everyone else, civil society would be less of an achievement than it is. But give some thought to Roger Williams, the somewhat obscure seventeenth-century Puritan evangelist and fanatic, pupil and secretary of Sir Edward Coke, friend of Milton, founder and governor of the colony of Rhode Island, and tireless and indomitable advocate of 'meer civility' as a necessary *vinculum societatis* (bond of society) in the face of multiple differences.

Unlike those few recent political theorists who have heard of him, prominent among them Martha Nussbaum,[88] who interpret him as an inspiring prophet of civility as a concomitant of mutual respect, the political theorist Teresa Bejan has recently pointed out that Williams was nothing of the kind.[89] It was lack of respect for beliefs other than his own that drove him and the problem that he sought to deal with.

The Puritan zealot appeared to dislike, to the point of disgust, the views of anyone who did not share his beliefs, and in Rhode Island, as well as in England, there were a lot of them. He expected he would not be alone in that sentiment. So rather than decree the implausible, in the variegated Rhode Island community he founded and governed, he decreed extraordinary and unprecedented freedom of religious belief, speech, and observance in the hope that the 'vinculum' 'might hold in the face of protracted fundamental disagreement and discord';[90] 'the virtue of civility in a tolerant society rested on the way in which the rules of respectful behaviour could be maintained no matter what one thought about others, their culture or their fundamental and sacred beliefs'.[91]

Bejan argues that Williams had recognised a truth for which there is more than enough evidence: that many of the harshest problems of social life, perhaps inexorable problems, come simply from the difficulties people have in living peacefully with others whose views, or whose religion, or whose nationality, they do not share. Of course, we can be directed to like them, but often that doesn't work. What to do? As Bejan interprets him, Williams makes this fundamental question central in a way many later enthusiasts for civility, who see it as part of a rosy, happy package, evade:

> [W]hen it comes to theorizing civility ... aspirations are not simply unrealistic; they are entirely inapposite. Civility emerges as an essential virtue in tolerant societies in response to a practical problem, not a theoretical one. In trying to make sense of others' different opinions, human beings conclude not that these differences are reasonable by-products of the burdens of judgment but that their opponents are bigoted, ignorant, malicious, even insane. We might hope – and strive – to do otherwise. But rather than conflating this aspiration with civility, political theorists must recognise the latter as the virtue called upon to fill the breach when reality fails to meet our expectations.[92]

The ambition here is not to outlaw conflicts or differences. Indeed civil society presupposes their existence. Some say it thrives on them. But it seeks to temper them. If it does so, something valuable has been achieved. It doesn't often come naturally. And it can go.

At present in a number of countries around the world, there are concerted and successful efforts to spurn civility and instead encourage Schmittian polarisation of society between friends and enemies, the true 'sovereign' (those who voted for the government), on the one hand, and 'elites', 'corporations', 'networks', 'traitors', on the other. No space in between, no complex differences of view or problems to deal with, no civil regard for those with whom one disagrees, but just hostilities, malignant versus pure motives, and only one winner to be left standing. And this is all before what can be said about refugees, immigrants, or George Soros.

Accompanying all this deliberate incivility and facilitated by it, as we have seen, are systematic and cumulative assaults on the integrity of major institutions that might support civility and civil society, among independent agencies of state such as courts, and NGOs, the media, and so on. Structures and institutions which used to support civil societies that appeared very successful now seem – variably – ineffectual against the growth of incivility on a grand scale. And they are under attack. This threatens civil societies, encourages polarised communities, and bodes ill for the tempering of power.

10.2.3 Polarised Communities

Tempered relationships are not to everyone's taste. In many places, today and always, societies are not interwoven by routinely civil exchanges and interchanges among citizens but by wary, hostile, and arbitrary manoeuvres, full of tension, fear, hatred, and contempt, frequently backed with authoritative encouragement and blessing.

A common source of hostility is social and cultural polarisation, whether based on inherited ancient (or purportedly ancient) ethnic, national, territorial, linguistic, or religious loyalties, differences and enmities, or contemporary disparities among groups, among them economic, regional, or educational. These divisions are frequently subject to political manipulation, exacerbation, and at times invention. Such divisions lead to bonds and to cleavages very different from civil ones. They tend to be intense, particularistic, exclusive, and intemperate. They represent 'not only different interests but, often ... different "metaphysical universes"'.[93]

In communities where such identifications and differences are intense and socially endorsed, civility in relations with outsiders is considered a vice of the weak, not a virtue of the strong. Commonly this is ideologised as natural and proper. When that is so, temperance is not a remedy in good odour; it is a bug not a feature. Those with a good or winning hand are commonly urged to strike rather than shake with it. Opponents without one's group, however defined, are enemies; those within are traitors.

Of course, such communities differ profoundly in detail. Indeed that is part of their stories. Each group considers its own legends, heroes, triumphs, injuries, and martyrs unique, as do their opponents. However, it is notable how similar the *structures* of polarised societies, divided between Us and Them, are. On the one hand, one's own nation, religion, class is quite remarkable and exceptional – indeed, uniquely so – sometimes in its achievements, at others in its victimisation, often both. All one need do is fill in the name, and the details of heroic exploits or fiendish victimisation, to find out which particular grouping we're talking about at the moment. One also needs, of course, to know the identities of the particular pollutant peoples who threaten to dilute 'our' purity. These differ enormously, though there are some useful ancient and multipurpose candidates in different parts of the world – Jews in Europe, Muslims in parts of South Asia, Chinese in other parts, and indigenes wherever they have been conquered. Skin colour is commonly a useful marker.

Polarised communities have been with us forever. In recent decades, however, forms of polarisation have been revived, with a new cast of heroes and villains. Some of the old suspects recur, but as well political movements of a decidedly 'anti-establishment' character have taken many countries by storm and many observers by surprise. Unlike some older polarities, they do not claim to represent part of the nation but the whole of it properly understood. In particular, they represent the true 'People' of the country, which, alas, also contains many other people. Of course, there are many precursors of these movements, but these are novel in several ways.

Because of the unique and intense link they claim with 'the People', these movements are commonly called 'populist'. Unlike their ancestors in the United States and Russia, who applied the term (populists, *narodniki*) proudly to themselves, it is today more commonly applied to them by others, rarely as a compliment.

Across eastern and western Europe, Asia, the Middle East, the Americas, and Africa, populist movements of the sorts discussed in Chapter 8 have sprung up in formerly and formally liberal democratic polities, have challenged their existing assumptions, offices and officers, and have frequently overwhelmed them. These challenges, and these successes, were rarely predicted, particularly since they so soon followed the (also unpredicted but also, for a time, apparently successful) wave of liberal democratic and constitutional enthusiasms, proclamations, and institution-building that marked the 'transitions to democracy and the rule of law' which peaked in the 1990s. In several countries – among them what seemed to be the most successful of early post-communist 'transitional' states, such as Hungary and Poland – such parties have won elections several times.

Again, each example is itself, but contemporary populist forms of polarisation have many structural features in common. On the one hand are 'the People' whose traditional values have been trashed, jobs taken, nation undermined, future derailed. The main overarching trait of true People seems to be that they are *authentic, uncontaminated* but exploited 'sons of the soil' (daughters too, so long as they come in second place to sons, bear children, and have no fluid or binary gender proclivities or attachments).

Of course, ordinary standard-issue democrats also claim to represent the people. However, populists' relationship to their *demos* is typically distinctive and selective: not all people, not even all citizens or electors, qualify, just followers and similars. As the political theorist Nadia Urbinati nicely observes: 'Populism may be identified with a process of *extraction* of the "true people" from the empirical people.'[94]

Thus, when his party was defeated in the 2002 Hungarian elections, the later Prime Minister Viktor Orbán, claiming to represent 'the civic Hungary' against cosmopolitan elites, explained in an open-air rally after the election:

> The civic Hungary is not the one smaller or bigger part of this country. The civic Hungary is the whole. ... It may be that our parties and our representatives are in opposition in the National Assembly, but we who are here on the square will not and also cannot be in opposition, because the homeland cannot be in opposition.[95]

If part of the people manages to form the whole of the true People, what about the others, the non-People people? These are inferior because they differ politically, ethnically, religiously, educationally, genderly, regionally, or in some other disdained way, and of course if they oppose the People's vessels. As Jarosław Kaczyński characterised detractors who criticised the Polish government abroad:

> In Poland, there is a horrible tradition of national treason, a habit of informing on Poland to foreign bodies ... And that's what it is. As if it's in their genes, in the genes of Poles of the worst sort. And that worst sort is at the moment extraordinarily active because it feels threatened ... scared that times are changing and there will come a time, as there should, when a *different* type of person, that is to say people with higher motivations, patriotic motivations will be raised to the top and that will affect every branch of life.[96]

A key motif of modern populist regimes is that opponents are not merely people who disagree about issues, as is to be expected in a democracy and a civil society, as over time opinions change and power flows one way and then another. They are *enemies* who must be vanquished, traitors who must be exposed. Not killed or gaoled for the most part, which is so far a salutary distinction between the modern wave of populists and many of their bloody predecessors (and contemporaries), but hounded, abused, harassed, and excluded, all of these often by legal means.

A pivotal category among the non-'People' people are *elites*. They are not hard to identify. They are to be found in prominent political and economic positions; they live in cities, particularly capital and large ones; they typically have been to universities – many are 'experts' or listen to experts; they like to travel; and they know too many languages. They are at home everywhere but at home, where instead they promote alien and degenerate ways of living, loving, and thinking. They tend to be vaccinated.

Among their other and many vices, these elites are alleged to coagulate into 'castes' that dominate politics, law, and the economy. They run the institutions and call the shots, furthering their own interests, and the interests of those with a stake in the existing system, over the interests of the People.

None of this is a recipe for civil society or tempered power, at least in relation to non-true People. That follows partly from the denigratory nature of populist attitudes themselves, which might well, as is often alleged,[97] be generated from below, as a result of social, economic, educational, regional, and/or cultural differences, inequalities, and dissatisfactions. However, these tectonic layers do not just quake and generate deep fissures and dislocations on their own. They have promoters, shapers, and *leaders*.[98] And populist leaders are hostile to temperance, at least in relation to the powers they seek to wield. Which takes us to politics.

10.3 Polities

As well as supporting and sustaining cultural and social frameworks, and however counter-intuitive to many of its proponents, civil society depends upon a well-functioning state, that is, a state that is in good shape, one whose power is well tempered. More counter-intuitive still, the state must be strong. Moderated, disciplined, limited, channelled in the exercise of its power, not necessarily big but strong.

This is so, notwithstanding that the dissident rhetoric of 'anti-political politics' sought relentlessly to pit 'civil society against the state', for reasons that are obvious but were in part misleading. All the more so in the versions that came to be supported by those western libertarians drawn to the Thoreauian nonsense that 'that government is best which governs least' and to his extension – truly nonsense on stilts – that 'that government is best which governs not at all'.[99]

In the counter-position of state and civil society there is a deep truth and a deep falsehood. The truth is that civil society only exists when there is room for clear distinctions between state and civil society. As the Polish philosopher Leszek Kołakowski has argued, it is precisely the annihilation of this distinction which defines totalitarianism.[100] The contrast on which *Solidarność* insisted – between a society independent of the state and one which is chewed and swallowed up by it – was absolutely central to the anti-communist revival of 'civil society', and rightly so. More generally, the distinction between civil society and the state was crucial not only to anti-communist dissidents but also to civil society discourse at least since the eighteenth century.

However, the transformation of legitimate distinctions and differences of emphasis into false dichotomies is unfortunate. For the distinction between civil society and the state can be understood in two very different ways: on the one hand, as one between hostile forces; on the other hand, as one between parts of an organism – bone and muscle, say. When a civil society is weak and/or the state is seeking to crush it, the distinction is of the first sort; when the civil society is in good shape, and the state provides indispensable infrastructure for it, the second sense applies.

For very obvious reasons, *Solidarity* told us far more about the first sense than the second. The belief that civil society and the state are naturally pitted against each other, in a zero-sum encounter which one side can win only at the other's expense, is eminently understandable and largely justified in the circumstances of revolutionary opposition, but not everywhere and not ideally. It tells us more about what the relationships between states and civil societies should not be than what they should. For just as societies are of many kinds, so are states. And these differences are not unrelated.

10.3.1 Despotisms

The French intellectual historian Blandine Kriegel has eloquently insisted that 'the state' is a remarkably heterogeneous category.[101] Within that category, there are many variants. In place of the in principle anti-political and anti-state bias of many civil society activists, then, we need qualitative distinctions: what kinds of governmental activities, undertaken in what kinds of ways, by what kinds of states, are helpful, indeed essential, for their power to be reliably tempered and for them to undergird the routine civility of social practices? What sorts of competences is it important to encourage among officials of state, not merely what are the ways in which these officials might be constrained? These are not easy questions to answer, and I do not have all the answers, but they are important because we know that some sorts of governments and activities can be indispensable and others ruinous for social civility and the tempering of power.

The social historian Michael Mann has made a suggestive distinction between what he calls despotic power – 'the range of actions which the elite is empowered to undertake without routine, institutionalized negotiations with civil society' – and infrastructural power – 'the capacity of the state to actually penetrate society, and to implement logistically political decisions throughout the realm'.[102] For the release and development of social and economic energies, he and several of his colleagues argue, as well as for political decency and social civility, it is infrastructural power that is crucial. Traditional despotic states combined arbitrariness and lack of political or legal limits with chronic incapacity to mobilise social energies and make use of social potential. As Mann's colleague John Hall puts it, they sat like capstones atop the societies they dominate; they did not penetrate organically and effectively into the social structure. They dominated from above but did little to contribute from within.[103] Most modern dictatorships do the same.

The moral of this historically anchored line of argument is that 'strong states are not only those which are able to control the population within their boundaries and thus extract the necessary material and human resources. They are also those which rely least on arbitrary and unstable forms of control such as terror or physical force.'[104] They provide predictable, reliable frameworks of laws and trustworthy undertakings. They cooperate with major social forces in ways on which both sides can rely. They can penetrate the society without fraud and force and extract resources from it without coercion. Rather than exercise power *over* society, strong but limited states exercise it *through* society.[105] On this view, the infrastructural role of states is indispensable for the existence of strong modern societies. Strong societies, in turn, can provide the economic base for strong states. So, power restrained is power, in crucial infrastructural senses, strengthened.

This, I imagine, is only the beginning of the sorts of qualitative distinctions which might bear on our subject. What seemed true – even obvious – at the end of history is more uncertain, certainly more contested, today. Perhaps, as I worried in Chapter 6, China's combination of overwhelming dictatorship with selective quasi-legality and unprecedented, digitally empowered surveillance will alter the picture, though there are few other examples and the price is very high. For the moment, I hang on to the thought that a state whose power is effectively tempered is likely to be more effective and its citizens more productive than its opposite and also, not coincidentally, altogether nicer to live with.

If we ask what the political conditions of tempered power are, it is not much of a surprise to learn that dictatorial, despotic, tyrannous (and other pejoratively qualified) political orders are rarely listed among them. We have seen enough examples in this book alone, and it makes sense. If tempering power depends on power checking power 'in the arrangement of things', as Montesquieu insisted, then these polities are unlikely to be much into that. Such 'arrangements' defy their logic.

10.3.2 Democracies

Democracies, many have believed, are different. Certainly, in the excitement of the 'third wave'[106] of twentieth-century democratisation it was common to join democracy and the rule of law as two of three virtuous circles that were inexorably linked. Country after country was exhorted to welcome 'democracy, human rights and the rule of law',[107] the assumption apparently being that they all bring each other joy, or at least bring *us* joy and do each other no harm. Certainly on the crest of the third democratic wave there were few voices speaking against combining democracy and the rule of law.

And there is something in it. The German social philosopher Jürgen Habermas argues for an *internal* normative connection and also a practical empirical one between public rights anchored in popular sovereignty and democracy and private rights protected by the rule of law. On the one hand, in the absence of pre-modern traditional moral sources of legitimation, Habermas argues that today we must answer

> the legitimation question by referring, on the one hand, to the principle of *popular sovereignty* and, on the other, to the *rule of law* as guaranteed by human rights. The principle of popular sovereignty is expressed in rights of communication and participation that secure the public autonomy of citizens; the rule of law is expressed in those classical basic rights that guarantee the private autonomy of members of society.[108]

There is an insightful practical observation that undergirds the argument:

> [P]rivate and public autonomy mutually presuppose each other in such a way that neither human rights nor popular sovereignty can claim primacy over its counterpart.
>
> This expresses the intuition that, on the one hand, citizens can make adequate use of their public autonomy only if, on the basis of their equally protected private autonomy, they are sufficiently independent; but that, on the other hand, they can arrive at a consensual regulation of their private autonomy only if they make adequate use of their political autonomy as enfranchised citizens.[109]

If the philosophical connection for which Habermas argues might stand or fall with the distinctive argumentation of his 'discourse theory' in which it is embedded, the practical link can be appreciated from many points of view. Thus, Stephen Holmes has long argued that democracy is enabled by the rule of law, which in turn is supported by democracy. Thus, if the people are to be effectively engaged in rule, and not merely permitted to cast a vote every now and then for someone they don't know for reasons they don't understand, that will involve more than provision of polling booths. For citizens to be informed, to participate politically, to choose intelligently, to *engage* in political choice and maybe life, a lot is required. As Holmes explains: 'The protection of private rights provides a crucial precondition for "positive liberty" in both senses. If the police can smash down doors at midnight and drag away families to unknown dungeons or graves, a citizen's chances for "personal fulfilment" will be drastically curtailed, as will his desire to participate actively in public life.'[110]

On the other hand, democracy can be a major potential source of check on arbitrary power. Maravall gets the point, though he somewhat simplifies it: 'citizens have two instruments to protect them: first, to throw the rulers out of office at election time; second, to enforce, through institutions, legal limits to the political discretion of incumbents between elections. The first protection is provided by democracy; the second, by the rule of law.'[111]

Indeed, not merely is it the case that democracy can support the ideal of the rule of law; on many views that, and not personal fulfilment or even political participation as a good in itself, is the primary good it offers. This is a central argument of Philip Pettit's republicanism. Election of governments is one function we expect from the *demos*, but it is not the only, nor necessarily the most important one: *contestation* is equally so.[112] The first goal of political arrangements, on this reading, is non-domination. For that to be freely available and readily accessed, the sway of arbitrary power is its perennial, indeed conceptual, antithesis. To be free *is* to be without subjection to arbitrary power.[113] They cannot live together. However, law is often not enough; the availability of popular contestation of public decision-making is crucial. So, in so far as they approach their goals or ideals, democracy and rule of law are helpmates not enemies. They are both key modes of tempering power.

Indeed, particularly after the 'third wave' it was often said you can't have one without the other.[114] But we have. Thus, Benjamin Constant, French liberal of the French revolutionary and Napoleonic eras, already delivered an early and profound reflection on modernity and freedom, his lecture on 'the liberty of ancients compared with that of moderns',[115] in 1819. He argued that the form of democracy practised by 'the ancients' – the Greek city states, and especially Sparta – was democracy *pur sang* but lacked and had no appreciation of constraints on the power of the *demos*, which was necessary to ensure 'the liberty of the moderns'. Indeed it could not have coexisted in pure form with such constraints, to which few of the ancient Greeks in any case gave any thought; they were no part of the ancient ideal. As one modern scholar reads and reiterates Constant's argument, '[i]n Ancient Athens, the people, the Demos, *hoi polloi*, were politically dominant and nothing was there to restrain them. There was no Constitution, laws could be annulled or nullified by a temporary majority, there were no checks and balances. Athens was an illiberal democracy.'[116] Not the last.[117]

Conversely, those eighteenth-century 'foreign observers of English manners', whom Dicey proudly quoted as finding England to be 'a country governed, as is scarcely any other part of Europe, under the rule of law',[118] were not praising it as a democracy, which it was not at all in the eighteenth century, and was only becoming in the nineteenth, and which few of them would have thought praiseworthy. But they had a point. In England, over centuries, power was less arbitrarily wielded and law more of a constraint on rule than in, say, France then,[119] or Russia then or now, and than in many other states in the world. The English had long considered that a public ideal.[120] There were numerous countervailing forces that tempered power in England, and that were praised for doing so, but the rule of the people was not until relatively recently among them. And, *pace* Dicey, England was not unique in having traditions, institutions, social arrangements, and practices that effectively limited arbitrary power in the pre-modern and pre-democratic era, which was long and full of more or less ruly autocracies. Think late eighteenth- and nineteenth-century Prussia with Frederick the Great's Constitution declaring him 'the first servant of the state', or the Austro-Hungarian empire – not democracies, but not tyrannies either. After democracy's ancient rise and demise, however, it took a much longer time for it to re-emerge and to be praised than did hostility to arbitrary power.

Even where democracy and the rule of law coexist, moreover, the marriage has not always been easy. Many thinkers have argued that tensions between democracy and the rule of law are conceptually, or in principle, or in fact, hardwired. Alexis de Tocqueville and John Stuart Mill worried about the 'tyranny of the majority' in democracies, and some more recent partisans of the rule of law warned of 'elective dictatorship',[121] in circumstances where parliaments are commonly dominated by governments who will stop at little to curry favour with electors. Such partisans of the rule of law seek to bolster what they see as the essential dyke-like functions of unelected judges, bills of rights, commissions of inquiry often headed by judges and staffed by experts, and other 'independent' institutions to stem the surging tides of democratic and populist demands that wash against them.

These controversies continue, and they have come to be joined and are likely to be accelerated by unpredicted developments in the democratic world. When the end of history had just begun, it appeared that contemporary liberal democratic political orders had come to manage to combine both democracy and the rule of law. Perhaps cultural and social supports were uncertain in new democracies, such as post-communist ones, though even there, there was a lot of confidence about. Many were confident that such gaps could be filled with the right institutional architecture, transported from 'old' democracies such as the United States and Britain and thick on the ground in western Europe and elsewhere.

And those old democracies were thought for a moment to be on clover. Not only were they blessed with the extensive constitutional instrumentarium of elections, constitutions, parliament, and courts but they also had dense thickets of unwritten rules of the game, embedded in cultural norms, patterns, and precedents of accepted and acceptable norms of how officials, elected and appointed, should behave. After all, as Levitsky and Ziblatt observe, 'gatekeeping institutions go back to the founding of the American republic'.[122] Today, however, the gates are swinging about, and many of the keepers have left or lost their jobs. And not only in America.

At the end of the twentieth century, Fareed Zakaria coined the term 'illiberal democracy', a mutation that he feared was growing all around us.[123] While 'for a century in the West, democracy has meant *liberal* democracy – a political system marked not only by free and fair elections, but also by the rule of law, a separation of powers, and the protection of basic liberties',[124] this was decreasingly the case. Instead, '[t]oday the two strands of liberal democracy, interwoven in the Western political fabric, are coming apart in the rest of the world. Democracy is flourishing; constitutional liberalism is not.'[125] As a result, though 'we live in a democratic age',[126] this is not necessarily something to boast about: 'The tendency for a democratic government to believe it has absolute sovereignty (i.e. power) can result in the centralization of authority, often by extra-constitutional means and with grim results.'[127] If Zakaria's observation was controversial in 1997, it had become less so thirty years later.

10.3.3 Populisms

The 'No Kings' protest movement in the United States slightly misnames its target.[128] Long-established monarchies were often stabilised and their powers tempered by old traditions, customs, aristocratic powers, regional and religious authorities, and other sources of power that could check power. In any event, kings are a wilting force in the modern world, most prominently found as figureheads, with little power and wayward families. Donald Trump, by contrast, knows no tradition. He is a charismatic leader, for whom whatever 'has been written' has no bearing on what 'I say unto you'.[129] He might find he cannot do whatever he wants, but not for want of trying nor simply because it is not in keeping with traditional expectations of the position he fills. Perhaps the slogan should be 'No Democrators', though it doesn't roll off the tongue.

It does, however, point to something new. As we have seen, twenty-first-century populist regimes in many countries, which only a short time before had seemed to be paragons of democracy and rule of law, came to boast of their democratic credentials while busily and often effectively subverting constraints on the power of 'the sovereign people', or more accurately their elected representatives, themselves. Courting of the sovereign and winning support through elections is popular among twenty-first-century populists. Legal (and other) constraints on their ability to wield arbitrary power are, by contrast, anathema to them: any such institutionalised intermediation would, it is often said, put unelected legal elites, 'castes of jurists', typically in service of themselves and also monied or otherwise sullied elites, in the way of 'the will of the people'. And what democrat could support that? In many so-called democracies, new and old, this institutional, cultural, and normative architecture of temperance seems to be collapsing or in many eroding dramatically.

Perhaps 'collapsing' is the wrong word. The institutions remain; they just seem unable, and their occupants unwilling, to do what they were set up to do. 'Erosion' is not perfect either. Whatever the intrinsic weaknesses and failings of existing sources of temperance, and they are likely to be many, not yet fully understood, their fate in the modern world is not likely to be determined by natural processes of erosion alone. Maybe a phrase sometimes used – hollowing out – serves best to remind us that both endogenous and exogenous processes are at work.

Often modern illiberal populists are alleged to be anti-institutional, and they are, but with a twist: they are not anarchists. On the contrary, their hostility to institutions is balanced, as it were. As we saw in Chapter 8, on the one hand some institutions, particularly those that watch out for untempered power, might need to be shut down, and if they are not taken down they at least need to be shaken up – their infected cadres purged and replaced, activities disassembled and reassembled. On the other hand, many need only to be thoroughly purged, cleansed, and then reprogrammed. Come victory (not through revolution, to repeat, but election), those institutions might survive populist transformation if they can be reshaped and repurposed, but they are on notice that they are not to get in the way. Anyway, many of their newly appointed and under-qualified incumbents can be relied upon to have no incentive to get in the way.

It is common in contemporary discussions of these trends to speak of democratic or constitutional or rule of law 'backsliding'.[130] It is not hard to see why. The bracketed adjectives capture both the fact that what had seemed to be fundamental, and in many countries stable, conditions of democracy (e.g. free elections) or constitutionalism (a binding legal frame, often with rights-guaranteeing provisions) and rule of law (courts, regular laws, legal argument) are being hollowed out, and that is often being accomplished by measures originally devised, and until recently thought, to serve them. The noun suggests a process of sliding back to something before it started. The adjectives are fine with me; the noun – both its elements – less so.

First of all, backsliding might simply suggest regression in these domains, which certainly has occurred. However, to the extent that the word is understood to suggest reversion to something that existed before, it misleads. What we are witnessing in many parts of the world is novel in many respects, in some perhaps unprecedented. What emerges from this process might not be recognisable to anyone who lived before it. At the (real) risk of hyperbole, but not without (also real) apprehension, the question can re-emerge:

> what rough beast, its hour come round at last,
> Slouches towards Bethlehem to be born?[131]

Secondly and much more important, the metaphor of 'sliding' fails to capture the active, energetic, relentless *agency* involved. We speak of 'backsliding', 'decay', 'erosion', 'decline'; all of which might well apply to internally driven, perhaps organic, regression. I'm not as young as I used to be; some might say I'm 'decaying', 'declining', maybe even 'backsliding'. I don't like to hear that but, no worries, my hearing is not what it used to be either. But everyone loves me, so my decay is my own affair, not down to others. But living as we do at the end of the end of history we can see that not everyone loves the ideal of the rule of law, even if they maintain an instrumental toleration for many instruments that have been supposed to serve it. It has real enemies, in many places resolute and energetic in pursuit of subversive activities and ends, that these organic and solipsistic metaphors fail to capture. We need a language that can capture and a practice that can respond to active and hostile subversion and indeed sabotage. Even if we stick with 'back', 'lash' seems a more apt coupling than 'sliding'.

Many sorts of malaise are alleged to afflict modern liberal democracies, beset by pains of globalisation, cultural disorientation and dissatisfaction, loss of sense of place and confidence, inept political performance, and many other things. There is plenty of evidence that such sources of dissatisfaction exist,[132] and it is at least plausible that they have contributed to the shifting and unstable soil on which democratic politics now wobbles. That must be acknowledged. Causes of social dissatisfaction can be many, deep, and some at least can be laid at the door of existing systems and elites.

However, the causal story explaining the present challenges to the rule of law ideal in contemporary democracies in terms of surges of dissatisfaction from below is not self-evident, nor is it sufficient to explain modern tendencies.[133] Of course, subverters must have supporters, particularly when they are elected in free (but commonly not fair) ballots, but the role of fomenters and exploiters of dissatisfaction, the leaders of the movements which sow distemper, should never be underplayed. They might be responding to real dissatisfactions, but they are not *just* responding. Moreover, and perhaps more sinister, apart from how they gain power where they do, there is a separate and even more fundamental issue: to explain what, once in power, they *do* with that success. Populist leaders, elected by dissatisfied electors, often unmoor their subsequent activities from whatever it was that explained their election. And what they then do has consequences of its own.

Often we – including their electors – do not know what populist parties will do until they have the power to do it. At times, as with the populist governments in Hungary (Fidesz) from 2010 and Poland (PiS) between 2015 and 2023, many of their most radical measures in power were not foreshadowed – indeed were concealed – before they were elected. But then the rules of the game could be changed.

It is plausible that there would be no Trump without many disappointments and disturbances, beyond his strange charisma, that had nothing to do with him but predisposed his voters to support him. And he was in a way candid about his intentions, though so inconsistent about which ones he would back that it was hard to know. However, it is also true that many of his fervent supporters might be surprised by what he has got up to in his second term, when he was freed from 'adults in the room'. One pervasive and, in its extent, unprecedented characteristic of this phase, despite all the vaunted institutions, written and unwritten rules, traditions and social arrangements, is his intemperate, indeed arbitrary approach to the deployment of power domestically. In the world-reaching implications of that, he stands out. But he is not alone. Not even lonely.

Contemporary populist politics are rarely temperate. They are angry, they are fomented, they are directed, they are institutionalised, and they are *led*. The Leader claims to be the People's embodiment or at least their vessel, and his (almost always so far; I can think of less than a handful of exceptions) is key. As Hugo Chávez self-effacingly explained in his 2006 closing campaign speech:

> I swear that ... when you are re-elected, because you are not really going to re-elect Chávez. In truth, you are going to re-elect yourselves, the People are going to re-elect the People. ... Chávez is nothing but an instrument of the people.[134]

This humble-brag conception of the Leader's role has implications. Courting the sovereign People and winning support through elections and referenda, not all of them spurious, is popular among modern populists. Constraints on their ability to wield arbitrary power are, by contrast, anathema to them. Any such institutionalised intermediation would put unelected legal elites – 'castes of jurists' typically in service of themselves and the monied or otherwise sullied elite – in the way of the will of the People. Liberal emasculations therefore not only block the state but deny the democratic will of the people as expressed in the decisions of its representatives. What democrat could support that?

If the leader is *the* instrument of the true People, then it is not obvious who else, what else, should have authority to get in the way of the People's person. And so, again and again, this is the trend among contemporary populists-in-power. One might focus, as lawyers typically do and I did in Chapter 8, on the undermining of legal and constitutional institutions. These ways are many, systematic, and reach from top to bottom: the legal complex, constitutional courts, ordinary courts, legislative processes, and many other components of the legal complex.

However, illiberal populists do not stop at instrumentalising legal institutions. They engage in attacks on independent media, the 'civil' service,

NGOs, local government, independent protestors, and so on. Populist intemperates are well aware that legal institutions are not all that matters in the achievement of the rule of law ideal. That is why they go after so many other institutions, actors, and activities. As Sajó and Tuovinen have pointed out:

> The attack on courts is just the tip of the iceberg … The rulers of the emerging illiberal regimes are suspicious of all autonomous social entities like education, including higher education and research. Some churches, NGOs and cultural institutions are ostracized, others are made loyal and dependent with financial sticks and carrots. Public broadcasting is controlled in the name of 'national interest first' by personnel cleansing. The private media are domesticated through takeovers and administrative means (threats of license revocation, non-renewal, special tax, carrots of government advertisement).[135]

There is one thing in common between all these targets: potentially critical independence from the Leader. And that goes for virtually every other institution that feels the lash of populist whips. Though these measures are authoritarian, they are not totalitarian; they are not interested in controlling every aspect of life. So not every sort of independence matters to them. Just those sorts that might 'check power in the arrangement of things'.

Thirty-odd years after the third wave, this is the (or, one might hope, just a) wave of our future.

10.4 Connections

According to Barry Commoner, the 'First Law of Ecology' is that everything is connected to everything else.[136] Perhaps that might be adapted as the first law of tempering power. For realisation of that ideal requires complicity among elements from many domains – legal, cultural, social, political, and others that I have no competence to discuss. These include the economy and, if we are to believe Montesquieu, climate as well. Indeed in these times of rapid climate change that might prove to be a deeply prescient insight.[137]

Commoner helps in another way too. The title of his book is *Closing the Circle*. Coincidentally, I had in mind as the title for this chapter 'circles, vicious and virtuous' but then coming across his first law and looking into his book I found another more apt metaphor. At one point, Commoner observes, 'the operation of the whole of human society … is not a simple circular process, but rather a complex, multiply branched – network'.[138] So too, that precious but only occasionally reached ideal of human society, well-tempered power. Notwithstanding the exaggerations of various determinists – economic, cultural, social, political, legal, and others – significant connections rarely point in any one direction, or simply revolve, either virtuously or viciously. They branch out in many, have multiple reciprocal interactions and effects, and are subject to deliberate and fortuitous changes.

One example might serve, and again it comes from Montesquieu. Like Tocqueville after him, Montesquieu insisted that moderation in politics depended upon the existence of independent intermediate powers, and it also depended on laws. However, neither was self-sustaining. Each required the support of the other, and other supports as well. None could stand without the others.[139] That is not always the way we think about subjects that matter to us. Just as too much discussion of law has ignored the variable extent and significance of its embedded interactions with social and political institutions, common culture, and ways of life, so conversely, altogether too little discussion of culture, democracy, and civil society mentions law at all. Montesquieu, on the other hand, insists *both* on the importance of independent social groups *and* on the legal institutionalisation of their entitlements, as intertwined and mutually reinforcing restraints on power.[140] We should heed him.

Civil society crucially depends on interpersonal trust, particularly among strangers, as it does on trust in institutions, but these are chancy without many intervening complicities between law, cultures, societies, and politics. These, in turn, if they are to contribute effectively to tempering power, need to be administered in ways that accord with that spirit. All this needs to be lubricated by facilitating cultural norms, products of all sorts of inheritance and agency, old and new. For a great deal of the work goes on in people's heads, and few are conscious how much those heads are full of cultural gifts, burdens, values, and commonplaces that have taken residence there uninvited and unannounced, but not without pervasive effects.

One limitation of the *Solidarity* interpretation of 'civil society' was that it was conceived in *opposition to* the state. Under communist rule, this was understandable and appropriate: the communist state actually *was* the enemy of an independent society. In conditions of war, social unity against an opponent is appropriate. However, it is not productive of civil association in times of peace or democracy. In times of peace, it can spawn – and in Poland arguably has drawn upon (and spawned) – traditions less of civil society than intolerant communities. Moreover, translated into democratic conditions, civil society is dependent on support and cooperation from state institutions, and the reverse is also true.[141] A strong civil society depends upon the support of a strong state and law, which perform indispensable infrastructural functions for it. In turn a strong civil society both supports such a state and limits the power of incumbents of state positions. Connections, often tensions, but not contradictions.

Again, a political order exercising reliably tempered power might well draw support from resources offered by law and institutions of particular character, interpreted and implemented in a certain spirit. But for law and those institutions to contribute effectively to tempering power, they must reach and have sway over powerful forces and actors. And for people to believe that is the way things work and rely upon it or have their imaginations of what's possible framed by it, that too takes us beyond the internal arrangements of legal things. Circles upon circles, branch after branch, sometimes vicious, sometimes virtuous, often bits of both. Hard to make one's way through it all without getting dizzy or scratched. But we must try.

11

Conclusions

> No, the struggle between the devil and God in history is not a merry spectacle. The only comfort we have comes from the simple fact that we are not passive observers or victims of this contest but participants as well, and therefore our destiny is decided on the field on which we run. To say this is trivial, and, as many trivial truths, worth repeating.
>
> Leszek Kołakowski, 'Politics and the Devil'

Over a decade ago, John Braithwaite spoke at a conference I co-organised on media, democracy and the rule of law.[1] His remarks had the apparently innocent title 'Is Separating Powers a Rule of Law Issue? The Media Case'. Perhaps not appreciating that he was about to change my life, Braithwaite pointed out that though many people speak of the rule of law as a 'good thing for its own sake', it was not that. Rather, he contended, it 'is best thought of as part of a separation of powers rather than the reverse'.

This book has not been about separation but tempering of power, and I would now want to take Braithwaite's insight in that direction. I would substitute tempering for separation not as a replacement for it but as the reason for it. Like the rule of law itself, separation of power is not a self-validating goal. We seek it as a key ingredient of tempered power, liable to make it both more effective and less open to arbitrary abuse.[2]

That substitution was not, however, even in my mind at the time. I was moved by something else in Braithwaite's talk: the switch of means and end. Why should the order matter? What difference could it make? According to Braithwaite: 'Conceiving the separation of powers as a rule of law question constrains … imagination in how to struggle for more variegated separations of powers. It tracks political thought to a barren, static constitutional jurisprudence of a tripartite separation of powers.'[3] Substitute 'tempering' for 'separation' and that is the argument of this book.

By the time of that conference, I had become convinced of the arguments in Chapters 3 and 4 of this book, that the rule of law should be approached teleologically rather than anatomically: start with end not means. However, what I thought I believed was that this was a better way to get a handle *on the rule of law*: ask what you want the rule of law for; only then can you get right what it should involve.

Braithwaite's comment nudged me to move – again slowly – in another direction. I came to ask why, if so much else beyond law is always involved in the achievement of tempered power, and such things will vary, we should assume that law (still less any specific configuration of law) should be our starting point and central focus. Its role will have to be estimated and established again and again.

Ultimately I suggest that we would think better about the rule of law by displacing it from the centrality it has come to assume by those who discuss it. If you start with conventional rule of law presumptions, you are likely to be limited in where you look for what you need, what might need fixing, and what might fix it. Yet the challenges of untempered power are too complex, too varied, and too many for the ideal to be pursued that way. There might be other ways to achieve it; a lot else will always be needed to redeem it; and there are circumstances where one wants the end but law is not much of a means to it. The role that law can and should play will have to be discovered. It cannot be assumed. What *can* be assumed is that it will vary, and so will that of other elements, with different circumstances, times, conditions, and contexts.

So, as this book attests, I have come to believe that my long interest in the rule of law was contingent not necessary, or at least derivative not primary. Tempering power is the goal; rule of law is one means, often important, never adequate on its own, and in many contexts possibly not relevant to the problem in hand. It depends.

If whatever we take to be the rule of law fails to contribute to tempering power, we should look elsewhere. In any event, since it always needs help, we need to appreciate the role of other sources and resources. We need to think of the rule of law, and value it, as a variably configured and varyingly significant part of inheritances, arrangements, institutions, and actions that together might add up to contribute to the tempering of power. We should not assume it is sufficient, or even first among others, in achieving that goal. Sometimes it is indeed first, but not always. And it always needs others. These are truisms, but it is remarkable how much rule of law talk appears to go on as though they were not even true.

The rule of law is not to be loved just for what it is, as one might love a beautiful piece of music or a dear friend, but appreciated for its promise to help us gain something valuable to us. Since it doesn't always deliver, and never does so on its own, we should avoid glorifying it as though it was an end in itself or a sufficient condition for what we want from it. It is a variably effective means to an almost always desirable end. When in good shape its contribution to that end will often be precious, but it is the end, not the means, that matters most. For the vulnerabilities to arbitrary power, that people have suffered from and wrestled with over millennia, do not change so much.

Much contemporary discussion of the rule of law, still more infatuation with it, seems to me myopic and misleading. The question always should be: what does it contribute to what we want? If the answer is 'heaps', I commend it and believe we all should. But law should be viewed not as the assumed centrepiece of power-tempering policy, to which other measures are secondary or supplementary addenda, but as one implement among several of potentially unique importance in some respects and circumstances but dependent for its success on many other things, and frequently not more important for the achievement of its own goal than they.

The importance of tempered power varies less. We would have less reason to be fond of the rule of law if we believed it was not especially successful in tempering power. Tempered power would still matter just as much, though, pretty well however we gain it. To the extent that the rule of law helps us achieve this goal – as it often crucially does – I still embrace it with enthusiasm, but that qualification matters. Less the passion my friends have attributed to me,[4] more a grateful appreciation for its potential to contribute to what is really at stake.

Late in his very long life, Isaiah Berlin recalled: 'I have lived through most of the twentieth century without, I must add, suffering personal hardship. I remember it only as the most terrible century in Western history.'[5]

I only overlapped with Berlin for half of that century, the better half, and my own life has been much easier than his or most people's. But anyone who was alive then, and already alas even those born yesterday, should need no reminders of the availability and potential horrors of untempered power, nor of the untempered zeal of many who would seek their power to be beyond tempering.

Given that these are the latest centuries we have, no one devoted to tempered power can rely on any Whiggish deliverance, emancipatory historical script, universal happy ending. As we have seen, there are many powerful forces that might assault, subvert, or undermine the tempering of power. Nothing guarantees it. The very notion, let alone reality, has often been radically, even tragically, maligned, rejected, ignored, or overwhelmed. There is little reason to believe this is about to change any time soon.

Favourable inheritances, circumstances, and conditions are a huge bonus, hard to make up. Those lucky enough to benefit from them should count their blessings. However, before we advise those without such blessings to hope for a few hundred good years,[6] we should remember that we simply do not know if any of these impediments is decisive, and we won't unless someone tries to break through them.[7] History is not destiny; our circumstances are not necessarily our fate.

As Giuseppe di Palma has persuasively argued, '[h]ard facts do not mean necessity'.[8] And as he demonstrates in rich and arresting detail, '[w]hatever the historical trends, whatever the hard facts, the importance of human action in a difficult transition should not be underestimated'.[9] World history has had more than enough bleak moments, but they have not always led to disaster. Neither paralysing humility nor excessive hubris is appropriate.

People are not just creatures of their environments but contributors and creators as well. Cultural traditions and we who inhabit them and are inhabited by them change, mix, borrow, learn, and develop. The lack or weakness of favourable conditions does not mean that the ideal of the rule of law is out of one's grasp.

One of the most disabling conditions in hard places and times is that what are often good grounds for caution in practice are taken to be sufficient grounds for despair in principle. Despair is, of course, readily available and often understandable in hard times, but it is not a useful default position and should be resisted. And lazy determinism is rarely adequate justification for it.

Cultures, societies, and polities are never immobile. Once upon a time, people believed in witches. That changed. Since ancient Greece, there were no democracies until the end of the eighteenth century. That changed. And at that time no women could vote. That changed. Moreover, as di Palma pithily observes, 'if democracy was fortuitous in its cradle, why then should it not be fortuitous elsewhere? Why should paths to democracy elsewhere necessarily replicate a first path, or fail if unable to?'[10] Despair would not have helped South Korean democrats, for example, for many years under an anti-communist autocracy, for some years a whisker away from pulverisation by a communist dictatorship, now a resilient democracy instead. True, it suffers from political polarisation, wayward presidents, and difficult neighbours, but it is not alone in that. There was a time when no Germans were Nazis, then many were, and most are not now. Indeed, the spirit and practice of temperance is strong in modern Germany, though the rise of the far-right populist Alternative für Deutschland (AfD) party suggests both that not everything has changed and that more change is in the wings.

The price of liberty is still eternal vigilance. The space in which one acts is never empty, and it is important to pay attention to what forms and fills it – if only because you will be affected by it, whether you pay attention or not. Better to be prepared. A corollary is that sustenance and (re-)generation of the ideal of the rule of law, particularly where it has been undermined, neglected, or rejected, will often require a complex, lasting struggle on many fronts. It will certainly not spring automatically out of political dictation, however easily it might be damaged by such dictation.

Given what is pitted against the achievement of that ideal, then, one cannot rely on it just happening naturally or for that matter legally. Among many other things, it needs strong and widespread conditions and commitments that are often contested and not always available or sufficient. In principle, it is always possible that the law will be undercut by inconsistent norms or overwhelmed by more powerful ones. Conversely, ideas about law, cultural norms, institutions, modes of interaction, and political learnings that support tempered power might come to reinforce each other. Where that is the case, something significant and good is happening. It should be encouraged, supported, and celebrated, in every way one knows, for it is unlikely to happen on its own and it may not last.

So, the absence or weakness of congenial conditions is no reason to avoid seeking to develop congenial institutions and practices. Indeed, realistic awareness that easy roads are rare might help prevent a fall into despair if reforms work less well or less quickly than one had hoped. There is more to do.

Now that the ideal of the rule of law is increasingly and vocally challenged, though, those committed to it will have to do more than offer technical assistance. They need to explain why it matters. And that gives us one more reason to prefer teleology to anatomy. Anatomy, after all, can be done quite satisfactorily on a corpse. However, for an ideal to make a difference, it needs to be alive. Those animated by the ideal of the rule of law need to think more about how to animate (or reanimate) it.

Assaults on the major institutions, cultural dispositions, and social and political arrangements that might temper power, whether they be independent courts or journalists, or associations, or civil servants with an ethos of independent service, or a public culture of temperance, or a textured and tolerant civil society, or all of the above, attack the central ideal for which people have appealed to the rule of law. At its core, this has to do with hostility to the arbitrary – whether uncontrolled, unpredictable, unrespectful, or ungrounded – exercise of power. Those values need defenders, *champions* indeed, when they are threatened. And hopefully they might get them, since populist demagogues often overreach and 'the people' get restless.

But champions won't do it on their own, and it is unlikely that they will persuade huge multitudes with purely legal arguments, which in any event often won't be there, since again 'abusive constitutionalists' often find ways of negotiating such arguments with plausible, if fraudulent, ease. So, legal punctiliousness is no sufficient answer to these highly manipulative uses and abuses of legalicism, if I may be allowed an infelicity, against the rule of law ideal.

So, those who seek to defeat populist and authoritarian intemperance will need to do more than object to (il-)legal tactics and manoeuvres, particularly given the many unanticipated consequences of legal interventions, so many indeed that we might be well advised to anticipate them.[11] What is needed is tempered militancy all the way down.[12]

For it is not *ultimately* about law. Legal and other temperers need to spread the wealth: don't just talk to each other (though that has its own importance) but to the society they inhabit, and indeed to the wider world. As much as legal experts, citizens need to understand the point of the rule of law, even if they don't know any law, and be encouraged to defend and sustain it against those keen to subvert it.

Just as *Solidarity* once brought people together by expanding their understandings of what underlay the arbitrary indecencies of communist power, so today opponents of arbitrary power will need, above all and in every (non-arbitrary) way they can, to expose what is at stake.

Untempered power is often scary and when powerful enough almost always dangerous. Simple as that. It is in *everyone's* interest that power be tempered (though intemperates are reluctant to admit it), and so it is in *everyone's* interest to seek out every which way that can be done.

In 'Politics as a Vocation', one of his last lectures, delivered just after the First World War ended and a year before he died, Max Weber reflected that:

> Politics is a strong and slow boring of hard boards. It takes both passion and perspective. Certainly all historical experience confirms the truth – that man would not have attained the possible unless time and again he had reached out for the impossible. ... Only he who in the face of all this can say 'In spite of all!' has the calling for politics.[13]

What Weber says of politics in general is true of commitment to tempered power in challenging times. I fear those are our times, and I hope we find plenty of people with such a calling.

NOTES

Chapter 1

1. William Partlett, *Why the Russian Constitution Matters: The Constitutional Dark Arts*, Hart, Oxford, 2024, 60.
2. Parkes and Deakin were architects of Australian federation; Bakunin, anarchist leader, contemporary of Marx; Lenin, leader of the Russian Revolution of 1917.
3. Robert Haupt, 'It's NO WAY to Run a Country', *Sydney Morning Herald*, 9 October 1993, p. 27.
4. Ibid.
5. See Partlett, *Why the Russian Constitution Matters*, chaps. 4–8.
6. See Laura Engelstein, *Slavophile Empire: Imperial Russia's Illiberal Path*, Cornell University Press, Ithaca, 2009; Jeffrey Kahn, 'Vladimir Putin and the Rule of Law in Russia', (2008) 36 *Georgia Journal of International & Comparative Law*, 511–558; Jeffrey Kahn, 'The Search for the Rule of Law in Russia', (2006) 37 *Georgia Journal of International Law*, 353–409; Richard Pipes, *Russia under the Old Regime*, Penguin, Harmondsworth, 1974.
7. See David Neal, *The Rule of Law in a Penal Colony*, Cambridge University Press, Cambridge, 1991. I have discussed some of the implications of this work in my 'The Grammar of Colonial Legality: Subjects, Objects, and the Australian Rule of Law', in Geoffrey Brennan and Francis G. Castles, eds., *Australia Reshaped: 200 Years of Institutional Transformation*, Cambridge University Press, Cambridge, 2002, 220–260.
8. Martin Loughlin, 'The Rule of Law: A Slogan in Search of a Concept', (2024) 16 *Hague Journal on the Rule of Law*, 509–523.
9. Gerald J. Postema, *Law's Rule: The Nature, Value, and Viability of the Rule of Law*, Oxford University Press, Oxford, 2022, ix.
10. See Thomas Carothers, 'The Problem of Knowledge', in Thomas Carothers, ed., *Promoting the Rule of Law Abroad: In Search of Knowledge*, Carnegie Endowment for International Peace, Washington, DC, 2006, 15–28, at 15. See also Deval Desai, *Expert Ignorance: The Law and Politics of Rule of Law Reform*, Cambridge University Press, Cambridge, 2023.
11. See Mila Versteeg and Tom Ginsburg, 'Measuring the Rule of Law: A Comparison of Indicators', (2017) 42 *Law & Social Inquiry*, 100–137.
12. David Nelken, 'Contesting Global Indicators', in Sally Engle Merry, Kevin E. Davis, and Benedict Kingsbury, eds., *The Quiet Power of Indicators: Measuring Governance, Corruption, and Rule of Law*, Cambridge University Press, Cambridge, 2015, 317–338.

13. Nyasha Weinberg, 'Chasing Reality: Rule of Law Measurement Is Lagging Years behind Current Developments', *Verfassungsblog*, 30 July 2020, https://verfassungsblog.de/chasing-reality/.
14. See Montesquieu, *The Spirit of the Laws*, eds. Anne M. Cohler, Basia C. Miller, and Harold S. Stone, Cambridge University Press, Cambridge, 1992, pt. 1, bk. 5, chap. 14, 63.
15. See Thomas Hobbes, *Leviathan*, ed. C. B. Macpherson, Penguin, London, 1968, chap. 13.
16. See John Locke, *The Second Treatise of Government, in Two Treatises of Government*, ed. Peter Laslett, Cambridge University Press, Cambridge, 1988, chap. XI, s. 137; Philippe Nonet and Philip Selznick, *Law and Society in Transition: Toward Responsive Law*, Routledge, London, 1978, 36–37, 39, 44.
17. See Daron Acemoglu and James A. Robinson, *The Narrow Corridor: How Nations Struggle for Liberty*, Penguin, London, 2020, on 'Paper Leviathans', 344–436.
18. See Nick Cheesman, *Opposing the Rule of Law: How Myanmar's Courts Make Law and Order*, Cambridge University Press, Cambridge, 2015; Nick Cheesman, 'Law and Order as Asymmetrical Opposite to the Rule of Law', (2014) 6 *Hague Journal on the Rule of Law*, 96–114; Donald C. Clarke, 'Order and Law in China', GW Law School Public Law and Legal Theory Paper No. 2020-52, 25 August 2020, https://papers.ssrn.com/sol3/papers.cfm?abstract_id=3682794; Moritz Rudolf, 'Xi Jinping Thought on the Rule of Law', German Institute for International and Security Affairs (SWP), SWP Comment No. 28, April 2021, www.swp-berlin.org/publications/products/comments/2021C28_Jinping_RuleOfLaw.pdf.
19. See Harold Berman, *Law and Revolution, Vol. I: The Formation of the Western Legal Tradition*, Harvard University Press, Cambridge, MA, 1983; Berman, *Law and Revolution, Vol. II: The Impact of the Protestant Reformations on the Western Legal Tradition*, Belknap Press, Cambridge, MA, 2006; Fernanda Pirie, *The Rule of Laws: A 4,000-Year Quest to Order the World*, Profile Books, London, 2022.
20. See Douglass C. North, John Joseph Wallis, and Barry R. Weingast, *Violence and Social Orders*, Cambridge University Press, Cambridge, 2009; Acemoglu and Robinson, *The Narrow Corridor*.
21. Graham Greene, *A Sort of Life*, Vintage Books, London, 1999, 120.
22. Philippians 4:6–7.
23. See Heinz Popitz, *Phenomena of Power*, trans. Gianfranco Poggi, Columbia University Press, New York, 2017, 42: 'Only rarely has it been possible even just to pose the question of how to constrain institutionalized violence, in a systematic and effective manner. This has only taken place with the Greek *polis*, republican Rome, a few city-states, and the constitutional states of the modern era.' For a more ecumenical view, see Pirie, *The Rule of Laws*.
24. See, for example, Marc Hertogh, 'A Sociology of the Rule of Law: Why, What, Where? And Who Cares?', (2013) 34 *Recht der Werkelijkheid*, 42–46; Martin Krygier, 'Still a Rule of Law Guy', (2013) 34 *Recht der Werkelijkheid*, 47–55; Richard Sannerholm, 'A Rule of Law Guy', (2019) 11 *Hague Journal on the Rule of Law*, 315–320.
25. Nick Cheesman and Ronald Janse, 'Martin Krygier's Passion for the Rule of Law (and His Virtues)', (2019) 11 *Hague Journal on the Rule of Law*, 251–508; 'A Passion for the Rule of Law: In Conversation with Martin Krygier', Australian National University School of Regulation and Global Governance website, video, https://bit.ly/44hkvzm.

26. I discuss some of these concerns in *Between Fear and Hope: Hybrid Thoughts on Public Values*, ABC Books, Sydney, 1997; *Civil Passions*, Black Inc., Melbourne, 2005, and 'An Intimate and Foreign Affair', in Ann Curthoys and Joy Damousi, eds., *What Did You Do in the Cold War, Daddy?* New South Publishing, Sydney, 2014, 23–56.
27. For example, Martin Krygier, ed. *Marxism and Communism: Posthumous Reflections on Politics, Society, and Law*, Rodopi, Amsterdam, 1994; Martin Krygier and Adam Czarnota, eds., *The Rule of Law after Communism*, Dartmouth, Aldershot, 1999; Adam Czarnota, Martin Krygier, and Wojciech Sadurski, eds., *Rethinking the Rule of Law after Communism: Constitutionalism, Dealing with the Past, and the Rule of Law*, Central European University Press, Budapest, 2005; Wojciech Sadurski, Adam Czarnota, and Martin Krygier, eds., *Spreading Democracy and the Rule of Law? Implications of EU Enlargement for the Rule of Law, Democracy and Constitutionalism in Post-Communist Legal Orders*, Springer Verlag, 2006; Martin Krygier, Adam Czarnota, and Wojciech Sadurski, eds., *Anti-constitutional Populism*, Cambridge University Press, Cambridge, 2022;
28. See Martin Krygier, 'Institutional Optimism, Cultural Pessimism and the Rule of Law', in Martin Krygier and Adam Czarnota, eds., *The Rule of Law after Communism*, Dartmouth, Aldershot, 1999, 77–105.
29. I was encouraged in this belief by Whit Mason's insistence that what I took to be mere theorising bore closely on what he was intensely engaged with in practice. See Martin Krygier and Whit Mason, 'Violence, Development, and the Rule of Law', in George Mavrotas, ed., *Security for Development: Confronting Threats to Survival and Safety*, Global Development Network, Edward Elgar, Cheltenham, 2011, 129–170, and Whit Mason, ed., *The Rule of Law in Afghanistan: Missing in Inaction*, Cambridge University Press, Cambridge, 2011.
30. See Krygier, Czarnota, and Sadurski, *Anti-constitutional Populism*.
31. Martin Krygier, 'The Quality of Civility: Post-Anti-Communist Thoughts on Civil Society and the Rule of Law', in András Sajó, ed., *Out of and into Authoritarian Law*, Kluwer, Amsterdam, 2002, 221–256; 'The Rule of Law and State Legitimacy', in Wojciech Sadurski, Michael Sevel, and Keven Walton, eds., *Legitimacy: The State and Beyond*, Oxford University Press, Oxford, 2019, 106–136; 'Legal Pluralism and the Value of the Rule of Law' in Andrew Halpin and Nicole Roughan, eds., *Jurisprudence without Borders*, Cambridge University Press, Cambridge, 2017, 294–325; 'Polish Lessons: Backsliding, Sabotage and the Rule of Law', in Aleksandra Gliszczyńska-Grabias and Uladzislau Belavusau, eds., *Constitutionalism under Stress: Essays in Honour of Wojciech Sadurski*, Oxford University Press, Oxford, 2020, 79–94; 'The Grammar of Colonial Legality: Subjects, Objects, and the Australian Rule of Law', in Geoffrey Brennan and Francis G. Castles, eds., *Australia Reshaped: 200 Years of Institutional Transformation*, Cambridge University Press, Cambridge, 2002, 220–260; (with Mason), 'Violence, Development, and the Rule of Law'; 'The Rule of Law: Legality, Teleology, Sociology', in Gianluigi Palombella and Neil Walker, eds., *Relocating the Rule of Law*, Hart, Oxford, 2008, 44–69, 'Marxism, Communism, and the Rule of Law', in Martin Krygier, ed., *Marxism and Communism: Posthumous Reflections on Politics, Society, and Law*, Rodopi, Amsterdam, 1994, 135–168; (with Adam Czarnota), 'After Postcommunism: The Next Phase', 2006, 2 *Annual Review of Law and Social Science*, 299–340; 'Hart, Fuller and Law in Transitional Societies', in Peter Cane, ed., *The Hart–Fuller Debate in the Twenty-First Century*, Hart, Oxford,

2010, 107–134; 'Democracy and the Rule of Law', in Jens Meierhenrich and Martin Loughlin, eds., *Cambridge Companion to the Rule of Law*, Cambridge University Press, Cambridge, 2021, 406–424; 'Tempering Power', in Michael Adams et al., eds., *Bridging Idealism and Realism in Constitutionalism and the Rule of Law*, Cambridge University Press, Cambridge, 2016, 34–39; 'The Spirit of Constitutionalism', Jakub Urbanik and Adam Bodnar, eds., *Περιμένοντας τους Βαρβάρους. Law in the Days of Constitutional Crisis: Studies Offered to Mirosław Wyrzykowski*, C. H. Beck, Warsaw, 2021, 343–358; 'Illiberalism and the Rule of Law', in András Sajó, Renata Uitz, and Stephen Holmes, eds., *Routledge Handbook on Illiberalism*, Routledge, London, 2021, 533–553; 'Transformations of the Rule of Law: Legal, Liberal, Neo', in Ben Golder and Daniel McLoughlin, eds., *The Politics of Legality in a Neoliberal Age*, Routledge, London, 2017, 19–43; 'The Challenge of Institutionalisation: Post-Communist "Transitions", Populism, and the Rule of Law', (2019) 15 *European Constitutional Law Review*, special issue on Populism and Constitutionalism, 544–573; Krygier, Czarnota, and Sadurski, *Anti-constitutional Populism*; 'The Ideal of the Rule of Law and Private Power', in Mark Tushnet and Dimitry Kochenov, eds., *Research Handbook on the Politics of Constitutional Law*, Edward Elgar, Cheltenham, 2023, 14–29; '"What's the Point of the Rule of Law?" The Baldy Center's 40th Anniversary Conference: Tempering Power', (2019) 67 *Buffalo Law Review*, 743–791; 'The Rule of Law: An Abuser's Guide', in András Sajó, ed., *The Dark Side of Fundamental Rights*, Eleven International Publishing, Utrecht, 2006, 129–161.

32. 'Trump's America: Fear, Polarisation, and The Future (Ezra Klein)', *The Rest Is Politics: Leading*, podcast, 14 April 2025, https://bit.ly/4pSERGR.
33. See Martin Krygier, 'Marxism and the Rule of Law: Reflections after the Collapse of Communism', (1990) 15 *Law and Social Inquiry (Chicago)*, 633–663, followed by five responses and my rejoinder, 'Marxism, Communism, and Narcissism', (1990) 15 *Law and Social Inquiry*, 709–732.
34. See, for example, Krygier, 'Marxism and the Rule of Law', and, to a slightly less extent, Martin Krygier, 'Rule of Law', in Neil J. Smelser and Paul B. Bates, eds., *International Encyclopedia of the Social and Behavioral Sciences*, Elsevier Science, Oxford, 2001, vol. 20, 13403–13408.
35. Tom J. Palmer, 'Limited Government and the Rule of Law', in *Cato Handbook for Policymakers*, 8th ed., Cato Institute, https://bit.ly/4k1ZIGC.
36. 'Factors of the Rule of Law', World Justice Project, https://bit.ly/3LOfWXe; 'As an idea about government, the essence of the rule of law is that all authority is subject to, and constrained by, law' (Murray Gleeson, 'Courts and the Rule of Law', The Rule of Law Series, Melbourne University, 7 November 2001, https://bit.ly/4k1ZMGm).
37. 'What Is the Rule of Law', United Nations and the Rule of Law, www.un.org/ruleoflaw/what-is-the-rule-of-law/.
38. Acemoglu and Robinson, *The Narrow Corridor*, 24.
39. Google Books Ngram Viewer, 'tempering power', https://bit.ly/4jXe3Uy.
40. Google Books Ngram Viewer, 'rule of law', https://bit.ly/3ZtK3Gu.
41. See Petra Bard, *Rule of Law: Sustainability and Mutual Trust in a Transforming Europe*, Eleven, The Hague, 2023; John Braithwaite, *Macrocriminology and Freedom*, ANU Press, Canberra,2021; Postema, *Law's Rule*; Gregory Shaffer and Wayne Sandholtz, eds., *The Rule of Law under Pressure: A Transnational Challenge*, Cambridge University Press, Cambridge, 2025; András Sajó, *Militant Rule of Law*, Cambridge University Press, Cambridge, 2026.

42. See Chapter 8.
43. John Locke, *An Essay Concerning Human Understanding*, Clarendon Press, Oxford, 2011, 10.
44. Montesquieu, *The Spirit of the Laws*, pt. 2, bk. 11, chap. 20, 186.

Chapter 2

1. Pirie's *Rules of Law* documents 'A 4,000-Year Quest to Order the World'.
2. See Julian A. Sempill, 'Ruler's Sword, Citizen's Shield: The Rule of Law and the Constitution of Power', (2016) 31 *Journal of Law and Politics*, 333–415, at 336–337.
3. See Gianluigi Palombella, *È possibile una legalità globale? Il Rule of law e la governance del mondo*, Il Mulino, Bologna, 2012; Martin Krygier, 'Rule of Law (and Rechtsstaat)', in James D. Wright, ed., *International Encyclopedia of the Social and Behavioral Sciences*, 2nd ed., Vol 20, Elsevier, Oxford, 2015, 780–787.
4. Mirko Canevaro, 'The Rule of Law as the Measure of Political Legitimacy in the Greek City States', (2017) 9 *Hague Journal on the Rule of Law*, 211–236; Julian A. Sempill, 'The Rule of Law and the Rule of Men: History, Legacy, Obscurity', (2020) 12 *Hague Journal on the Rule of Law*, 511–540.
5. See Pirie, *Rules of Law*.
6. A search of Google Ngram for 'rule of law' finds nothing before the eighteenth century, apart from a small and mysterious blip between 1512 and 1517, and a large one between 1638 or 1640–1646 unreached again until about 1990, when the term begins its late twentieth-century surge. I have no idea what the first blip signifies. The second might well reflect the huge debates surrounding the English Civil War. The third is the subject of this chapter.
7. Albert Venn Dicey, *Introduction to the Study of the Law of the Constitution*, 10th ed., Macmillan & Co., London, 1961.
8. See Judith Shklar, 'Political Theory and the Rule of Law', in *Political Thought and Political Thinkers*, ed. Stanley Hoffmann, University of Chicago Press, Chicago, 1998, 21–37, at 26.
9. See Anna Wierzbicka, *Imprisoned in English: The Hazards of English as a Default Language*, Oxford University Press, Oxford, 2013.
10. See Sempill, 'Ruler's Sword', 338–340; Jeremy Waldron, *The Rule of Law and the Measure of Property*, Hamlyn Lectures, Cambridge University Press, Cambridge, 2012, 8.
11. See, for example, Jeremy Matam Farrall, *United Nations Sanctions and the Rule of Law*, Cambridge University Press, 2007, 22; UN Doc. A/63/226 (6 August 2008) Strengthening and coordinating United Nations rule of law activities: Report of the Secretary-General, 6.
12. See Balakrishnan Rajagopal, 'Invoking the Rule of Law in Post-Conflict Rebuilding: A Critical Examination', (2008) 49 *William and Mary Law Review*, 1347–1376.
13. Charles T. Call, ed., *Constructing Justice and Security after War*, United States Institute of Peace, Washington, DC, 2007, 4.
14. Brian Z. Tamanaha, *On the Rule of Law*, Cambridge University Press, Cambridge, 2004, 1.
15. Farrall, *United Nations Sanctions*, 22.

16. Vladimir Ilyich Lenin, 'The Proletarian Revolution and the Renegade Kautsky', in *Collected Works, Vol. 28: July 1918–March 1919*, ed. Jim Riordan, Progress Publishers, Moscow, 1974, 227–325, at 236.
17. Robert Cordy, 'Gulags Give Way to the Rule of Law', *Boston Herald*, 18 November 2002, A25; quoted in Tamanaha, *On the Rule of Law*, 2.
18. Actually, that is not very close. If Trump had known, he might have been relieved to learn the deeper meaning of his slogan. See Cheesman, *Opposing the Rule of Law*, and Cheesman, 'Law and Order'.
19. See Krygier, Sadurski, and Czarnota, *Anti-constitutional Populism*.
20. See Julian Scholtes, *The Abuse of Constitutional Identity in the European Union*, Oxford University Press, Oxford, 2023.
21. András Sajó, *Ruling by Cheating: Governance in Illiberal Democracy*, Cambridge University Press, Cambridge, 2021, 285.
22. See 'President Repeatedly Responds "I Don't Know" to Constitutional Questions', *New York Times*, 4 May 2025, www.nytimes.com/live/2025/05/04/us/trump-news#trump-meet-the-press-interview-due-process.
23. See Deval Desai, *Expert Ignorance: The Law and Politics of Rule of Law Reform*, Cambridge University Press, Cambridge, 2023.
24. See Rudolf, 'Xi Jinping Thought on the Rule of Law'.
25. See Martin Krygier, 'The Rule of Law after the Short Twentieth Century: Launching a Global Career', in Richard Nobles and David Schiff, eds., *Law, Society and Community: Essays in Honour of Roger Cotterrell*, Ashgate, Farnham, 2014, 327–46. Revised and updated in Piotr H. Kosicki and Kyril Kunakhovich, eds., *The Long 1989: Decades of Global Revolution*, CEU Press, Budapest, 2019, 161–86. This chapter draws on that article.
26. Ronald Janse, 'Why Did the Rule of Law Revive?' (2019) 11 *Hague Journal on the Rule of Law*, 341–48, at 344.
27. See Douglass C. North, *Institutions, Institutional Change and Economic Performance*, Cambridge University Press, Cambridge, 1990; David M. Trubek and Alvaro Santos, eds., *The New Law and Economic Development: A Critical Appraisal*, Cambridge University Press, Cambridge, 2006.
28. Janse, 'Why Did the Rule of Law Revive?'.
29. See, for example, Samuel Huntington, *The Third Wave: Democratization in the Late Twentieth Century*, University of Oklahoma Press, Norman, 1991.
30. This and the next section draw on Krygier, 'The Rule of Law after the Short Twentieth Century'.
31. Hobsbawm popularised the term in his *The Age of Extremes: The Short Twentieth Century 1914–1991*, Michael Joseph, London, 1994. It was coined by the Hungarian historian Ivan T. Berend. Poles might plausibly argue it ended on 4 June 1989, when the first semi-free elections in communist Poland were lost by the communists. Internationally, the symbol most associated with it is the fall of the Berlin Wall on 9 November of the same year. However, those like Hobsbawm, for whom communism rose and fell with the Soviet Union, stick with his dates. At this distance, any of these will do.
32. Tony Judt, 'The Rediscovery of Central Europe', (Winter 1990) 119 *Daedalus*, 23–54, at 25.
33. Kenneth Jowitt, *The New World Disorder: The Leninist Extinction*, University of California Press, Berkeley, 1992, 284.

34. Hobsbawm, *The Age of Extremes*, 4.
35. David Trubek, 'The "Rule of Law" in Development Assistance: Past, Present, and Future', in David M. Trubek and Alvaro Santos, eds., *The New Law and Economic Development: A Critical Appraisal*, Cambridge University Press, Cambridge, 2006, 74–94, at 78.
36. Francis Fukuyama, 'The End of History?', (1989) 16 *The National Interest*, 3–18, and *The End of History and the Last Man*, The Free Press, New York, 1992.
37. Veronica L. Taylor, 'Frequently Asked Questions about Rule of Law Assistance (and Why Better Answers Matter)', (2009) 1 *Hague Journal on the Rule of Law*, 46–47.
38. See Claude Karnoouh, 'Postcommunisme/Communisme: Le Conflit des interpretations', Collegium Budapest, Discussion Paper No. 21; Krygier and Czarnota, 'After Postcommunism'.
39. See Chapter 8, and Krygier, Czarnota, and Sadurski, *Anti-constitutional Populism*; Wojciech Sadurski, *A Pandemic of Populists*, Cambridge University Press, Cambridge, 2022.
40. Adam Taylor, 'There Was an "Epidemic" of Coups in 2021: The New Year Hasn't Cured the Political Turmoil', *The Washington Post*, 4 January 2022, https://bit.ly/49QQTMk. See also Sadurski, *A Pandemic of Populists*.
41. See 'Discrediting Democracy in "Sharp Power" Battle of Ideas', Democracy Digest, 1 November 2021, www.demdigest.org/discrediting-democracy-in-sharp-power-battle-of-ideas/.
42. Charles Kupchan, *No One's World: The West, the Rising Rest, and the Coming Global Turn*, Oxford University Press, Oxford, 2012.

Chapter 3

1. Jørgen Møller, 'The Advantages of a Thin View', in Christopher May and Adam Winchester, eds., *Handbook on the Rule of Law*, Edward Elgar, Cheltenham, 2018, 21–33, at 23–24.
2. John Finnis, *Natural Law and Natural Rights*, 2nd ed., Oxford University Press, Oxford, 2011, 270.
3. See Rufus E. Miles, Jr., 'The Origin and Meaning of Miles' Law', (1978) 38 *Public Administration Review*, 399–403.
4. Norman Marsh, ed., *The Rule of Law in a Free Society: A Report on the International Congress of Jurists, New Delhi, India January 5–10, 1959*, International Commission of Jurists, Geneva, 2.
5. See Dicey, *Introduction to the Study of the Law of the Constitution*.
6. Though modern usage in the English-speaking world is attributed to Dicey, the phrase appears earlier: 'The precise issue we raise is this – that throughout our empire the British rule shall be the rule of law.' Frederic Harrison, *Martial Law: Six Letters to 'The Daily News'*, The Jamaica Committee, London, 1867, 4, quoted in Dylan Lino, 'The Rule of Law and the Rule of Empire: A. V. Dicey in Imperial Context', (2018) 81 *Modern Law Review*, 739–764, at 739. See H. W. Arndt, 'The Origins of Dicey's Concept of the "Rule of Law"', (1957) 31 *Australian Law Journal*, 117–123.
7. Judith N. Shklar, 'Political Theory and the Rule of Law', in *Political Thought and Political Thinkers*, ed. Stanley Hoffmann, University of Chicago Press, Chicago, 1998, 21–37, at 26.

8. Lino, 'The Rule of Law and the Rule of Empire', 742.
9. Tom Bingham, *The Rule of Law*, Allen Lane, London, 2010, 8.
10. Joseph Raz, 'The Rule of Law and Its Virtue', in *The Authority of the Law: Essays on Law and Morality*, Clarendon Press, Oxford, 1979, 211. Jeremy Bentham, *Principles of the Civil Code*, cited in Timothy Endicott, 'The Coxford Lecture: Arbitrariness', (2014) 27 *Canadian Journal of Law and Jurisprudence*, 49–71, at 52–53.
11. Lon L. Fuller, *The Morality of Law*, rev. ed., Yale University Press, New Haven, CT, 1969.
12. See Fuller, *The Morality of Law*.
13. See Kristen Rundle, *Revisiting the Rule of Law*, Cambridge University Press, Cambridge, 2023, n. 71: 'Fuller actually used the term "rule of law" very rarely in his writings, but notably did so in relation to his eighth principle of congruence between official action and declared rule: "if the Rule of Law does not mean this, it means nothing."' (Fuller, *The Morality of Law*, 210). That he used the phrase of this principle is notable, given he did not use it of the others, and also because it is different from all of them. It has not to do with formal elements of rules but of a government's acts in conformity to its 'declared rule'.
14. See H. L. A. Hart's book review 'Fuller: *The Morality of Law*', (1965) 78 *Harvard Law Review*, 1281–1296, at 1286: 'Poisoning is no doubt a purposive activity, and reflections on its purpose may show that it has its internal principles. ("Avoid poisons however lethal if they cause the victim to vomit", or "Avoid poisons however lethal if their shape, color, or size is likely to attract notice").'
15. 'A blackmailer would fail in his dastardly objective unless he made his instructions clear and unambiguous.' Ronald Dworkin, 'The Elusive Morality of Law', (1965) 10 *Villanova Law Review*, 631–639, at 634.
16. See Martin Golding, *Philosophy of Law*, Prentice Hall, Englewood Cliffs, NJ, 49–50.
17. See Andrei Marmor:

    > A remarkable consensus prevails in the literature about what the rule of law actually requires. It is widely agreed that the rule of law requires that laws be publicly promulgated, be reasonably clear and not self-contradictory, and have general and prospective application; that the application of laws be administered by impartial and independent courts which are reasonably accessible to all; that people ought to be given adequate opportunities to comply with the law; that laws are not be changed too frequently; and other, similar principles.

    USC Legal Studies Research Paper, No. 08–6, 2. https://bit.ly/4qdyMVJ.
18. Jeremy Waldron, 'Thoughtfulness and the Rule of Law', *British Academy Law Lecture: February 1, 2011*, 3, republished in Waldron, *Thoughtfulness and the Rule of Law*, Harvard University Press, Cambridge, MA, 2023, chap. 1. These lists were all preceded by the eighteenth/nineteenth-century legal reformer Jeremy Bentham's list of seven. See Jeremy Bentham, 'The Power of Laws over Expectation', in his *Principles of the Civil Code*, cited in Endicott, 'The Coxford Lecture: Arbitrariness', 52–53.
19. Jeremy Waldron, 'The Rule of Law and the Importance of Procedure', in James Fleming, ed., *Getting to the Rule of Law*, New York University Press, New York, 2011, 3–31, reprinted in his *Thoughtfulness and the Rule of Law*, chap. 7.
20. See Martin Krygier, 'False Dichotomies, Real Perplexities and the Rule of Law', in András Sajó, ed., *Human Rights with Modesty: The Problem of Universalism*, Martinus Nijhoff, Leiden, 2004, 251–277.

21. See Chapter 8, and Krygier, 'The Spirit of Constitutionalism'.
22. Marsh, *The Rule of Law in a Free Society*, 3.
23. Raz, 'The Rule of Law and Its Virtue', 211.
24. See Krygier, 'Rule of Law (and Rechtsstaat)', 783–784; 'The Rule of Law: Pasts, Presents, and Two Possible Futures', (2016) 12 *Annual Review of Law & Social Science*, 199–229, at 213–215.
25. See James E. Fleming, ed., *Getting to the Rule of Law: NOMOS L*, New York University Press, New York, 2011.
26. Francis Fukuyama, *The Origins of Political Order*, Farrar, Straus & Giroux, New York, 2011, 214; see also his *Political Order and Political Decay: From the Industrial Revolution to the Globalisation of Democracy*, Farrar, Straus & Giroux, New York, 2014, 37.
27. See David Trubek, 'The "Rule of Law" in Development Assistance: Past, Present, and Future', in David M. Trubek and Alvaro Santos, eds., *The New Law and Economic Development*, Cambridge University Press, 2006, 74–94, at 84.
28. F. Charles Sherman, 'Law and Development Today: The New Developmentalism', (2009) 10 *German Law Journal*, 1257–1273, at 1264.
29. See Paul W. Kahn, *Origins of Order: Project and System in the American Legal Imagination*, Yale University Press, New Haven, CT, 2019.
30. Sannerholm, 'A Rule of Law Guy', 316.
31. See Lino, 'The Rule of Law and the Rule of Empire'.
32. Richard Sannerholm, 'Rule of Law after War: Ideologies, Norms and Methods for Legal and Judicial Reform', doctoral dissertation, Örebro University, 2009, 131.
33. Erik Jensen and Thomas C. Heller, eds., *Beyond Common Knowledge: Empirical Approaches to the Rule of Law*, Stanford University Press, Stanford, CA, 2003, 1–2.
34. Stephen Haggard and Lydia Tiede, 'The Rule of Law and Economic Growth: Where Are We?', (2011) 39 *World Development*, 673–685, at 673; Deval Desai and Michael Woolcock, 'The Politics of Rule of Law Systems in Developmental States: "Political Settlements" as a Basis for Promoting Effective Justice Institutions for Marginalized Groups', Effective States and Inclusive Development Working Paper No. 8, July 2012, 5; Kevin Davis and Michael Trebilcock, 'The Relationship between Law and Development: Optimists versus Skeptics', (2008) 56 *American Journal of Comparative Law*, 895–946. See the publications of the Thinking and Working Politically Community of Practice (TWP), for example Graham Teskey, 'Thinking and Working Politically: What Have We Learned since 2013?', December 2021. https://twpcommunity.org/latest-work.
35. See Deval Desai, *Expert Ignorance*, Cambridge University Press, Cambridge, 2023.
36. The traditional focus has been on state power. In Chapter 7 I argue that the ideal of the rule of law requires us to reach further, but even within states the forms of power the digital revolution has spawned have transformed many activities and functions of the state as well.
37. See Nicola Lacey, 'Philosophy, Political Morality, and History: Explaining the Enduring Resonance of the Hart–Fuller Debate', (2008) 83 *New York University Law Review*, 1059–1067, at 1072–1078.
38. See James C. Scott, *Seeing Like a State: How Certain Schemes to Improve the Human Condition Have Failed*, Yale University Press, New Haven, CT, 1988.
39. Sally Falk Moore, 'Introduction', in *Law as Process: An Anthropological Approach*, Routledge & Kegan Paul, London, 1978, 6.

40. Most recently, Krygier, 'Legal Pluralism and the Value of the Rule of Law'; 'The Rule of Law and State Legitimacy'.
41. Carothers, 'The Problem of Knowledge', 21. And for more recent self-conscious reflection, see Desai, *Expert Ignorance*.
42. See Chapter 10.
43. Lant Pritchett, Michael Woolcock, and Matt Andrews, 'Capability Traps? The Mechanisms of Persistent Implementation Failure', Center for Global Development Working Paper No. 234, 2010, 1.
44. Ibid., 4.
45. See Mason, *The Rule of Law in Afghanistan*.
46. Mark Fathi Massoud, *Law's Fragile State: Colonial, Authoritarian, and Humanitarian Legacies in Sudan*, Cambridge University Press, Cambridge, 2013, 206.
47. Ozan O. Varol, 'Stealth Authoritarianism', (2015) 100 *Iowa Law Review*, 1673–1742; Kim Lane Scheppele, 'Constitutional Coups in EU Law', in Maurice Adams, Anne Meuwese, and Ernst Hirsch Ballin, eds., *Constitutionalism and the Rule of Law: Bridging Idealism and Realism*, Cambridge University Press, Cambridge, 2017, 446–478; Scheppele, 'Autocratic Legalism', (2018) 85 *University of Chicago Law Review*, 545–583; Grażyna Skąpska, 'Znieważający konstytucjonalizm i konstytucjonalizm znieważony. Refleksja socjologiczna na temat kryzysu liberalno-demokratycznego konstytucjonalizmu w Europie pokomunistycznej', (2018) 7 *Filozofia Publiczna i Edukacja Demokratyczna*, 276–301; Alvin Y. H. Cheung, 'Legal Gaslighting', (2022) 72 *University of Toronto Law Journal*, 50–80; András Sajó and J. Tuovinen, 'The Rule of Law and Legitimacy in Emerging Illiberal Democracies', (2019) 64 *Osteuropa Recht*, 506–529.
48. David Landau, 'Abusive Constitutionalism', (2013) 47 *University of California, Davis, Law Review*, 189–260, at 189.
49. See Krygier, Czarnota, and Sadurski, *Anti-constitutional Populism*.
50. See, for example, Cheesman, *Opposing the Rule of Law*.
51. Bingham, *The Rule of Law*.
52. See, for example, Mason, *The Rule of Law in Afghanistan*.
53. See Cheesman, *Opposing the Rule of Law*.

Chapter 4

1. See 'Quote Origin: No One Wants a Drill. What They Want Is the Hole', Quote Investigator®, 23 March 2019, https://quoteinvestigator.com/2019/03/23/.
2. See Waldron, *Thoughtfulness and the Rule of Law*.
3. Philip Pettit, *Just Freedom: A Moral Compass for a Complex World*, Norton, New York, 2014, xix.
4. See Krygier, 'The Rule of Law: Legality, Teleology, Sociology'.
5. W. B. Gallie, 'Essentially Contested Concepts', (1955–1956) 56 *Proceedings of the Aristotelean Society*, 167–198, at 174.
6. Hilary Putnam, 'The Entanglement of Fact and Value', in *The Collapse of the Fact/Value Dichotomy and Other Essays*, Harvard University Press, Cambridge, MA, 2002, 28–45.
7. Raz, 'The Rule of Law and Its Virtue', 214.
8. See Section 8.3.

9. 'If we were asked to divide the objects we know into mountains and nonmountains, then we should certainly put Ayers Rock [Uluru] in the first category ... Nevertheless, from a scientific point of view, Ayers Rock is not a mountain, it is a *stone*.' Umberto Eco, *Kant and the Platypus: Essays on Language and Cognition*, Mariner Books, Boston, 2000, 225.
10. Jeremy Waldron, 'Is the Rule of Law an Essentially Contested Concept, in Florida?' (2002) 21 *Law and Philosophy*, 137–164, at 158.
11. Ibid.
12. Cited in Philip Selznick, *The Moral Commonwealth*, University of California Press, Berkeley, 1992, 454.
13. 'In politics, then, every enterprise is a consequential enterprise, the pursuit, not of a dream, or of a general principle, but of an intimation.' Michael Oakeshott, 'Political Education', in *Rationalism in Politics and Other Essays*, Liberty Press, Indianapolis, IN, 1991, 43–69, at 57.
14. Michael Polanyi, *The Tacit Dimension*, rev. ed., Chicago University Press, Chicago, 2009, 10. Italics in the original.
15. See Martin Krygier, 'Conservative Liberal Socialism Revisited', (2002) 11 *The Good Society*, 6–15, on which this paragraph draws.
16. Michael Oakeshott, 'On Being Conservative', in *Rationalism in Politics and Other Essays*, Liberty Fund, Indianapolis, 1991, 407–437, at 408.
17. See Krygier, 'The Challenge of Institutionalisation'; Krygier, 'Illiberalism and the Rule of Law'; Krygier, Czarnota, and Sadurski, *Anti-constitutional Populism*.
18. Giuseppe Tomasi di Lampedusa, *The Leopard*. Lebooks Editora, São Paulo, 2025, Kindle edition, 346.
19. James L. Gibson, 'Changes in American Veneration for the Rule of Law', (2007) 56 *DePaul Law Review*, 593–614.
20. See Amos G. Winter, Mario A. Bollini, Benjamin M. Judge, et al., 'Stakeholder-Driven Design Evolution of the Leveraged Freedom Chair Developing World Wheelchair', in *Proceedings of the ASME 2012 International Mechanical Engineering Congress and Exposition, Vol. 5: Education and Globalization; General Topics*, American Society of Mechanical Engineers (ASME), Houston, TX, 2012, 361–368, http://dx.doi.org/10.1115/IMECE2012-88881.
21. Frank Upham, 'Mythmaking in the Rule-of-Law Orthodoxy', in Thomas Carothers, ed., *Promoting the Rule of Law Abroad: In Search of Knowledge*, Carnegie Endowment for International Peace, Washington, DC, 2006, 75–104, at 76. This is an insight later developed impressively but with mixed practical take-up in the work of the Thinking and Working Politically Community of Practice (TWP). See Teskey, 'Thinking and Working Politically'.
22. Personal disclaimer: I participated for several years in enthusiastic attempts to 'build' constitutionalism and the rule of law in Myanmar. That is not a reason for shame but, alas, it is not a boast.
23. See Mason, *The Rule of Law in Afghanistan*.
24. Desai, *Expert Ignorance*, xvii.
25. Ibid., 10.
26. Unpublished observation at a 2003 workshop preparing Czarnota, Krygier, and Sadurski, *Rethinking the Rule of Law after Communism*.
27. See The World Bank, *World Development Report 2011: Conflict, Security, and Development*, The World Bank, Washington DC, 2011; Desai, *Expert Ignorance*.

Chapter 5

1. *Heydon's Case* (1584) 76 ER 637, at 638. As cited and discussed in Samuel L. Bray, 'The Mischief Rule', (2021) 109 *Georgetown Law Review*, 967–1013, at 990.
2. As a shorthand, I speak of 'remedy' to cover both avoidance of potential and remedy of actual mischief.
3. See John Philip Reid, 'In Legitimate Stirps: The Concept of "Arbitrary," the Supremacy of Parliament, and the Coming of the American Revolution', (1977) 5 *Hofstra Law Review*, 459–499; Sempill, 'Ruler's Sword'; David M. Beatty, *Faith, Force and Reason: An Armchair History of the Rule of Law*, University of Toronto Press, Toronto, 2022, Pirie, *The Rule of Laws*; Postema, *Law's Rule*.
4. Aristotle, *The Politics*, in *The Politics and the Constitution of Athens*, trans. Jonathan Barnes and J. M. Moore; ed. Stephen Everson, Cambridge University Press, Cambridge, 1996, 88.
5. Locke, *The Second Treatise of Government*, chap. 11, s. 137. Italics in the original.
6. William Lucy, 'The Rule of Law and Private Power', in Lisa M. Austin and Dennis Klimchuk, eds., *Private Law and the Rule of Law*, Oxford University Press, Oxford, 2014, 41–66, at 44.
7. See Pirie, *Rules of Law*.
8. See Frank Lovett, 'Republicanism', in Edward N. Zalta and Uri Nodelman, eds., *The Stanford Encyclopedia of Philosophy* (fall 2022 ed.), https://plato.stanford.edu/archives/fall2022/entries/republicanism/.
9. Unless he moves into a palace, in which case, according to an allegedly Turkish proverb, he does not become a king but the palace becomes a circus.
10. Steven Lukes, *Power: A Radical View*, 3rd ed., Red Globe Press, London, 2021, 67.
11. See John Scott, *Power*, Polity Press, Cambridge, 2011, 1.
12. This is Gianfranco Poggi's formulation, *Forms of Power*, Polity Press, Cambridge, 2001, 25.
13. Norbert Elias, *What Is Sociology?*, Columbia University Press, New York, 1978, 74. Italics in the original.
14. Poggi, *Forms of Power*, 12.
15. Elias, *What Is Sociology?*, 74.
16. Elias, *What Is Sociology?*, 74.
17. Heinrich Popitz, *Phenomena of Power: Authority, Domination, and Violence*, Columbia University Press, New York, 2017, 18. Italics in the original.
18. F. A. Hayek, *The Road to Serfdom*, 50th anniversary ed., with a new introduction by Milton Friedman, University of Chicago Press, Chicago, 1994, 159.
19. Alexander Hamilton, 'New York Assembly: First Speech on the Address of the Legislature to Governor George Clinton's Message', quoted in Lawrence Goldman, editor's 'Introduction', to Alexander Hamilton, James Madison, and John Jay, *The Federalist Papers*, Oxford World's Classics, Oxford University Press, Oxford, 2008, xxxii. Italics in the original.
20. See, for example, Samuel Arnold and John R. Harris, 'What Is Arbitrary Power?', (2017) 10, *Journal of Political Power*, 55–70; Endicott, 'The Coxford Lecture: Arbitrariness'; Frank Lovett, 'What Counts as Arbitrary Power?' (2012) 5 *Journal of Political Power*, 137–152; Assaf Sharon, 'Domination and the Rule of Law', in David Sobel, Peter Vallentyne, and Steven Wall, eds., *Oxford Studies in Political Philosophy*, Vol. 2, Oxford Academic, Oxford, 2005, chap. 5.

21. See, for example, Paul Gowder, *The Rule of Law in the Real World*, Cambridge University Press, Cambridge, 2016, 50.
22. 'I shall not today attempt further to define the kinds of material I understand to be embraced within that shorthand description ['hard-core pornography'], and perhaps I could never succeed in intelligibly doing so. But *I know it when I see it*, and the motion picture involved in this case is not that.' Stewart, J., in *Jacobellis* v. *Ohio* (1964) 378 U.S., at 197.
23. *Akhil Bharatiya Upbhokta Congress* v. *State of Madhya Pradesh* (2011) 5 SCC 29 [65].
24. Philip Pettit, *Republicanism*, Cambridge University Press, Cambridge, 1997, 55.
25. Thomas Hobbes, 'Of the Natural Condition of Mankind as Concerning Their Felicity and Misery', in *Leviathan*, Basil Blackwell, Oxford, 1946, chap. 13, 80–84.
26. Locke, *The Second Treatise of Government*, chap. XI, s. 137. Italics in the original.
27. Aristotle, *The Politics*, 106.
28. Samuel Johnson, *A Dictionary of the English Language*, https://johnsonsdictionaryonline.com/views/search.php?term=arbitrary.
29. See Chapter 3.
30. Adrianan Lanni, 'Classical Athens' Radical Democratic "Rule of Law"', in Jens Meierhenrich and Martin Loughlin, eds., *The Cambridge Companion to the Rule of Law*, Cambridge University Press, Cambridge, 2021, 25–38.
31. Charles McIlwain, *Constitutionalism: Ancient and Modern*, Cornell University Press, Ithaca, NY, 1940; Palombella, *È possibile una legalità globale?*.
32. See Reid, 'In Legitimate Stirps'; John Philip Reid, *The Rule of Law and the Jurisprudence of Liberty in the Seventeenth and Eighteenth Centuries*, Northern Illinois University Press, DeKalb, 2004.
33. Locke, *The Second Treatise of Government*, chap. XI, s. 137. Italics in the original.
34. Reid, *Rule of Law*.
35. See Gianluigi Palombella, 'The Rule of Law as an Institutional Ideal', in Leonardo Morlino and Gianluigi Palombella, eds., *Rule of Law and Democracy*, Brill, Leiden, 2010, and, taught by Palombella, Krygier, 'Rule of Law (and Rechtsstaat)'.
36. See F. A. Hayek, *Law, Legislation and Liberty, Vol. 1: Rules and Order*, University of Chicago Press, Chicago, 1973; Hayek, *Law, Legislation and Liberty, Vol. 2: The Mirage of Social Justice*, University of Chicago Press, Chicago, 1977; Hayek, *Law, Legislation and Liberty, Vol. 3: The Political Order of a Free People*, University of Chicago Press, Chicago, 1979; Eugene Kamenka and Alice Erh-Soon Tay, 'Beyond Bourgeois Individualism: The Contemporary Crisis in Law and Legal Ideology', in Eugene Kamenka and R. S. Neale, eds., *Feudalism, Capitalism and Beyond*, 1975, 128.
37. See Kenneth C. Davis, *Discretionary Justice*, LSU Press, Louisiana, 1969, 216–217; Mortimer R. Kadish and Sanford H. Kadish, *Discretion to Disobey: Study of Lawful Departures from Legal Rules*, Stanford University Press, Stanford, CA, 1973. See also Edward L. Rubin, 'Law and Legislation in the Administrative State', (1989), 89 *Columbia Law Review*, 369–426.
38. For the distinction between 'the flexible and the arbitrary' as a key insight of the American constitutional framers, see Stephen Holmes, 'In Case of Emergency: Misunderstanding Tradeoffs in the War on Terror', (2009) 97 *California Law Review*, 301–355, at 322. See too Postema, *Law's Rule*, 30.
39. Waldron, 'The Rule of Law and the Importance of Procedure', 16.
40. Avishai Margalit, *The Decent Society*, Harvard University Press, Cambridge, MA, 1996.

41. Joseph Raz, 'The Law's Own Virtue', (2019) 39 *Oxford Journal of Legal Studies*, 1–15, at 5.
42. Montesquieu, *The Spirit of the Laws*, pt. 2, bk. 12, chap. 4, 189.
43. Philip Selznick, *Law, Society, and Industrial Justice*, University of California Press, Berkeley, 1969, 13.
44. See Paul Blokker, 'Populism, COVID-19, and the Rule of Law: The Cases of Hungary and Poland', (2021) 15 *Politics: Rivista di Studi Politici*, https://doi.org/10.4000/151i7.
45. See Max Weber, *Economy and Society*, Vol. 2, Bedminster Press, New York, 1968, 809–811.
46. See Martin Krygier, 'Subjects, Objects, and the Colonial Rule of Law', in *Civil Passions: Selected Writings*, Black Inc., Melbourne, 2005, 56–91.
47. See Jothie Rajah, *Authoritarian Rule of Law*, Cambridge University Press, Cambridge, 2012.
48. Leonard Krieger, *An Essay on the Theory of Enlightened Despotism*, University of Chicago Press, Chicago, 1975, 52, 56.
49. Max Weber, *Economy and Society*, Vol. 3, Bedminster Press, New York, 1968, 1115.
50. Joseph de Maistre, *The Executioner*, trans. Richard A. Lebrun, Penguin Books, Aldershot, 2013, 29.
51. He was writing of the German concept, the *Rechtsstaat* (state of law, law-governed state), which is not identical to rule of law but it is close and in these quotations interchangeable. See Krygier, 'Rule of Law (and Rechtsstaat)'.
52. Carl Schmitt, *Legality and Legitimacy*, trans. Jeffrey Seizer, Duke University Press, Durham, NC, 2004, 20.
53. Carl Schmitt, *Political Theology*, trans. George Schwab, University of Chicago Press, Chicago, 1985, 15.
54. Postema, *Law's Rule*, 87.
55. See Fuller, *The Morality of Law*.
56. Ibid., 162–163.
57. See the discussion in Kristen Rundle, *Forms Liberate: Reclaiming the Jurisprudence of Lon L. Fuller*, Hart Publishers, Oxford, 2012, 107.
58. Evan Fox-Decent, 'The Fiduciary Nature of State Legal Authority', (2005) 31 *Queens Law Journal*, 259–310.
59. Gowder, *The Rule of Law in the Real World*, 40.
60. See Palombella, 'The Rule of Law as an Institutional Ideal'.
61. See Hayek, *Law, Legislation and Liberty, Vol. 3*, 41; F. A. Hayek, *The Constitution of Liberty*, Routledge & Kegan Paul, London, 1976, 215, 221.
62. Waldron, 'The Rule of Law and the Importance of Procedure'.
63. See especially Rubin, 'Law and Legislation in the Administrative State'. For a critique of Rubin, see Lisa Burton Crawford, 'The Problem of Complex Legislation', (2024) 30 *Legal Theory*, 1–21.
64. Compare with Krygier, 'The Grammar of Colonial Legality'.
65. After Pettit, *Republicanism*.
66. Judith N. Shklar, 'The Liberalism of Fear', in *Political Thought and Political Thinkers*, ed. Stanley Hoffman, University of Chicago Press, Chicago, 1998, 3–20, at 3.
67. Pettit, *Republicanism*, 86; Palombella, 'The Rule of Law as an Institutional Ideal'.
68. Palombella, 'The Rule of Law as an Institutional Ideal', 24.
69. Mary Wollstonecraft, *The Vindication of the Rights of Women*, W. W. Norton, New York, 1967.

70. Pettit, *Republicanism*, 69. See also his *On the People's Terms*, Cambridge University Press, Cambridge, 2012, chap. 1.
71. In her *Political Thought and Political Thinkers*, 3–20.
72. Joseph Priestley, *Political Writings*, ed. P. N. Miller, Cambridge University Press, Cambridge, 1993, 35.
73. John Emerich Edward Dalberg, Lord Acton, letter to Archbishop Creighton (Cannes, 5 April 1887), https://oll.libertyfund.org/title/acton-acton-creighton-correspondence:

    > I cannot accept your canon that we are to judge Pope and King unlike other men, with a favourable presumption that they did no wrong. If there is any presumption it is the other way against holders of power, increasing as the power increases. Historic responsibility has to make up for the want of legal responsibility. Power tends to corrupt and absolute power corrupts absolutely. Great men are almost always bad men, even when they exercise influence and not authority: still more when you superadd the tendency or the certainty of corruption by authority. There is no worse heresy than that the office sanctifies the holder of it.

    I doubt that 'great men are almost always bad men', but the argument is no weaker without that claim.
74. See Reid, 'In Legitimate Stirps'; Reid, *Rule of Law*.
75. Adam Smith, *An Inquiry into the Nature and Causes of the Wealth of Nations*, Vol. 1, Liberty Classics, Indianapolis, 1981, 26.
76. See Stephen Holmes, *Passions and Constraint*, University of Chicago Press, Chicago, 1995; Holmes, 'In Case of Emergency'.
77. Kaczyński was simply an elected member of the Polish *Sejm*, or Parliament, neither president nor prime minister.
78. PiS *Program 2011 r. Nowoczesna, Solidarna, Bezpieczna Polska*, Warsaw 2011, 17, quoted in Karol Muszynski, 'Socjologia prawa a kryzys konstytucyjny w Polsce. Między "imposybilistycznymi" rządami prawa a "silnym" systemem politycznym' (copy on file with the author), 5.
79. 'Czy Polska jest państwem prawa?' Wykład na Uniwersytecie Jagiellońskim *Presje Teka* XXIV Klubu Jagiellońskiego (2011), 222–229, at 227.
80. 'Kaczyński Announces Aim to Change Polish Constitution', Radio Poland, 2 May 2016, cited in Bojan Bugarič, 'The Populists at the Gates: Constitutional Democracy under Siege', September 2017, https://bit.ly/45uTj0w.
81. See Oliver Smith, 'Naypyidaw, Myanmar: The World's Weirdest Capital City', Traveller, *The Sydney Morning Herald*, 15 May 2009, www.traveller.com.au/naypyidaw-myanmar-the-worlds-weirdest-capital-city-hleexe.
82. See Darrick Danta, 'Ceausescu's Bucharest', (1993) 83 *American Geographical Society*, 170–182.
83. See Holmes, 'In Case of Emergency'.
84. Simone Weil, 'The Needs of the Soul', in *Simone Weil: An Anthology*, ed. Siân Miles, Penguin, London, 2005, 105–140, at 107.
85. Brian Tamanaha, 'Why Sovereigns Are Entitled to (Horizontal) Benefits of the International Rule of Law', in Gregory Shaffer and Wayne Sandholtz, eds., *The Rule of Law under Pressure: A Transnational Challenge*, Cambridge University Press, Cambridge, 2025, 87–110, at 96–99.
86. See Krygier, 'Transformations of the Rule of Law'.

87. See Martin Krygier, 'Domestic Abuse: Populists and the Rule of Law', Institute for Human Sciences (IWM), www.iwm.at/publication/iwmpost-article/domestic-abuse-populists-and-the-rule-of-law; András Sajó, 'The Rule of Law as Legal Despotism: Concerned Remarks on the Use of "Rule of Law" in Illiberal Democracies', (2019) 2 *Hague Journal on the Rule of Law*, 371–376.
88. Krygier, 'The Rule of Law: An Abuser's Guide', 141.
89. Pettit, *Just Freedom*, xix.

Chapter 6

1. These terms are, in turn, from Palmer, 'Limited Government and the Rule of Law'; 'Factors of the Rule of Law', World Justice Project; Gleeson, 'Courts and the Rule of Law'; 'What Is the Rule of Law', United Nations and the Rule of Law.
2. See N. W. Barber, *The Principles of Constitutionalism*, Oxford University Press, Oxford, 2018, drawing on the classic account of McIlwain, *Constitutionalism*. See also Palombella, 'The Rule of Law as an Institutional Ideal'.
3. Thucydides, *History of the Peloponnesian Wars*, trans. Martin Hammond, Oxford University Press, Oxford, 2009, 302.
4. Reid, *Rule of Law*, 12.
5. See also Gerald J. Postema, *Bentham and the Common Law Tradition*, Clarendon Press, Oxford, 2022.
6. Hayek, *The Road to Serfdom*, 159.
7. Hayek, *Law, Legislation and Liberty, Vol. 3*, 128.
8. Shklar, 'Political Theory and the Rule of Law', 24–25.
9. Ibid., 36.
10. Shklar, 'The Liberalism of Fear', 9.
11. Selznick, *The Moral Commonwealth*, 175.
12. Jeremy Waldron, '*Political* Political Theory: An Inaugural Lecture', (2013) 21 *Journal of Political Philosophy*, 1–23.
13. See Jeremy Waldron, *Law and Disagreement*, Oxford University Press, Oxford, 1999.
14. See Bernard Williams, 'The Liberalism of Fear', in *In the Beginning Was the Deed: Realism and Moralism in Political Argument*, Princeton University Press, Princeton, NJ, 2005, 52–61.
15. Muszynski, 'Socjologia prawa a kryzys konstytucyjny w Polsce', 5.
16. Schmitt, *Legality and Legitimacy*, 20.
17. See Nadia Urbinati, *Me the People*, Harvard University Press, Cambridge, MA, 2019.
18. Raz, 'The Rule of Law and Its Virtue', 224.
19. Ibid., 228.
20. See Postema, *Law's Rule*, 23: 'The rule of law is concerned not with the abuse of *law*, but rather with the abuse of *power* in social life.'
21. Mao Tse-Tung, 'Problems of War and Strategy' (November 6, 1938), *Selected Works*, Vol. 2, Pergamon Press, Oxford, 1965, 224.
22. John Rawls, *A Theory of Justice*, Oxford University Press, Oxford, 1971, 238.
23. On relationships between the rule of law and constitutionalism, see Krygier, 'Tempering Power', 34–59.
24. H. L. A. Hart, *The Concept of Law*, Clarendon Press, Oxford, 1961.

25. See Krygier, *Between Fear and Hope*, especially chaps. 2 and 5.
26. Stephen Holmes, *Passions and Constraint*, University of Chicago Press, Chicago, 1995.
27. Holmes, 'In Case of Emergency'.
28. Acemoglu and Robinson, *The Narrow Corridor*, 24.
29. Ernest Gellner, *Conditions of Liberty: Civil Society and Its Rivals*, Hamish Hamilton, London, 1994, 8.
30. Acemoglu and Robinson, *The Narrow Corridor*, 24.
31. Ibid., 341.
32. Ibid., 345.
33. On which, see Stephen Holmes, 'What Russia Teaches Us Now: How Weak States Threaten Freedom', *The American Prospect*, no. 33, July/August 1997, 30–39.
34. Holmes, *Passions and Constraint*. The term is later used to make a similar point by Barber: '[n]egative constitutionalism builds upon, or implies, an impoverished account of the state' (*The Principles of Constitutionalism*, 5).
35. See David Stark and Laszlo Bruszt, *Postsocialist Pathways*, Cambridge University Press, Cambridge, 1998, chap. 6. See too Martin Loughlin, *The Idea of Public Law*, Oxford University Press, Oxford, 2003 and Jon Elster, *Ulysses Unbound: Studies in Rationality, Precommitment, and Constraints*, Cambridge University Press, Cambridge, 2000.
36. Holmes, *Passions and Constraint*, 109.
37. Stephen Holmes, 'Constitutions and Constitutionalism', in Michel Rosenfeld and András Sajó, eds., *The Oxford Handbook of Comparative Constitutional Law*, Oxford University Press, 2012, 189–216, at 192.
38. Locke, *Second Treatise of Government*, chap. 6, s. 57.
39. Jeremy Waldron, 'Constitutionalism: A Skeptical View', NYU School of Law, Public Law & Legal Theory Research Paper Series, No. 10–87, December 2010, 25.
40. Ibid., 26.
41. Ibid., 25.
42. Allegedly by the French Physiocrat Vincent de Gournay in 1745. See Martin Krygier, 'State and Bureaucracy in Europe: The Growth of a Concept', in Eugene Kamenka and Martin Krygier, eds., *Bureaucracy: The Career of a Concept*, Edward Arnold, London, 1979, 1–33, at 22.
43. Montesquieu, *The Spirit of the Laws*, pt. 1, bk. 4, chap. 9, 28.
44. Ibid., pt. 1, bk. 6, chap. 14, 63.
45. Aurelian Craiutu, *A Virtue for Courageous Minds: Moderation in French Political Thought, 1748–1830*, Princeton University Press, Princeton, NJ, 2012, 49.
46. Barber, *The Principles of Constitutionalism*, 70–71.
47. Stephen Holmes, 'The Constitution of Sovereignty in Jean Bodin', in *Passions and Constraint*, 100–133.
48. Hilton L. Root, *Political Foundations of Markets in Old Regime France and England*, University of California Press, Berkeley, 1994, 156.
49. Ibid., 214.
50. The last few paragraphs are drawn from my Australian Broadcasting Commission radio lectures (the Boyer lectures); Krygier, *Between Fear and Hope*; 112–113.
51. Stephen Holmes, *The Matador's Cape: America's Reckless Response to Terror*, Cambridge University Press, Cambridge, 2007, 6.
52. See Paul van Tongeren, 'Nietzsche's Revaluation of the Cardinal Virtues: The Case of Sōphrosýnē', (2001) 3 *Phromimon*, 128–149.

53. See Helen North, *Sōphrosýnē: Self-Knowledge and Self-Restraint in Greek Literature*, Cornell University Press, Ithaca, NY, 1966.
54. See *Collins English Dictionary*, s.v. 'Temper', www.collinsdictionary.com/dictionary/english/temper. Cited in John Braithwaite, 'Tempered Power, Variegated Capitalism, Law and Society', (2019) 67 *Buffalo Law Review*, 527–594, at 533.
55. Actually,

> Cicero suggests 4 different translations of *sōphrosýnē*, that all have their own connotations: *moderatio* which means moderation in the sense of control and restrain; constantia, which means being (remaining) unperturbable or undisturbed; *frugalitas*, which means frugality and thrift; and the fourth one, which became the most influential: *temperantia*, which means of course temperance. But temperance has in Latin, certainly in Cicero's Latin the connotation of: 'the right mixture', the right balance; *temperare* means to mix different liquids in the right proportion.

Tongeren, 'Nietzsche's Revaluation of the Cardinal Virtues', 133.
56. Helen North, 'Sōphrosýnē', in P. P. Wiener, *Dictionary of the History of Ideas*, Vol. 4, Charles Scribner's Sons, New York, 1973, 365–378, at 367.
57. Helen North, 'A Period of Opposition to Sôphrosynê in Greek Thought', (1947) 78 *Transactions and Proceedings of the American Philological Association*, 1–17, at 3.
58. See Waldron, 'Thoughtfulness and the Rule of Law'; Waldron, 'Constitutionalism: A Skeptical View'.
59. Henry Bracton, *De legibus et consuetudinibus Angliæ* (Bracton on the Laws and Customs of England), Bracton Online, vol. 2, 110, https://amesfoundation.law.harvard.edu/Bracton/.
60. Nichols Aroney, 'Subsidiarity, Federalism and the Best Constitution: Thomas Aquinas on City, Province and Empire', (2007) 26 *Law and Philosophy*, 161–228.
61. Gerhard Dohrn-van Rossum, *History of the Hour: Clocks and Modern Temporal Orders*, University of Chicago Press, Chicago, 1996, 5.
62. Quentin Skinner, 'Ambrogio Lorenzetti and the Portrait of Virtuous Government', in *Images of Politics, Vol. 2: Renaissance Virtues*, Cambridge University Press, Cambridge, 2004, 39–92, at 85.
63. Wikipedia, s.v. 'Tempering (metallurgy)', https://en.wikipedia.org/wiki/Tempering_(metallurgy).
64. John Braithwaite, 'Hybrid Politics for Justice: The Silk Road for Restorative Justice Part II', (2017) 5 *Restorative Justice*, 7–28, at 25; Braithwaite, 'Tempered Power'.
65. John Braithwaite, 'Tempering Martin', (2019) 11 *Hague Journal on the Rule of Law*, 277–281, at 280. I discuss the distinction between despotic and infrastructural power, made first by Michael Mann, *Sources of Social Power*, Vol. 1, Cambridge University Press, Cambridge, 1986, 477.
66. Martin Krygier, 'Jak temperować władzę', in Jacek Żakowski, ed., *Wirus 2020*, Sic, 2020, 103–113.
67. Ibid., 103.
68. See Section 6.1.
69. Selznick, *The Moral Commonwealth*, 174.
70. Philip Selznick, 'Legal Cultures and the Rule of Law', in Martin Krygier and Adam Czarnota, eds., *The Rule of Law after Communism*, Aldershot, Ashgate, 1999, 21–38, at 26.

71. Ibid., 25–26.
72. See Eugene Bardach and Robert A. Kagan, *Going by the Book*, Temple University Press, Philadelphia, 1982.

Chapter 7

1. See Guillermo O'Donnell, 'Horizontal Accountability in New Democracies', (1998) 9 *Journal of Democracy*, 112–126.
2. For deep insights into differences between the conception of the rule of law, on the one hand, and *Rechtsstaat* and allied continental conceptions, on the other, see Palombella, 'The Rule of Law as an Institutional Ideal', and Palombella, *È possibile una legalità globale?* See also Krygier, 'Rule of Law (and Rechtsstaat)'.
3. William Blackstone, *Commentaries on the Laws of England*, University of Chicago Press, Chicago, vol. 1, 17 (first published in 1769).
4. See Martin Krygier, 'Common Law', in Edward Craig, ed., *Routledge Encyclopedia of Philosophy*, 10 vols., Routledge, London, 1998, 1:440–446.
5. Tamanaha, *On the Rule of Law*. And see Brian Tamanaha, 'Tempering Arbitrary Power: A Moral Theory of the Rule of Law', (2023) 38 *Constitutional Commentary*, 129–159; Tamanaha, 'Vertical and Horizontal Dimensions of the Rule of Law', (2024) 73 *Emory Law Journal*, 1216–1247.
6. Lisa M. Austin and Dennis Klimchuk, eds., *Private Law and the Rule of Law*, Oxford University Press, Oxford, 2014, 5.
7. Julian Sempill, 'The Lion and the Greatest Part: The Rule of Law and the Constitution of Employer Power', (2017) 9 *Hague Journal on the Rule of Law*, 283–324, at 289–291; Sempill, 'What Is the Rule of Law? Political, Traditional, Rhetorical', in Michael Sevel, ed., *The Routledge Handbook of the Rule of Law*, Routledge, London, 2024, 57–73, at 68.
8. Max Weber, 'Politics as a Vocation', in *From Max Weber*, ed. H. H. Gerth and C. Wright Mills, Routledge & Kegan Paul, London, 1948, 77–128, at 78. Weber's immediate 'today' was 1919, just after the First World War. There is no reason, today, to give an end date to his comment.
9. Gianfranco Poggi, *The State: Its Nature, Development, and Prospects*, Polity Press, Cambridge, 1990, 9.
10. Weber, 'Politics as a Vocation', 78.
11. Tamanaha, 'Vertical and Horizontal Dimensions of the Rule of Law', 1224.
12. Gowder, *The Rule of Law in the Real World*, 9.
13. Poggi, *The State*, 73.
14. Jan Zielonka, *The Lost Future and How to Reclaim It*, Yale University Press, New Haven, CT, 2023, 175.
15. See Kevin Aquilina, 'Bill No. 125: The Latest Nail in the Rule of Law Coffin', *The Malta Independent*, 9 February 2025.
16. Gowder, *The Rule of Law in the Real World*, 53.
17. Paul Gowder, 'Finding Leviathan in Hegel: The Private Rule of Law and Its Limits', (2024) 43 *Law and Philosophy*, 669–688, at 680.
18. Ibid., 685.
19. Selznick, *Law, Society, and Industrial Justice*.
20. Elizabeth Anderson, *Private Government: How Employers Rule Our Lives (and Why We Don't Talk about It)*, Princeton University Press, Princeton, NJ, 2017.

21. Max Weber, *The Protestant Ethic and the Spirit of Capitalism*, trans. Talcott Parsons, Unwin University Books, London, 1971, 182–183. The original term Weber used, however, was '*stahlhartes Gehäuse*' (housing hard as steel).
22. Peter F. Drucker, *The Concept of the Corporation*, Mentor Books, New York, 1964, 18–19.
23. Selznick, *Law, Society, and Industrial Justice*, 36.
24. Ibid., 246.
25. Selznick, *The Moral Commonwealth*, 300–301.
26. Anderson, *Private Government*, 70–71.
27. Ibid., 67.
28. Karl Marx and Friedrich Engels, 'Manifesto of the Communist Party', in *Political Writings, Vol. 1: The Revolutions of 1848*, ed. David Fernbach, Penguin, Harmondsworth, 1973, 62–98, at 69.
29. Though, for some qualification of this 'vulgar Marxist' claim, see his *The Eighteenth Brumaire of Louis Bonaparte*, Foreign Languages Press, Paris, 2021.
30. Krygier, 'Marxism and the Rule of Law'.
31. I, of course, am alluding to the much bowdlerised passage in the afterword to *Capital*, in which Marx suggests that Hegel gets the mechanism of history half-right but has the relationship between ideas and the material development of the world upside down: 'With him it is standing on its head. It must be turned right side up again, if you would discover the rational kernel within the mystical shell'. Karl Marx, *Collected Works, Vol. 35: Capital, Vol. 1*, Lawrence & Wishart, London, 2010, 19.
32. Postema, *Law's Rule*, 34.
33. Julian A. Sempill, 'What Rendered Ancient Tyrants Detestable: The Rule of Law and the Constitution of Corporate Power', (2018) 10 *Hague Journal on the Rule of Law*, 219–253. See also Sempill, 'The Lion and the Greatest Part'.
34. See Martin Krygier, *Philip Selznick: Ideals in the World*, Stanford University Press, Stanford, CA, 2012, chaps. 7 and 9.
35. See Lauren B. Edelman, *Working Law*, University of Chicago Press, Chicago, 2016.
36. Sempill, 'What Rendered Ancient Tyrants Detestable', 230.
37. Ibid., 248.
38. Seth Lazar, 'Automatic Authorities: Power and AI', in Arathi Sethumadhavan and Mira Lane, eds., *Collaborative Intelligence: How Humans and AI Are Transforming Our World*, MIT Press, Cambridge MA, 2024, 37–60, at 37.
39. Scott Veitch, 'Martin Krygier and The Rule of Law', Glasgow University Law School, 11 June 2024 (unpublished text on file with the author).
40. Quoted in Frank Pasquale, *The Black Box Society: The Secret Algorithms That Control Money and Information*, Harvard University Press, Cambridge, MA, 2015, 187.
41. Postema, *Law's Rule*, 263.
42. See too Paul Gowder, *The Networked Leviathan: For Democratic Platforms*, Cambridge University Press, Cambridge, 2023.
43. Jamie Susskind, *Digital Democracy: On Freedom and Democracy in the 21st Century*, Bloomsbury, London, 2022, 41.
44. See Simon Chesterman, 'Through a Glass, Darkly: Artificial Intelligence and the Problem of Opacity', (2021) 69 *American Journal of Comparative Law*, 271–294, at 274. And see Gilad Albiri, 'Public Constitutional AI', Peking University School of Transnational Law Research Paper, SSRN, (2024), https://papers.ssrn.com/sol3/papers.cfm?abstract_id=4874670: 'The complex, non-linear nature of deep learning

models makes it nearly impossible for humans to fully comprehend their decision-making processes, even with complete access to their architecture and training data. While proprietary and complexity opacity can be addressed through legal means or expert consultation, the inherent natural opacity of deep learning models presents a more fundamental problem.'

45. Pasquale, *The Black Box Society*, 61.
46. Ibid., 217.
47. See Mustafa Suleyman (with Michael Bhaskar) *The Coming Wave: AI, Power and Our Future*, Vintage, New York, 2024, 114.
48. See Chesterman, 'Through a Glass, Darkly, 274. And see Albiri 'Public Constitutional AI'.
49. Shoshana Zuboff, *The Age of Surveillance Capitalism: The Fight for a Human Future at the New Frontier*, Profile Books, London, 2019, 10.
50. Susskind, *Digital Democracy*, 219.
51. Ibid., 73.
52. See Yoshua Bengio, 'AI and Catastrophic Risk', (2023), 34 *Journal of Democracy*, 111–121, at 112.
53. See Royal Commission into the Robodebt Scheme, *Report*, Commonwealth of Australia, Canberra, 2023, https://robodebt.royalcommission.gov.au/publications/report; Rick Morton, *Mean Streak*, 4th Estate, London, 2024. See also 'Post Office Horizon Scandal: Why Hundreds Were Wrongly Prosecuted', BBC News, 22 April 2021, www.bbc.com/news/business-56718036; 'Dutch Scandal Serves as a Warning for Europe Over Risks of Using Algorithms', *Politico*, 29 March 2022, https://bit.ly/3Z5zmtA.
54. See the 'Glossary of Key Terms' at the start of Suleyman's *The Coming Wave*, xiii, which lists as a term of art for his book, 'the containment problem': 'Technology's predisposition to diffuse widely in waves and to have emergent impacts that are impossible to predict or control, including negative and unforeseen consequences.'
55. See Michael Veale, Kira Matus, and Robert Gorwa, 'AI and Global Governance: Modalities, Rationales, Tensions', (2023) 19 *Annual Review of Law and Social Science*, 255–275.
56. See Michael Guihot and Lyria Bennett Moses, *Artificial Intelligence, Robots and the Law*, LexisNexis, St Leonards, NSW, 2020, 108.
57. Susskind, *Digital Democracy*, 246.
58. See Peter R. Evans, Dietrich Rueschmeyer, and Theda Skocpol, eds., *Bringing the State Back In*, Cambridge University Press, Cambridge, 1985; Linda Weiss, *The Myth of the Powerless State*, Polity Press, Cambridge, 1998.
59. Michael Walzer, *Thick and Thin: Moral Argument at Home and Abroad*, University of Notre Dame Press, Notre Dame, IN, 1994, 37.
60. See Martin Krygier, 'Publicness, Privateness and "Primitive Law"', in Stanley I. Benn and G. F. Gaus, eds., *Public and Private in Social Life*, Croom Helm, Kent, 1983, 307–340.

Chapter 8

1. See Stephen Macedo, *Liberal Virtues*, Oxford University Press, Oxford, 1990.
2. Montesquieu, *The Spirit of the Laws*, pt. 1, bk. 2, chap. 1, 10. Italics in the original.

3. Hobbes, *Leviathan*, chap. 13, 82.
4. Locke, *The Second Treatise of Government*, chap. XI, ss. 124–126. Italics in the original.
5. See Section 6.2.
6. See Pirie, *Rules of Law*.
7. Lenin, 'The Proletarian Revolution and the Renegade Kautsky'.
8. See Karl Schlögel, *Moscow, 1937*, Polity Press, Cambridge, 2012, 125–143, 510–537.
9. See Nicolas Werth, 'A State against Its People: Violence, Repression, and Terror in the Soviet Union', in Stéphane Courtois, Nicolas Werth, Jean-Louis Panné, Andrzej Paczkowski, Karel Bartošek, and Jean-Louis Margolin, *The Black Book of Communism*, ed. Mark Kramer; trans. Jonathan Murphy, Harvard University Press, Cambridge, MA, 1999, 33–268.
10. Mervyn Matthews, *Party, State, and Citizen in the Soviet Union: A Collection of Documents*, Sharpe, Armonk, NY, 1989, xxxvii.
11. Alvin Cheung, 'Abusive Legalism', doctoral dissertation, New York University, 2020, chaps. 3–4.
12. Alexandr Solzhenitsyn, *The Gulag Archipelago, 1918–1956: An Experiment in Literary Interpretation*, Vols. 1–2. Harper & Row, New York, 1973, 60.
13. Attributed to long-time Italian premier, Giovanni Giolitti.
14. Cheung, 'Abusive Legalism', 73. Italics in the original.
15. See Krygier, 'Domestic Abuse', 1.
16. Vladimir Ilyich Lenin, 'The Trade Unions, The Present Situation and Trotsky's Mistakes', Speech Delivered at a Joint Meeting of Communist Delegates to the Eighth Congress of Soviets, Communist Members of the All-Russia Central Council of Trade Unions and Communist Members of the Moscow City Council of Trade Unions, 30 December 1920, V. I. Lenin Internet Archive (www.marx.org) 2002, www.marxists.org/archive/lenin/works/1920/dec/30.htm.
17. See Partlett, *Why the Russian Constitution Matters*.
18. Ibid., 11.
19. See Tom Ginsburg and Tamir Moustafa, eds., *Rule by Law: The Politics of Courts in Authoritarian Regimes*, Cambridge University Press, Cambridge, 2008.
20. See Waldron, *Thoughtfulness and the Rule of Law*, chap. 10: 'Rule *by* Law: A Much Maligned Proposition'.
21. Jothie Rajah, *Authoritarian Rule of Law: Legislation, Discourse, and Legitimacy in Singapore*, Cambridge University Press, Cambridge, 2012.
22. Ibid., 44.
23. Plan on Building the Rule of Law in China (2020–2025), https://bit.ly/3OhcRj2.
24. Randall Peerenboom, 'The Transformation of State Socialist Rule of Law into Party-State Socialist Rule of Law in the Xi Jinping Era of Comprehensive Rules-Based Governance', (2025) 17 *Hague Journal on the Rule of Law*, 221–276, at 269.
25. Taisu Zhang and Tom Ginsburg, 'China's Turn toward Law', 59 *Virginia Journal of International Law*, 306–389, at 321.
26. Ibid., 317.
27. See Donald C. Clarke, 'Is China a Dual State?' GW Law School Public Law and Legal Theory Paper No. 2022-74 (2022), https://ssrn.com/abstract=4317126.
28. Cited in Peerenboom, 'The Transformation of State Socialist Rule of Law', 240.
29. See Zeming Liu and Benjamin L. Liebman, 'Redefining Law in China', (2025) 73 *American Journal of Comparative Law*, 672–735.

30. Sida Liu and Terence C. Halliday, *Criminal Defense in China: The Politics of Lawyers at Work*, Cambridge University Press, Cambridge, 2016, 64.
31. Zhang and Ginsburg, 'China's Turn toward Law', 376. And see Xiaobo Zhai, 'Law in the Shadow of the Political', in Brian Christopher Jones, ed., *Democracy and Rule of Law in China's Shadow*, Hart Publishing, Oxford, 2021, 197–217.
32. Locke, *The Second Treatise on Government*, chap. VII, s. 93. Italics in the original.
33. Ernst Fraenkel, *The Dual State: A Contribution to the Theory of Dictatorship*, Cambridge University Press, Cambridge, 2017 (first published in 1941).
34. Franz Neumann, *Behemoth: The Structure and Practice of National Socialism*, Oxford University Press, New York, 1942.
35. See Rudolf, 'Xi Jinping Thought on the Rule of Law'; Ji Li, 'The Evolving Rule of Law with Chinese Characteristics and Its Impacts on the International Legal Order', in Gregory Shaffer and Wayne Sandholtz, eds., *The Rule of Law under Pressure: A Transnational Challenge*, Cambridge University Press, Cambridge, 2025, 431–457. See Cora Chan, 'From Legal Pluralism to Dual State: Evolution of the Relationship between the Chinese and Hong Kong Legal Orders', (2022) 16 *Law & Ethics of Human Rights*, 99–135; Hualing Fu, 'Between the Prerogative and the Normative States: The Evolving Power to Detain in China's Political-Legal System', (2022) 16 *Law & Ethics of Human Rights*, 61; Susan H. Whiting, 'Authoritarian Legality and State Capitalism in China', (2023) 19 *Annual Review of Law and Social Science*, 357–373; Clarke, 'Is China a Dual State?'. And see Serdar Tekin, 'The Dual State in Turkey', (2022) 34 *European Journal of Turkish Studies*, https://doi.org/10.4000/ejts.8000.
36. Fraenkel, *The Dual State*, 71.
37. See Fu, 'Between the Prerogative and the Normative States'; Eva Pils, 'China's Dual State Revival under Xi Jinping', (2023) 46 *Fordham International Law Journal*, 339–376. But see Samuli Seppänen, 'The Party State', in Mark Tushnet, Cora Chan, Madhav Khosla and Benjamin Liebman, eds., *The Oxford Handbook on Law and Authoritarianism*, Oxford University Press, Oxford, in press.
38. Wojciech Sadurski, *Poland's Constitutional Breakdown*, Oxford University Press, Oxford, 2019, 7.
39. See Rosalind Dixon, 'Rule of Law Teleology: Against the Misuse and Abuse of Rule of Law Rhetoric', (2019) 11 *Hague Journal on the Rule of Law*, 461–464; Rosalind Dixon and David Landau, '1989–2019: From Democratic to Abusive Constitutional Borrowing', (2019) 17 *International Journal of Constitutional Law*, 489–496. See also Kim Lane Scheppele, 'The Rule of Law and the Frankenstate: Why Governance Checklists Do Not Work', (2013) 26 *Governance: An International Journal of Policy, Administration, and Institutions*, 559–562.
40. In Poland, teams within the judiciary orchestrated hate (in Polish *hejt*) campaigns against judges and others who resisted them.
41. Huntington, *The Third Wave*.
42. See references in Chapter 3, Note 47.
43. Scheppele, 'Autocratic Legalism', 547.
44. Benjamin Constant, *Political Writings*, Cambridge University Press, Cambridge, 1993, 95 Quoted in András Sajó, *Ruling by Cheating*, Cambridge University Press, Cambridge, 2021, 12.
45. See Partlett, *Why the Russian Constitution Matters*.
46. See Gianluigi Palombella, 'The Abuse of the Rule of Law', (2020) 12 *Hague Journal on the Rule of Law*, 387–397.

47. Tarunabh Khaitan, 'Killing a Constitution with a Thousand Cuts: Executive Aggrandizement and Party-State Fusion in India', (2020) 14 1 *Law & Ethics of Human Rights*, 49–95, at 93.
48. See Steven Levitsky and Lucan Way, 'The New Competitive Authoritarianism', (2020) 31, 1 *Journal of Democracy*, 51–65.
49. Sajó, *Ruling by Cheating*, and *Militant Rule of Law*.
50. See the excellent discussion by Palombella, 'The Abuse of the Rule of Law'.
51. Leszek Garlicki, 'Jak Zjednoczona Prawica podbija sądy i jak one się bronią' ['How Does the United Right Overtake the Courts and How They Defend Themselves'], *Oko Press*, 31 August 2020, https://oko.press/jak-zjednoczona-prawica-podbija-sady-i-jak-one-sie-bronia-przenikliwy-esej-prof-garlickiego/.
52. Sadurski, *Poland's Constitutional Breakdown*, chap. 3, 79. And see Chapter 4 for the measures undertaken to undermine the independence of judges and prosecutors.
53. See Krygier, Czarnota, and Sadurski, eds., *Anti-constitutional Populism*.
54. Sadurski, *A Pandemic of Populists*, 54.
55. Khaitan, 'Killing a Constitution with a Thousand Cuts'.
56. See Scholtes, *The Abuse of Constitutional Identity in the European Union*.
57. Sadurski, *Poland's Constitutional Breakdown*, 6. Italics in the original.
58. Ibid.
59. Kim Lane Scheppele, Dimitry Kochenov, and Barbara Grabowska-Moroz, 'EU Values are Law, After All: Enforcing EU Values through Systemic Infringement Actions by the European Commission and the Member States of the European Union', (2020) 38 *European Yearbook of International Law*, 3–121, at 98.
60. See Philip Selznick, review of '*The Morality of Law*', (1965) 30 *American Sociological Review*, 947–948.
61. See especially Rubin, 'Law and Legislation in the Administrative State', and Crawford, 'The Problem of Complex Legislation'.
62. Fuller, *The Morality of Law*.
63. Waldron, Waldron, *Thoughtfulness and the Rule of Law*, chap. 10: 'Rule *by* Law: A Much Maligned Proposition'.
64. See Kristen Rundle, 'The Impossibility of an Exterminatory Legality: Law and the Holocaust', (2009) 59 *University of Toronto Law Journal*, 65–125, and see her *Forms Liberate: Reclaiming the Jurisprudence of Lon L. Fuller*, Bloomsbury, London, 2012; and *Revisiting the Rule of Law*.
65. See Krygier, 'Hart, Fuller and Law in Transitional Societies'.
66. Fuller, *The Morality of Law*, 207.
67. Fuller, *The Morality of Law*, 162.
68. Fuller, *The Morality of Law*, 162–163, emphasis added.
69. Though see Rubin, 'Law and Legislation in the Administrative State', and Crawford, 'The Problem of Complex Legislation'.
70. See Raz, 'The Rule of Law and Its Virtue', 213: 'the law should be such that people will be able to be guided by it ... : the law must be capable of being obeyed'.
71. And it would appear, the later Raz. See Raz, 'The Law's Own Virtue'.
72. See Sempill, 'Ruler's Sword', 333.
73. See Thomas Adams, 'The Rule of Law and Respect for Persons', in Geneviève Cartier and Mark Walters, eds., *The Promise of Legality: Critical Reflections on the Work of TRS Allan*, Cambridge University Press, Cambridge, 2025, 103–116.

74. See Krygier, 'Illiberalism and the Rule of Law', especially 543–549; Taisu Zhang, 'Authoritarian Legality', (2024) 32 *Asia Pacific Law Review*, 311–321.
75. Otto Kirchheimer, *Political Justice: The Use of Legal Justice for Political Ends*, Princeton University Press, Princeton, NJ, 1961, 287.
76. Julian Sempill, 'Law, Dignity and the Elusive Promise of a Third Way', (2018) 38 *Oxford Journal of Legal Studies*, 217–245, at 230.
77. Finnis, *Natural Law and Natural Rights*, 273.
78. Fuller, *The Morality of Law*, 40.
79. Krygier, 'Rule of Law', 13406.
80. Postema, *Law's Rule*, 56.
81. Ibid., 55.
82. Kim Lane Scheppele, 'Worst Practices and the Transnational Legal Order (or How to Build a Constitutional "Democratorship" in Plain Sight)', Working Paper, 2016, archived at http://perma.cc/Q266-MJEK.
83. John Braithwaite, 'Rules and Principles: A Theory of Legal Certainty', (2002) 27 *Australian Journal of Legal Philosophy*, 48–81, at 54, and see Bardach and Kagan, *Going by the Book*.
84. John Braithwaite and Valerie Braithwaite, 'The Politics of Legalism: Rules versus Standards in Nursing-Home Regulation', (1995) 4 *Social and Legal Studies*, 303–347, at 336–337.
85. John Braithwaite, 'Hybrid Politics for Justice: The Silk Road for Restorative Justice Part II', (2017) 5 *Restorative Justice*, 7–28.
86. Carol Heimer, 'The Routinization of Responsiveness: Regulatory Compliance and the Construction of Organizational Routines', American Bar Foundation Working Paper No. 9801, n.d., 6, 7.
87. Steven Levitsky and Daniel Ziblatt, *How Democracies Die*, Viking, New York, 2018, 99.
88. See Hart, *The Concept of Law*, chap. 7.
89. See A. R. Amar, *America's Unwritten Constitution*, Basic Books, New York, 2012.
90. See Martin Krygier, 'Law as Tradition', (1986), 5 *Law and Philosophy*, 237–262, and Krygier, 'Thinking Like a Lawyer', in Wojciech Sadurski, ed., *Ethical Dimensions of Legal Theory*, Rodopi, Amsterdam 1991, 67–90. And see Section 8.5, this chapter.
91. See Marcin Matczak, 'The Clash of Powers in Poland's Rule of Law Crisis: Tools of Attack and Self-defense', (2020) 12 *Hague Journal on the Rule of Law*, 421–450, https://papers.ssrn.com/sol3/papers.cfm?abstract_id=3677796, and Sajó, *Militant Rule of Law*.
92. Wojciech Sadurski, 'Hercules or Sisyphus? On the Legacy of Statutory Lawlessness in Post-autocratic Poland: A Letter from Princeton', *Verfassungsblog*, 12 April 2024, https://bit.ly/3ZeTGJ7; Sadurski, 'Sisyphean Democracy', *Democracy Project*, 17 September 2025, https://democracyproject.org/posts/sisyphean-democracy.
93. Samuel Issacharoff, *Democracy Unmoored: Populism and the Corruption of Popular Sovereignty*, Oxford University Press, Oxford, 2023, 97.
94. Sajó, *Militant Rule of Law*, 361.
95. Ibid., 13.
96. See Attila Vincze, 'Rule of Law Compliance beyond Ticking Boxes', (2025) *Hague Journal on the Rule of Law*, https://doi.org/10.1007/s40803-025-00255-6.
97. Sajó, *Militant Rule of Law*, 370.

98. See Kim Lane Scheppele, 'Blinded by Legality: The Venice Commission's Change of Heart on Restoring the Rule of Law in Poland', *Verfassungsblog*, 23 December 2024, https://verfassungsblog.de/blinded-by-legality/; Scheppele, 'The Rule of Law Writ Large: The European Union and Its Rogue Member States', in Gregory Shaffer and Wayne Sandholtz, eds., *The Rule of Law under Pressure: A Transnational Challenge*, Cambridge University Press, Cambridge, 2025, 251–283; Wojciech Sadurski, 'Judicial Review versus Populist Authoritarianism', (2025) 3 *Comparative Constitutional Studies*, 81–105. See Krygier, 'The Spirit of Constitutionalism'.
99. See Maciej Kisilowski, 'Militant Public Administration', *Verfassungsblog*, 6 June 2024, https://verfassungsblog.de/militant-public-administration/.
100. Upham, 'Mythmaking in the Rule-of-Law Orthodoxy', 76.
101. Scheppele, 'Worst Practices and the Transnational Legal Order'.
102. See Massoud, *Law's Fragile State*.
103. Cheesman, *Opposing the Rule of Law*, 259.
104. Montesquieu, *The Spirit of the Laws*, pt. 1, bk. 6, chap. 14, 60.
105. Oakeshott, *Rationalism in Politics and Other Essays*, 61.
106. Ibid., 121.
107. Kamenka and Tay, 'Beyond Bourgeois Individualism', 128.
108. Clifford Geertz, *Local Knowledge: Further Essay in Interpretive Anthropology*, Basic Books, New York, 1983, 215.
109. For more on law's traditionality, see H. Patrick Glenn, *Legal Traditions of the World: Sustainable Diversity in Law*, 5th ed., Oxford University Press, Oxford, 2014; Krygier, 'Law as Tradition', Krygier, 'The Traditionality of Statutes', (1988), 1 *Ratio Juris*, 20–39; Krygier, 'Thinking Like a Lawyer'.
110. J. H. Merryman, *The Civil Law Tradition*, 2nd ed., Stanford University Press, Stanford, CA, 1985, 2.
111. See Sida Liu, 'Between Rules and Power: Finding a Place for Lawyers in the Sociology of Professions', in Richard L. Abel, Ole Hammerslev, Hilary Sommerlad, and Ulrike Schultz, eds., *Lawyers in Twenty-First-Century Societies*, Vol. 2, Hart Publishing, Oxford, 2022, 445–460.
112. Adam Czarnota and Martin Krygier, 'From State to Legal Traditions? Prospects for the Law after Communism', in Janina Frentzel-Zagórska, ed., *A One-Party State to Democracy: Transition in Eastern Europe*, Rodopi, Amsterdam, 1993, 91–112.
113. Smith, *An Inquiry into the Nature and Causes of the Wealth of Nations*, vol. 1, 26.
114. Emile Durkheim, *The Division of Labor in Society*, The Free Press, New York, 1984, 161.
115. Postema, *Law's Rule*, 39–45. See too Stephen J. Toope, *A Rule of Law for Our New Age of Anxiety*, Cambridge University Press, Cambridge, 2023 on law's 'anchoring practices'.
116. Postema, *Law's Rule*, 41. Italics in the original.
117. *Whitney* v. *California*, 274 U.S. 357, at 375 (Brandeis, J., concurring).
118. Postema, *Law's Rule*, 41–42.
119. Neil MacCormick, *Rhetoric and the Rule of Law*, Oxford University Press, Oxford, 2005, 14.
120. Montesquieu, *The Spirit of the Laws*, pt. 2, bk. 11, chap. 14, 155.
121. See Krygier, 'Tempering Power', 34–39.

Chapter 9

1. Center for the Study of Law and Society, University of California, Berkeley.
2. Philip Selznick, 'Jurisprudence and Social Policy: Aspirations and Perspectives', (1980) 68 *California Law Review*, 206–220, at 216. Compare with Lon L. Fuller, 'Some Unexplored Social Dimensions of the Law', in Arthur E. Sutherland, ed., *Path of the Law from 1967*, Harvard University Press, Cambridge, MA, 1968, 57–70:

   > The intensified interest in the sociology of law that has developed in recent years has come to assume the proportions of something like an intellectual movement. In the United States this movement has found a kind of sloganized expression in the title, *Law and Society* ... It would be captious indeed to pick any serious quarrel with this innocent renaming of the familiar. ... At the same time there are, I believe, some dangers in this new title and in the allocation of intellectual energies it seems to imply. By speaking of law *and* society we may forget that law is itself a part of society, that its basic processes are *social* processes, that it contains within its own internal workings social dimensions worthy of the best attentions of the sociologist. (70; italics in the original)

3. Center for Advanced Study in the Behavioral Sciences (CASBS), Palo Alto, California.
4. Robert F. Schoeni, James S. House, George A. Kaplan, and Harold Pollack, eds., *Making Americans Healthier: Social and Economic Policy as Health Policy*, Russell Sage Foundation, New York, 2010, 10.
5. Marc Galanter, 'Justice in Many Rooms: Courts, Private Ordering, and Indigenous Law', (1981) *Journal of Legal Pluralism*, 1–47, at 17. Compare Selznick, 'Sociology and Natural Law', 84: 'education, politics, religion, and other social activities are found outside of the specialized institutions established to deal with them. Sociology has located these phenomena "in society," that is, in more informal and spontaneous groupings and processes.' Selznick thought the same was true of law.
6. Galanter, 'Justice in Many Rooms', 20. For a more recent and remarkably wide-ranging discussion of the literature exploring 'non-official sites of legal production [that] have always existed and still exist (outside and) inside the West', see Mauro Bussani, 'Strangers in the Law: Lawyers' Law and the Other Legal Dimensions', (2019) 40 *Cardozo Law Review*, 3125–3184, at 3128.
7. Leon Petrażycki, *Law and Morality*, Routledge, London, 2017.
8. Eugen Ehrlich, *Fundamental Principles of the Sociology of Law*, Harvard University Press, Cambridge, MA, 1936, xv.
9. Bronisław Malinowski, *Crime and Custom in Savage Society*, Routledge, London, 2017 (first published in 1926), 37.
10. Leila Chirayath, Caroline Sage, and Michael Woolcock, 'Customary Law and Policy Reform: Engaging with the Plurality of Justice Systems' World Bank Legal Department Paper, 2005, 3, quoted in Brian Tamanaha, *Legal Pluralism Explained: History, Theory, Consequences*, Oxford University Press, Oxford, 2021, 208.
11. Moore, 'Introduction', 2–3.
12. Moore, chap. 2: 'Law and Social Change: The Semi-autonomous Field as an Appropriate Subject of Study'.
13. Margalit, *The Decent Society*, 138.
14. See Robert H. Mnookin and Lewis Kornhauser, 'Bargaining in the Shadow of the Law: The Case of Divorce' (1979) 88 *Yale Law Journal*, 950–997.

15. See Scott Burris, Peter Drahos, and Clifford Shearing, 'Nodal Governance' (2005) 30 *Australian Journal of Legal Philosophy*, 30–58.
16. See, for example, Vladimir Gel'man, 'The Unrule of Law in the Making: The Politics of Informal Institution Building in Russia', (2004) 56 *Europe-Asia Studies*, 1021–1040.
17. Moore, 'Introduction', 4.
18. Actually some would. See Rubin, 'The Rule of Law in the Administrative State'.
19. See, for example, Julia Berg and Clifford Shearing, 'Governing-through-Harm and Public Goods Policing', (2018) 679 *Annals of the American Academy of Political and Social Science*, 72–85.
20. Moore, 'Introduction', 7.
21. Gunther Teubner, 'Legal Irritants: Good Faith in British Law or How Unifying Law Ends Up in New Divergences' (1998) 61 *Modern Law Review*, 11–32. And for the wider theoretical context, see Nofar Sheffi, 'Societal Constitutionalism, Reviewed and Re-Viewed', (2025) 21 *Annual Review of Law and Social Science*, 35–53, https://doi.org/10.1146/annurev-lawsocsci-062124-122245.
22. For a classic reflection on the interaction of novel legal irritants with just such a legal background, see E. P. Thompson, *Whigs and Hunters*, Harmondsworth, Penguin, 1977.
23. See Alena V. Ledeneva, *Russia's Economy of Favours*, Cambridge University Press, Cambridge, 1998, and Ledeneva, *How Russia Really Works: The Informal Practices That Shaped Post-Soviet Politics and Business*, Cornell University Press, Ithaca, NY, 2006.
24. See Galanter, 'Justice in Many Rooms', 17.
25. Moore, 'Introduction', 29–30.
26. See Gillian K. Hadfield and Barry Weingast, 'Microfoundations of the Rule of Law', (2014) 17 *Annual Review of Political Science*, 21–42; Lant Pritchett and Michael Woolcock, 'Solutions When the Solution Is the Problem: Arraying the Disarray in Development', Centre for Global Development Working Paper No. 10, September 2002, 17, http://papers.ssrn.com/sol3/papers.cfm?abstract_id=1106236.
27. Moore, 'Introduction', 2.
28. See William Felstiner, Richard Abel, and Austin Sarat, 'The Emergence and Transformation of Disputes: Naming, Blaming, Claiming…', (1980) 15 *Law & Society Review*, 631–654.
29. Catherine R. Albiston, Lauren B. Edelman, and Joy Milligan, 'The Dispute Tree and the Legal Forest', (2014) 10 *Annual Review of Law and Social Science*, 105–131.
30. Though not always to citizens and increasingly to administrative agencies. This, as Edward Rubin argues brilliantly, much complicates the Fullerian and similar understandings of the rule of law. See Rubin, 'Law and Legislation in the Administrative State'.
31. Mnookin and Kornhauser, 'Bargaining in the Shadow of the Law'.
32. See Berg and Shearing, 'Governing-through-Harm and Public Goods Policing', 78: 'A governing-through-harm approach, in contrast to a governing-through-crime approach, does not establish a solution prior to the issue being canvased and understood.'
33. Angelo Golia, Jr, and Gunther Teubner, 'Societal Constitutionalism: Deconstruction of Statecentrism and Construction of a Constitutional Theory for the Digital Age', in Giovanni De Gregorio, Oreste Pollicino, and Peggy Valcke eds., *The Oxford Handbook of Digital Constitutionalism*, Oxford University Press, Oxford, in press, 6

34. See Gunther Teubner, *Constitutional Fragments: Societal Constitutionalism and Globalization*, Oxford University Press, Oxford, 2012; Sheffi, 'Societal Constitutionalism'.
35. See Shaffer and Sandholtz, *The Rule of Law under Pressure*, 17; Terence J. Halliday and Gregory Shaffer, eds., *Transnational Legal Orders*, Cambridge University Press, Cambridge, 2015.
36. See Burris, Drahos, and Shearing, 'Nodal Governance'.
37. Braithwaite, *Macrocriminology and Freedom*.

Chapter 10

1. See the Law in Context series page, Cambridge Core (online), www.cambridge.org/core/series/law-in-context/387EA14AA111E65AB0120DA893AFAFCB.
2. E. P. Thompson, *Whigs and Hunters: The Origin of the Black Act*, Allen Lane, London, 1975.
3. Ibid., 191–192.
4. E. P. Thompson, *The Making of the English Working Class*, Victor Gollancz, London, 1963.
5. Thompson, *Whigs and Hunters*, 188–189.
6. According to his wife, the section was added at her prompting after 'a very heated discussion' with her led him 'to rethink the question'. Letter to Daniel H. Cole, cited in Cole, '"An Unqualified Human Good": E. P. Thompson and the Rule of Law', (2001) 28 *Journal of Law and Society*, 177–203, at 183.
7. Thompson, *Whigs and Hunters*, 264–265.
8. Ibid., 265.
9. Ibid., 266.
10. Things changed, of course, very soon after.
11. Nancy Lee Peluso, 'Whigs and Hunters: The Origins of the Black Act, by E. P. Thompson', (2017) 44 *Journal of Peasant Studies*, 309–321, at 310.
12. Much of this section is adapted from sections 1–3 of my 'Well-Tempered Power: "A Cultural Achievement of Universal Significance"', (2024) 16 *Hague Journal on the Rule of Law*, 479–507.
13. Thompson, *Whigs and Hunters*, 260.
14. Ibid., 265.
15. Ibid., 267.
16. Ibid., 260.
17. Ibid., 260.
18. Ibid., 262.
19. See Krygier, 'Thinking Like a Lawyer'.
20. Thompson, *Whigs and Hunters*, 263.
21. See Terence C. Halliday, Lucien Karpik, and Malcolm Feeley, eds., *Fighting for Political Freedom: Comparative Studies of the Legal Complex and Political Liberalism*, Hart Publishing, Oxford, 2007; Lucien Karpik and Terence C. Halliday, 'The Legal Complex', (2011) 7 *Annual Review of Law and Social Science*, 217–236. See also Postema, *Law's Rule*, and Toope, *A Rule of Law for Our New Age of Anxiety*.
22. See 'History of the Phrase 'How Many Divisions Has the Pope?', World Histories, https://wordhistories.net/2019/08/23/how-many-divisions-pope/.

23. See Thompson's student and colleague, Douglas Hay, 'Property, Authority, and the Criminal Law', in Douglas Hay et al., eds., *Albion's Fatal Tree: Crime and Society in Eighteenth Century England*, Verso, London, 1965, 1–63.
24. Thompson, *Whigs and Hunters*, 264.
25. E. P. Thompson, 'The Rule of Law in English History', (1979) 10 *Bulletin (Haldane Society of Socialist Lawyers)*, 7–10, at 8.
26. Thompson, *Whigs and Hunters*, 261.
27. Ibid.
28. Ibid., 264.
29. Ibid., 261. Compare with Thompson, 'The Rule of Law in English History', 8:

> This rhetoric was deeply believed. But for the belief to endure, it must sometimes be seen to be so. And it must be supported on occasion in the courts. In London 200 years ago you would have found many coal-porters, Covent Garden workers, and tailoring and hatting artisans, profoundly filled with the notion that they were free born Englishmen, and clamorous on occasions to assert these rights.

30. Thompson, *Whigs and Hunters*, 262–264.
31. See Quentin Skinner, *Liberty as Independence: The Making and Unmaking of a Political Ideal*, Cambridge University Press, Cambridge, 2025.
32. Thompson, *Whigs and Hunters*, 263. In all these references to 'notion', the emphasis is mine.
33. Ibid., 265.
34. Ibid., 268.
35. See Daniel H. Cole, cited in Cole '"An Unqualified Human Good": E. P. Thompson and the Rule of Law', 178.
36. Toope, *A Rule of Law for Our New Age of Anxiety*, 217.
37. See Gianfranco Poggi, *The Development of the Modern State*, Hutchinson, London, 1978.
38. Jürgen Habermas, 'Law as Medium and Law as Institution', in Gunther Teubner, ed., *Dilemmas of Law in the Welfare State*, De Gruyter, Berlin, 1986, 203–220, at 212.
39. See Glenn, *Legal Traditions of the World*; Pirie, *Rules of Law*.
40. See David Neal, *Rule of Law in a Penal Colony*, Cambridge University Press, Cambridge, 1991.
41. Adam Czarnota and Martin Krygier, 'From State to Legal Traditions?'.
42. See Pirie, *The Rule of Laws*, chap. 3 (on Imperial China). See Pipes, *Russia under the Old Regime*; Kahn, 'The Search for the Rule of Law in Russia'; Kahn, 'Vladimir Putin and the Rule of Law in Russia'; Engelstein, *Slavophile Empire*. See Samuel E. Finer, *The History of Government, Vol. 3: Empires, Monarchies, and the Modern State*, Oxford University Press, Oxford, 1999, 1306–1307: 'the most striking and important contrast between Russia and the rest of Europe was that the country had no tradition of what we have called "law-boundedness". … In effect, until as late as the mid-nineteenth century, Russia did without systematized laws, a legal profession, and the law-boundedness that was the essential characteristic of the western state tradition.'
43. See Nonet and Selznick, *Law and Society in Transition*, 34.
44. See Hart, *The Concept of* Law, 55.

45. See, for example, Ledeneva, *Russia's Economy of Favours*; Ledeneva, *How Russia Really Works*.
46. See Section 4.4, p.303.
47. Kahn, 'The Search for the Rule of Law in Russia', 357.
48. Marek Zirk-Sadowski, 'Transformation and Integration of Legal Cultures and Discourses: Poland', in Wojciech Sadurski, Adam Czarnota, and Martin Krygier, eds., *Spreading Democracy and the Rule of Law? Implications of EU Enlargement for the Rule of Law, Democracy and Constitutionalism in Post-Communist Legal Orders*, Springer, Dordrecht, 2006, 299–311, at 300.
49. Geertz, *Local Knowledge*, 215.
50. Neal, *Rule of Law in a Penal Colony*, xi. Neal's argument was heavily influenced by Thompson, *Whigs and Hunters*, and mine in turn by Neal.
51. Ibid., 62.
52. See Krygier, 'The Grammar of Colonial Legality'.
53. Martin Krygier, 'Neighbours: Poles, Jews, and the Aboriginal Question', (2002) 29 *East Central Europe/L'Europe du Centre Est. Eine wissenschaftliche Zeitschrift*, 297–309; Krygier, 'False Dichotomies, Real Perplexities and the Rule of Law'; Krygier, 'The Grammar of Colonial Legality'; Krygier (with Robert van Krieken), 'The Character of the Nation', in Robert Manne, ed., *Whitewash: On Keith Windschuttle's Fabrication of Aboriginal History*, Black Inc., Melbourne, 2003, 81–108.
54. Marc Galanter, 'Why the "Haves" Come Out Ahead: Speculations on the Limits of Legal Change', (1974) 9 *Law and Society Review*, 95–160.
55. Reid, *The Rule of Law*, 75–79.
56. See Steven Hahn, *Illiberal America: A History*, W. W. Norton & Co., New York, 2024.
57. See Louis Hartz, *The Liberal Tradition in America*, Harcourt, Brace & World, New York, 1955.
58. See Hahn, *Illiberal America*, 129–136, for the young Lincoln on Native Americans and 'the colored race'.
59. 'Avant que la société puisse être libre, il faut qu'elle soit': Raymond Aron, 'La définition libérale de la liberté: I: A propos du livre de F. A. Hayek "The Constitution of Liberty"', (1961) 2 *European Journal of Sociology/Archives Européennes de Sociologie/Europäisches Archiv für Soziologie*, 199–218, at 215.
60. 'manières collectives d'agir ou de penser': Emile Durkheim, *Les règles de la méthode sociologique*, Kindle Edition, UltraLetters, 2013 (first published in 1894], loc. 512.
61. Gianfranco Poggi, *Durkheim*, Oxford University Press, Oxford, 2000, 89.
62. Ibid., 85.
63. The first was revealed in the presidential election itself; the second in a post-coup referendum and then plebiscite which he was alleged to have won by Stalinesque margins.
64. Karl Marx, author's preface to the second edition of *The Eighteenth Brumaire of Louis Bonaparte*, 14. The three 'swindlers' were Napoleon III and his co-conspirators, Emmanuel Joseph Sieyès and Pierre-Roger Ducos.
65. According to Friedrich Engels, letter to Conrad Schmidt, 1890, 'Marx used to say, commenting on the French "Marxists" of the late [18]70s: "All I know is that I am not a Marxist"', Marx/Engels Internet Archive, www.marxists.org/archive/marx/works/1890/letters/90_08_05.htm.

66. Marx, *The Eighteenth Brumaire*, 56.
67. For an illuminating discussion of this determination to find economic causes for political events, see Raymond Aron's comparison between the explanations of Tocqueville and Marx, 'The Sociologists and the Revolutions of 1848', in *Main Currents in Sociological Thought*, vol. 1, Penguin, London, 1965. See also Martin Krygier, 'Marxism and Bureaucracy: A Paradox Resolved', (1985) 20 *Politics*, 58–69.
68. Marx, *The Eighteenth Brumaire*, 108–109.
69. Ibid., 109–110.
70. See Hannah Arendt, *The Origins of Totalitarianism*, World Publishing Co., Cleveland, OH, 1958.
71. Adam Michnik, 'A New Evolutionism', in *Letters from Prison and Other Essays*, trans. Maya Latynski, University of California Press, Berkeley, 1985, 144.
72. See Jacek Kuroń, 'Polityczna opozycja w Polsce' ['Political Opposition in Poland'], in *Polityka i odpowiedzialność*, Aneks, London, 1984, 107–123.
73. Adam Michnik, 'The Prague Spring Ten Years Later', in *Letters from Prison and Other Essays*, trans. Maya Latynski, University of California Press, Berkeley, 1985, 158.
74. See Antony Black, *Guilds and Civil Society in European Political Thought from the Twelfth Century to the Present*, Methuen, London, 1984; Dario Castiglione, 'History and Civil Society: Outline of a Contested Paradigm', (1994) 40 *The Australian Journal of Politics and History*, 83–103; Manfred Riedel, 'Gesellschaft, Bürgerliche', in Otto Brunner et al., eds., *Geschichtliche Grundbegriffe*, Vol. 2, Klett, Stuttgart, 1975, 719–800.
75. See Zbigniew Rau, ed., *The Reemergence of Civil Society in Eastern Europe and the Soviet Union*, Westview Press, Boulder, CO, 1991; Vladimir Tismaneanu, *Reinventing Politics: Eastern Europe from Stalin to Havel*, The Free Press, New York, 1992.
76. See Dominique Colas, *Civil Society and Fanaticism: Conjoined Histories*, trans. Amy Jacobs, Stanford University Press, Stanford, CA, 1997, 39–40: 'Devoid of context, no longer linked to a particular period or a precise doctrine, gushing out of everyone's mouth at once, "civil society" … has become a label for all sorts of goods, and in certain cases even a mark for intellectual emptiness. … "[C]ivil society" allows people to speak without knowing what they are saying, which in turn helps them to avoid arguing with each other.'
77. On better government, see Robert D. Putnam, *Making Democracy Work: Civic Traditions in Modern Italy*, Princeton University Press, Princeton, NJ, 1993; on better societies, see Putnam, *Bowling Alone: The Collapse and Revival of American Community*, Simon & Schuster, New York, 2000.
78. This argument draws on Krygier, 'The Quality of Civility'.
79. See Richard Rose, *Distrust as an Obstacle to Civil Society*, Centre for the Study of Public Policy, University of Strathclyde, Glasgow, 1994.
80. One of the most influential of these ways was derived from the advocacy of 'civic association' in Putnam's *Making Democracy Work*, and the sprawling literature devoted to it. It is not immediately obvious why, but it was at the very least a sign of the times when it was published (1993), that such a specialised tome should have engendered the extraordinary resonance it did.

81. Sheri Berman, 'Civil Society and the Collapse of the Weimar Republic', (1997) 49 *World Politics*, 401–429, at 402.
82. Dylan Riley, *The Civic Foundations of Fascism in Europe: Italy, Spain, and Romania, 1870–1945*, Verso, London, 2019.
83. Berman, 'Civil Society', 424.
84. And perhaps intrinsically more democratic. Compare with Christopher Bryant's remark that civility 'remains a fundamentally democratic idea. Courtesy was for the court; gentility was for the gentry; civility is for all citizens.' Bryant, 'Civil Nation, Civil Society, and Civil Religion', in John A. Hall, ed., *Civil Society: Theory, History, Comparison*, Polity Press, Cambridge, 2013, 145.
85. Hobbes, *Leviathan*, chap. XI, 'Of the Difference of Manners', 63.
86. Edward Shils, 'The Virtue of Civil Society', (1991) 8 *Government and Opposition*, 3–20, at 14. I am much influenced by this essay, as well as by three unpublished typescripts on civil society that Professor Shils kindly sent me shortly before his death.
87. John A. Hall, 'In Search of Civil Society', in John. A. Hall, ed., *Civil Society: Theory, History, Comparison*, Polity Press, Cambridge, 11–41, at 15.
88. Martha Nussbaum, *Liberty of Conscience: In Defense of America's Tradition of Religious Equality*, Basic Books, New York, 2008.
89. Teresa Bjan, *Mere Civility: Disagreement and the Limits of Toleration*, Harvard University Press, Cambridge, MA, 2017.
90. Ibid., 52.
91. Ibid., 74.
92. Ibid., 161.
93. Adam B. Seligman, *The Idea of Civil Society*, The Free Press, New York, 1992, 165.
94. Urbinati, *Me the People*, 78.
95. Viktor Orbán, 'Orbán Viktor beszéde a Dísz téren 2002. május 7', 2002, http://mkdsz1.freeweb.hu/n22/orban020507.html, quoted in Seongcheol Kim, '… Because the Homeland Cannot Be in Opposition: Analysing the Discourses of Fidesz and Law and Justice (PiS) from Opposition to Power', (2021) 37 *East European Politics*, 332–351, at 337.
96. Jarosław Kaczyński, interviewed on program *W Punkt, Telewizja Republika*, 11 December 2015, www.youtube.com/watch?v=LCK_biZe_KU.
97. Thomas Carothers and Brendan Hartnett, 'Misunderstanding Democratic Backsliding', (2024) 35 *Journal of Democracy*, 24–37; Francis Fukuyama, Chris Dann, and Beatriz Magaloni, 'Delivering for Democracy: Why Results Matter', (2025) 36 *Journal of Democracy*, 5–19.
98. See Larry M. Bartels, *Democracy Erodes from the Top: Leaders, Citizens, and Challenge of Populism*, Princeton University Press, Princeton, NJ, 2023; Thomas Carothers, 'Beyond Performance: Why Leaders Still Matter', (2025) 36 *Journal of Democracy*, 20–22.
99. Henry David Thoreau, *Civil Disobedience*, Dover Publications, New York, 1993, 1:

> I heartily accept the motto, – 'That government is best which governs least'; and I should like to see it acted up to more rapidly and systematically. Carried out, it finally amounts to this, which also I believe, – 'That government is best which governs not at all'; and when men are prepared for it, that will be the kind of government which they will have.

100. Leszek Kołakowski, 'Hope and Hopelessness', (1971) 17 *Survey*, 37–52.
101. Blandine Kriegel, *The State and the Rule of Law*, trans. Marc A. LePain and Jeffrey C. Cohen, Princeton University Press, Princeton, NJ, 1995.
102. Michael Mann, 'The Autonomous Power of the State: Its Origins, Mechanisms and Resources', in his *State, War and Capitalism*, Blackwell, Oxford, 1988, 1–31, at 32; italics in the original. See also his *Sources of Social Power*, Vol. 1, Cambridge University Press, Cambridge, 1986, 477. Here, and more crisply, Mann contrasts 'power over civil society, that is, *despotism*' and 'the power to coordinate civil society, that is, *infrastructural power*.'
103. John A. Hall, *Powers and Liberties: The Causes and Consequences of the Rise of the West*, Penguin, London, 1985. See too Adam Czarnota and Martin Krygier, 'Revolutions and the Continuity of European Law', in Zenon Bankowski, ed., *Revolutions in Law and Legal Thought*, Aberdeen University Press, Aberdeen, 1991, 90–112.
104. Linda Weiss and John M. Hobson, *States and Economic Development*, Polity Press, Cambridge, 1995, 3.
105. Ibid., 168.
106. Huntington, *The Third Wave*.
107. See, for example, Ken Macdonald, 'Democracy and Human Rights Are Vital for the Rule of Law: And So Is Legality', *South China Morning Post* (online), 4 September 2017, www.scmp.com/comment/insight-opinion/article/2109596/democracy-and-human-rights-are-vital-rule-law-and-so; Democracy International, 'Human Rights and Democracy', www.democracy-international.org/human-rights; Council of Europe, 'State of Democracy, Human Rights and the Rule of Law (2017)', https://edoc.coe.int/en/an-overview/7345-pdf-state-of-democracy-human-rights-and-the-rule-of-law.html.
108. Jürgen Habermas, 'On the Internal Relation between Rule of Law and Democracy', (1995) 3 *European Journal of Philosophy*, 12–20, 15–16. See also Habermas, *Between Facts and Norms*, Polity Press, Cambridge, 1996, chaps. 3–4. Italics in the original.
109. Habermas, 'On the Internal Relation between Rule of Law and Democracy', 17, 18.
110. Ibid., 28–29.
111. José María Maravall, 'The Rule of Law as a Political Weapon', in José María Maravall and Adam Preworski, eds., *Democracy and the Rule of Law*, Cambridge University Press, Cambridge, 2003, 261–301, at 261.
112. See Philip Pettit, 'Democracy Electoral and Contested', (2000) 42 *Nomos*, 105–144.
113. In Philip Pettit, *On the People's Terms*, Cambridge University Press, Cambridge, 2012, 58, Pettit decides no longer to use the republican term 'arbitrary', as he used to, since he believes it has strayed from referring above all to 'uncontrolled' power as it did and as it does for him and has come to be confused with 'not subject to established rules' and 'wrong or objectionable'. He prefers to stick to 'uncontrolled' and has come to prefer that word for clarity. I stick with 'arbitrary', both because it is a term deep and resonant in rule of law traditions and to denote the four forms of the exercise of power, discussed in Chapter 5, that different strands of those traditions have found objectionable: uncontrolled, unpredictable, unrespectful, and ungrounded. Notwithstanding this verbal difference, there is no substantive difference between us. We both object to uncontrolled exercise of power, and I have no doubt Pettit also objects to unpredictable, unrespectful, and ungrounded power as well.

114. Democracy International, 'Human Rights, Democracy, and Rule of Law'.
115. Benjamin Constant, 'The Liberty of the Ancients Compared with That of Moderns (1819)', The Online Library of Liberty, http://oll.libertyfund.org/titles/constant-the-liberty-of-ancients-compared-with-that-of-moderns-1819.
116. Aristides N. Hatzis, 'The Illiberal Democracy of Ancient Athens', SSRN, 2016, 3, https://papers.ssrn.com/sol3/papers.cfm?abstract_id=2810070.
117. See Fareed Zakaria, 'The Rise of Illiberal Democracy', (1997) 76 *Foreign Affairs*, 22–43.
118. See Dicey, *Introduction to the Study of the Law of the Constitution*, 186–187.
119. See Root, *Political Foundations of Markets in Old Regime France and England.*
120. See Reid, *Rule of Law.*
121. 'Lord Hailsham: Elective Dictatorship', BBC, 14 October 1976, and see Hayek, *Law, Legislation and Liberty, Vol. 3*, 101.
122. Levitsky and Ziblatt, *How Democracies Die*, 39.
123. Zakaria, 'Illiberal Democracy'.
124. Ibid., 22.
125. Ibid., 23.
126. Ibid., 42.
127. Ibid., 30.
128. In this section, in using the term 'populisms' I am speaking not of all movements that have been called, or have called themselves, populist. My focus is on the authoritarian populist movements and regimes that have become widespread in recent years, which I discuss in Chapter 8, and that I have elsewhere called 'anti-constitutional populists'. See Krygier, Czarnota, and Sadurski, *Anti-constitutional Populism.*
129. Weber, *Economy and Society*, 1115.
130. Nancy Bermeo, 'On Democratic Backsliding', (2016) 27 *Journal of Democracy*, 5–19; Laurent Pech and Kim Lane Scheppele, 'Rule of Law Backsliding', *Verfassungsblog*, 2 March 2018, https://verfassungsblog.de/what-is-rule-of-law-backsliding/.
131. Yeats, 'The Second Coming'.
132. See Pippa Norris and Ronald Inglehart, *Cultural Backlash: Trump, Brexit, and Authoritarian Populism*, Cambridge University Press, Cambridge, 2019.
133. See Bartels, *Democracy Erodes from the Top*; Carothers and Hartnett, 'Misunderstanding Democratic Backsliding'.
134. Closing speech of the candidate for re-election, 'Discurso de cierre de campaña del candidato a la reelección', *Apporea*, 27 November 2006, www.aporrea.org/oposicion/a27627.html.
135. Sajó and Tuovinen, 'The Rule of Law and Legitimacy in Emerging Illiberal Democracies', 519.
136. See Barry Commoner, *The Closing Circle: Nature, Man and Technology*, Bantam Books, New York, 1974; Jonathan D. Phillips, 'Why Everything Is Connected to Everything Else', (2023) 54–55 *Ecological Complexity*, 1–10.
137. See Ralf Michaels, 'Climate's Empire in Comparative Law', (2023) 28 *Tilburg Law Review*, 1–19.
138. Commoner, *The Closing Circle*, 113.
139. See Charles Taylor, 'Modes of Civil Society', (1990) 3 *Public Culture*, 95–118, at 105.
140. Compare with Jean L. Cohen and Andrew Arato, *Civil Society and Political Theory*, MIT Press, Cambridge, MA, 1994, ix: 'Modern civil society is created

through forms of self-constitution and self-mobilization. It is institutionalized and generalized through laws, and especially subjective rights, that stabilize social differentiation. While the self-creative and institutionalized dimensions can exist separately, in the long term both independent action and institutionalization are necessary for the reproduction of civil society.'

141. See Martin Krygier, 'Virtuous Circles: Antipodean Reflections on Power, Institutions, and Civil Society', (1997) 11 *Eastern European Politics and Societies*, 36–88.

Chapter 11

1. With Jan Zielonka, Professor of European Politics, University of Oxford.
2. Though that was not his subject then, Braithwaite assures me he has no objection to my redirection of his argument. In his recent writings, tempering power has become a central theme. With 400 references in his astonishing 800-page *Macrocriminology and Freedom*, where he explores an extraordinary range of routes to temper power in a multifarious variety of contexts, the idea has been launched. See also Braithwaite, 'Hybrid Politics for Justice'; Braithwaite, 'Tempering Martin', 280; Braithwaite, 'Tempered Power'.
3. The talk has not been published, but Braithwaite kindly gave me his speaking notes, which I have on file.
4. Cheesman and Janse, 'Martin Krygier's Passion for the Rule of Law (and His Virtues)'.
5. Quoted in Hobsbawm, *The Age of Extremes*, 1.
6. This is one crude, but not totally fanciful way to read Putnam, *Making Democracy Work*.
7. For why we don't know and why we should try, see Giuseppe di Palma, *To Craft Democracies*, University of California Press, Berkeley, 1990.
8. Ibid., 8.
9. Ibid., 9.
10. Ibid., 17.
11. See the excellent discussion of many of these consequences in Mark Tushnet and Bojan Buarič, *Constitutionalism and Its Discontents*, University of Chicago Press, Chicago, 2025.
12. Including, for example, Kisilowski, 'Militant Public Administration'; Jakub Drożdż, 'Resilient Diplomacy against the Populist Capture', *ResearchGate*, July 2024, https://bit.ly/46eosWg.
13. Weber, 'Politics as a Vocation'.

INDEX